Laurie Cabot's
Book of Shadows

by Laurie Cabot

with

Penny Cabot

& Christopher Penczak

**COPPER
CAULDRON**
PUBLISHING

Credits

Cover: Derek Yesman and Daydream Designs

Editing: Tina Whittle

Proofreading: Alura Rose, Karen Ainsworth, Lisa Bland, Steven "Ven" Brady, Becky Hobson, Helen LaGod, Chris LeVasseur, Silver Lyons, Raye Snover, Deborah Stelhorn, Rowann Stormbender, Virginia Villarreal

Interior Art: Christopher Penczak. Cabot Altar photo courtesy of Rory McCraken and Terra Nova Creative. Cabot Crest courtesy of Derek Yesman and Daydream Designs

Layout & Publishing: Steve Kenson

Acknowledgements: Special thanks to...

Jean Renard, Tom Cowan, and Jean Mills.

James Cabot Daly, particularly for his work on the Cabot Tradition Code of Ethics. Used by permission of the Cabot Kent Hermetic Temple.

Kip Ellis for his work and research focused on gathering, organizing, and expanding upon the first degree materials for the official Cabot Academy Witchcraft One Teacher's Manual, and in particular for his teachings on Universal Light. These materials have been adapted in this Book of Shadows with his kind permission.

Candy-Jeanne Burke HPS and Dana Burke HP for the Cabot Call of the God, and Cabot Call of the Goddess, reprinted here with their kind permission.

Patricia A. Barki for creation of the Cabot Kent Hermetic Temple Law Memorandum. Used by permission of the Cabot Kent Hermetic Temple.

Memie Watson for the Cabot Clergy Training Materials, Cabot House Blessing Ritual, Spell of the Crone, What It Means to be a High Priestess/High Priest in the Cabot Kent Hermetic Temple, and all of her service to the community. All reprinted with her kind permission.

Silver Lyons for inspiring the Parallel Universe Meditation Technique.

ISBN 978-1-940755-05-2, First Printing, Printed in the U.S.A.

Disclaimer

This book and all spells, rituals, formulas, and advice in it are not substitutes for professional medical advice. Please confer with a medical professional before using any herbs, remedies, or teas in any manner. Unless specifically indicated, formulas are not intended to be consumed or ingested. The publisher and author are not responsible for the use of this material.

The Book of Shadows

The moment I open this book and turn the pages,
I am enchanted by the light of the Universe.

All the majick that I set upon enters my body, mind, and spirit,
conjuring the majick of its light, the planets, and the stars.

The music of the spheres reaches into our future
and into the many worlds we shall live.

I shall be careful not to move the Moon
or change the course of other worlds around us
for surely it will change the course of my blood.
Then no longer can the planets help me.

May the Gods and Goddesses hear my voice.

Table of Contents

Foreword

Witchcraft came to me at the perfect time. Like so many of us, I was in the right place, at the right time, with the right teacher who could help me have the eyes to see and the ears to hear. I started as a skeptic, and in some ways, I still am. Yet the formula of starting with the science of Witchcraft, the understanding of its principles and philosophies, was what I needed to bridge the gap between skeptic and Witch. If we had started with the gods, with the rituals, or even with spells, I would not have made the leap. The intellectual understanding, comparing ancient philosophy to cutting-edge physics and creating a platform for a rational modern person to be able to experience and embrace majick (as the Cabots spell it) was the key that unlocked the doorway of the mysteries for me. Once I walked through, I could never go back.

As I got more involved in the romance of the Craft, the lore and cultures, the only thing I regretted from this modern approach was not having a traditional Book of Shadows. We were taught to make our own, mixing teachings with personal experiences and lore, becoming one part majickal journal, one part art project, and one part gigantic research project. Other Witches visit with their teacher and copy the foundational material of the Book of Shadows by hand, with special ink and incense burning, from their initiator's book. A tangible line is created. Being very modern in many ways, we did not do that. I had always wished for our tradition's Book of Shadows, particularly as we evolved and transformed over the years. Yet this personal approach created a wide range of lore and ways of doing things. Still, I longed for that book of majickally enchanted pages. Now I have it.

While we might not all be together at Laurie's kitchen table transcribing the book with Dragon's Blood ink and a quill pen, you do have in your hands what I longed to have—The Cabot Book of Shadows. Within are the teachings, lore, and material of the three degrees of the Cabot Tradition of Witchcraft, starting with Witchcraft I as a Science, Witchcraft II as an Art, and Witchcraft III as a Religion. This book is an alchemical amalgam of Laurie's class hand-outs, material from her previous books and interviews, her teacher's manuals and instructional notes for certified teachers, recordings of her classes, and chats around the dining room table with her and Penny that I furiously transcribed, along with some additions from priestesses and priests of the Cabot Tradition, contributing to the public work and education of the Cabot-Kent Temple. This book is a treasure, for it records some of the most popular teaching stories from Laurie's career, things most of us only hear when we spend time in her presence, in class. They demonstrate the effectiveness and value of living a majickal life, and how things can still continually surprise and support us on the path.

In the first degree, our key is the science and our scientific understanding of how majick works. Those of us rooted in the modern worldview need a way to frame majick so it does not sound and feel utterly irrational. Many of us leave mainstream religions seeking something with more truth to it, and we can't trade one myth for another, particularly when we are not raised in the culture of that myth. So the understandings of modern science, particularly quantum physics and the holographic theory of the universe, give us a way to understand and express the majickal, even if modern scientists do not always like how metaphysicians co-op their terminology and ideas outside of the context of "pure" science. It also helps remind us that all the great Pagan philosophers of the ancient world, our spiritual ancestors as modern Witches, were considered the scientists of their day.

The function of the first degree is to generate self-esteem. Many people, myself included, come to Witchcraft with low self-esteem, yet we are seeking something nebulous, seemingly outside ourselves. Witchcraft teaches us to seek within to find the answers, feeling our connections to the universe through the Divine Mind. By fulfilling the task of psychic development through meditation, light energy work, and vision work, we learn how to become a Witch. The connection occurs through our actions. We open to the "sight" which is not really sight at all, but an inner vision and knowing beyond the senses, using our psychic sixth sense. For me, this degree was utterly life changing and altered the course of my path forever.

In the second degree, our key is the art, as we learn to express ourselves through majick, ritual, and spellcraft. Our art becomes a means of communicating with the Divine. The function of the second degree is to take responsibility for our lives. Through the power of majick, with sufficient self-esteem, we can project for our future through spells and rituals, and balance our lives. By the power of the waxing Moon, we manifest and bring things we are lacking, things we need and want. By the power of the waning Moon, we banish excess and unwanted forces. We learn we have the power to shape our own lives through the task of manifestation before us, and through this holy work, we become priestesses and priests of our craft. The torch of light is passed from wand to circle, circle to wand. I hesitated taking this degree, rejecting the idea of being a "priest" until being convinced by my mother, who took Laurie's Witchcraft I and Witchcraft II classes with me. She wisely reminded me that it was vastly different to *be* a priest, rather than follow and obey a priest as we did when we were Catholic. Witchcraft empowered us. I soon began to embrace what I would think of as my Witch soul.

In the third and final degree, our key to approaching Witchcraft is the religion of the Craft. Religion is a difficult word. Those who left behind a dogmatic, prophetic religion may want nothing to do with religion when they seek majick. I know, for that was how I felt at one time. But there are many forms of religion, and by recognizing that our path is religious, we demonstrate that it should have the same rights and respect as any other by our society or government. Ours is a personal mystery religion, a tradition of inner transformation, not scripture and prophecy. Our spiritual ancestors were deeply religious, for religion was not separate from life. There was no secular society. Some of our ancestors practiced outside of the "official" religions of their lands, being the private practitioners of the crossroads and forests. Others were leaders of their community, advising chiefs and kings, running the seasonal celebrations and counseling the people. It is through that lens that we see our religion. While the first degrees are about self-esteem and self-responsibility, this third degree is about service to something beyond the self. It is service to the gods, and service to the community.

To be of service, we must quest for the Mystery that transforms us. In the Cabot Tradition, we look to the ancient mysteries of our people. These myths speak of cycles and seasons in the land, but also of the inner transforming cycles of our soul. We look to the search for the Child of Light, as in the stories of Mabon. We look to the rebirth of the child as wise one through the tale of Cerridwen and Taliesin. And we look to the mystery of healing the individual and the society through the quest for the Holy Grail, which is the cauldron of the underworld goddess and the cup of immortality from Arthurian myth. While we seemingly seek something outside of ourselves in myths of foreign lands, this degree teaches us to find the mystery within ourselves, and thus be healed, transformed, and able to serve the whole. We have the opportunity to become High Priestesses and High Priests. We have the chance to be ordained as ministers to the community, with legal as well as spiritual recognition. The light of our ancestors of Kent, the light of Excalibur, can be passed directly from sword to sword, guiding us. I came to this degree late, after spending a lot of time in other training and public service, but completion of this degree was a powerful shift in my own ministerial work and inner world contacts.

The material of the third degree, unlike the first and second, has shifted the most over the years, from an emphasis of the Egyptian mysteries to the Celtic, and Laurie and Penny have given me an opportunity to bring my experiences to expand and refine it, balancing the mystery of the high priest/ess with the community work of ministers. While much of Laurie's primary mission has been teaching the world the science of Witchcraft, Penny has focused deeply on the art, both the art of the Craft, and visual and mixed media mediums of expression. For me, I've been most concerned about the philosophies, culture, theories, and spiritual practices of Witchcraft, and the esoteric entities and non-ordinary realities we can commune with through trance. So out of the three degrees in this work, I've had the strongest hand in shaping the pattern of the third level into what it is now. I'm sure many who have gone through it in the past might not recognize all that is there now, but the core teachings and ideas are still the same. Laurie has been hugely influenced not only by her teachers, but by the esoteric works available in America at the time of her exploration, with the Antiquarian resources including Rosicrucianism and Theosophy, popular folklore, the Celtic revival, and later popular Paganism and Witchcraft. She has many of the same influences as other pioneers in the modern Craft.

Keeping with our modern trends, and with the spirit of transparency and openness, we've made the entire Book of Shadows available for initiates and non-initiates alike, to all those who seek to learn the ways of the Cabot Tradition of Witchcraft and learn from our founder, Laurie Cabot. Like any other Book of Shadows, this information is not complete. It is the notes to accompany the experience of the teacher, perhaps in a little more detailed form than many Books of Shadow, but incomplete still. For those who cannot study with a Cabot teacher, look to Laurie's previous five "how to" books for a more complete picture and to simulate being in the presence of a teacher. Yet books are no substitute for experience, so go out and do the rituals in this and other books, to experience them directly yourself.

While reading and working with the book does not confer membership in the terrestrial organization, the Cabot Tradition or the Cabot-Kent Hermetic Temple, the teachings are accessible to everyone, to have seeds of wisdom planted and transformative life-changing experiences begun. I hope this material is as profoundly helpful to you as it has been for me.

Blessed be,
Christopher Penczak

Introduction

People called to this path start to show an interest in Witchcraft in their own way. Some read a book, see a film, meet a Witch, or even visit Salem, Massachusetts, where America's most famous persecution and execution of those accused of Witchcraft took place some three hundred years ago. It awakens something in them.

For me it happened during history class in grammar school. When I was in school, we would have a week of history in one subject, and then move onto another. Of course we spent a week on the history of New England and the founding of the colonies. That led us to the Witch Trials of Salem, Massachusetts. I was seven or eight years old when I first heard about them. I remember my mother reading to me about it, and the two of us discussing it. While the texts said of course there were no Witches in Salem, she said, "They might not have been real Witches at all, but they could have been. And no one would ever know." I don't know how she could have known the "real" description of Witches. She was well read and knew a lot. I was too young to even really question her on it, but it always stuck with me – they could have been. I remember seeing a picture in the book, a house with gables upon it, and a woman looking out of the window. I thought to myself, "That poor woman." It all stuck in my mind. Every Halloween I wanted to be a Witch, though I often ended up as Little Bo Peep. I kept going back to the idea that "they could have been Witches." I guess with the way she said it, being a Witch didn't sound like a bad thing. They were not bad people; they were persecuted by others. That is where I first got the idea of Witches being good people to begin with, trapped in a horrible situation. What she said then, I say now. There could have been Witches. And no one would ever know.

My own path surprisingly led me to a real Witch, a woman named Felicity, when I was a young girl living in Boston. She worked at the public library where, in an effort to control my growing psychic abilities, my mother and I researched every esoteric concept in the library, attracting Felicity's attention. She was a Witch from Kent, England, and referred to her tradition, and her people, as the Witches of Kent. She came to America with her husband and ran a small coven with a few other women, very quietly, very secretly. She soon offered me her help, training and, finally, initiation as a Witch.

My own training in the Kent Tradition of Witchcraft led me to explore the science and philosophies behind majick and psychic phenomenon. I learned ancient Hermetic philosophy along with quantum science. I had to understand the science behind it. Soon I was teaching classes on Witchcraft as a Science, and my work evolved from my more private family tradition with my two daughters into the Cabot Tradition of Witchcraft, focused upon the Science, Art, and Religion of Witchcraft. It is one of the first American traditions of Witchcraft, rooted in my community work here in Salem, Massachusetts. Much later, we legally established a religious temple, and in honor of Felicity, it was named the Cabot-Kent Hermetic Temple.

When you read about Witchcraft, and you begin to try to practice, often times you're functioning without guidance. It is better to learn from a teacher, and follow a tradition, when possible but it is not always possible. You can learn from books until you find the right flesh and blood teacher. Books can be wonderful guides. Most traditions do not teach in the way we teach. We give you all the information. We allow you to walk with it, talk with it, and learn on your own so that you have the information by which to guide you. But you must be the one to practice it. You must apply it; otherwise the knowledge is useless. If you choose to be a Witch, please be dedicated. Then you will be able to put the book knowledge to best use.

I have always made crafty Books of Shadows for people to use. They contain blank pages for writing down your own spells and rituals, but are also filled with beautiful classical and medieval art, and a wide variety of teachings, lore, correspondences, and quotes throughout each section. I make them to inspire people to fill them up, to be collaborative works of art and majick. Sadly, not a lot of people write in the books. They won't fill in their own spaces, and that was not my intention. They are made for people to use and add to, like any Book of Shadows. We must take what we are given, add to it, and pass it onward to the next generation.

Since I didn't have a Book of Shadows from my teacher Felicity, as some other traditions of Witchcraft emphasize, I understand what it is like to not have a book from your teacher, and how special that can be when you do.

Now, a dream has come true to be able to collaborate with Christopher and to compile my own lore and teachings in a traditional Book of Shadows. This needed to be done, and I was unsure how it would happen. I projected my intention, and it came through in this form when I asked for someone to help me with it.

Since we now have our Temple legally established, it is important to have our lore preserved, and the mysteries, teachings, symbols, liturgy, and holidays clearly understood. We do things a bit differently from other Witches, and we need to have examples for people to inspire those seeking the Cabot Tradition of Witchcraft. This book can preserve the basic patterns, providing a foundation to inspire people forward.

For the Cabot Witches, this book is a reference, the foundation of the tradition. I hope they will add to it, as they will have their own spells and rituals they can add to the main body of work. Or they can have a supplemental book where they can keep the spells and rites they have done that worked, and cross out the ones that don't seem to work, creating their own lists of correspondences and formulas. This is the foundation for the teachings of the entire lifetime of the tradition thus far.

For others, this book is a compendium of lore, teachings, and majick. It shows you what is important to me, as a lifelong practicing Witch serving the public, and I believe it can be of service to you as well. It is more than just spells and charms; it is how to live your life as a Witch, to see through a Witch's eyes. I hope having the entire tradition in one place can be inspiring for not only Cabot Witches, but for other Witches so they can create their own traditions. I hope this documents what we do, so people can understand our practices and beliefs, at least for one version of Witchcraft, and can welcome us to the world.

— Laurie Cabot

First Degree: Witchcraft as a Science

Becoming a Witch

Opening the Sight — Psychic Development

Generating Self-Esteem

Witches and Witchcraft

Witchcraft is the description of our traditions and practices. We are Witches as our ancestors were Witches. Those who follow us will be Witches as well. We embrace this word for its majick and mystery, even though it is often misunderstood. In fact, perhaps no other word in the English language has been misused and misunderstood as blatantly as the word "Witch."

The definition of the word "Witch" has evolved over many centuries:

- The Anglo-Saxon "Wicca" or "Wicce" simply refers to "a male or female seer or person who can find out information by using majick."
- Both "Wyeh" in Saxon and "Wicce" in Old English means "to bend, turn or shape."
- The Germanic root "wit" means "to know."
- Druid, or "Drwyrd" originates from the Indo-European root word "deru," which has been translated as "firm" or "solid." The Indo-European root word "wid" means to know." Druids were a part of Witchcraft, not separate. They were Witches, and they were "law-givers."
- "Witchcraft" is an Anglo-Saxon word. "Druid" is a Celtic term.

No other original meanings of the words "Witch" or "Witchcraft" are known. "Witch" or "Witchcraft" does not describe majick or majick workers in any culture other than the Indo-European culture, even though specific Indo-European cultures have their own words that have been translated into the English word Witch. The Greek name for herbal Witches, *pharmacute,* is the root of our modern word pharmacy. In Latin, it would translate to the word *venefica,* who were often thought of as poisoners, but also associated with love potions, herbalism, and Venus. The Latin *saga* meant a psychic, seer, or fortune-teller. The Norse term, *völva,* or wand-bearer, refers to female sorcerers akin to what we think of as Witches today. The description of the Celtic priest-magicians known as the Druids, and their long-haired, black-robed Druidesses, points to the Celtic heritage of the Witch.

Since these words "Witch" and "Witchcraft" do not exist in any culture other than the Indo-European tribes, they have been used inaccurately throughout academia for hundreds of years to describe majick and majickal practitioners in other cultures, usually in a pejorative manner. For many, Witchcraft has become erroneously synonymous with harmful majick, and Witches synonymous with malefic practitioners, while other terms, such as "shaman" have been used, often erroneously as well, for healing and holy practitioners. Witches originally fulfilled these same holy functions in their own communities until a division grew between "official" state religions—including the then-growing Christianity—and majickal practices. Soon those majickal practices and their practitioners were consider illicit, and relegated to subordinate roles as local Wise Women and Cunning Men, until their original roles were almost forgotten, until the revival of Witchcraft as a religious tradition.

The laws and practices of Witchcraft are the same as the foundations of every religion in the history of the world. Witches do not worship Satan or devils, now or ever. We believe the only demons and devils are ignorance and fear. In the religion of Witchcraft, Witches honor a primal Goddess and a God, as well as the gods and goddesses of our ancestors. There is no evil god, devil, or demon in our pantheon. Since pure energies are incomprehensible to us as humans, we often visualize energy as color, or interpret energy and information in terms of archetype and entities. Fear-based people often make their own demons and devils, due to a lack of knowledge concerning mind-sight and the validity of un-manifested vibrations.

Witchcraft is considered by many to be a nature religion. As a science, it is the study of both the overt and hidden aspects of nature. Ancient magicians were often considered students of nature, and would study with the healers and wise women, the "Witches," beyond their school doors.

Early European cultures had similar beliefs to those of the Native Americans. Concepts like the sacredness of nature, the Earth as a living entity of which we are a part, our origin from the stars, and the hidden virtues found in plants, animals, and stones are universal, but the landscape, weather, food, resources, culture, language, and people shape the creation stories, mythology, and religious expression. The interactions between the goddesses and gods and humans shape those relationships and traditions.

The term Paganism is used quite a bit in our overall communities, but Paganism is not the same as Witchcraft. Paganism is a Latin term, usually referring to a "country dweller" or "people of the rustic land." As new religions like Christianity grew in popularity, those who retained the old traditions were equated with Paganism. Soon Paganism—and its northern equivalent, Heathenism, for the people of the heath—became synonymous with anything non-Christian. It became equated with Christian heresy, and many Christian denominations look at all non-Christian or non-monotheist traditions, including Buddhism, Hinduism, Daoism, Sikhism, and Jainism as Pagan. As people explored non-traditional spiritualities, they too used that definition and adopted into their personal spirituality any non-Abrahamic tradition as a part of their Paganism, even though technically it most correctly refers to European traditions.

During the Renaissance there was a strong revival of the ancient European Pagan art, literature, and philosophy, starting what we might think of as the Pagan Revival. Today those who reconstruct ancient Pagan traditions—including those practices of the Greeks, Romans, Egyptians, Norse, and Celts—in the modern world could be called Neopagan, or "New Pagan," though many prefer the term "reconstructionist."

Paganism is not the same as Witchcraft. I prefer the word Witchcraft to Wicca or Paganism. Many people mistakenly assume since Wiccans are Pagans, Wiccans, Witches, and Pagans are one and the same. They are not. There was a time when there were so few of us, it was easy to lump us all together, but now as our community grows, these distinctions are important. While Witches are technically Pagans, not all Pagans are necessarily Witches. Paganism can be used as an overall umbrella term for many of these European nature-based traditions, much like Christianity described a large number of religions and sects. Within Paganism are various types, including Witchcraft. While some have used Wicca synonymously with Witchcraft, Wicca can refer to both a very strict initiatory tradition from Britain, popularized in two strains known as Gardnerian and Alexandrian Wicca, and a form of solitary or eclectic practice with the concept of self-initiation, popularized by Raymond Buckland and even more so by the author Scott Cunningham. Wicca differs from the Witchcraft that I teach as part of the Cabot Tradition.

WITCHCRAFT AS A SCIENCE

On one fundamental level, Witchcraft is a science. It has underlying principles that can be understood and experimented with to learn their effectiveness. In the ancient world, many of our greatest philosophers, doctors, and early scientists were also magicians, interested in the ancient mysteries, the patterns of nature, and many things we would call Witchcraft today. Modern academics consider their supernatural leanings as a shortcoming of their time, a pseudo-science and superstition they would be free of had they lived in the modern era. But we believe they understood a great deal more than our modern scientists do today in terms of seeing a greater, holistic picture of the cosmos on all levels. They understood the subtle effects of energy, life force, nature, thought, word, and intention.

Today Witches look at the philosophy of the ancients to see how it relates to our modern understanding of science. Witches look at modern cutting-edge scientific principles, such as those found in quantum theory, to better understand the possible mechanisms of how majick and Witchcraft work.

What I call Witchcraft science is really a metaphoric connection between our modern understanding of science and what Witches have always done. While great ancient Pagan philosophers were the scientists of their day, they did not necessarily follow what we consider the modern scientific method. The idea of Witchcraft as a science, with natural laws and meaning, helps modern people understand the ancient principles of majick through the lens of science. You could say we use the poetry of modern science because that is the culture we live in right now.

One of the key teachings of Witchcraft is the knowledge of the brain and mind, and the difference between the two that is so often forgotten or misunderstood in our society. Witches know the brain and the mind are two separate entities.

- The brain is part of the organism—the physical manifestation.
- The brain receives information through the five physical senses.
- The brain is like a computer, programmed throughout life.
- The mind is the energy packet or aura (which may also be known as the soul).
- Through the invention of Kirlian photography, auras can be seen, and many scientists have accepted the existence of the aura as fact.
- The mind, in short, is the energy source tapped into the highest levels of Total Intelligence.
- The mind does not rely on the five senses; it knows all things.
- By using the brain as a filter for mind energy, one can be psychic and clairvoyant and able to take in knowledge and truth from the Universal Mind.

Witches know the levels of energy contained in the tools of Witchcraft, such as the popular use of herbs, woods, oils, stones, and metals in majick. We use these vibrations as catalysts for our mind energy. Since our brain is not programmed to recognize pure energy, we often visualize it, or use items that catalyze it for us. Thankfully psychic sciences and brave researchers are now focusing on the true abilities of humans. Perhaps one day all children will be trained in understanding how the brain and mind work together.

THE CABOT TRADITION OF WITCHCRAFT

The Cabot Tradition of Witchcraft is the first Witchcraft tradition to emphasize the science of the Craft, particularly the science of alpha as the heart of all majickal experiences. The tradition defines Witchcraft as a Science, Art, and Religion, with three degrees to explore each of these levels.

I founded the Cabot Tradition, building upon the foundation given to me by my own teacher, Felicity Bumgardner, who claimed descent from what she mysteriously referred to as the Witches of Kent, which is a southeastern county of England known for its Witchcraft lore and ancient stone sites including the White Cliffs of Dover, the Coldrum Long Barrow, and the Medway Megaliths, which includes Kit's Coty House. Felicity emigrated to the United States with her American husband and worked at the Boston Public Library, where she later met me as a teen, along with my mother, as we sought an explanation and assistance with my strong psychic gift. After some explorations in occultism, spiritualism, Theosophy, and ancient myth, I was soon training with Felicity and her coven, leading to my eventual initiation as a Witch.

Kent in England (highlighed)

Kent Coat of Arms

Bumgardner Coat of Arms

Being a modern woman, in my adulthood, I sought to add to the understanding of the occult folk magic I had learned and the techniques to increase and control my psychic power. I was soon exploring a scientific understanding of psychic phenomena and using it to craft my own brand of Witchcraft. By going public as a Witch in 1967, I found myself teaching this modern perspective of the science of Witchcraft. Rather than restricting it to only those joining a coven, I shared my Witchcraft with the public, through public education venues in both college and high school continuing education departments as well as directly with the public through my own shop, public rituals, and readings. I teach that one does not necessarily have to follow the religion of Witchcraft to benefit from the science of Witchcraft, opening the door of majick to many who would have otherwise never found it.

In the first degree, we seek to understand the science of Witchcraft through improving our psychic ability and being able to prove its validity to ourselves, and to others. We learn meditation through the use of the alpha state of altered consciousness. Through alpha meditation, we work with the concept of Universal Light to create majickal change. We learn the fundamentals of psychic diagnosis and psychic healing.

In the second degree of the Cabot Tradition, we seek to explore the art of Witchcraft through the use of sacred space and the majick circle ritual. We cast spells and learn the majick of nature found in herbs, oils, and stones.

In the third degree, we focus upon the Religion. We seek to explore the mystery of the Witch, to better ourselves as individuals, and to learn how to serve the greater community as Witches.

While all Witches are naturally guided by the teachings found in the Seven Hermetic Principles, Witches of the Cabot Tradition make a deep study of the seven laws, for they govern everything in the cosmos both on the physical and metaphysical planes. They are part of our understanding of the science of Witchcraft.

You might have noticed that Cabot Witches usually spell the familiar word magic as "majick." There are several different ways to spell this word, from the traditional "magic" to the esoterically popular Victorian spelling of "magick" with a K, popularized by the infamous magician Aleister Crowley. He did it to distinguish it from stage show illusionists, like Harry Houdini, and favored the use of the K, as the eleventh letter of the modern alphabet, due to some of the majickal associations with the number eleven.

I prefer the "majick" spelling for our work. In traditional numerology, the esoteric study of the vibration of the numbers associated with letters, words, and dates, majick with our spelling adds up to the number two.

1	2	3	4	5	6	7	8	9
A	B	C	D	E	F	G	H	I
J	K	L	M	N	O	P	Q	R
S	T	U	V	W	X	Y	Z	

M	A	J	I	C	K
4	1	1	9	3	2

$4 + 1 + 1 + 9 + 3 + 2 = 20$

$2 + 0 = 2$

Two is one of the primary numbers of majick, being the number of polarity and balance. Two signifies Yin and Yang, Goddess and God, light and dark, creation and destruction. The vocations of those associated with this number as their "life path" include healers, teachers, counselors, and creative artists such as musicians, designers, and architects. All of these relate to our associations with the Witch as healer, spiritual teacher, religious counselor, artist, ritual musician, and even the designer of temples and sacred sites. The number two, and therefore majick, has the theme of the Witch, of majickal creation, embedded right in it. We spell majick this way to keep its meaning even more special to us, to remember these things.

We believe that by our definition, all Witchcraft is Indo-European; our teachings originate with those who lived in the areas of Northern India and who migrated across Europe to what is now considered the Celtic and Germanic territories. For this reason, the Cabot Tradition embraces only the Celtic and Norse pantheons. We look to the myths of these traditions for wisdom and guidance, primarily focusing upon the Irish, Welsh, Scottish, and native British lore that has been transformed into the Arthurian myth cycle. We look to the ancient British tribes of the Dobunni and the Hwicce as our spiritual ancestors, tribes of Witches who are a part of our ancient history, and to what little lore remains from them. As the first scientific views on majick grew out of the European occult traditions, many of our practices are informed by British occultism and folklore, with our heritage from the Witches of Kent. While we work religiously with the Celtic gods, we recognize and honor all goddesses and gods, and can borrow majick and traditions from other cultures.

The first degree of the Cabot Tradition is not a religion course. As we divide the teachings into three distinct levels, it is perfectly acceptable to study this first degree regardless of faith or background. The religion of Witchcraft is reserved for the third degree, though aspects of ritual in the Art of Witchcraft can seem religious to some. We start with the science first because everyone can benefit from it. Witches, as a rule, will not and do not evangelize. No one is asked to convert. You will never hear me say that your current belief system, organized religion, or the faith you were brought up with is wrong. We encourage students to study as much as they can about any and all faiths. As we experience different religions and belief systems, we increase our own knowledge and learn more about our personal spirituality. You find out what works and doesn't work for you. I do wish everyone could take Witchcraft I or something like it to learn the benefits of meditation, alpha level, and self-healing, but not everyone is ready for it. Still, I think it can benefit any tradition or path, no matter the religion, or lack of one.

Some people enthusiastically embrace a new religion or lifestyle, sometimes without truly understanding it. We see that happen a lot in Witchcraft. People get excited about the cloaks, jewelry, and spells, focusing upon the aesthetics without understanding the heart of our tradition, its history and real meaning. Other people seem to be "professional seekers" always on the hunt for something new, but never committing to the practice of anything for a period of time. They never grow roots and develop. They never grow in a tradition. Most people tend to accept the ideas and morals they were raised with, often blindly following and asking no questions.

Those called to Witchcraft should seek and question and explore. Most Witches are educated not only about Witchcraft, and the associated traditions found in Paganism, but also in other religions, belief systems, and traditions of majick. We expect our Witches to be well-educated. I've found many Christians have not even read their own holy book or fully understand the meaning, history, and context of their scriptures. Most don't understand the underlying theology of the different denominations. They simply believe blindly or unconsciously. Most religions benefit from such unquestioning belief and devotion. While it is harder, we do not. Many Witches have read the Bible and sought to understand the history of it and its relationship to the ancient Pagan world of the Middle East. Because of this, Witches tend not to be dogmatic or zealous, realizing everyone has their own path and has to follow their own heart. We do not indoctrinate children, but expose them to our traditions and other traditions, so they can choose what is right for themselves as they grow older.

Part of our work as Witches today is developing the culture of Witchcraft. Culture socializes a religion and spiritual tradition. As modern Witches, we don't have a lot of music and art. American Witches in particularly are disconnected from the folklore and folksongs that inform our tradition, even through the Christian veneer. Without it, we are challenged to transmit the deeper meanings and culture of Witchcraft. We need to now develop more fine art and music to express our deep truths to each other and the world.

You could consider the Cabot Tradition an Aquarian Tradition, though we are not yet in the astrological Age of Aquarius, which will last roughly two thousand years. It is an age of seeking and asking questions, of non-hierarchical relationship, social consciousness, and shared power. We seek to empower individuals for themselves. We feel we are preparing the way for the Age of Aquarius.

Like the Aquarian ideal of universal sisterhood/brotherhood, we welcome women and men equally, and people from all walks of life. Among our members are doctors, bankers, salespeople, mothers, fathers, children, students, housewives, retirees, and professors in prominent colleges. Some are financially secure, and others are not. Some are married, while others are widowed or single. They come from many socio-economic backgrounds and reflect a rainbow of diversity.

The Glastonbury Phoenix – Sign of Aquarius in the Glastonbury Zodiac

The Majickal Journal

It is important to keep a majickal journal. It is the start of your own personal Book of Shadows. Many people don't start out as writers, but discover they can write by recording their thoughts, feelings, patterns, and life experiences. As you grow in your practice of Witchcraft, record all your meditations, psychic experiences, projections, spells, and rituals. As times goes on, when you review your journal, you'll be able to see how much was accurate, and how much you've changed with the practice of majick.

Personal Practice

Meditation is vital. You should practice at least three times per week. Most seasoned Cabot Witches meditate everyday, even several times a day, until alpha becomes second nature. It is only through the practice of meditation and majick that we grow, develop, and evolve. Just reading and thinking about it does not create change. They are not a substitute for actually doing it.

The Laws

Witches have two laws that make up our belief system. These laws work scientifically. The first is the Three-fold Law:

Everything we think and everything we do comes back to us three times.

If you don't believe this, take a look at your life, and you will see that you get a thump in the head now and then. When you feel that thump, you wonder why this had to happen to you. It might have been a passing thought, something you said, or a little lie you recently told. If you don't adhere to this law, the thumps continue, and it is not an easy thing to deal with. It relates to the Hermetic Principle of Cause and Effect. Remember, this world is not a dainty place. No one said it was going to be easy. It is not. If you wish, it is up to you to make it a dainty place. You have to abide by the rules so you can live in comfort and harmony. When you don't know the rules, and when your society avoids these rules and makes totally opposite ones, it can be hard to feel comfortable or harmonious. People in New England complain about the weather all the time. However, that is Mother Nature. The more you complain about the weather's changes, the more you are going to be feeling their effects. Your thoughts affect what is happening to a degree. When so many people complain, it becomes a "mass" thought and can bring weather changes.

Your thoughts do matter, more than you may think. Your thoughts are things that affect other things. These thoughts can be real. So be careful what you think.

The second law is from pre-Gardnerian times, however, Gerald Gardner publicized this law and made it a part of modern Witchcraft, and he also drew upon teachings from Aleister Crowley. The second law is:

Do what thou will and harm none!

Actually, it is more like all the Ten Commandments rolled up into one. It has a lot fewer words and may be easier to remember, but it is a difficult law to learn, love, and live. If you can learn your majick and exert control over yourself—thoughts, actions, and body—you will become happier, healthier, and things will come to you.

I have heard people twist this law around so it means something completely different. Read the above again and think of it carefully. If we are good at our majick, we do not have to do harm. If we are all part of the Earth, we are all necessary and should encourage the success of all. It is much better to handle our problems in a way that is beneficial for all. Wouldn't we want everyone who has difficulty with us to deal with us in that way, rather than wish harm upon us? It is never our job to punish, simply to transform an unhealthy situation when necessary.

To follow this law, many tend to alter or change their lifestyles. Some switch to a vegetarian diet to avoid eating other animals. Others choose to become vegan, a type of vegetarianism that excludes not only the ingestion of meat and meat by-products, but also the use of leather and other items made from an animal in any way. For example, they drink soy milk instead of forcing animals into a type of servitude for dairy production. Some do this out of respect for life, especially for animals who they feel are also co-creators of the environment and co-residents of the planet; for these vegans, their goal is to bring Earth back to the way it was. They are strong advocates of using no fur for clothes, are against factory farming, and protest animal testing in laboratories.

Their philosophy does not differ greatly from Witchcraft. Few people take this law to the max, but one needs to spend time really thinking and meditating about the ways one can follow these rules in life. Some Witches may interpret this as a reason to lose weight, quit smoking, or exercise more. The "harm none" includes that person closest to you: yourself. Again, in Witchcraft, all these choices are personal. No one will dictate the way you live, worship, or love.

NEUTRALIZATION

Why do we "harm none?" We do not harm anyone because we do not have to harm anyone. We don't have to use our majick in a hostile way...ever. It is not because we can't. We could, but at a price. Anger is a human thing, but there are consequences for every choice and action. Witches don't have to do anything harmful against another. We know how to neutralize energy and stop it. After neutralizing something, you can walk away from the situation and let it go. Neutralization shatters a stream of energy into pieces. Neutralization is done with the power of your thoughts, words, and with your mind.

To neutralize, you simply say, "I neutralize that (thought, statement, etcetera)." Neutralization can effectively erase the results of thoughts. Thoughts are the beginning of manifestation. When you realize that and utilize neutralization, you will make your life easier. Some Witches make the sign of an "X" in the air and imagine drawing a huge white "X" over a thought, statement, or situation. Neutralization can be even more effective when holding our Instant Alpha Trigger.

We have all heard people say, "That person is a pain in the neck" or "This job is a pain in the neck." People who overuse this phrase may end up with a stiff neck, tonsillitis, goiter, or a sore throat. Say it too much, and it becomes true. Watch how others use language. People who have a tendency to say everything is a "pain in the ass" have problems from that end. Monitor what you say and avoid dramatic description. Speak truly, clearly, and directly. Your brain, like a computer, processes your thoughts. It is affected by your words and your voice. Your body responds to programming. After a while, your projection begins to manifest. Sometimes with an instantaneous thought, the process happens instantly. When you blurt something out without thinking, you usually regret it. In most cases, the brain stops you from a faux pas with built-in neutralizers, though our affirmations in an alpha state of consciousness help us build up even stronger neutralizers. The information is first integrated before being verbalized. This process allows for more effective socialization skills.

Neutralize those things that are harmful. You do not have to do harm to anything. You can alleviate the effects in other, far more productive ways. How can you use this ability for good every day? When viewing an upsetting story on the news, you can become emotionally affected by it. Through this response, you may project the same problems back into the world. You may turn it off or neutralize that "bad" news. There are many ways to do this. The big white X can be envisioned over the picture in your mind, on a television screen, or over a newspaper story. Say out loud, "I neutralize this." You can add "It will not come to be again," or "It will not come to be," depending on the circumstances. Visualize this white X until the vision, television screen, or newspaper is out of focus.

Sometimes your brain gives you a little trouble. Whether it's an apple or an X, you may not be able to visualize what you want because you are not allowing it, for whatever reason. When I experience this, I quickly envision myself taking a big paintbrush and a bucket of white paint, "X-ing" it out, and painting it away. This helps to redefine the image and re-focus clearly on what I want to accomplish.

Graduates of Witchcraft II describe things as "correct" or "incorrect" when describing moral or ethical issues. We never use the words "negative" or "positive." Why? Negative and positive are not inherently evil or good, but simply ends of polarity. Start to use the words "correct" and "incorrect." Negative energy is not always bad, and positive energy is not always good; these are just colloquialisms. These terms are informal descriptions. Learn and understand negative and positive energy in a correct way. Witches use these terms in different ways than the general public does.

PROJECTION

Projection, or thinking things into existence, is a process. This topic naturally comes up with discussion of neutralization. Through neutralization, you avoid having any unwanted projections manifest in your life. Conscious projection yields helpful results for Witches.

Projection is a way of manifesting or thinking into reality things that will eventually come to be. In order for two-way communication to occur, the sender must be clear, and the receiver must be attentive. Professionals in psychology, education, and speech communication talk about the importance of really listening to what is said. An effective "active listener" uses different techniques to show the speaker that he or she is being heard. Why is this so important? It is estimated that people hear only about thirty percent of what is being said. When you hear Witches in Salem talking, you will often hear one of them reply to a statement with "I neutralize that thought." The first person may have said, "I am dying to see that movie, or "My son's sports addiction is going to kill me," or "If my husband asks me one more time, I'll yell my head off." We will say, "Come on, you are not dying to see that movie," or "Brian's love of the Red Sox isn't hurting anything but his wallet," or "Yelling your head off will be of little help and make a big mess!" Witches help each other, are careful of what others say, and catch these overdramatic statements. We all use them, but don't mean them, and absolutely do not want to project such ideas. After a while, you will monitor yourself, and after a statement like that, you will say, "I wonder how that happened?"

One day I was driving down Route 128 in Massachusetts, and we saw a crumpled barrier and lots of broken glass. I said that I wondered how that happened. I immediately caught myself and said that I didn't want to know. I neutralized that thought, because I knew how that happened and didn't need to experience it. What does that phrase really mean? It can mean that we want to experience it, or see it. We have to be very careful of both inner and outer dialogue.

Projection for the good of all is just as easy as projecting only for yourself. Once we start doing everything for the good of ourselves, we're always going to have opposition. You're always going to have a log in the road when you're driving. You're always going to have something that doesn't come through for you. It must be for the good of all. You need to understand the concept. When you start to really think about it and ask yourself "What does that mean?" you'll begin to understand it. I do what I do for the good of all people and all things on Earth. Why should I do that? What does the Earth do for me? What do people do for me? What does my boss do for me? That's how most people think. What's in it for me? What's in it for you is that when you do things for the good of all, you are successful. You get what is correct for you, and correct for all. You have to be careful what you want and how you want it. That is why you ask that any projection or spell is correct and for the good of all. You have to be careful. When you do that in the balance and harmony of the universe, there is harmony and balance in the universe. You may not see it or understand it because this place is so much of the time out of balance because of the way humans think. It takes into account the balance of the entire planet and all beings, and the cosmos.

LOVING YOURSELF

Before moving on to the importance of self-love, we must review the importance of inner dialogue. Inner dialogue affects projection, self-esteem, self-respect, and self-responsibility. To love oneself sounds egotistical, yet it is one of the most important steps to being a healthy human and an effective Witch. Inner dialogue often turns self-demeaning. Most of us say to ourselves that we don't know if we can do this or that, get this or that, or commit to this or that. We often beat ourselves up through inner dialogue. Reading books on your inner child or on being your own parent is a good idea. Take responsibility for how you feel, how you deal with your inner self, and how you project yourself. You have an obligation to accept your own choices and their results. Subsequent events, or what may happen, are caused by your actions and words. Choices affect your life, both the good and the bad aspects. There is no need to blame others or bemoan your fate. Take time to study your past behaviors and take control of your future. Both your own wishes, and those you accept from others, affect your life and self-esteem.

THE POWER OF "ALLOW" AND ITS TRUE MEANING

After the age of fourteen, we rarely hear the word "allow." Often "allow" is left out of people's vocabulary. You don't hear people say, "I will not allow this to happen," or "I will allow this in my life." Yet, "allow" is a very powerful word. Use it more often and become aware of your own power. As adults, we can control the things that affect us and our lives. How many times have you been pushed into things by another, and then wondered how you got there and why? You allowed the situation and accepted other choices over your own. When you realize you do not have to allow this behavior, it will stop. Only you can make it stop. It is hard to say "I am important," and "I can lead myself in the direction that is right for me," and "I know what is correct for me." These statements are the first steps to true independence in thought and action. You need and want to follow your own heart, knowledge, and instincts to function as a healthy adult.

CARING WHAT OTHERS THINK

Most of us are easily demeaned by others; what you should look like, what you should act like, what is right and wrong, what you should study, where you should go, how you should feel, what a good mother is like...it goes on and on. Remove the judgmental word "should" from your vocabulary. If you are a fully functioning, healthy adult, you know what is right and wrong, and don't need to be reminded about what you should do in any situation. Should, according to the *American Heritage Dictionary* is the past tense of shall:

1. Used to express obligation or duty.
2. Used to express probability or expectation.
3. Used to express conditionality or contingency.
4. Used to moderate the directness or bluntness of a statement.

"Should" implies you may not be bright enough to take the appropriate action. Our language has dropped the word "shall" in its modern form; I think it's time we also get rid of the past tense.

Once you find out that you can change, and that one person could conceivably change the whole world by thoughts and actions, you see everything about life in a renewed and different way. Things can change. You can change. This is powerful and possible. Some people may not want to make major changes, and that is okay. You may want to keep things going in the current direction. Each one of us can decide what we want to do and use our majick to accomplish what we need to accomplish.

HEALTH IN THOUGHT, ACTION, AND BODY

Keep your thoughts, actions, and body healthy. If you can put food in your mouth psychically and physically, heal yourself psychically and physically, earn a living and put a roof over your head, you are doing a service to the universe. You are independent and can provide for your own basic needs. This means that you take care of yourself and are then able to help others. To help yourself and then reach out to others is the best goal that anyone can have.

These goals have to be in this order. If you don't love yourself first, you cannot love anyone else. That is the bottom line. One of the most important things to learn and meditate on is that loving yourself is important. Realize that you are worthy of your love. You also deserve love from others. Forget what the media portrays as the best looking specimen. Life is not dainty, and life is not always easy. If you can learn your majick and exert control over yourself—thoughts, actions, and body—you will become happier, healthier, and things will come to you. Think about how it would feel to have control in your own personal space and to be able to trust yourself. When you control yourself, just this little improvement can improve society as a whole. You are doing something good, healing yourself, and experiencing happiness and joy. Some people have never felt these sensations and emotions; they have never felt this good. They may feel they were never allowed to, or they were afraid to, but that is now past. Feeling good, for any time at all, is one of the most wonderful things on Earth…to smile, to be truly happy. These are the things that this science can give to you.

Through these laws, exercises, and ideas, you can get closer to inner and outer happiness. Society will still step on you now and then, but you will be better prepared for the downs when you recognize and control the ups in your life. After this course, you will be better equipped to spring back. You will know and understand the balance of life, and live your life better. You will feel more comfortable and more in tune with the aging cycle. You recognize the energies of the Sun and Moon, the day and night, and the changing of the seasons. You also learn to accept that which you can't control. If it's raining, bring an umbrella. Snowing? Get out the shovel. Deal with your decisions and accept the consequences. You are responsible for how you feel and how you act.

A MAJICKAL ATTITUDE

Keeping a majickal attitude in all that you do is important if you want to live a majickal life. You experience life in the manner in which you approach it. If you want your majick to be successful and help you, you need to be able to see the majickal possibilities and lessons in everything you do. Everything is majickal. Everything is spiritual. Everything is listening to you and if you listen closely, you can hear it communicating with you. A good Witch knows how to develop this relationship with everything and everyone. You must expect your majick to succeed —and it will!

WHAT IS "NATURAL?"

We live in a modern society. Urbanites and suburbanites are more common than farmers. That does not make the world less majickal. You can still do majick whether you live in a high-rise or a log cabin. Many Witchcraft authors stress the importance of what is natural. Guess what? Cement is natural. Even polyester is natural. It is made out of petroleum. There is really nothing on the Earth that doesn't have its beginning in something natural. It is all about how you perceive it. Through the science of Witchcraft, our bodies become in synch with the changing of the tides and seasons. Pay attention to the Moon, stars, and astrological aspects. You live in a changing world, but are present in a season. Enjoy the present, the past, and the future. These are the gifts that I give you, and the knowledge you give to yourself after completing the first degree.

BRAIN WAVES AND THE ALPHA STATE

Our brainwaves are measured in cycles per second (cpc), also known as hertz (htz), and we recognize four main brain wave states. Whenever a state is dominant in our brain, we experience that level's perception of reality and awareness. The names for the different cycles are as follows:

Beta (24–14 cps): Active, alert, waking, logic, reason, linear thought
Alpha (14–07 cps): Rest, daydream, intuition, psychic information, inner visions, creativity
Theta (07–03 cps): Withdrawal from senses, clear inner visions, bodily control
Delta (03–00 cps): Deep trance, deep sleep, astral travel, muscle atrophy, no linear thought

Beta is the most active, alert state. The activity decreases as the cycles decrease. Alpha level is the key to psychic and majickal experiences. Brainwave rates in alpha are 14-7 cycles per second. During sleep, you automatically go into alpha. Alpha is your resting level. You automatically go into alpha when you allow your mind and body to rest, such as during a nap. If you close your eyes and relax for over three minutes, you are in the alpha state. Alpha is something you naturally do every day and night. Reaching the alpha state is not as hard as you think. You simply may not feel it or realize it when you first start to practice.

The relaxation and clearing benefits of alpha contribute to your health. If you do nothing else with alpha but meditate and lower your blood pressure, that is fine. It will keep you rested. Every fifteen minutes in alpha is equal to three hours of sleep. The ability to work at alpha level is the springboard to all majick. It can assist you in doing so many things. When you are in alpha and receiving information, you retain that information at a rate of almost one hundred percent.

Here are three major facts regarding alpha:

1. During sleep, everyone experiences alpha, regardless of the differences in the visions.
2. There are differences in how one experiences or perceives information in dreams, and you find these same differences in how individuals receive information in alpha.
3. You may not consciously feel yourself entering an alpha state.

When you reach alpha, intentionally or otherwise as you relax or go to sleep, your brain waves slow down and you start seeing pictures on the screen of the mind. Whatever you are thinking about—or whatever comes in—can be seen on this screen. Your awareness of these visions is heightened. A picture of an Australian Aborigine may come onto your screen. You may never have seen an Aborigine before. You decide that he must be a Native American. You stereotypically put a loin cloth on him and place a tomahawk in his hand. You put a horse under that man and find yourself being chased by a tomahawk-wielding Indian on horseback, all through your unconscious interpretation.

After learning alpha, you know how to deal with this, and realize that it may not be what you thought it was. You then say, "Where are you from?" You then might see a big rock like the image of Uluru, also known as Ayer's Rock, an aboriginal sacred site in Australia, or hear the word "Australia." Now you have clues as to who and what that person really is.

Until you learn to use alpha, you will turn the images you see into recognizable people, places, or things from your culture. This is what you know, how you have been taught, and how you have programmed your brain in the past. We often work in familiar images and stereotypes.

Alpha can be used for practical purposes. You want to use every bit of energy, intelligence, and knowledge you have to make life better and easier for yourself and others. You have to develop the skill. Study the Crystal Countdown, learn the numbers, and practice it daily, not sporadically. We all have busy lives and little time for ourselves. Five minutes during lunch break, or before preparing dinner, can be worked into the busiest schedules.

Working at alpha level will change your life for the better. It is like any physical exercise, but this is for your brain. Alpha is a part of a system that helps you direct and control energy for a specific purpose. Whether you send a message or do a healing, you simply transfer energy. We believe it is in the form of light energy. Pythagoras, who some sources say was trained by the Celts, is the father of this system. Alpha training may have been a part of Celtic knowledge passed down through the centuries, but there is no hard evidence of this. In any case, it is a part of our majickal heritage today, and should be used to better our lives and make the world a better place.

ALPHA AND THE DREAM STATE

When you go into alpha to sleep, your body goes through the same cycles and shifts as when you consciously put yourself into alpha. After the alpha state, while asleep, you enter a REM sleep level. REM stands for "rapid eye movement." In REM sleep, you experience night visions, commonly known as dreams and nightmares. Everyone has their own dreams and visions. Some dream only in black and white, while others dream in color. Some hear clearly in their dreams; others do not. Some people easily remember their dreams, and others don't. Some remember every single dream. Science has not been able to explain these individual differences. Dreams can be prophetic, but more often, dreams are your brain sorting and deliberating your emotional concepts.

This skill of stopping our vision and asking questions, peeling away the layers of our own culture and expectations, is also a useful skill with our dreams. Many cultures have recognized that by remaining in alpha during a bad dream, we can turn the results of the dream into a pleasurable experience.

For example, you dream you are chased by a tomahawk-wielding madman, jump off a cliff... and land on a giant trampoline! The director says "good work" and you have started a new career. Or a big bear is chasing you in the woods. It comes closer and closer and...licks you on the face! You pet it, now realizing that he is the lost bear from the petting zoo. You take him back to his home, get a big reward, and have a special relationship with bears from then on. Let's get back to the Aborigine. What is it, really, that is on your screen? Why, of all things, is an Aborigine standing there? Sometimes it can be a spirit, a projection from another person, or you, mind-traveling, envisioning an Aborigine. We don't know for sure which it is in every case. Is it just your imagination? Imagery is imagery. It does not mean the vision is false, not there, or not real. You can't tell whether it is an imagined or actual Aborigine. We have no idea how the picture, place, person or thing got on your screen.

Some people report having lucid dreams. These people can ask and get information on whether this person, place, or thing is in existence now, or why it is there, but most people do not experience it. You may be able to achieve this to an extent in alpha. Either way, do not worry. If it is a spirit, because you have your protection shield, nothing is going to harm you in alpha. All you are going to do is see the image. If it is a spirit, it may be someone who wants to give you knowledge.

I have been consciously using alpha for years, communicating with people alive and not alive. I have never had a problem. Don't listen to movie plots where people have horrible things happen to them. For example, *The Amityville Horror* was a hoax. Residents of that area say there is no truth to the story. We even called the Archdiocese of the Roman Catholic Church in the area, who would have had to approve all exorcisms. We performed other independent research, and there is no truth to that story. People will go to such lengths to make stories like that seem real. Hollywood will spend lots of money for stories like that for a real profit.

If you do pick up a spirit who wants to show their image to you, they are simply communicating. Nine out of ten times, you will not be picking up a spirit, but someone asleep, who is also in alpha. For some reason, their brain waves get caught up with yours and, like a radio, you have picked up this person. If you believe in demons and devils—although Witches do not— you might see one on your screen, but it is of your own making. I have done a lot of work with police who are looking for information about people who have passed on. Never, not even during a murder investigation, have I had a demon, devil, or angry, nasty spirit around me in my entire life. Never. Spirits are always at their highest level. When they have done something bad, they can't believe that they were once capable of doing such a thing. After death, people have a completely different focus.

The Devil didn't do it! Witches do not believe in a Devil who makes you do something or entices you to think incorrectly. We all have a choice. We are here to learn to act correctly, instead of incorrectly. We can do evil; anyone can do evil. It is in your best interest, however, to choose to act and think in a correct manner. This is not because of a vengeful deity or a judgmental priest; it is because of the Three-fold Law. Remember, this law states that whatever you do will return to you three times. I personally would prefer to have three good things return to me than to face the consequences and have a triple whammy for some irresponsible act. This is your choice—and your challenge.

Dreams and Déjà vu

We review our problems during our nightly dream state. Your brain sorts the information you received that day into categories, as a computer would. In alpha, the brain activity is the same as while sleeping. When tired or stressed at the office, sit down and count into alpha for five minutes. You will receive more rest in those five minutes than you may get by sleeping all night long! Try the Apple Meditation and remember Total Health Clearance (both of which you will learn shortly). Many ask if the information received during dreams is similar to that received during alpha. In alpha, you consciously seek information. In the dream state, it is presented to you through subconscious or other means. Sometimes you do receive information in a dream.

Déjà vu occurs when information from an earlier dream is presented to you in a waking state, yet you forgot the dream or parts of it. Suddenly, something (or someone) looks or feels familiar; you just cannot place how. Some people have taken my night class after working all day. A few actually snored through their alpha exercises! The fact is that while sleeping, they still hear everything and comprehend the exercises. When you are in alpha and receive information, you retain that information at a rate of almost one hundred percent. This is significant, because the average person, at work or in class, retains information from an oral source at about thirty percent. When you retain things so completely, they remain in your long-term memory. This is why we have to be so careful about what we say to ourselves.

For example, if you have a dream where you are in Chicago and you see a building with two stone steps and the number upon the door is clearly 1840, you might be experiencing mind travel or time travel in the dream. Then, a year later, you visit Chicago and find yourself in front of that same building, with the same number. You don't consciously remember the dream as a dream, but feel a sense of déjà vu, a vague familiarity that seems significant.

There are groups that offer "total mind control." One thing they say to cover themselves legally is that you can do no harm in alpha. They claim that it won't work, but this is false. Of course, you can do harm in alpha. How could you do harm through thoughts, but not in alpha? Of course you could. The reason you don't is simply because you don't have to. You can put up shields and protect yourself in a number of ways. With so many other reasons to go into alpha, it is senseless to waste this skill doing something wrong. You are learning alpha to use it for your own advantage, and for the advantage of others, and for the world.

USING ALPHA MEDITATION: THE CRYSTAL COUNTDOWN

Here are important points to memorize before going into alpha through the use of the Crystal Countdown Meditation:

1. Always practice alpha with your eyes closed.
2. You will see your screen (of the mind) in front of you, between your eyebrows, where the third eye would be.
3. Visualize each color on your screen as you count down. Try remembering things associated with that color to help you.
4. Do not try to physically use your eyes; use your mind's eye. Many people perceive or "see" in different ways. The more you practice, the more you perfect your own method of perceiving at a mind level.

5. You count down, visualizing colors and numbers, but you still may not physically feel any change when you enter alpha. You will hear things in your environment and be aware of your surroundings; you will not become catatonic or hypnotized. It is easy to reach alpha level, but bells don't ring when you are doing it correctly.

6. Alpha is not dangerous. Do not be afraid of "letting go" any more than you would be afraid of letting go when going to sleep. Alpha affects your brain in a helpful way, much like sleep, except that you remain conscious.

7. Don't try too hard. Don't try to force anything. Enjoy the experience and sensations. When you try too hard to "see" and don't really understand it's with the mind's eye, you can stress yourself out.

The Crystal Countdown Meditation

The Crystal Countdown is the crystal rainbow of light that is your aura, and light carries information. The spectrum of light enters your pineal gland. Your psychic ability is stimulated, and you receive information. This meditation helps you activate your mind's eye. The Crystal Countdown can slow down your brainwaves into alpha.

Sit quietly in a chair and close your eyes. Take a deep breath and relax. Relax all the muscles around your eyes and eyelids. Relax your jaw. Feel the warmth on the top of your head and feel warmth over your forehead down your face and shoulders, down your spine, over your arms and fingertips. Feel the warmth down your thighs and your shins, over and under your feet. Relax.

Look up at the screen of your mind's eye; keep your eyes closed and relax. You are using your brain and not the muscles in your eyes. Look at the screen of your mind. See the number seven and see the color red. See the number six, and see the color orange. See the number five, and see the color yellow. Number four is green; see the color green. Number three is blue; see the color blue. Number two is indigo; see the midnight sky. Number one is orchid; see the orchid. You are now in alpha level. Continue to count from ten to one, at which time you will be in a more perfect level. Ten, nine, eight, seven, six, five, four, three, two, one. You are now at your innermost level where everything you do will be accurate and correct and this is so.

7 is Red

6 is Orange

5 is Yellow

4 is Green

3 is Blue

2 is Indigo

1 is Orchid

At this point, you would do any meditative work you desire, including following your inner visions, healing, psychic work, or speaking to spirits. Alpha presents a perfect opportunity to program yourself. You may want to work on weight loss, smoking, or self-esteem. I use alpha for meditation. I work health cases and do healings. You can use alpha as a sleep aid. When done, count yourself back up.

To count up, erase your screen with your hand. Give yourself Total Health Clearance by placing your hand above your head and with a sweeping motion bring it down in front of your body, and at your solar plexus push the hand out and away from the body.

Count from one to ten without colors. Count from one to seven without colors. Open your eyes.

When you count down correctly, once you get to "number one is orchid," you are in alpha. It is that simple. Memorize the colors and numbers to effectively count down. Practice the colors and numbers and learn to affect your brainwaves. You are adjusting the flow of energy and lowering the number of cycles per second of activity in the brain. Both numbers and colors affect light in the brain. A specific color produces a specific effect. If you had a spectrum (rainbow of colors) that went from red to orchid, and you, with eyes open, stared at each color, one at a time, you would automatically lower your brain waves.

You can see the red seven, and all the other colors, in any way you choose. A big black seven can appear on a red background, or you may want a seven drawn in red. You can see yourself writing the seven or painting it in red. It can be a hollow seven and you can color it in with red. Or a white seven that changes to red. Any method works.

Recall the color red. Think of a stop sign, an exit sign, your favorite red sweater, a red apple or a rose, anything that is red. Take it from your memory and place it on your screen. Use that to create the red seven. For orange, try a pumpkin, carrot, or an orange citrus fruit. For yellow, use the image of a canary, banana, lemon, or the Sun. For green, work with the image of grass, a leaf, a green traffic light, or an emerald. For blue, use an image of the sky, a clear blue lake, or the tropical ocean. For indigo, work with the image of an eggplant or a deep night sky. The indigo puts you into a deep alpha, but the last color, orchid, lifts your awareness a bit, into a more appropriate mode for majickal working. For orchid, use a light lilac, a pale lavender, or the actual traditional orchid flower.

Review the colors and numbers in your mind until you feel comfortable with the countdown, then move on, but continue to practice them daily.

When counting yourself up from alpha, it is not necessary to use colors. Count from one to ten and then from one to seven, without colors. After practicing alpha for a while, your brain waves automatically adjust to an active (beta) state as you come out. The more you practice, the easier it becomes to change your beta to alpha states.

Be patient with yourself. I have never had a student who was unable to achieve alpha. Visualization is something we do naturally. Sometimes visualization feels threatening because it is a new sensation. Sometimes it is hard to accept what you are seeing, because you have not been taught that what you "see" or visualize is correct. Some of us have to "re-program" our thinking. We have to learn to let go of the restrictions that society, parents, and schools have put on us. If you can dream, you can visualize. You will find alpha is a truly enjoyable experience. We spend three quarters of our sleep resting in alpha.

THE MIND SCREEN OR THIRD EYE

Remember, do not try to use your physical eyes, for the majick is not happening with your physical eyes. It is occurring through the power of the screen of your mind. The mind screen is also known as the third eye. You imagine it in front of you, but between your brows, where if you literally had a third eye, it would be looking. When you use your imagination, you are engaging the screen of your mind. Whenever someone says, "picture this," you are using the screen of your mind.

Using the mind's eye is not as hard as it sounds. We use our mind's eye every day in a variety of ways. Think of a red fire engine. You saw one in your mind, right? When we recall, we use our mind's eye. Each major energy point within the body is associated with a gland or organ; the third eye is associated with the pineal gland, a vestigial third eye with rods and cones much like our own physical eyes which can sense the changes in light in the environment. When we visualize light, it senses that as well, and we perceive it as the screen of our mind. Memory and imagination engage the third eye. Try one more...a grey elephant. Would you be able to describe this elephant to me? Of course you could. That is the power of alpha.

At first, it will seem harder to you to do these exercises with your eyes closed than with your eyes open, simply because we are not used to doing these recall exercises without physical sight. We taught ourselves to daydream in school with our eyes open. You will eventually learn to consciously reach alpha with eyes closed.

Third Eye Mandala

If you put your finger in the middle of your head on the crown (the top of your head) and went straight down through the largest, thickest bone of the body—the butterfly bone—while also going straight through the middle of your forehead, the point of intersection between these two lines is a little pea-shaped gland called the pineal gland. This gland has light coming through it. For years scientists have said we can't reach that part of the brain because it's too dense. The bone is too dense. Well, Witches and mystics have been teaching it as the physical location of the third eye. We've been teaching for centuries that light comes through that gland, the pineal. Scientists have discovered it is sensitive to changes in light, but we know it also sees universal light, the psychic light from which we do our psychic reading and project our majick.

TOTAL HEALTH CLEARANCE

One way to protect yourself from unwanted or lingering psychic energy or information is Total Health Clearance. This should become an automatic habit whenever you are about to come up out of alpha. Even if you are going into alpha to meditate, it is wise to give yourself Total Health Clearance. No matter what work you are doing in alpha, give yourself Total Health Clearance before the count-up.

Put one hand over the crown chakra (above your head) and bring your hand down in front on your face, palm facing you, and then push outward, palm outward, as you reach the level of your solar plexus, or chest. Say to yourself:

I am giving myself Total Health Clearance.

Total Total Health Clearance, through the use of your own hand, is a way to heal yourself. It ensures that anything brought up on your screen will not affect you. For example, if you do not do a Total Health Clearance, and you have been working on a healing case where the person has a cold, you may experience the sniffles for about five minutes. Again, this won't hurt you, but there is no need to experience this. We often pick up other people's energies and feelings. Some people experience this in everyday life. By standing next to a person with a cast on their arm, some sympathetically feel some pain. When they walk away, it goes away. We are sensitive to others' information and energies, but most of us are unaware of this.

CONTROL

Some people feel that they have to control everything around them, in their lives and in others' lives. The truth is that no one can control everything. It is impossible; such action only leads to frustration. At some point, you just have to let go. It is not healthy to worry about the things you have no control over. Part of learning alpha is also learning to let go. Overcome the urge to control and let the brain take over to go into alpha. Do not be upset if it doesn't come to you easily. It takes some people longer to get used to alpha than it takes others. Once you get it, though, you will never have a problem with the process again. After much practice, many of the people with difficulty wonder how they ever had any trouble at all.

THE APPLE

The apple is a sacred Witch symbol. Avalon, which is the land of the Witches, means "Isle of Apples." If you cut an apple in half crosswise, you'll see the five seeds in the center creating a five-pointed pentacle around the core.

The Apple Meditation

To perform the Apple Meditation, follow the steps for the Crystal Countdown. Once in alpha, look on your psychic screen. Draw the energy and aura of an apple onto your screen by visualizing it using all the senses. The apple is real. It may be from your neighbor's kitchen or drawn from a grocery store across the country, but the apple is real and you are drawing upon its energy and image through the screen of your mind.

With your eyes closed, bring the apple clearly into focus. Reach up on the screen of your mind and touch the apple. Grasp the apple with your forefinger, middle finger, and thumb. These fingers are acupressure points which activate the mind's eye. A blind person can "see" colors, shapes, and forms by using the tip of their index finger. The middle finger is an acupressure point for recall of what you see or feel in the mind's eye. Use both together to retain what you are getting psychically.

Cup the apple in your hand. Feel how round and smooth it is. Examine it closer. There may be ridges and bumps. The skin is smooth and may be green, red, or yellow.

Before counting yourself up, erase the apple by using your hand as if erasing a blackboard. As you clear your screen, you erase the aura of the apple and eliminate the image. By using your hands, you are learning to integrate physical movement while in alpha.

In essence, you draw in the energy of a real apple from somewhere in the world. Information on the taste, smell, touch, and sound of the object on our screen also enters through the aura and the solar plexus. "Gut feelings" occur when we receive information through our solar plexus. The more skilled you are in alpha, the better you will successfully perform the Witchcraft techniques of psychic diagnosis, healing, mind travel, manifestation, and any other form of majick. The Apple Meditation is excellent practice.

Sometimes the image on the screen of your mind looks like a real apple. Other times, it may be more like a picture or a sketch of an apple. Sometimes the apple is cloudy or less distinct. These are normal experiences. The more you practice, the more you allow a clearer apple to appear. Clarity differs from person to person, from vision to vision. A vision may not be clear, but the information and energy are still there. Let the energy come through. Don't try to force it into a clear image. It may be a form, shape, or shadow, distinct or indistinct. Using your hands and fingers helps bring it into focus and offers further information on shape, color, and texture. Use your hands when you erase your screen. This action helps you clear for the next working.

A professional yoga teacher was taking this course to see what Witches do. She and her husband, an opera singer, lived in the beautiful town of Newburyport. She was thrilled to learn about alpha and the Apple Meditation, but her tenor husband was not enthused. He was disgusted with the idea of Witchcraft classes. The couple liked to meditate under a particular tree in the yard. She went to sit under the tree to practice her Apple Meditation. She received a really nice apple on her screen. After she was finished, he went out to spend some time meditating under the tree. In just a few minutes, though, he came back in the house. He looked so frustrated, and she asked him what was wrong. He told her that every time he closed his eyes, he saw an apple! She had forgotten to erase the apple from her screen and it affected him, showing the reality of our psychic experiences beyond our own imagination.

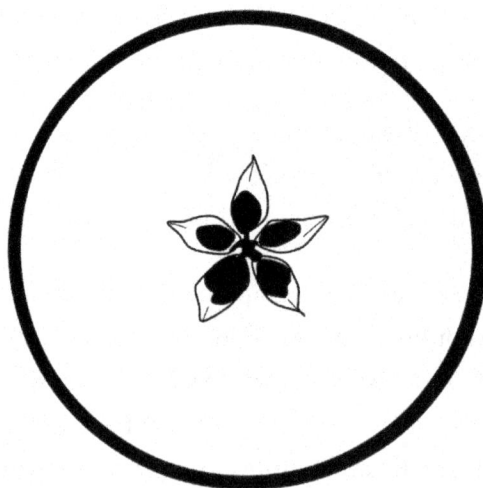

Apple with Seed Pentagram

THE PENTACLE

The Pentacle is the symbol of the Witch. It is also the sign of universal wisdom and protection. It is a five-pointed star, also known as a pentagram or pentalpha, in a circle. Enclosed in the circle is what makes it a pentacle, a symbol of the Witch and her path. The five points are for the five physical senses through which earthly knowledge enters the world, while the circle is the secret sixth sense we discover in alpha, our psychic sense. The points of the pentagram also embody the five elements—earth, water, air, fire, and spirit. These stand for your body, emotions, mind, vitality, and invisible spark, respectively. All things are made from the five elements.

While the pentacle is a symbol of the art and religion of Witchcraft, it is also a symbol of our science and requires no "faith" to use. The circle reflects and refracts all light from any angle. The five-pointed star depicts a human figure, with two arms, two legs, and the head, surrounded by the circle, which is also a symbolic of Total or Divine Intelligence, the Goddess and God. Here is the point where the mystic center is found, the point of consciousness between the normal human consciousness, the deep unconscious, and the higher self.

The pentacle follows scientific principles. It is like a printed circuit. You don't have to be a Witch to understand or enjoy its significance or effects. It is also a symbol of protection. It gives us information, guiding us and helping us to grow.

The pentacle is a type of talisman, a ritual object that by its very nature produces energy for a specific desired effect. Some talismans are based upon their geometry and symbolism. Others are enchanted by a Witch, and can be made from stones, herbs, roots, wood, bone, metal, paper, or even a photograph or drawing. Ritual jewelry often is used as a talisman for the active Witch.

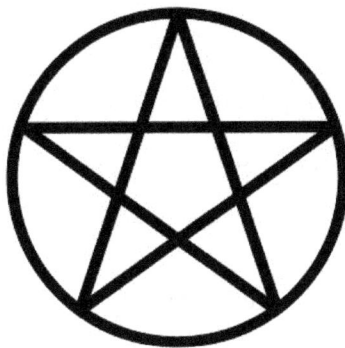

The Pentacle

While anyone can wear a pentacle, a pentacle pendant is particularly a sign of a Witch, and an appropriate piece of jewelry to wear both as a student and graduate of the First Degree. Often a pentacle or pentagram ring is used as the sign of a Second Degree Witch, and a talismanic bracelet as a subtle sign of the Third Degree Witch, though we have also used crown or star rings.

AFFIRMATIONS AND BENEFICIAL PHRASES

The world responds to your thoughts. When you think negatively, you can set up some roadblocks for yourself, but when you think positively, you will find the results can be truly wonderful. By using affirmations in the alpha state, you can reprogram your thinking and transform your life.

We react to thoughts and words. That is why we need to learn to love ourselves. Self-love is not egotistical. Saying "I love you" to yourself every day is learning to give and accept love, and it helps you learn how to give and receive love from others. Practicing healthy self-love can assist you in entering into and sustaining healthy friendships and romantic relationships. During this alpha meditation, you will repeat beneficial phrases that you can use every day. You may choose to repeat these to yourself as often as you like, or do this meditation when you need self-healing and self-love. Healthy self-love strengthens your intuition, perception, and power. It heightens all your abilities. It enables you to function at peak performance. It will make you wiser in many ways and more confident. Witches know they need to be confident and believe in themselves in order to do majickal workings.

Affirmation Meditation

Sit quietly in a chair and close your eyes. Take a deep breath and relax. Relax all the little muscles around your eyes. Relax your jaw. Use the Crystal Countdown to put yourself into alpha level. Listen to these beneficial phrases and repeat them to yourself after you hear them:

- I am gaining better control of my thoughts, words, and actions. Thoughts are a form of action.
- I better understand all forms and flows of energy both inside and outside of my body.
- I improve my psychic ability every day.
- I understand that thoughts and words are powerful, and are forms of action; I'm responsible for all of my own actions.
- I will always use energy in a correct manner for the good of all.

- Every time I go into alpha, all my bodily functions improve: my eyesight, my hearing, and my vision.
- Every day in every way I'm feeling better, I am better, and I'm getting better.
- I'm becoming more of a genius every day.

Feel your body becoming infused with pink light. Enjoy its warmth and blanketing effect. Experience feeling good all over, in every cell of your body. Enjoy the safety and comfort of self-love and self-esteem. When you are finished, give yourself Total Health Clearance. Count up from alpha. Open your eyes. You are learning to take better care of yourself with healthy self-love.

Here are some alternative beneficial phrases that can also be repeated in alpha:

- I am now gaining control and understanding of energy levels outside of the body.
- My intelligence is expanding, and this is so.
- By functioning at these levels of mind, I have the ability to use my psychic senses.
- I have the control and responsibility for my actions.
- I will always use energy in a correct manner for the good of all.
- I am getting better every day in every way.
- I am achieving my goals.

As you continue to work through Witchcraft I and practice all the exercises, your self-esteem will increase. Attitude toward self-esteem does matter, but this is within your control. Attitude makes things happen through manifestation. If you direct the energy of your aura into a specific area, using words and visualizations for change, it happens. It is as simple as that. When you allow energy to come into the screen of your mind, you take that information and filter it. Our brain can only take in and process a certain amount of information at a time. Majickal people can allow the information flow through their minds all the time. They process what they need, and discard what is not necessary. Change your attitude, and take charge of your life.

A person at one of my workshops for the first time observed that she felt a lot of Witchcraft was "self-help." Witches may have been the first group to practice self-help. There is nothing wrong with self-help. Witches try to be of service to the universe and take care of themselves. Before you take care of others, you have to make yourself a vessel of power, balance, and harmony. "Self" is not "selfish." There is a difference. Any good idea about self-help—getting straightened out, in harmony, empowered or feeling good about ourselves—should be considered and utilized. If that is what some people see in my classes and workshops, that is fine. Nothing will help, however, if you do not do the work. This is especially true about alpha and the Crystal Countdown. All of us have to follow the system and practice the process. You must use the colors and numbers in the correct sequence to achieve the alpha state of consciousness. This is how you achieve alpha to effectively do majick and healing.

The Majick Mirror Exercise

This is an easy exercise that you do when you get up in the morning. During your daily hygiene, look at yourself in the mirror for a long time and say, "I love you." Turn on the radio, the tap, or shower if you must, but say it out loudly. Your voice has to be heard by your brain. Try these affirmations:

- I love you.
- You are wonderful.
- You deserve the very best.

Say these sentences every day. These are beneficial phrases or mantras. The first few times you will feel foolish or strange. Everyone does. Two weeks later, it won't bother you as much. By three weeks, some people find that they actually look forward to "talking" to the mirror. This exercise affects you in positive ways. The majick mirror helps us align the three core selves needed to be successful in our majick and our lives:

1. Esteem
2. Confidence
3. Love

The very best can be available for everybody. You deserve your portion of the very best. By saying this again and again, it goes into the brain. Very few parents or spouses will tell you that you deserve the very best. Very few people can tell themselves that they love themselves and mean it. You need this information to heal, succeed, and do majick. You need confidence to help yourself and to help others.

Majick Mirror

OUR LANGUAGE, OUR SELVES

We have to be careful what we say to ourselves and to others. Watch your language, the influence of advertising, and your inner thoughts. Psychologists and psychiatrists are aware of the effect of words and beneficial phrases. Here are some phrases medical professionals have found useful in difficult situations:

- I cannot accept your behavior (right now).
- I cannot accept what you are saying to me (right now).
- You are being very hard on yourself.

These phrases can help defuse an unpleasant situation, extinguish chronic complaining, and decrease psychologically abusive statements. Say no more, and just walk away. When you use these phrases, do not look the person in the eye, but look at their eyebrow area. This shows that you will not respond in the manner that they wish and discontinue this interaction. While this seems cold in some instances, it will be beneficial to both parties if the interaction is not continued.

INSTANT ALPHA, RECALL, AND PROGRAMMING MECHANISM

Instant Alpha is a form of eyes-open alpha. Witches use Instant Alpha to manifest something quickly, such as a parking space on a busy street. We all need things manifested in our daily lives, and Instant Alpha can help us to do this.

Instant Alpha is a quick way to achieve alpha without the Crystal Countdown. It should be used only in emergencies. In this case, an emergency can be defined as any situation in which you would not be able to take the time to use the Crystal Countdown. This would include any situation where you cannot close your eyes.

A popular story recorded in my book, *The Power of the Witch,* shows the power of Instant Alpha. Four Witches were driving to a restaurant for dinner. We got to the parking lot, and there were no spaces left. Each of us turned to one another and said, "I thought you would take care of the parking space." We went around the corner again. This time, all four of us crossed our fingers and projected. When we returned, there were four spaces in front!

Another one of my favorites is the story of little Jay. A Witchcraft student of mine successfully taught her toddler alpha. It enabled him to fully relax and sleep easily at night and for naps. As a distraction, while driving around doing errands, she taught little Jay to use Instant Alpha. She gave Jay the "job" of zapping parking spaces. A child that age has not been programmed to disbelieve in the majickal powers of the mind. Little Jay was successful most of the time. To this day, because of his mother's teachings, he has resisted societal and cultural programming that certain things are not possible or that his goals can't be achieved in a variety of ways. Most people are indoctrinated by their parents into disbelieving both the possibility of majick and their own psychic abilities. Abilities that are not acknowledged, encouraged, and developed eventually become suppressed and wither.

Instant Alpha uses the trigger of the index and middle fingers crossed, as with the "lucky sign" which is in truth an ancient hand gesture for granting wishes by balancing the energy field and entering into a light state of alpha. With intention we program it to fulfill our projections.

Instant Alpha Programming

Using the Crystal Countdown, enter into alpha level. Cross your index and middle finger on your dominant hand and say to yourself: "Whenever I cross my index and middle fingers, it will be a trigger for Instant Alpha."

I use it in various ways:

* getting parking spaces;
* relaxation, better health and blood pressure reduction;
* better reading comprehension and retention;
* remembering important information from lectures or conversations;
* better recall while taking tests;
* removal of bad habits and development of correct behavior;
* sending light and energy;
* anything my mind creates as a use.

With your trigger programmed, give yourself Total Health Clearance, and count up from alpha level.

From that time on, anytime you need to attain alpha instantly, in an emergency or in a majick circle, you will be in that state. Your eyes may remain open.

Use your Instant Alpha trigger in daily life. Every time you project for something say, "I ask that this be correct and for the good of all." Majick is always done in for the good of all and to harm none. With all intentions, always project for the end result, not the means by which it comes to be.

When you use Instant Alpha to get a parking space, always project for an empty parking space. Do not pick out a car and project that it moves. Let the All decide what is needed to happen to make that space available. You cannot make deals with Deity; it does not work. Use Instant Alpha to project for many things, including ritual and practical purposes. It may be inappropriate during an important meeting to close your eyes. In a true emergency, when there is no time to waste and you cannot slowly go into alpha, use Instant Alpha.

BIOFEEDBACK AND BODY CONTROL

Your brain is like a computer, and you can put the image you want up on the screen of your mind. We only use ten percent of our brain, so brain energy fuels our majickal workings. The science of Witchcraft is nothing more than this. A student nurse who took this class proved that he could control his heart rate in an experiment. He had challenged his professor's assertion that the heart is an involuntary muscle whose rate cannot be changed. We can affect the health of ourselves and others. Through alpha, you can will yourself to better health. None of this is mysterious; you don't have to believe in a certain way to understand this information. This is all a part of a science.

THE EMERALD TABLET

Witches and magicians, scientists and philosophers have always been in awe over the concept and significance of the Emerald Tablet. This tablet was where Hermes Trismegistus engraved his precepts. On this tablet he wrote the truths regarding honesty, philosophy, alchemy, the Earth's beginning, and the Hermetic Laws. The name Trismegistus means "thrice-great" and Hermes Trismegistus was the ancient father of occult wisdom, astrology, and alchemy, associated by the Egyptians with Thoth, and by the Greeks with Hermes.

Stories of the Philosopher's Stone and the Emerald Tablet show the hidden meaning of alchemy: a mastery of mental forces which allows you to change your mind's vibrations. It had nothing to do with changing metal into gold.

With the Emerald Tablet Meditation, you will be able to retrieve wisdom and answers to any questions or challenges that may appear in your life. Like with Instant Alpha, you are going to program yourself so you will be able to calmly receive and retrieve wisdom and information.

The Emerald Tablet Meditation

To perform the Emerald Tablet Meditation, follow the steps for the Crystal Countdown. Once in alpha, turn your left hand upward in your lap. We receive information from the left side of our body and send from the right. Rest your hand in your lap. In the palm of your hand, visualize a faceted emerald the exact size of your palm.

The point of the emerald comes out of the back of your hand. In your palm it is smooth, polished stone. This green gem is called the Emerald Tablet. It immediately warms to the touch of your hand and almost seems to vibrate and pulse, as if alive. You can actually touch the tablet with your right hand, feeling its smoothness and sensing its power and wisdom. Notice that the emerald extends to a point, like a diamond, which passes harmlessly through your hand. Examine it thoroughly. This emerald in your hand can answer questions and can heal.

If you have a question, you can look into the emerald with your mind's eye and see if you can get an answer from the crystal. It will be accurate and correct information. It is a portal to Divine wisdom. Whenever you need it, it will be there. Gaze into the shiny depth of the emerald and ask your question. Understand that you might not get the information immediately. It can come to you in dreams, meditation, and symbolism, but you will always get an answer to your question. If you have a need for healing, you can ask the crystal to heal you.

Remember to perform your Total Health Clearance after each question, to clear yourself before asking a new question, with new information.

If you feel comfortable with the emerald in your hand and you would like it to remain there, you can say it is fixed. If you feel uncomfortable, you can take the emerald out of your hand and call to it again when needed. Give yourself Total Health Clearance. Count yourself up from alpha to beta, counting one to ten and then one to seven.

Your Emerald Tablet is now available and always at hand; use it anytime to better understand a situation or yourself. Getting answers to tough questions in life helps us in making the correct decision. Correct actions help us to lead healthier lives.

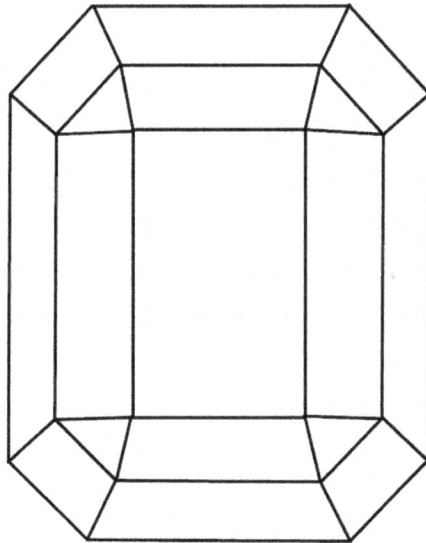

Faceted Emerald

THE SEVEN HERMETIC PRINCIPLES

Cabot Witches follow the Seven Hermetic Principles. There is a book you will read many times over—*The Kybalion* by Three Initiates. The Seven Hermetic Principles are described in this mysterious book, published by Yogi Publications in 1908. As you go through your life as a Witch, practicing your majick and logging your results, parts of this book will become clear to you. In the beginning, much of the book will probably not make much sense. Don't let it frustrate you. As you have learned alpha, use alpha when reading it. As you return to the text throughout your years practicing Witchcraft, your majickal workings will correlate with the principles in *The Kybalion*.

The Principle of Mentalism

"THE ALL is MIND; The Universe is Mental."

The Principle of Correspondence

"As above, so below; as below, so above."

The Principle of Vibration

"Nothing rests; everything moves; everything vibrates."

The Principle of Polarity

"Everything is Dual; everything has poles; everything has its pair of opposites; like and unlike are the same; opposites are identical in nature, but different in degree; extremes meet; all truths are but half-truths; all paradoxes may be reconciled."

The Principle of Rhythm

"Everything flows, out and in; everything has its tides; all things rise and fall; the pendulum-swing manifests in everything; the measure of the swing to the right is the measure of the swing to the left; rhythm compensates."

The Principle of Cause and Effect

"Every Cause has its Effect; every Effect has its Cause; everything happens according to Law; Chance is but a name for Law not recognized; there are many planes of causation, but nothing escapes the Law."

The Principle of Gender

"Gender is in everything; everything has its Masculine and Feminine Principles; Gender manifests on all planes."

It has been speculated that its author is William Walker Atkinson, who wrote under many secret pseudonyms. The work bears an uncanny resemblance to the writings of the anonymous *Arcane Teachings*, which later showed up at *The Secret Doctrine of the Rosicrucians* by Magus Incognito. While having a modern origin, these seven principles sum up the core ideas found in much longer Hermetic wisdom attributed to the Emerald Tablets; they provide a strong foundation for Witches today in understanding the ancient philosophies that govern our majick.

Another excellent resource on Hermetic and esoteric traditions is the classic tome *The Secret Teachings of All Ages* by Manly P. Hall. In it, he collects much valuable lore on majick, alchemy, healing and Hermeticism.

HERMES TRISMEGISTUS

Our beliefs rest upon the foundation of the Hermetic Laws. Although conceived of thousands of years ago, these principles parallel the theories of the new physics today. In the past, Pythagoras, the Druids, and secret mystery traditions followed these laws, as many people still do today. Quantum physics has its origin in the teachings of Hermes, as the Logos, or Word of God, made flesh. Christians applied the images associated with Hermes to Jesus, but Hermes was the original world teacher.

Hermes might have been a universal Indo-European god who taught astrology, alchemy, and many majickal practices. These universal truths are seen in many religions, including Native American beliefs. Whether Hermes was a human, several humans, or a god, he and his writings are considered the roots of astronomy, chemistry, and physics. Hermes Trismegistus, the triple wise one, was known to the Egyptians as Thoth, to the Romans as Mercury, and to the Greeks as Hermes. Whatever name he went by, his descriptions for Earth, mind, and spirit are grounded in scientific fact. You can experience Hermes in alpha meditation, accessing this universal world teacher's wisdom.

Hermes Meditation

Use the Crystal Countdown to enter into alpha state, making sure you relax your body.

Picture yourself sitting or lying on a coarsely woven blanket, on a beach of beautiful light-colored sand. The water glistens, and the air is warm, with a gentle breeze. You are enjoying the hot Sun on your body, and you are very comfortable. The sound of the waves on the shore is almost lulling you to sleep.

You become more alert as a figure dressed all in white comes walking towards you. As the figure approaches, you realize it is a man. Notice what he is wearing as he comes closer.

He is right before you now. Look at his facial features. His eyes seem to dance, and he smiles. He asks what it is that you wish. You tell him your name, and explain that you have wanted to meet him. He sits down next to you and listens as you tell him why you wanted to contact him. Ask questions now, such as these:

What is your name?

What should I call you?

How may I access your wisdom and power in my life?

What can I do for you here on Earth?

What changes should I make to become a better person?

Do you have any advice for me?

When you are ready, finish your conversation with Hermes, thank him, and bid him goodbye. Give yourself Total Health Clearance and count yourself up from alpha.

Thoth *Mercury* *Hermes Trismegistus*

Polarize Yourself For Balance

To polarize yourself, follow the steps for the Crystal Countdown. Once in alpha, picture a rod with a sphere at either end. Mentally turn the rod around one hundred and eighty degrees—even physically gesture with your hand—and say to yourself:

I polarize all positive and negative energies that are imbalanced in my mind, brain and body.

To correct this, I turn this pole (visualize turning the pole).

I have now corrected all negative and positive energies to balance my mind, brain, and body.

So Mote It Be!

Count yourself up from alpha, giving yourself Total Health Clearance.

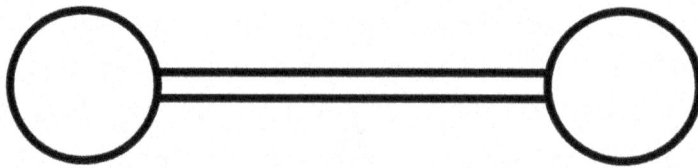

Polarizing Rod

Positive Breathing: To Counterbalance A Negative Condition*

1. Sit in a comfortable position. Take three deep, easy breaths.
2. Make sure your hands are in your lap and your feet are squarely on the floor.
3. The index finger, middle finger, and thumb of each hand must be held touching each other in a sort of triangle composed of the first two fingers and thumb.
4. Take a deep breath and hold it to the count of seven six more times (seven times total).
5. Put the whole procedure out of your mind.

In chronic situations, this exercise may be repeated. Always wait at least two hours before repeating treatments. The earlier you treat yourself when falling out of balance, the easier it is to come back to normal. This is helpful in dealing with depression.

Negative Breathing: To Counterbalance An Over-Positive Condition*

1. Sit comfortably as in the previous treatment.
2. This time your feet should be touching each other, squarely on the floor.
3. Hold your hands in front of your body at chest level; thumb touching thumb and each finger touching its corresponding finger on the other hand.
4. Close your eyes and take a deep breath. Exhale slowly.
5. When the air is completely out of your lungs, hold it for the count of seven.
6. Breathe in and out easily and slowly for five to six seconds until you are again relaxed.
7. Repeat, holding your breath out for the count of five.
8. Repeat this entire procedure seven times, then stop, breathe normally and put the entire exercise out of your mind.

This treatment is also good for the common cold if used in the early stages of infection. The cold symptoms are outward evidence of your system's attempt to rid itself of an invasion by certain types of micro-organisms. This treatment usually subdues these germs in about six to eight hours.

* Drawn from *Wisdom of the Mystic Masters* by J. Weed, published in 1974.

THE MALE AND THE FEMALE

According to the Arthurian legends or Grail myths, when the male ignores the female, the land declines into the wasteland. In other words, when you ignore the Goddess (or the female), everything around disintegrates and turns to waste. There has to be a balance in life; to recognize the Goddess as well as the God, the female as well as the male. Both energies must be present for fertility. This is an ecological lesson. Most native religions recognize this. When you have only a male or female as the highest deity, the balance is neither recognized nor honored.

An imbalance shows in all things. In our society, women make a fraction of every dollar a man makes. If it were the opposite in our culture, the men would go to war, yet women allow it. Men have not been trained in equality due to their religious upbringing. Judaism, Christianity, Buddhism, and Islam all teach that the male is superior. For seventeen hundred years, Christianity has taught this belief to its followers. That is a lot of programming, generation after generation, throughout the world.

If women are less worthy than men, why can the DNA structure of life only be carried by a woman? The man carries the X chromosome from his female ancestors. We are all equal, made of the same thing. It seems the ancients knew more about these things than we do.

These facts are why partnership between male and female is so important. Both women and men have to recognize this, and then they can benefit from it. The equality of men and women is more than a political or ethical issue. There must be a balance between the sexes, between the energies.

You have learned to use your mind, specifically how to develop your mind's energy in this course. This awareness of polarity should be studied, and there should be a balance of all extremes within us all.

Many state that we are all born women, being "female" in the womb for the first ten days. This is not necessarily true, though it has a truth to it. Once the unfertilized egg is fertilized, genetically we are male or female, but until the male Y chromosome activates the genes for the development of male hormones to give shape to the fetus, structurally we are female. Though until the hormone development takes place, it can be quite difficult to tell what species the fetus is, let alone gender. However, the "default" state of being—particularly for mammals—is female, giving rise to the notion of the Goddess as foremost the force of life.

I don't expect you to share the Cabot Witches' religious belief systems when in the First Degree, but it is important to understand balance and energy transfer. Whether you are male or female, understanding the polarities and the need for balance is a form of empowerment. Honing the skills you have learned will help. Each of us has certain abilities, and in this way, we complete one another. Remember, everything is connected.

One thing I like best about our beliefs and our science is that we can understand people and the life cycle better. Sometimes the world is not a dainty place, but each one of us can work to make it better and enjoy the time we spend here.

Many people experience things that they don't understand. It may mean they are psychic, but you have to ask, "So what?" That is why I started teaching this class. People have sporadic experiences: hearing things, déjà vu, seeing a ghost, or receiving information that they had no way of knowing. People don't want to be at the mercy of such events. The skills you have learned will help you control your abilities and to use them for good and correct reasons.

BEING PSYCHIC

Some people say it is not wise to find out about your future. Others ponder if that information is really valuable. Why wouldn't you want to know? I'd want to know. Some things, even death, can be changed at certain points. For example, if a person in danger changes plans or location, the future changes. If it is not meant to be, it does not have to happen. A good psychic who sees danger can warn a person.

Three times in my forty years of reading, I have seen specific danger and warned my client. A client from Iowa had a nine-year-old nephew. I saw the father working on a farm with machinery. I told my client that if this child was climbing around equipment, a fatal injury could occur. I found out later that my client had not warned other family members. The child had climbed up on a four-hundred-pound wheel to play and was crushed. Psychics can offer knowledge; sometimes it is useful information. Though no psychic can claim one hundred percent accuracy, the rate can be around eighty percent. Psychics are human beings who have learned to use an ability everyone could potentially use. Psychics have learned to use their brains and direct their thoughts, and that is what you are learning through this course.

LIFE FORCE: CHI, KI OR PRANA

Witches use life force in our majick. We have a natural life force in our body. Through breathing, eating, exercise, meditation, and majick, we can increase or deplete that life force. Ancient healers had a great understanding of life force. The words they used for it often related to the breath, as the invisible energy is carried on the breath. In China and in Chinese practices and medicine, it is known as *Chi,* divided into masculine active energy known as *Yang,* and feminine receptive energy called *Yin.* In Japan, the same energy is known as *Ki.* In India, life force is known as *Prana.* No matter what name you use for it, we work with energy as a part of our psychic development and often recognize this energy as light and vibration. When we integrate this energy into ourselves, it becomes a part of our life force. Witches train themselves to increase and clear our energy whenever possible.

UNIVERSAL LIGHT

All colors are made up of light. Light travels one hundred and eighty-six thousand miles per second. It is a scientific fact that all types of light, visible and invisible, have an effect on people. Moonlight and sunlight also affect people, both physically and mentally. We live awash in a sea of energy. Much of what Witches use in our majick is an invisible frequency of "psychic" light that corresponds to the colors of the visible spectrum we can see. By learning to work with this inner universal light, we can create changes in ourselves, others, and our environment. Colored light becomes the means by which we transmit information and intention to manifest.

Everything around you has its own aura, its own energy field of vibrations we can experience as colored lights. The aura is the field of our consciousness, including our thoughts, emotions, memories, and future possibilities. We can "read" the aura's information on the past, on the current state (including our health and well being), and look to possible futures. The aura is generated by the spiritual centers known as *chakras* in Hindu traditions. It is your personal "packet" of universal light energy, though most people do not know how to work consciously with their own aura and the auras of others. Through Witchcraft, we learn to project our awareness to other places. We learn to charge our aura directly as a shield. We learn to read the aura and transmit energy to and from the aura for healing.

Many cultures recognize the existence of the third eye, one of the seven major chakras. Some people believe it "sees" changes in light and allows "sight" in the mind. Scientists in the 1970s formally discovered the pineal gland, located approximately where the third eye is supposed to be, but further inside the brain. Ancients understood the pineal gland's role in psychic work on some level. The importance of colored light and its effect on the pineal gland allows us to consciously attain the alpha state. From a Witchs' perspective, the pineal gland allows you to draw light and information in on any subject you wish, or to heal yourself. It also enables you to send light out with your mind to heal others. You may project a certain color for healing, or draw it in to achieve goals or affect yourself. When you have your eyes closed and "see" something on the screen of your mind, you are creating that image with the light of the pineal gland. It can read universal light energy.

We also sense light energy with our hands. Hands are sensors that send information to the brain so it can process the information. We receive light through our solar plexus. You will understand energy work when you complete your health cases. Through the use of energy, you can not only receive an image of a person, but can examine their body through the touch of your hands. Mind and sight are supplemented through touch.

Some scientifically-minded Witches and mystics think the Higgs Boson, also known as the "God Particle," is tied to our understanding of psychic or universal light, fundamental to our universe and present everywhere. Is this an aspect of the Total Intelligence that Witches work with in our majick and light? Possibly. Is this the means by which we can gain information and manifestation across time and space through alpha? Thus far, it's pointing in the direction of our understanding, but it's also important to remember we are not professional physicists. We are using the understanding and poetry of science to better understand ourselves and our majick.

When transferring energy, psychic colored lights are used:

Emerald Green
- Heals, takes away pain
- Treats minor ailments including colds, minor cuts, bruises, first degree burns, sunburns, allergies, stubbed toe, sinus headache

Red-Orange

- For critical/life threatening problems
- Critical healings including diabetes, cancer, infection, some broken bones
- Often asthma, sometimes allergic reactions
- Heart, circulatory, respiratory and neurological problems
- Serious viral or bacterial complications
- Migraines

Bright Pink

- Self-love, self-esteem

Ice Blue

- Anesthetizing, pain relief, pain reduction
- Be careful using this color for back problems. When the pain is gone, people tend to overuse the muscles again, resulting in further damage or injury.

Electric Blue

- Total Intelligence

Violet

- Psychological Balance
- Do not use if you are unsure or unfamiliar with psychological/psychiatric problems. Use of this color often causes those severely affected to act out during the balancing process.

Dazzling White

- Enlightenment

Brilliant Gold

- Tao, Spirituality, God/Goddess
- Total Intelligence

Bright Orchid

- Force, The All

While other colors are used in majick, these are the common colors we use for healing in the first degree. Your mind and your light are more important than any other tools you can gather.

"WHITE" AND "BLACK" LIGHT

When I go into alpha, sometimes I see white light. What is it? "White light" has become part of New Age terminology. New Agers and Witches may use the same terms, but in some cases, they mean different things. White light contains all colors. Black is an absence of color. On a physical plane, black is the absorption of all colors, and white is the reflection, or absence, of all colors. Wearing black is like wearing a rainbow; you absorb all colors. Wearing white, your clothing reflects and refracts all light.

HEALING WITH COLOR

Visualize the affected area bathed in the appropriate color of light. If the wound is bleeding, visualize the closing and healing of the wound. If the wound is infected or looks red, visualize the cleaning and sterilizing of the wound. Always go into alpha to send colored light and perform a Total Health Clearance before coming out of alpha. Sending light is always done in correctness and for the good of all. Every time you send light say, "I ask that this be correct and for the good of all."

We must let the Universal Mind, Total Intelligence, create this healing. The ways and the means (how it happens, why it happens, where it happens, when it happens, if it happens) must be arranged by the higher realms. Some religions believe that death is predetermined, or that one has to live in pain for karmic reasons. Witches in the Cabot Tradition believe that people do not have to live in pain.

Perform color healing every three days; do not do it every day. This gives the body a chance to absorb the light and its benefits while rebuilding the affected area. This is not dissimilar to physical workouts where top trainers tell athletes to do heavy weight training every other day. "Time off" allows the body to have a chance to adjust, develop, build, and heal. If it is a critical situation, you may send red-orange light once a day for the first week.

Make your healing fit the problem. If it is a collapsed lung, visualize the lung filling up with air. Many people ask, "In a critical situation, should you wait to ask the patient for permission to do a healing?" I never ask. If the healing is not correct, it simply won't happen. You can never heal someone against their will. If the recovery is not for the good of all, something else will occur. You will not keep someone from going on to Summerland if it is their correct time to do so. Have no vanity if the healing succeeds, and no guilt if it does not. It is not in your hands; this is where your sense of God has to come in. Throughout your life, you will "save" some, and do the dramatic healings. Some of the results you will never see, but simply sense.

Healing Light Meditation

Now we are going to visualize our healing lights. To send yourself or others healing light, use the Crystal Countdown to achieve alpha level.

The first light is a clear emerald green. Envision on the screen of your mind clear emerald green light, which is for minor ailments. As soon as you've got a good view of the emerald light and can feel its vibration, allow yourself to absorb the amount of green light you need and then erase it from your screen.

Red-orange is for critical healing only and life-threatening issues; red-orange light is a color like glowing coals in a fire. Once you have a clear view of that color, you may erase it, using your hands to clear the screen of your mind.

Bright pink light is for self-love and self-esteem. While you visualize your pink light, think of the grumpy person and send the pink light to the grumpy person; fill their house, their office, their car, their body, their mind with pink light for the good of all. Every time we send light to someone, we ask that it is correct and for the good of all. As soon as you've seen this, you may erase it.

Ice blue light is like the depths and crevices in an iceberg; it is for anesthetizing, pain relief, and pain reduction. As soon as you have gotten a real good view of it, you can erase the color with your hand.

Electric blue, dazzling white, brilliant gold, and bright orchid are the colors of Total Intelligence: the Dao, the Force, the All, the God, the Goddess, and the Universal Mind. Absorb the light and pass it through your body and your mind.

Now give yourself Total Health Clearance and count yourself up.

THE CHAKRAS

The chakras are the energetic centers of the body, where we process different levels, or colors, of light energy. Today we associate the seven centers with the seven colors of the rainbow, just like the seven colors of the Crystal Countdown. Using the Crystal Countdown, you activate these seven centers of consciousness. The lowest—at the feet—is red, and the highest—at the crown of the head—is orchid, or sometimes described as brilliant white. Each one is associated with a place in the body, and organs within the body. Imbalances in these levels of consciousness can result in imbalances in health.

Location	Color	Principle	Body
Feet/Root	Red	Grounding	Feet, Legs, Perineum, Reproductive System, Eliminative System, Skeletal System
Belly/Sacral	Orange	Trust	Spleen, Lower Digestive System, Kidneys
Solar Plexus	Yellow	Power	Upper Digestive System, Liver, Gall Bladder, Pancreas, Muscular System
Heart	Green	Love	Thymus, Heart, Lungs, Circulatory System, Immune System
Throat	Blue	Communication	Thyroid, Mouth, Teeth, Tongue, Vocal Cords, Jaw, Nervous System
Brow/Third Eye	Indigo	Vision	Pineal, Nervous System
Crown	Orchid/White	Enlightenment	Pituitary, Endocrine System

Chakras

THE PINK STAR

Self-esteem and self-love are at the core of successful majick and good living. These feelings are prerequisites for all spells. They strengthen beliefs and knowledge that are correct, and you want to do the best for yourself. Self-esteem is basic to Witchcraft because majick can only be successful for those who know that they deserve the very best.

One of the most important colors is a bright pink, used for self-love and self-esteem. It is useful to project onto grumpy or depressed people and affects outlook and interactions. Studies have shown that the color of a room can induce a change of attitude in as little as fifteen minutes.

Anger comes from low self-esteem. Study your own emotions for a moment. In situations where you have been verbally threatened, you feel angry. When we are critical or criticized, when we feel insecure or unloved, it is because of a loss of self-esteem. This goes back to childhood. The first two emotions a child learns are like and dislike, or love and hate. Young children can neither fully identify their feelings, nor categorize the vast variety of human emotions. To children, love is life and hate is death. Love is comfortable; hate is not. Love and hate are the most intense feelings experienced by humans of any age. One craves love and avoids feelings that hate can bring, such as anger. Eventually, through becoming conditioned to hate, one hates oneself. Love is life. It is a primal instinct that you learned before you could speak. Dissatisfaction with self causes discomfort. By changing your attitude, you will feel more comfortable, raise your self-esteem, and replace that unease with feelings of love.

The Pink Star Meditation clears your mind and removes the mental obstacles that prevent successful majick. Remember, self-esteem is the only true healer.

The Pink Star Meditation

Lie down and close your eyes and count yourself into alpha level using the Crystal Countdown. Visualize the sky and the cosmos around us. See the lights of the universe, the God and the Goddess, the Force, the All.

Allow white light to come soaring in from the cosmos. A huge ball of white light appears at your feet. It encompasses your feet, and in the center of it is a red stone. Allow the light to travel up your body, stopping at each chakra. Let it empower you.

The light comes from the universe into the foot chakra and travels upward into the spleen. In this ball of white light is a glowing orange stone; it empowers you. The light comes pouring in from the cosmos through the foot chakra, the spleen chakra, into the solar plexus. The ball of white light now moves upward into the solar plexus and in the center is a yellow stone. The light again begins to pour in from the Force, the All, the God, the Goddess. Upward into the heart chakra the ball of white light comes pouring in, and in the center of it is an emerald green stone. The light comes in from the cosmos pouring through the foot chakra, the spleen chakra, upward into the solar plexus, and into the heart. It now travels upward into the throat chakra, and in the center of this ball of white light is a sapphire blue stone. The light comes cascading and pouring in from the cosmos, traveling through the chakras into the forehead, and inside this ball of beautiful white light is an indigo stone. The light travels upward into the crown chakra, and the crown chakra becomes orchid and silver, and white light exits through the top, forming a crown like a petaled flower. The flower begins to move and turn. The shape of the petaled flower helps to float you into the solar system. Let your consciousness float on the flower's petals and travel through space. Travel past the Sun, all the planets. We are in places unknown to us.

As we look ahead, we see a bright pink star. Its rays extend far out into space, and we are moving towards the pink star. Let the rays touch you. Feel its power drawing you in closer and closer to its center. Feel the warmth and exhilaration from this pink light, giving you self-esteem and self-love. You are now filled with self-esteem and pink light. You are now One with the entire Universe, the All, the God and the Goddess, the Force. You and the cosmos exist in perfect harmony and perfect love.

While inside the pink star, reach out and grasp two handfuls of pink light. You are now deciding to return to earth. The petals of the crown chakra begin to help you float back to earth with your body and hands full of pink light. Notice the depth of the cosmos and all the heavenly bodies as you pass.

Return to earth, re-enter your physical body through the crown of your head. With your eyes still closed, see two people to whom you would like to give a gift of self-love. Picture them on your mental screen. Take one handful of pink light, and speak the name of one of the individuals. Place the light inside his or her solar plexus and watch the pink light spread throughout the body, and then do the same for the other person.

Give yourself Total Health Clearance. Open your eyes and affirm that you are becoming more self-confident and that you have learned how to have healthy self-love and self-esteem.

Sending Pink Light

You can also project pink light, and transfer energy without visiting the Pink Star, though the Pink Star Meditation is an important meditation to practice.

Pick an unhappy friend, family member, or co-worker. Go into alpha and project pink light to this person. You don't have to say or do anything different. Use your psychic ability. Watch that person's demeanor and interaction with others. You will find that such work can make a difference, sometimes quite a significant difference, in a person. You will see your majick working.

If you'd like to help yourself with work-related stress, have something bright pink on or near your desk to remind you of self-healing. When stressed, gaze deeply at that object. People have found that this actually lifts the moods of others in their area, too. Anything pink will work: flowers, paper, pink stones, whatever you wish.

PROSPERITY MAJICK

We all want wealth and prosperity, and there are many get-rich-quick schemes out there, from scams to spells that promise you power and wealth. The truth is the primary goal in life is balance between spiritual wealth and material wealth. That being said, a degree of prosperity and wealth is needed to bring a less stressful, more fulfilling life. Money can bring stress into our lives, and worrying or obsessing about money is not correct.

Balancing spiritual and material needs is not easy. The Principle of Polarity states that neither extreme wealth nor extreme poverty is a comfortable lifestyle. We want to live a comfortable life. However, some people are so down on themselves, they believe they will never have enough. Their expectations may be too high or not high enough. Make sure you do not create your own psychic road blocks and obstacles to prosperity. A balance between prosperity and spirituality can be achieved. The only limits to majick are self-imposed. All our limitations come from a lack of self-esteem. Self-esteem and self-love are at the core of success majick, and successful living.

Certain colors can keep you focused on prosperity. You can incorporate them in your working environment, clothing, and home.

- Royal Blue, Purple, and Turquoise: These are Jupiter colors. They symbolize success, influencing people in high places, good fortune, and new beginnings.
- Gold, Yellow, and Light Orange: These are the colors of the Sun. Use them for health, wealth, success, and victory. Gold also brings strength. Yellow brings information, news, and sometimes useful gossip.
- Pink, Green, and Copper: These are Venus colors. They are the colors of love. Love is a goal some of you may have, but these colors can also be used for money, prosperity, growth, and fertility.

Money is an indicator of success and a symbol of worth. When something is given away for free, people are suspicious and wonder if it has any value at all. Take a moment and listen to the following statements:

- Money seekers are hedonists. They just want pleasure.
- Money corrupts.
- Relationships always break up due to money.
- You don't need money to be happy.
- Money is the root of all evil.
- The best things in life are free.
- Rich people become corrupt and selfish.
- To be spiritual you must give up all your material possessions.

If you tended to agree with these statements, you may have created barriers to your own prosperity through your attitude about money. Change that by doing majick. Money spells and prosperity majick help you project for the wealth you need and accept the reality of money at the same time.

Prosperity Meditation

Enter into a relaxed alpha state through the Crystal Countdown. Envision yourself surrounded and filled with one of the prosperity colors. Choose the one that is right for you. If in doubt, start with royal blue. Then repeat the following affirmations:

- Money enables me to obtain the goods and services I need and helps provide these services to the world.

- Money is an acceptable form of exchange throughout the world.
- Money is neutral and can be used for good.
- I create my own financial situation.
- I deserve prosperity.

Visualize yourself living with both prosperity and spirituality. What would that look like? How would you feel? Relax into this new image of yourself and let these words become part of your attitude. Soon you will be able to draw to you what you need to improve your financial situation. When we think we don't deserve things, we project those beliefs into our lives instead of improving our lives. Sometimes the best things elude us because we believe we do not deserve them. The truth is simple: you state your own limits and impose your own barriers.

Give yourself Total Health Clearance and count up from alpha level.

PROTECTION SHIELDS AND WHITE LIGHT PENTACLES

Witches use protection shields around their bodies, homes, possessions, animals, families, and friends. Protection shields appear in your mind's eye as though you are sitting inside an enormous crystal egg. This crystal light extends above your head and beyond your fingertips. Reach out in front of you and to the sides, behind you, and below your feet. The crystal light surrounds you completely. The crystal light is called a shield. This shield becomes a filter. This shield allows only psychic energy and physical energy that you need or want to pass through. Your shield stops any energies that are evil or harmful, or incorrect for you in any way.

Often we do not recognize or know harmful energies. Many times things or situations that feel correct can be harmful. Positive energies do not always affect you correctly. Negative forces are not always bad or evil. These energies and forces are simply opposite polarities. In other words, they are the same energies at the opposite ends of the spectrum. Your protection shield strengthens your intuition and perception. It makes you wiser in many ways and less afraid of the unknown.

Witches know they never need to do evil or harm to protect themselves. Witches know they can neutralize harmful energies coming from any person, place, or thing. Witches dissipate harmful energy or polarize it into constructive energy. We do not have to do harm.

This shield will last forever, and at any time you feel like renewing your shield or placing one on others, use the Crystal Countdown and cast your shield.

Protection Shield Meditation

Get to alpha level through the use of the Crystal Countdown and reach your innermost level.

You are now placing your protection shield. Envision yourself inside a giant crystalline egg that shields you from all harm. The crystal shield is forming around you now. Visualize with your mind's eye a crystal egg. The crystal light extends beyond the reach of your fingertips. You can see the sparkling crystal light around you. Your protection shield is in the shape of an egg, enclosing your feet, head, hands, and body. You are completely enclosed by your shield.

After the shield is up, while still in alpha, look at your shield carefully. It is like looking through a crystal ball or a real crystal. There are inclusions in real crystals and in your protection shield. It does not have to be only pure white or clear light; it can also be a mixture of colors.

Take a good look at it. Feel the energy and the protection. With your mind's eye, explore the shield around you. Hold your hands out in front of you to test the shield's distance. You want to put your hands up above you and see how far up it goes. How far beyond your hands does it go? Put your hand straight down beside you and see how far below your feet it goes.

Sit within your crystal light. Enjoy the safety and comfort of the crystal shield. With your mind's eye, place a white light pentacle—a five-pointed star in a circle—above your shield, below your shield, on each side of you, in front of you, and in back of you.

While you are resting in your shield, you are going to repeat in your mind:

"This shield will protect me from all negative and positive energies and forces that may come to do me harm. This shield will protect me from all negative and positive energies and forces that may come to do me harm. This shield will protect me from all negative and positive energies and forces that may come to do me harm. This shield is fixed. And it is so."

These words will help the brain draw in the energy to put up the shield. Words help direct the brain to perform a task.

Take a few moments to place a shield around anyone or anything important to you. I may place this shield around my family, animals, home, car, and place of work. Just as you did for yourself, imagine creating a crystal egg to protect these things.

You can envision a white light pentacle at the front door of your home, on the floor and ceiling, and on all four walls. Like the shield, a white light pentacle is for protection. Envision them on your car—white light pentacles in front, behind, under, and over, the shield all around. These shields are fixed.

Stay inside your protection shield and relax in alpha. Enjoy the safety and the peace of the crystal light. While you're in your shield, bathe yourself in pink light, the top of your head right down through your body just like a CAT scan or MRI. Put that light right through you, all the way through your aura and energy well to the bottom of your feet. That pink light for self-esteem and self-love. You're empowering yourself.

Give yourself Total Health Clearance and count yourself up from alpha level to waking consciousness.

You only need to do this exercise once, but periodically check on your shield and reinforce it while you are in alpha. If you share your experience with others, please don't be alarmed if people describe shields that are different from yours. Everyone sees their shields a little differently. This is normal.

Once you have your shield around you, sense it, even when you are out of alpha. Take your hand and feel the energy. Take your hand and rub it on your thighs; feel your trousers or shirt. You think you are feeling the fabric, but you are really feeling your fingers. You cannot feel the fabric. You can only get a sensation from your fingers. Our fingers are our sensors.

Speaking molecularly, you are not able to touch the table, the fabric, or the chair you are sitting on. There is molecular space between everything. You actually condense light energy, aura, and oscillation of objects. Everything has an aura, or oscillation of energy, around it. An object's information is actually above its surface, a few inches or more, in light form. You can try to touch it, but all you really do is condense your own aura and the energy of the object.

An object's energy can actually travel through your hand. Karate experts can break wood with their hands. The only way to accomplish this is to envision the hand moving through the wood before it is hit. If the person does not do this, the wood will not break—the person could even break his hand—yet experts easily break thick boards. I used to make the students in my religion classes accomplish this. By trying it themselves, they understood their abilities. This exercise illustrates the compression of energy and light, which causes sound. It also underscores the importance of the mind in daily living and majick working.

Think about the importance of the mind in the following scenario: one day you have a pocketful of money and want to go to the mall. You are in the kitchen, immersed in envisioning how you will spend the three thousand dollars in your pocket. As you reach for your coat, you hit your hand hard on the wall. You hear a crack; it was a hard hit, but you don't feel a thing. Off to the mall! The next day, you realize you should have paid off a few bills. Worse, everything you bought does not fit. You go and return some of the items. You reach for your coat, and bang! It is not such a loud noise as yesterday, but you hit your hand on the wall again. It hurts! You grab your hand and hold it and run to the refrigerator for ice. What is the difference? Why was there no pain the first time, but incredible pain after the second hit? Attitude and energy go together. Your thoughts matter and make things happen. Your aura goes in and out, oscillating. When you feel good and project outward, your aura does the same and extends far from your body. If you hit something (like a block of wood, or a wall), compression of the object by your aura results in your hand not being hurt. It is as simple as that. When you are depressed and suffering from low self-esteem, the opposite effect occurs. You draw your aura in. When you hit that wall or piece of wood, the energy of the object smacks your hand, and there is not enough aura to compress it.

Energy flows in and out. You can draw in energy, and you can also project energy out. There are easy exercises to develop your control over the flow of energy. Stand with arms outstretched. Draw in energy through your solar plexus and send it out through your hands. This helps you stay strong and enables you to keep your aura extended. It reduces the chance of harm if you do collide with an object. The whole point of this lesson is to understand the flow and intake of energy and the importance of our mindset on that flow of energy. This also illustrates why we have to keep our self-esteem level up. Haven't you ever noticed that depressed people who see themselves as victims seem to continually have "bad luck" or have bad things happen to them? This is no coincidence. Low self-esteem and depression not only feel bad, but can do bad things to us.

You don't have to constantly remember your shield for it to work. Enjoy your protection shield. You will forget about it as you go through your day, but it will still be there and work for you. In this sense, it is like your aura. Both are always there. When you put the shield up and say, "It will stay there forever," your brain will process this and put up the shield. Sometimes, we don't know what can help or hurt us, and your shield can help to process the information.

Many people confuse their aura and their protection shield. While connected, they are not the same thing. Your aura contains your particular life information and energy. Simply an energy packet, the aura is not necessarily directed to do anything. The aura can scatter, but that depends on your attitude or mood. Your shield is directed; it is pure light.

A direct shield in place can alert and protect you from harmful forces or energies. You can put a shield of protection around your animals, house, or car. For example, I hate flying. When I get into an airplane, I place a white light pentacle on the nose, on the tail, on each wing, and on the sides of the craft's body. Then I put a shield around the whole plane. I think flying bothers me the most because you are completely out of control when you are in a plane. You sit down in your seat, and fate takes over. Whatever is going to be, is going to be.

I had a student who always sped to class from work, and then sped home. The night we had put up protection shields, we finished later than usual, and off she flew. As she was driving down the turnpike, she felt a tap on her shoulder. She slowed down and looked in the rear view mirror, frightened that someone was in the back seat of the car, but there was no one there. She finally decided that it was just her imagination and dropped the pedal down. As she got zooming along again, she felt another tap on her shoulder. Now she was even more scared. She got back into the outside lane and pulled over on the side of the road. She got out of the car and looked in the back seat to make sure nothing was there. She was terrified, and drove under the speed limit in the outside lane. She was sure that if she felt the tap again, she would die of fright. A few miles down the road, she came to a fourteen-car pile-up on the turnpike. A huge truck had jackknifed and caused a domino effect with fourteen cars behind it. If she had stayed at her speed, she might have been right in the middle of this crash.

She believes if she hadn't put her protection shield up that night, the results would have been tragic. Who or what was tapping her on the shoulder? She unconsciously scared herself for protection. These things do happen, and protection shields do work. I love sharing these stories because they show how people use their abilities to help themselves.

Another time, a friend took my classes as a diversion, while her husband was caring for his dying mother in Florida. After classes were over, her husband needed her. This woman does not fly or drive, so she took a bus to Florida. In Georgia, she had to transfer buses. They got there at night, and the only gas station in this desolate area was closed.

Nervously, she and the other transferring passengers hurried to the second bus. Once seated, she realized she had left her backpack behind. She ran to get it, but missed her transfer. She was stuck at the station alone. She put her back against the wall and kept a constant watch. She was understandably terrified and said that all she could think of was a pentacle. She reviewed her exercises for Witchcraft I to calm her nerves. Shortly, another bus came along. About twenty minutes down the highway, the bus that she had missed was upside down in a ditch. Many passengers had been injured. She believes that if she had gotten on that bus, she would have been hurt. She attributes her safety to her protection shield.

THE IMPORTANCE OF A BALANCED SHIELD

A friend of mine had been getting some unwanted attention from a student. He was concerned about this personal safety and his professional status. To make matters worse, a truck had hit the utility pole outside his house and had ruined his wiring. He wondered if these two problems were somehow related and came to me for advice. He had taken Witchcraft I, and I asked him if he had put up a shield. He replied that yes, he had put up a positive shield. I explained to him that a positive shield simply would not work. My friend had been putting up a positive shield around himself and his house for the last month. Why was this wrong? A shield must contain both positive and negative energy. If you put up only one, you will receive the other. My friend's whole house had to be re-wired. The electric company couldn't believe it. The negative energy, let loose from the accident, had burnt out every wire!

We need both positive and negative. There must be a balance. We always need harmony and balance. Negative and positive are not evil or good, but are simply forces or energies. You need them both to keep out all harm. This brings us to an important question: How do we know what is harmful? We often don't know. I can't immediately identify a dangerous person or situation. Even as a psychic for other people, I sometimes overlook what my intuition tells me. You can avoid a problem. Simply protect yourself from all negative and positive energies that may come to do you harm. This is a prevention, not a cure. It does not mean you will never get into an accident or become a victim of a crime. You will be less likely to be hurt when such things do occur. Protection shields just make life easier. We can harm ourselves. It is really important to recognize self-abuse and self-harm, because a shield for incoming energy usually won't work when we are doing something to ourselves.

Everything flows in positive, negative and neutral waves.

BORN VICTIMS?

Responsibility for one's thoughts and actions is a major issue. We all know people who appear to be victims. Somehow, these people draw in negative energy. Others are accident-prone. As you study our own behaviors, you learn to avoid these pitfalls.

Often, these people accept the role of victim. The U.S. government, along with medical professionals, performed a study with both victims of assault and convicted perpetrators of these types of crimes. Researchers took candid photos of the recurrent victims while they conducted daily affairs. The group of pictures was shown to the criminals. "Control" photos of people who had never been victims of assault were interspersed in the series. The researchers discovered that criminals could correctly identify the victims every single time! The victims demonstrated stances, facial expressions, and particular ways of walking that indicated lack of self-reliance and self-esteem.

One of the best ways to avoid appearing as a victim is to study a form of martial arts. Any age group can take lessons. Tai Chi is the easiest on the body. You do not have punch or spar, and the movements are soft and fluid. The martial arts enhance your reflexes and build up the chi force (energy) in your body. You will be able to react more quickly and walk more confidently. Your aura will be stronger. Since you will not look or act like a victim, you will be less likely to be attacked.

MIND TRAVEL VS. ASTRAL TRAVEL

Mind travel is distinct from astral travel. Astral travel happens sporadically. Some people like to practice astral travel—where one leaves the body and goes into another plane. It is a difficult technique to master because you have to attain a delta state of consciousness and let go of the body altogether.

Mind travel is easier; you just send your mind where you wish to go. I do a lot of police work. Sometimes you have to go to a certain room, travel through walls, locate yourself in the scene and be able to describe to the authorities any and all furniture and distinctive markings in the environment.

When performing the Crystal Door Mind Travel technique, think about your intention, where you want to go. To help someone, you might have to go someplace you have never been. If you have the address, think about the address as a focus. Go into alpha and use the Crystal Door to reach it. Affirm you will remember everything, and when you come back, write down all the details and even draw a little map. Just like psychic diagnosis, you can gain information that your conscious mind will have no way of knowing until you access it in alpha.

Crystal Door Mind Travel Meditation

To perform the Crystal Door Mind Travel Meditation, follow the steps for the Crystal Countdown to reach alpha level. Once in alpha, picture a crystal door in the center of the screen of your mind. You picture a crystal door at a forty-five degree angle. It may be a little dot at first, far, far away. Yet you know it is there. You leave your body with your mind. You go into a tunnel, and go up, up, up. Keep going and going, traveling faster than the speed of light. Keep your mind's eye on that dot...the door. Do not look at any images that are on either side of you. These distractions are merely brain-oriented images. You may feel some pull or force on your face. Go through the door, which will take you where you desire to go.

After traveling forward for a period of time, come backwards to the starting point. You can use the door to travel wherever you want. The door can connect you to any place and any point in time. This time, you may feel the force against the back. Return from the crystal door back to where you began, uniting your mind with your bodily awareness. Let the energy come down through your head, shoulders, stomach, legs, and to your toes. Then count up from alpha.

Mind travel is a useful skill. The exercise trains the mind's eye to go anywhere you wish it to be. When I was in England, I was called by a representative of Johns Hopkins University, who was working with a patient who could not be diagnosed. They called me, and I was able to do the diagnosis over the phone. I had to travel, with my mind, to that bed at Johns Hopkins.

Do not be confused by what is really happening here. Your spirit is not traveling in and out of your body; it is just in your mind's eye. We often think of using our feet or fingers, but don't often think of using our minds and imagery to an advantage.

All kinds of images come into your mind every day. We pay attention to the ones that seem meaningful to us. As you practice these different meditations, notice how much information you can receive from your mind's eye.

Druid Candle Meditation

Follow the steps for the Crystal Countdown to reach alpha level. Picture a white candle in the center of the screen of your mind, a beautiful white candle with a flickering flame. Hold the candle perfectly still and concentrate on the candle and only the candle for a period of time. If you cannot center and still the candle, polarize yourself for balance, using the vision of the rod with two spheres, one at each end. When you have successfully polarized and balanced your energy, erase the bar, look at the candle, and it will remain still.

After polarization, you should be able to keep focus on the candle for a longer period of time. When done, erase the image from the screen of your mind and count yourself up from alpha.

THE OTHERWORLD

Witches also believe there is another world, a sacred place. When you "go into spirit" (meaning you die), you are at your highest level. Witches believe in a place called Summerland, a land of milk and honey. Often called Avalon in the Celtic British traditions, it is associated with the mysteries of King Arthur, and also Tara, the home of the gods in the Irish Traditions. Everyone has three choices once in the afterlife of the Summerland.

1. You can stay there and rest.
2. You may choose to come back and stay with loved ones, as a ghost, to help your family or others.
3. You can be reincarnated.

To us, reincarnation is a choice. You may choose to come back, work on the Earth, and help the living. My experiences with the dead have led me to the belief that ghosts are never truly "stuck" here on Earth. It's a choice, even if they are not conscious they have made a choice. Sometimes what seems to be a ghost is a really hologram of the past, repeating over and over again. Such astral holograms give the appearance of a mindless entity stuck in a loop, but their spirit is not really there. Poltergeists are not the deceased. Usually a poltergeist manifests from a person who is alive and psychically powerful, but disturbed. There is no reason to fear ghosts.

SPIRITS AND GUIDES

Witches believe our world intersects with many other worlds, and those worlds are populated by a variety of entities. Some were human and might be again, but many were never human. Some of these spirits become guides or allies in our human work, either due to our karma together, or through their desire to aid our evolution. Often we experience these guides in pairs, one male and one female, and many compare them psychologically to the *anima* and *animus* of Jungian psychology. Other entities want little to do with humans, at least initially, and their trust must be earned.

Sometimes when in alpha, we can encounter such entities. It can be helpful to have a working understanding of them before trying to communicate, and to make contact first with our own familiars and guides.

Ghosts and Ancestors: These spirits are those of the human dead. Those still on the earthly plane are often considered ghosts, though there is a difference between a spirit who is seemingly in distress and those that have consciously come back. Distressed spirits are more rare than movies and TV would lead you to believe, as most have chosen to remain with loved ones for helpful reasons. When we encounter them in the Otherworld by projecting our mind to the Otherworld, we experience them in the ancestral realm.

Faeries: Faerie are the elder race that predates humanity. They are a nearly immortal race of beings of light who dwell within the Earth and are intimately connected with nature. Faeries come in all sizes, from small winged creatures to giants, and a powerful form is one we might think of as elves. Faeries can be amazing teachers, healers and partners in majick if you approach them with respect and offerings. Be aware that Faery culture is quite different from that of humans, and their sense of morality is different from ours as well.

Elves: Elves are a type of faeries, though they differ from our popular ideas of the Little People. They live on another plane, the realm of enchantment known as Elphame, or simply Faerie. They tend to be tall, beautiful, and ethereal. They can be like idealized, majickal humans from another time. Some even believe elves, or those with elf blood, still walk among us.

Elementals: Elementals are spirits tied to one of the four elements—earth, air, fire, or water. They take the form of dwarves, gnomes and goblins (earth), sylphs or winged faeries (air), salamanders and drakes (fire), or undines/merfolk (water). They each reside in their own realm that intersects with our own, and they share some similar attributes to, but are different from faeries.

Dragons: Dragons are terrestrial spirits mixing all four elements, though they can choose to specialize in an element. They are ancient and wise creatures, associated with the energy or life force of the Earth itself—the ley lines, known as Dragon Lines in the East.

Familiar Spirits and Totems: Animal spirits reside in the other worlds and can take on mythic proportions and power. Our Celtic ancestors venerated the power of animals as both living creatures and spiritual entities, with many deities associated with specific totemic animals. An animal spirit that guides you is often called a totem, though in Witchcraft traditions, it can also be referred to as a familiar. Familiars can be both spirit animals and living flesh and blood members of your household.

Ancient Ones: The Ancient Ones are our ancient ancestors of power and blessings. These are the Witch ancestors who now reside on another plane but who answer our calls for majickal aid. They can be the heroes of our myths and stories, residing between the realm of the human dead and the gods.

Deities: The gods reside on another plane. Many are ancient ancestors who have grown so powerful that we see them as gods. Others are manifestations of nature, and others still are reflections of the great Goddess and great God of the Divine Mind.

Majick Room and Spirit Guide Meditation

Use the technique of the Crystal Countdown to enter your innermost alpha level. Meditate upon the beauty of nature, on your own inner majickal place, and make contact with your spirit guides.

Envision walking into a scene from nature where everything is beautiful. The sky is clear; the Sun is shining. The breeze is perfect. All the flora is around you; the Earth is under your feet, and you can feel the Sun and breeze on your face and arms as you walk into your nature scene. It is a beautiful place, very comforting. Here you find Mother Nature at her best. Sometimes you can even watch things grow or a piece of bark fall off a tree. The sound of water is like music.

There's a hill, and you climb up to the top. Once you're at the top of the hill, look around you. Look at all the neighboring beauty around you and far off to the edge of the Earth. You can see the edge of the Earth—how wonderful this is—and you can feel the sunlight on your face and the warmth and a slight breeze as you look to the edge of the Earth.

You start to see clouds forming, billowing clouds growing larger. They get darker, grey and black, and come rolling in towards you. The clouds get larger and come faster, rolling right over your head, shutting out the light, and the breeze suddenly feels colder. A mist of rain comes down and you can feel it on your face and arms as it hits the Earth around you. It rolls and rumbles, and all of a sudden it goes beyond you, behind you, as it rolls away.

The Sun comes out again, and now you can see the sparkles of water like diamonds on your arms and on the leaves. You can smell the Earth where the water hit the ground and now the Sun warms it. The land smells good and clean. You look at the edge of the Earth again, and far away, you see a rainbow forming. It's growing upward and upward into the sky, getting bigger and clearer. It's arching right over you. It's coming down right on top of you. Now you are standing right at the end of the rainbow, and the rainbow light is constantly pouring into your body. It feels so comfortable now. The rainbow dissipates, and you can sit on the ground and look off into the sky and all around you.

Suddenly there is a rumble or a roar. It sounds like a train is coming, and it gets louder and louder. The rumble gets closer, and the Earth is starting to shake beneath you. You can feel the Earth moving underneath you. It gets a little bit violent, but then all of a sudden, a fissure opens. The Earth cracks open to your left, and you can look down inside the Earth.

The shaking has stopped. The noise has stopped. You can look inside the Earth and see the layers of stone and sand. You stand up, and you know that the earth is steady. Turn and go down the back of the hill, where a meadow of wildflowers extends beyond the bottom of the hill to the edge of a deep forest.

Walk through the flowers, looking at all the flora: the leaves, the petals, the colors. The Sun is shining on the flowers, so beautiful. You get the scent of the flowers, and you're walking toward the forest. You go amongst the trees, stepping inside the forest, and as you walk along, the Sun shines down through the leaves onto the floor of the forest. The ferns, the roots of the trees, and the pathway—scattered with pine needles and fallen leaves—are illuminated. You walk along, and the forest starts to get denser. The leaves shut out the sunlight. It gets darker as you walk deeper into the woods. Soon you can hardly see your hands in front of you, and you must watch your footing, so that you don't trip on the roots of the trees. Put your hands on the trees as you go by— one to the next, and to the next. It's too dark to go any farther. Put your back to the tree and slide down to the floor of the forest. You look up into the canopy of the leaves, and through an opening, you can see that it is night-time. The sky is deep indigo, and there are a million stars. You've never seen so many stars. They're bright. You look back down into the wooded area. You can't see yourself. You can't go any further.

All of a sudden, far off in the dense wood, you see a sparkle of light. The light starts to travel in and out of trees, coming closer, and closer. Behind the tree next to you, a little grinning face peeks around and takes a good look at you. It's a fairy, a wood fairy, and there she is. As quickly as she sees you, she turns around and goes back. The light dwindles back and forth, back and forth, and back into the woods. She is gone. You are in the dark again, so you must be careful of your footing. You don't want to trip and fall, so you put your hands on the trees as you go by one by one.

There is a spark of light on the floor of the forest. A dapple of light is coming down. Now you're beginning to see. You can see the trees now. It is getting lighter and lighter as you walk outward. Now the light comes down in shafts like a cathedral, hitting the floor of the forest. You look forward as you are walking forward; now you can see the edge of the forest and the meadow. The sunlight is shining in the meadow. You walk out of the woods and into this meadow again.

Now you are going to take a stroll. You need to find a doorway; it will be under a tree, or behind a huge stone, or in the side of a cliff. Find the doorway, and when you do, open the door. There will be steps going down. Go down the steps to find another door that will open into your majick room.

You find a spacious room, large and empty. You walk into the room. Immediately you realize you need a throne, a wonderful chair to sit in. Envision something comfortable so you can create your room and do your majick in it. Sit in your new chair and manifest a table. Then manifest a chair to your right and a chair to your left. Now start deciding what else it is that you want in your majick room.

Do you want a time machine? Do you want a library with ancient or modern books or both?

Do you want a computer or something even better? Do you want a fireplace where you can put your cauldron? Do you want a table where you can mix your oils and herbs? Perhaps a cabinet full of essential oils and all the herbs hanging up that you can gather when you need them?

Do you have a familiar? Is it a black cat? Is it a small dragon? Where is your broom? Where is your wand? Your majick chalice? How many do you have?

And where do you do your healing? What majickal things do you use to heal? Do you have a place in your majickal room where you heal yourself?

Look at the curtain across the room, a beautiful curtain. What is behind it? Your guides are there.

You are going to open the curtain now while you're sitting in your chair. Ask your female guide to enter the room now. Open the curtain and she enters. Ask her to sit next to you and talk to her.

When you are ready, open the curtain again and ask your male guide to come in. Have him sit next to you in the other chair. Speak to him. Greet him. Say hello. Ask his name.

Make sure you look at their clothing and appearance. Learn all the details you can about each one.

When you are finished with your conversations you can ask them to leave and ask them to return again so you can get to know each other even better. Close the curtain.

Take one last look around your majick room for now. You are going to leave it, but keep the fire going and tell your familiar to take good care of the space while your gone. Open the door and climb up the stairs. Open the door to the outside and step outside. Now close the door. And remember where you found the door. Only you know where it is. You are going to walk back into nature again.

You are going to feel the Earth under your feet, and you're going to walk back into this room and sit in the chair you are physically sitting in. Feel the energy return to your body. Give yourself Total Health Clearance and count yourself up. When done, open your eyes.

Make sure in particular with this meditation to record your experiences in your majickal journal.

SPEAKING TO THE DEAD

You can speak to those who have crossed over using the science of alpha. The dead are simply in a different dimension, and when you can perceive the hidden light of that reality, you can communicate with them, just like any spirit guide. The methods of communication with the dead include:

- Enter into alpha, and call the name of the person you wish to speak with to the screen of your mind, as you would for the health cases later in this degree.

- Use your Instant Alpha Trigger, and look just behind, to the left or right of the person you are "reading" for, and you might see, feel, or hear their personal dead who still walk with them. Often those on the person's left side are from their mother's lineage, and those on the right are from their father's, but friends can appear on either side, above, or next to the person.

- Go to your majick room and open the curtain, asking that the deceased come through the curtain, instead of your usual male and female guides. You can even ask your familiar to "fetch" the person from the spirit world and help them find you.

Rituals to speak with the dead can be more elaborate, with incense, oils, food, water, and candles, but they are not always necessary. Alpha is the key to true and clear communication.

When you are done conveying any messages from the ancestors, make sure to give yourself Total Health Clearance.

Don't try to edit what you are being told, even if it makes no sense to you. You'll often be more right than you know. In one of my first mediumship sessions, I read a woman whose son was recently deceased. She was desperate to communicate with him. At the end of the session, the boy's spirit told me, "Tell my Mother I feel like Highlander. I'm going to live forever." I thought how strange that was and decided it must be my imagination. That makes no sense. But I felt I should tell the mother anyway. She began to cry and told me that was the last movie they saw together. That bit of information verified everything else for her and she knew I was really talking to the spirit of her son. So I learned a valuable lesson that day.

THE EGYPTIAN SUN

The Egyptians worshipped the Sun. Witches worship the Sun in a way. They follow the Sun as the father, the Moon as the mother, and observe the cycles of the year. These aspects are similar to the Egyptian belief system. Witches often borrow from different magical systems. We can all benefit from many of the beautiful rites and beliefs from ancient Egypt. There is something to the importance of the Sun's power. Solar energy positively affects the mind and body.

All of nature manifests as the Egyptian gods, each part taking the name of an Egyptian deity. The primary Egyptian Sun god is Ra, with manifestations of Amon Ra, as well as the lion-headed goddess Sehkmet and the hawk-headed Horus. Isis is the greater mother goddess of the Egyptians, partnered with her brother-husband Osiris, the lord of fertility and the dead. They raise the child Horus to be the new leader of Egypt, but come into conflict with Horus' uncle, the god Set. Thoth is the Egyptian god of wisdom and learning. He helps Horus and Isis. Isis becomes the greatest of magicians, learning the secret name of the creator Sun god Ra, and with that name, she can make anything happen.

The Egyptian Sun meditation combines the life-giving power of the Sun with a vision of the Temple of Isis, an encounter with the Goddess. While Isis might not be a part of your belief system, focusing your meditation upon her connects you to the majick and mystery of the Great Mother.

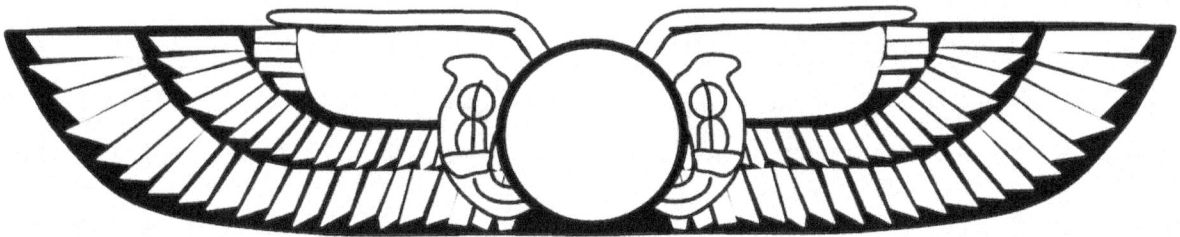

Egyptian Sun Symbol

Egyptian Sun Meditation

The ancient Egyptian Sun meditation will give you sight and psychic strength. Witches use this meditation any time we need to rejuvenate our powers. To perform the Egyptian Sun Meditation, follow the steps for the Crystal Countdown. Once in alpha, perceive the Egyptian Sun, approximately seven feet above your head, as a perfect glowing fiery orb. Visualize the glowing Sun above your head. Sit up straight with your eyes closed. Place your hands, palm upward, at shoulder level, with your fingers pointing away from you. Touch your feet together parallel on the floor. This is the Egyptian goddess position. See with your mind's eye the bright shining Sun.

One ray of the Egyptian Sun streams down into the top of your head and into your pineal gland.

The second ray, like a laser, comes down through the thyroid gland into your neck.

The next ray of light comes down into your heart, bringing golden light into your body.

The next ray penetrates your solar plexus, and the last golden ray enters into your body.

As you hold your palms upright at your shoulders, one ray of light lasers into the palm of your right hand, and the next one touches the left hand.

Golden rays pulsate through your body, pouring through your blood, your nervous system, and every muscle, every cell in your body. They give you psychic and physical strength. Feel the bright light traveling through your entire body. You begin to feel the energy tingling in your hands and in your fingertips. When you feel the warmth in your hands, cross your hands and place them on your chest. Hold the energy inside of your body. This is the Egyptian God Position, like an Egyptian mummy. Enjoy the bright healing and strengthening light.

Look around you, and then look toward the sky. Great white pillars of the Isis temple loom upward, and the black doves of Isis flutter skyward, rising in perfect formation, into the blue and shining light. Isis is before you on her golden throne. She rises to her feet. On her head is a golden disc, and the sunlight pours down through the top of the temple, striking the Sun disc and showering sunlight back onto you. The Goddess spreads her golden wings and steps toward you. She wraps her wings around you and whispers, *"Napu kanapu rah. Napu kanapu rah. Napu kanapu rah."*

Isis raises the power and energy to bring the golden light into your life. "Come upward with me," she says in your ear. Holding you with her golden wings: one, two, three, four, five, six, seven, eight, nine, ten. You are flying with Isis. One, two, three, four, five, six, seven. The Goddess Isis is with you. Let yourself slowly float back to the floor of the temple. Continue to feel the energy and power and love of the Goddess. Relax in alpha; enjoy the safety and peace of the crystal light, and the Egyptian Sun.

When you are finished, give yourself Total Health Clearance. Count yourself up from alpha. Open your eyes.

Isis

You have learned the ability to travel to different dimensions. You have met the goddess Isis. You have used alpha. This ability will assist you in all aspects of your life. You are also probably wondering what is whispered in the meditation. I invoke the energies of various Egyptian Gods and Goddesses through whispering their names. I use the names Isis, Amun Ra, and in particular Nepukanepu Ra, which means "one with the Sun." It was a name for Tutankhamun and helps make us one with the Sun for this meditation, and through the mediation of Isis. Names can be included in the meditation and do not have to be a part of your belief system or religion. These are used to help envision. Names have the power to help evoke energies, and the power of name majick was a huge part of Egyptian majickal practices. To know the secret name of something, the Ren, means you have power over it. How we name ourselves, and accept our own names, gives us power over ourselves.

THE METALS

Each of the ancient metals is said to have a majickal power associated with a planet. We know each metal has a vibration, but tuning into the metal itself when in alpha helps us understand the vibration and energy of the metal. When we focus upon it on the screen of our mind, we can bring those beneficial qualities to ourselves and our lives.

The Metal Meditation

You can perform the Metal Meditation either as part of the Egyptian Sun meditation, within the Temple of Isis, or as a separate meditation. To begin, count yourself down to alpha level using the Crystal Countdown.

In front of you on your screen, put a ball of gold, a huge ball of solid gold the size of a basketball. Open that ball and go inside with your mind, inside the golden ball. See if it is warm or cold. How does the gold feel? Is it soft? Hard? What molecular structure does gold have? What configuration does it take? Can you taste it? Does it feel good to you? Does it empower you? Take all of that information from the gold and close the ball of gold back up again and erase it from your screen.

Now we are going to place a ball of silver on the screen, a ball the size of a basketball, right in front of you on your screen. Open that ball of solid silver and look inside with your mind. Is it warm or cold? Is it soft? Is it sharp? Can you hear a sound? Does it make a sound? Can you taste it? And what is its molecular structure? What does the configuration of its molecular structure look like to you? When you are finished, you may close the ball and erase it from your screen Use your hands to wipe it away.

Next we are going to put up a ball of copper. Did you know that copper is ruled by Venus? Place a basketball-sized sphere of copper on the screen of your mind. Open the ball of copper and look inside. Is it smooth? Is it sharp? Does it taste good? Does it have a sound? Does it have a molecular structure of any kind? You can close it and erase it from your screen. Give yourself Total Health Clearance and count yourself up.

| *Alchemical Symbol for Gold* | *Alchemical Symbol for Silver* | *Alchemical Symbol for Copper* |

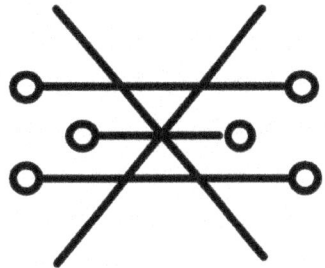

KINESTHETIC TESTING

Kinesthetic testing, also known as kinesiology, or more simply as muscle testing, is the process of testing the body's response to certain substances and information. While our conscious and unconscious minds can sometimes fool or confuse us, the body's response to things can be more direct. We use muscle testing in the Cabot Tradition to show students the mind-body-spirit connection, as well as demonstrate on a practical level that some substances, in particular metals, resonate better with individual Witches for their health and well being.

To test someone using kinesiology, have the person you are testing take their dominant arm and place it parallel with the ground, outward from the body. The tester counts to three, and then puts downward pressure on the arm, to gauge how much strength the person to be tested has in that arm. Rest a moment and gather a small amount of gold jewelry and a small amount of silver jewelry, without any stones or crystals. Have the person being tested close their eyes, and then place one of the metals in the non-dominant hand and hold it against the solar plexus. Then have the person being tested assume the testing position with their dominant hand out; repeat the count to three and place downward pressure on the extended arm. Note how easy or difficult it is to push the arm down based upon that particular metal. Results will be immediate. It will not require extended pressure. Rest, but have the person being tested keep their eyes closed, not knowing what metal was just tested. Repeat with the second metal and notice the difference in the results.

Usually, most people are strengthened by one metal and weakened by the other. Some are strengthened by both or weakened by both, but more often than not, one metal will be dominant in an individual. Usually the qualities of that metal are needed in the person's make up, instead of the qualities they are in tune with. For example, psychic people often resonate with gold as their needed metal, while those who not as psychic in their natural life, often test well for silver. Ultimately we seek balance between the qualities of gold and silver. I wear a pentacle that has both gold and silver.

Psychic Diagnosis and Health Cases

Psychic diagnosis and healing is a powerful skill. You have this talent, lying hidden inside of you. It is a natural ability. After practicing Witchcraft as a science, through the Cabot Tradition techniques, these abilities emerge. You can envision someone on the screen of your mind and accurately diagnose what is wrong, Then you can send healing light and energy. After practicing this technique for some time, you will see the results and understand that nine out of ten times or more, healing takes place. Not everyone will be healed. This is a fact. Some people are beyond our ability. Some take a journey that does not include healing.

There are reasons for not getting well or healing. People tell me that the thought of doing a case is like walking on fire. You have to truly believe, and use your mind over matter. When it works, you will love yourself more. You will realize your worth. You will help others and help yourself.

Do not feel bad if you are ill. We are responsible for our health condition to an extent. Sometimes we cannot be healed, or there may be a reason why we are sick. We can also allow ourselves to become ill. Don't feel guilty, but feel empowered to reject illness when possible. We don't catch colds; we accept them. There are viruses and bacteria—all sort of bugs—flying around in the air. Sometimes we get them; sometimes we don't. Why do we "catch" cold? We may be under biological or psychological depression or stress. We don't consciously decide to get sick. The relaxation and clearing benefits of alpha contribute to your health. If you do nothing else with alpha but meditate and lower your blood pressure, that is fine. It will keep you rested. Every fifteen minutes in alpha is equal to three hours of sleep. You may not enjoy working health cases; however, you need to learn how to diagnose and use alpha in order to progress in Witchcraft. The ability to work cases is the springboard to all other majick. It can assist you in doing many things.

Guidelines For Working A Health Case

Work with a partner. One person works three cases; the other is the guide. After that person has worked at least three cases, switch roles. The caseworker goes into alpha through the Crystal Countdown. When you are ready, the helper gives you the name, age, sex, and location of the case to be worked.

At the count of three, the image of (repeat to self) name, age, and location will appear on the screen of your mind.

1-2-3 (snap your fingers)

Start to feel the facial features of the subject. The helper should be patient and encouraging, but do not give hints. Do not say "no" or "you are wrong." These phrases may intimidate the caseworker and cause their brain to doubt. Try "I don't have that information" or "look closer" to guide another when working a health case in alpha.

Heal the person with the necessary colored light. State: "I ask this to be correct and for the good of all."

Remember your colors:
- Green – minor ailments
- Red-Orange – healing critical only
- Bright Pink – love, life, light, self-love
- Ice Blue – anesthetizing
- Electric Blue/Dazzling White/Orchid/Brilliant Gold – Total Intelligence levels, God/Goddess

Concentrate on areas of concern. When you are done, erase the image from the screen with your hand and give yourself Total Health Clearance. Relax for a few minutes and go on to a new case.

When the worker has completed giving impressions of the three cases, count up and discuss the cases with the guide. If information came through that was unknown, write it down. The information could be past, present, unknown, or future conditions. When others work on the same case, you can compare notes to verify.

Helpful Hints:

- If you have the person on the screen of your mind, scan it up and down a few times.
- Verify the facial features.
- Perhaps you are immediately attracted to a particular area—check it out.
- You can use your hands to draw in energy.
- Verbalize what you see and describe texture or color. What you see could be clues to abnormalities or health issues.
- After checking the brain, put on the subject's head and walk with the person for a total experience (see Putting on the Head and Connecting With the Body, following).
- If you are not visualizing, ask the Universal Mind to give you the necessary information.
- Don't be afraid to state your first impression—it is often correct.
- "Guessing" is not necessary, and in fact, is not a correct technique. The better way to get information is to focus on seeing and examining the body, as well as "asking" the subject to clarify or explain what is wrong.
- Relax and enjoy!
- Every time you aid another's health and give yourself Total Health Clearance, you reinforce your own good health.

Health Case Sequence

- Head and skull
- Brain and eyes
- Neck and down the spine
- Initial broad sweep of torso for immediate information
- Limbs and then digits
- Major body systems

- Circulatory including heart and blood vessels. Checking the blood.
- Respiratory including lungs
- Digestive system, upper and lower
- Reproductive system
- Elimination system
- Immune system
- Skeletal system
- Muscular system
- Nervous system
- Endocrine system
- Micro-organisms (internal flora)

Why Use Your Hands?

You use your hands in alpha during health cases, during the Apple Meditation, and other exercises. Your index finger is for sight, to see items in the mind's eye. The middle finger is used for recall. Through the use of your hands and fingers, you have recall and sight to work better in alpha.

The pointing and index fingers should be used to outline the shape of the face when calling the name of a subject and drawing the person onto the mind screen. The correct positioning of hands and fingers is essential for accuracy, and it is important that students keep their hands and their focus up in front of the "third eye," being sure to use broad gestures with the hands in tracing the outline of the face. As the outline of the face is traced, students should look for characteristics of the hair and face, and the general shape of the head.

Checking the Blood

It is also crucial that students check the blood of the subject using a method that psychically draws "blood" into a glass tube, which is shaken and observed for unusual color or material that can be seen floating in the blood. Information will be obtained when doing this that points to and informs about many systemic abnormalities, as well as the presence of medications or toxins in the body.

Putting on the Head and Connecting With the Body

Students should be reminded they can put on the "head" of the subject as well, to look with or connect with the subject's body. This allows you to do things such as looking through another's eyes, breathing with their lungs, or walking with their gait to better understand the nature and aspects of health problems.

SELF-PROTECTION WHEN HEALING

When working a health case or seeking information, energy flows from you to that person. Their inner energy, or aura, sends a message or information about their health, pain, or happiness, and you receive the data. After a while, you will be able to shut off or decrease the flow of information. That is important. You don't want to overload yourself with someone else's emotions or pick up the pain of their conditions. You don't want such oversensitivity that you pick up emotions and pain from anyone your pass on the street. Some people may be on prescription medication today because they cannot control the flow of information from stimuli in their environment. They are not in control of their chemistry or ability. This is not to say that drugs, such as antidepressants, are always bad or unneeded. For example, scientists now agree with Witches in the beneficial effect of St. John's Wort for calming nerves.

LAYING ON OF HANDS

Though laying on of hands has been popularized by many modern religions, Witches too perform healing through this practice. When healing someone in person, it can be helpful to transfer the energy via touch. I was asked to do that once for a woman who had gone deaf in one ear. I held my Instant Alpha Trigger and then touched her ears. I envisioned the energy of the universe going to her to heal her, and imagined while in alpha that she could hear perfectly well. She later came back and said that the healing had worked and that she had regained a significant amount of hearing. Not all laying on of hands works so well, as you can never tell who is ready to receive healing, and who only believes they are ready.

To use this method, enter into alpha state either through the countdown or through your trigger. Then, if possible, touch the afflicted area of the person. Imagine the light of the universe going to heal this person, choosing the appropriate color. Imagine them in your mind's eye, fully healed and well. Follow your intuition on how long you should keep your hands upon the person. When done, make sure you give yourself Total Health Clearance.

BEING A HEALER

Many have described me as a healer. Yet, in reality, I am not. No one can heal anyone else. One sends healing energy, and the other person is responsible for accepting that energy. Some will not accept healing energy. Whether the person gets better or not, it is not a reflection on you. The person will only absorb the healing energy you send when he or she is ready. Usually, people absorb it. Some do not want to be healed, and there is nothing you can do about it. Do not call yourself a healer. Healing happens through you, not by you. We take energy through us and direct it to help a person, animal, or situation. Using pink light is a perfect example of this. You affect the person's grumpy mood, and then alter the situation, environment, and atmosphere. If you only make one person less grumpy, that in itself can be a miracle. If we all worked on making each other feel better, there would be no hatred, no fears, and no wars.

HEALING OUR CHILDHOOD

A big part of our personal healing is understanding our relationship with our parents and how they have both helped us and harmed us. While most parents don't intend to harm their children, some don't know any better. Our society doesn't teach people how to be parents, to the detriment of children. Parents may be immature themselves, having not done their own healing and introspection. Even the best parents can unconsciously do these things and not realize it, but we bear the consequences and have the responsibility to heal.

When I moved to Salem, Massachusetts, as a single mother of two young girls, I realized how much some of my experiences with my own parents, whom I loved very much, were still influencing me in a harmful way. Things parents say to us can be detrimental, even when not intentional. I needed to find a way to free myself from any unhealthy and untrue images of myself and embrace the woman I was to fully understand who I would be.

My mother would say things to me like, "You never finish anything." Not true. I finished many things that were important to me, but not all the things she thought were important. She had lots of projects for me, but because of that, I had in my head this idea that I couldn't finish anything on my own. But when I looked back, I realized I finished many things successfully. She didn't realize the difference between what she wanted and what I wanted, and over time, her words were battering my self-esteem. Without even realizing it, I was hurt.

My father thought he was a jokester, but his kidding was also hurtful. My mother liked to make clothes. She was not a professional seamstress, but she made elegant gowns better than most things available in a store. My mother would have me dress up and show me off to my father, saying things like, "Doesn't she look pretty?" He'd respond with "Pretty awful and pretty apt to stay that way." I carried around this idea, even as a little girl, that I wasn't attractive, and only as I grew older did I understand I was beautiful.

So when I arrived in Salem, I created a little ritual. I divided paper into two columns. I wrote down all the things I could remember my mother saying that were detrimental to me now on the left column. Then I wrote down all the things I could remember my father saying that were detrimental beneath it. In the right hand column, I wrote down next it what I thought about what they said now, as a grown woman. Was it true? Was it fair? Was it false? With this exercise, I could see the truth better. I could understand what was real and what I had to take responsibility for versus what were their projections and not true for me. This simple act helped set me free.

Along with this writing exercise, we can do meditations to find and parent our own inner child and help heal ourselves, regardless of our upbringing.

Inner Child Healing Meditation

This meditation is to take responsibility for the care, love, and nurturing of your inner child, the child-self within you. Use the Crystal Countdown to enter into a deep state of alpha, relaxing fully but keeping your awareness.

You will be traveling back in time. Go back to a time that you remember when you were a child and it was your birthday. Walk into the room and see whoever is there, see what is going on. There you are, a little you, at your birthday.

Walk up to yourself as a child, hold out your hand, and say to your child self, "I am your parent now. I want you to come with me."

Take your child's hand, and walk out of that room and out of the house. Hold the hand tightly and walk around the corner until you cannot see the house anymore. Sit down, and bring your child to stand directly in front of you.

Look at your child and say, "I am your parent now. I love you. I'm going to take care of you. I won't let anyone harm you."

Hold out your arms. Look at your child. Notice your face when you were young, the sincerity, the love and the care. Put your arms around your child-self and bring the child towards you. Embrace each other, repeatedly telling the child, "I love you. I'm going to take care of you. I'll never let anyone harm you again."

Hold the child within you. You are a parent to that little person. The child is an important part of you. Hang on to the child in your heart. Cross your hands across your chest, touching your own grown body, your grown-up self. You are now also touching the child within.

Give yourself Total Health Clearance and count up from alpha.

GENETIC MEMORY

Genetics is more than just eye color or body shape. Genetic memory has many layers; that is why we cannot be sure about reincarnation. Are you recalling a life you lived before or receiving information from genetic memory? You may feel particularly close to Egypt or may relate to the ways and culture of the American Indian. Some explain these feelings as reincarnation. Others say it is genetic memory. I believe it can be both.

How can someone who goes into alpha to work cases access information from someone who died? You can receive information from genetic memory. I have, many times, been asked to work a case on someone who has passed away. These people, now deceased, tell everything that happened, what their life was like, and what they did. Where does that information come from? Some call it the Akashic Records. I say it is from energy packets of light that carry your information forever. You have an energy packet of light now with your information. That is why someone in Australia can pick you up on their screen while you are both in alpha. These packets offer a chance to engage in important communication. The skill involved in alpha teaches important control for visioning, dreaming, and living a full life.

Past Life Regression

Initially you are going to want to decide which incarnation you wish to observe. You may choose to witness your most recent existence or perhaps the existence in which you were happiest. Once you have set your intention, you may begin. Preferably you should work with a partner who records the details of what you are experiencing as you are going through the exercise.

Start by counting yourself down into alpha level using the Crystal Countdown. You are then going to let yourself leave your body and exit a door that leads outside. After exiting, you are going to turn around and psychically affix a glowing white pentacle to the door. You will then feel yourself ascending, taking note of the building's features as you rise high above the building.

When you have found yourself above the building, panoramically view the city around you, looking in all directions and taking note of all that you see. You are then going to look down at the roof below and see a large glowing white pentacle affixed to the rooftop below you. This pentacle will be your "launching pad" as well as the "landing pad" during the meditation.

See yourself rising over seven hundred feet in the air above the rooftop. When you have reached this height, affirm your intention to witness your past life by stating aloud, "I am now going to land in a past life that is (add here the type of existence you wish to observe that you have decided upon)."

You are going to then descend towards the white pentacle which you have fixed upon the rooftop. When you have landed, look down at your feet and note the type of footwear you are wearing, if any at all. Then notice the type of clothing you are attired in, taking note of what you see. You are then going to allow yourself to receive the information that will inform you of which incarnation you are witnessing. This might include what time period or year it was when this life was occurring, where you were, how old you were, and any other details.

Then put yourself onto the screen of your mind and observe the events of this life as if watching a movie. You can ask to witness what was occurring at various ages, different events, and, perhaps most importantly, the karmic lessons of this incarnation.

If you are at the point of death, are in pain, or are experiencing any disturbing visions, immediately neutralize what you are seeing, give yourself Total Health Clearance, and count yourself back up from alpha.

After you have witnessed as much of this incarnation as you wish, allow yourself to rise upwards to a height of seven hundred feet once again. From this apex, look downwards at the white pentacle which you have affixed to the rooftop and state aloud, "I am now going to return to my current existence."

Allow yourself to slowly descend until you have landed safely upon the white pentacle on the rooftop. Then descend and land in front of the door to which you fastened the other white pentacle. Enter the building and see yourself returning to your corporeal body, physically wiggle your fingers and toes to adjust to the reentry. Give yourself Total Health Clearance and the count yourself back up from alpha level.

Have your DNA analyzed through the services available today. Learn more about who you are and where you come from. You are a composite of all your ancestors, known and unknown. Some ancestors were more majickal. Others were more in tune with nature. Some might have been more mathematical or scientific, others more artistic. You can draw from your genetic background with your majick and kindle gifts you did not know you had, quietly lurking within your DNA and genetic memory. Many believe the ancient Scottish people have genetic links to Egypt, through the Princess Scotta. Others believe Witches have a connection to Faeries through the "faery blood." You never know what blessings might be lurking in your own DNA.

WEATHER MAJICK

Weather majick is the act of changing the weather around you, either for an immediate change or for a long-term weather intention at a specific date, time, and place. Though some can't believe it, you can change the weather. It is one of the classic powers of the Witch. However, you have to be careful with this. If you change the weather in one place, it affects the weather in another. This is true of all majickal workings. One change can affect something else which affects something else and so on, just like dominoes! Make sure all weather majick projections are done with the intention of the highest good, harming none. My teacher Felicity had us call up the wind on a still day, and we'd blow feathers for our spells into the wind. Calling up a simple wind is a good way to start exploring weather majick. Hold your Instant Alpha Trigger and call to the wind. Imagine it coming and how it would feel upon your skin, and in a few moments, there it will be.

ANIMAL COMMUNICATION

Through the science of alpha, you can both gain information from, and communicate with, animals. The best animal communicators use alpha, whether they know it or not. Through this altered state, we can connect through the screen of our mind to the animal. The animal can be present, or we can simply have the name or photograph of the animal from someone. We can then use the same techniques we use for the health cases to gain information about not only the animal's physical condition, which can be verified, but also a sense of their emotional and mental state, and whatever they wish to communicate to their human companions.

When physically working with an animal, we can use our Instant Alpha Trigger to attain a trance state with our eyes open, touching the animal if possible. We can project our own thoughts to the animal in words, or better yet, in pictures, as images are the universal language to non-verbal species. We can then wait and receive information that our brain can interpret as images, words, or feelings, relaying what the animal might wish to convey. Don't be surprised if the animal is surprised that you are communicating. It doesn't happen all that often, so animals don't come to expect it from humans anymore.

Using a combination of the mind travel and health case techniques, Witches can locate lost animals by gaining a better understanding of the environment the animal is in by perceiving its surroundings. A pendulum can be swung over a map to narrow down possible locations, dowsing for the location of the animal.

These techniques can help bond you to a flesh-and-blood living familiar, developing a majickal relationship with an animal in your life that will enhance your Craft and the quality of your life.

As with all uses of alpha, make sure to give yourself Total Health Clearance when completing any work with animal communication.

Penny's Universal Sky Exercise

Penny actually learned this many years ago in an astronomy class, but immediately saw the application of it in our Witchcraft studies.

Find a spot where there is as little urban light pollution as possible, such as a field, mountain, or beach. Lie down flat on the ground and extend your arms straight out forward at the sky. Stay this way for fifteen minutes while staring at the universe and the stars. Within fifteen minutes, you will begin to feel the sensation that your back is glued to the Earth and you are hanging from the planet above the void. Your perspective of gravity has changed, and you now have the understanding of how vast our universe is.

TELEPATHY AND EMPATHY

Just as we can project our thoughts and specific information to our animal companions, receiving their thoughts and information in return, we can send our thoughts to other people and pick up on the thoughts of other people. When we pick up on thoughts and ideas, we call this skill telepathy. When we pick up on the emotions of other people, we call it empathy or being an empath. Many people who are naturally gifted in empathy have quite a difficult time distinguishing their own moods and emotions from others, so proper shielding is important, as is the ability to ground. By knowing ourselves, we can better and more quickly separate our own thoughts or feelings from those we might be picking up from others.

Telepathy works best between two people who can cooperate consciously at alpha level. Work with a willing partner and explore trying to send thoughts to one another. It can be done silently in the same room, but also over wide distances. You can also use this technique to send information or images through to another's dreams at night. Keep a notebook to record your impressions, both in your telepathic practice sessions and in your dreams, and see if you have any success sending or receiving the thoughts, images, and information with another.

SUN SIGN ASTROLOGY

Sun sign astrology begins with knowing the astrological sign the Sun occupied when you were born. The sky is divided into twelve sections, and each of those sections has been associated with a zodiac constellation, although today, the signs really have more to do with the seasons and our position in space. Each of the twelve signs is associated with a positive or negative polarity, often equated with masculine or feminine gender. Each sign is associated with one of the four classic elements of fire, earth, air, and water, plus one of three other qualities: cardinal, meaning the energy begins things; fixed, meaning the energy sustains; and mutable, meaning the energy of this sign ends or adapts. The Sun occupies cardinal signs during the official start of a season, fixed signs in the middle of a season and mutable signs at the end of the season. Each sign is also linked to a planet that "rules" it, meaning it influences that sign because they have so much in common.

Sign	Gender	Element	Quality	Planet	Dates
Aries	Male	Fire	Cardinal	Mars	Mar 21 – Apr 20
Taurus	Female	Earth	Fixed	Venus	Apr 21 – May 21
Gemini	Male	Air	Mutable	Mercury	May 22 – Jun 21
Cancer	Female	Water	Cardinal	Moon	Jun 22 – Jul 22
Leo	Male	Fire	Fixed	Sun	Jul 23 – Aug 22
Virgo	Female	Earth	Mutable	Mercury	Aug 23 – Sep 23
Libra	Male	Air	Cardinal	Venus	Sep 24 – Oct 23
Scorpio	Female	Water	Fixed	Mars/Pluto	Oct 24 – Nov 22
Sagittarius	Male	Fire	Mutable	Jupiter	Nov 23 – Dec 21
Capricorn	Female	Earth	Cardinal	Saturn	Dec 22 – Jan 20
Aquarius	Male	Air	Fixed	Uranus	Jan 21 – Feb 19
Pisces	Female	Water	Mutable	Neptune	Feb 20 – Mar 20

If you are born on a cusp, meaning the day of transition between one sign to the next, you might have to consult an astrological ephemeris, or a practicing astrologer, with your birth time and place to determine which sign you truly are.

Learning about your own birth sign is a wonderful start to the path of self-discovery and introspection. Explore the strengths, weaknesses, tendencies, and lessons associated with each of the Sun signs. This could be the start of a more in-depth study of astrology, and the possibility of learning your entire birth, or natal, chart and the position of all the planets when you were born. A thorough understanding of the planets and signs in astrology will be of great help to you in the Second Degree.

CELTIC TREE SIGN ASTROLOGY

Different from traditional Sun sign astrology is what has become known as Celtic Tree sign astrology. While some claim it is an ancient practice, it is really a modern system using ancient Celtic symbols and myths, and can be used to attune us to the ways of the Celts. As the Cabot Tradition is rooted in the Celtic culture, knowing your Celtic Tree sign can be an excellent introduction to the Celtic world for beginners. It can give you different information than your traditional Sun sign does, and many majickal people find it more accurate and helpful on their path.

Essentially the three-hundred-and-sixty-degree circle of the sky is divided not into twelve equal sections, but thirteen, each named after thirteen of the Irish Celtic Ogham. The Ogham are a system of divination and lettering based upon mostly straight lines. While each has a wide range of associations, the most popular associations with each symbol is a majickal tree.

The idea of a tree-based astrology seems to have been started by the author Robert Graves in his book, *The White Goddess*. Modern astrologers such as Helena Patterson have built upon it, but most today agree that this does not resemble any traditional Celtic forms of astrology from antiquity. Still it is a system we have access to, one that can prove helpful for modern Celtic Witches.

Tree	Ogham	Dates	Planet	Totem	Qualities	Stone	Deity
Birch	Beth	Dec 24 – Jan 20	Sun	Eagle, Stag	Ambitious, successful, Family responsibility	Quartz	Taliesin
Rowan	Luis	Jan 21 – Feb 17	Uranus	Dragon, Crane	Visionary, Humanitarian, Controversial, Opinionated	Peridot	Brigid
Ash	Nion	Feb 18 – Mar 17	Neptune	Seal, Seahorse	Artistic, Sensitive, Compassionate, Realistic	Coral	Lir
Alder	Fearn	Mar 18 – Apr 14	Mars	Bear, Fox	Warrior, Leader, Competitive, Impatient	Ruby	King Arthur

Willow	Saille	Apr 15 – May 12	Moon	Serpent, Hare	Psychic, Mystical, Hidden, Mysterious, Emotional	Moonstone	Morgan le Fey
Hawthorn	Uath	May 13 – Jun 9	Vulcan	Bee, Owl	Charisma, Craftsmanship, Strategy, Leadership	Topaz	Govannan
Oak	Duir	Jun 10 – Jul 7	Jupiter	Wren, Horse	Optimistic, Charming, Successful, sacrifice	Diamond	Dagda
Holly	Tinne	Jul 8 – Aug 4	Earth	Cat, Unicorn	Strong Will, Values, Loyal, Historical, Pretentious	Carnelian	Danu
Hazel	Coll	Aug 5 – Sep 1	Mercury	Salmon, Crane	Communication, Wisdom, Good Memory, Challenging	Amethyst	Ogma
Vine	Muin	Sep 2 – Sep 29	Venus	White Swan	High Emotions, Restless, Gentle, Angry, Sad	Emerald	Guinevere
Ivy	Gort	Sep 30 – Oct 27	Transpluto (Sparta)	Butterfly	Justice, Responsibility, Shrewd, Manipulative	Opal	Arianrhod
Reed	Ngetal	Oct 28 – Nov 24	Pluto	Hound, Owl	Personal Power, Magnetism, Imaginative, Obsessive	Jasper	Pwyll
Elder	Ruis	Nov 25 – Dec 23	Saturn	Raven, Horse	Transformative, powerful, disciplined, adventurous	Jet	Pryderi

Modern practitioners of this system have converted the whole system of astrology, creating birth charts and describing them in terms of the thirteen "tree" signs. Start with this introduction, and learn more about the majick associated with each of the trees as you continue your studies in the subsequent degrees of the Cabot Tradition.

ROSICRUCIAN YEARLY LIFE CYCLES

As I have also studied with a Rosicrucian Master and have found Joseph Weed's book *Wisdom of the Mystic Masters* quite helpful, I teach some of the esoteric ideas found in Rosicrucianism to my students. The Rosicrucians extend much of what we have learned from the Hermetic Principles. They teach a seven-part cycle that occurs to us every year. If you understand your cycles, you can more easily work with the energies flowing in your life.

To calculate your seven part cycle, start with your birthday and count 52 days. Seven periods of fifty days, or (7 x 52 = 364), is just a day short of a year. For example, my birthday is March 6.

First Cycle	Sun Cycle	March 6 – April 27
Second Cycle	Moon Cycle	April 28 – June 18
Third Cycle	Mars Cycle	June 19 – August 9
Fourth Cycle	Mercury Cycle	August 9 – September 30
Fifth Cycle	Jupiter Cycle	October 1 – November 21
Sixth Cycle	Venus Cycle	November 22 – January 12
Seventh Cycle	Saturn Cycle	January 13 – March 5

Once you've calculated this, you don't have to do it again as its the same every year, with a slight adjustment for leap years.

First Cycle	Building, Opportunity, Power, Influence, Ask Favors, Change Jobs
Second Cycle	Quick Changes, Short Travel, Transient Work, No Longer Term Change
Third Cycle	Discernment, Good Judgment, Overcome Past Obstacles, Avoid Arguments
Fourth Cycle	Mental and Spiritual Period, Writing, Creativity, Optimism, Good Impulses
Fifth Cycle	Greatest Success in All Things, Confidence, Benevolence, Growth
Sixth Cycle	Rest, Relaxation, Leisure and Amusement, Continue Business, Short Trips, Friendships, Art, Music, Literature
Seventh Cycle	Removal of Unnecessary, Distress, Seeming Difficulties Leading to Better Things, Exercise Good Judgment, Easily Discouraged, Don't Be Impulsive

Along with this yearly cycle of the planets following what you will later learn as the pattern of the planetary days of the week, there is also a lifetime cycle.

Planet	Period	Ages
Moon	Personal Growth	Birth to 4 Years Old
Mercury	Education	5 – 14 Years Old
Venus	Emotion	15 – 22 Years Old
Sunday	Vitality	23 – 42 Years Old
Mars	Ambition	43 – 57 Years Old
Jupiter	Reflection	58 – 69 Years Old
Saturn	Resignation	70 + Years Old

Now with an understanding of the planetary energies in your life, you can better plan your year for your success and spiritual growth.

THE CRYSTAL WHEEL

The Crystal Wheel is a psychic construct of etheric crystals placed seven hundred feet above the city of Salem, Massachusetts, around the entire perimeter of the city. The wheel was psychically constructed in 1975 by the Black Doves of Isis coven of the Cabot Tradition. Born from the traditions of various majickal lodges such as the Rosicrucians, who offered circles of solace for petitioners within and beyond their tradition, the Crystal Wheel serves the same purpose. You can go there to seek solace and help, or you can go to offer solace and help to others in need. It is a place of healing and energetic exchange for the highest good. Anyone who needs emotional, physical, or spiritual healing may meditate on this wheel. All the Witches who attend the Crystal Wheel become a conduit so that universal information can answer questions and send the proper majick to whoever enters the wheel. We put ourselves there so we can become a conduit of the universal mind. Anyone who wants to meditate and come to the Crystal Wheel above Salem in our sky, we will be there for you. If you have questions, if you have issues or problems you want solved, we're there to help the universal mind help you solve those problems.

The Witches of the Cabot Tradition focus upon the Crystal Wheel every Thursday, the day of good fortune, at 10:00 p.m. Eastern time. We ask those who would like to participate to perform this meditation at the same time, adjusting for local time zones. You may come to the wheel as often as you wish. The circle usually lasts an hour but you can join for as long as you'd like, from just a few minutes to the full hour. All helps the work of the Crystal Wheel.

Healing lists are collected weekly by the Priests and Priestesses of the Cabot-Kent Hermetic Temple, as people place their names via social media. Each week we add the names of anyone you wish for us to concentrate on. We place all the names into a cauldron for this purpose. There is no need to tell us why anyone needs assistance when you offer the name. Just the name will suffice.

Meditations to help you join in are transcribed and posted on the same media outlets. They are used as a focus for those who will be sent the appropriate energies by the Witches gathered psychically for the Wheel. Each Thursday we focus on a different color, and that too is posted, though you don't need to know the color of the week to join us and benefit from it.

Some people find it helpful to hold in their left hand a crystal of the appropriate color being focused upon for the week. Here are some suggestions.

Red	Ruby, Garnet, Red Jasper
Red-Orange	Carnelian
Orange	Orange Calcite
Yellow	Citrine, Yellow Topaz, Yellow Calcite
Green	Emerald, Malachite, Peridot, Green Fluorite, Green Tourmaline, Green Calcite
Pink	Rose Quartz, Kunzite, Pink Tourmaline
Blue	Lapis Lazuli, Turquoise, Sapphire, Sodalite , Blue Fluorite, Azurite, Aquamarine
Indigo	Sugilite, Iolite, Chariote
Orchid	Amethyst, Purple Tourmaline, Purple Fluorite
Gold	Pyrite, Gold

Silver	Silver, Moonstone

You can use a quartz crystal point as a focus for your work with the Crystal Wheel, imagining your crystal is one of the many crystals in the floating psychic wheel. Some special crystals have been charged by Priestesses and Priests of the Temple, and touched to the larger ritual crystal that is the focus for the Cabot Witches physically when working with the wheel. You can also look at a photo of the crystal as a way to anchor yourself to the wheel, but even that is not necessary. The etheric crystals exist on the astral plane and are accessible to anyone who comes with the intention of giving or receiving for the highest good.

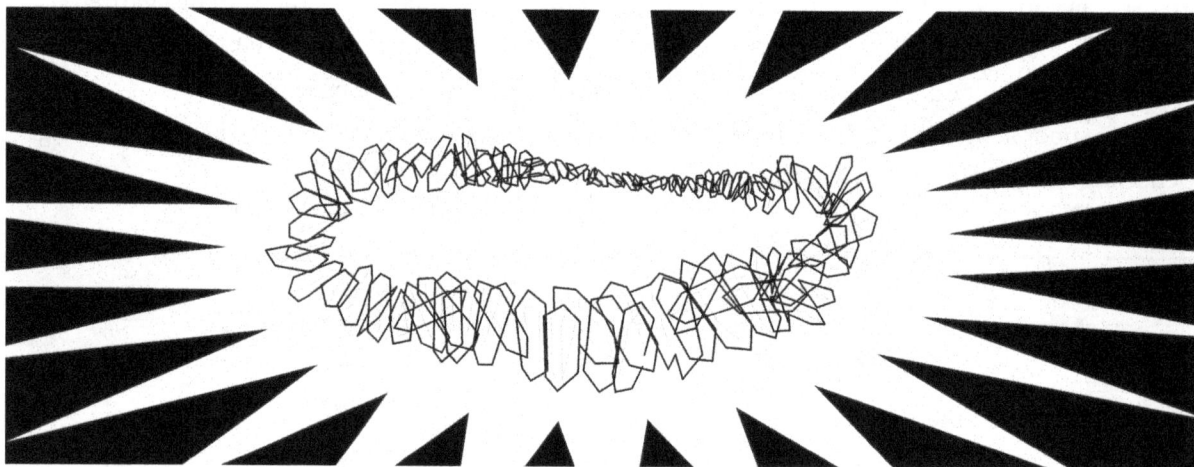

The Crystal Wheel

Crystal Wheel Meditation

Enter alpha using the Crystal Countdown. Imagine stepping outside of yourself, mentally rising up. Soon you are rising up and heading in the direction of Salem, Massachusetts, transporting yourself seven hundred feet above the city. There you see the giant Crystal Wheel above Salem, made of the most brilliant and beautiful crystals in a ring. You land safely upon the ring and sense it is filling with light, and as more and more people attune to it, adding light or making healing requests.

Once on or in the ring you may psychically sense the presence of other people. This is totally normal, so do not fear. You might even recognize specific people. Now you can request answers from the elders or ancestors, ask for healing for yourself or a loved one, or simply pull in additional light into the circle from the All. This is done by visualizing the crystals and seeing them grow brighter as you call light from the universe into them. This light can come through you or be directed from you but in no way will it drain you of any energy whatsoever; your efforts are attracting more light into the circle for all to use, not taking any from you. Whatever your request, Cabot Witches always add, "And may it be for the good of all."

Spend as much time here with the Crystal Wheel as you feel is correct.

Then it is time to return back from the Crystal Wheel. With your intention, project your awareness back to where your physical body is located. Give yourself Total Health Clearance to remove any incorrect energy. Bring your awareness back to your body, and count up from your alpha level.

THE CABOT SASH

Once you successfully complete the Witchcraft I First Degree class, you are entitled to a Cabot Sash. This sash is worn during circle and at ritual, over your left shoulder, with the front a bit shorter than what falls to the back. It is in the Royal Stewart Plaid. We wear Royal Stewart Plaid because the Cabot Ancestors come from the McLaren Tribe. This tribe eventually became one with the Stewart Clan.

Ritual clothing is used in majick to focus and gather energy better. Cabots all dress the same in ritual because we collect our energy better through this connection. This gives power to our majick and strength to our ultimate goal in any given ritual setting. We always wear black—black everything. It must be solid black. We wear black because the color is a combination of every color in the spectrum. Black absorbs, making it perfect for our majickal rituals. In wearing black during ritual and majickal workings, we are drawing in the powers of the universe—the energies of the God/Goddess and The All.

The sash is often held in place with a crown-shaped pin. Cabots use crowns in our majick, jewelry, and ritual objects upon our altars. This crown represents sovereignty. To Cabots, sovereignty means not wielding your power over others or proving that our tradition is better than any other. It is about personal power. Owning this power means being responsible for your actions and your majick and admitting when you make a mistake. We must then learn from these mistakes. Mistakes are inevitable, as no one is perfect. The difference lies in accepting that you did wrong, seeking counsel, and fixing it, if you can. This can be difficult, as it takes a great amount of self-esteem to admit fault.

WITCHCRAFT I: WITCHCRAFT AS A SCIENCE
RECOMMENDED READING LIST

Power of the Witch by Laurie Cabot*

Love Magic by Laurie Cabot*

Laurie Cabot's Book of Spells and Enchantments by Laurie Cabot
     with Penny Cabot and Christopher Penczak*

The Kybalion by Three Initiates*

Stalking the Wild Pendulum by Itzhak Bentov*

The Tao of Physics by Fritzof Capra*

The Secret Teachings of All Ages by Manly P. Hall

The Holotrophic Mind by Stanislav Grof, MD

The Quantum Self by Dana Zohar

Wicca: A Guide for the Solitary Practitioner by Scott Cunningham

Earth, Air, Fire and Water by Scott Cunningham

The Inner Temple of Witchcraft by Christopher Penczak

Instant Magick by Christopher Penczak

The Witch's Shield by Christopher Penczak

The Mystic Foundation by Christopher Penczak

The Gates of Witchcraft by Christopher Penczak

Positive Magic by Marion Weinstein

Diary of a Witch by Sybil Leek

Astrology, A Cosmic Science by Isabel M. Hickey

The Celtic Lunar Zodiac by Helena Paterson

Celtic Magic by Edain McCoy

The Celtic Tradition by Caitlin Matthews

* Required Reading for the First Degree

Second Degree: Witchcraft as an Art

Becoming a Priestess or Priest of the Craft

Passing the Torch — Majickal Manifestation and Spellcraft

Taking Responsibility

THE ART OF THE WITCH

We seek to be artists in majick, but to truly be artists, we must be well aware of the theory. We must be grounded in our knowledge of the science of the craft, to know our own selves and experience the self-love and self-esteem that are the highest form of majick. We have learned the majick involving altered states of consciousness, including how to use the Crystal Countdown to enter into an alpha brainwave state. We have learned how to control our breathing, and how breath affects our energy and consciousness. We have learned the power of color and the influence of its vibration through an understanding of our body's energy centers (chakras), chi/prana, and by sending and receiving energy for healing through color. With those teachings, we can more effectively approach the art of the Witch.

In the Second Degree, we learn the mysteries of casting the Witch's majick circle, and how to do so specifically in the Cabot Tradition. The art of ritual has a psychology, a sociology, and a practice, and understanding its mechanics makes us better Witches. We learn the tools of the art used in ritual and spellcraft, including how to use herbs, stones, candles, and symbols in our spellcraft. The art of the Witch includes the making of the majick wand, and the crafting of potions, geometric talismans, amulets, and cord majick. We learn the influence of astrology upon our rituals and how to work at the most effective times. Through our majick, we can influence events, attract and manifest our goals, and banish harmful energies and forces.

Introspective skills are called for in our Craft as well. We learn the ways of crystal gazing, also known as scrying, to gain information. This can open our gifts of clairvoyance and clairaudience. We learn to dowse, and we develop the skill of automatic writing and "reading" objects through psychometry. We explore the role of tarot in our majick and Craft.

The practicing Witch does more than simple spells and divination. Through these arts, we grow in our self-confidence. We become steadfast, developing a stillness and sense of inner peace and calm that are unshakable. We further our self-esteem to a sense of total esteem. We gain greater abilities to focus our consciousness and attention and develop our own Witch Power.

In essence, we learn how to become practicing Witches, priestesses and priests of the Craft for our own betterment. These are lifelong lessons, and the more we practice majick, the more we learn and the more adept we become in our Craft.

THE TOOLS OF WITCHCRAFT

The Witch uses a wide variety of tools for ritual, majick, and divination. Some are considered to be traditional and "standard" ritual tools of the Witch and magician. Others, while majickal, also have a practical function beyond the main working tools. Some of the Witch's personal accoutrements are also majickal tools used in spells and rituals. They help establish a majickal atmosphere for the Witch. Certain tools are more often used in divination, but can also play a role in spellcasting, while other tools are really the ingredients and vessels for our spells, comprising our majickal apothecary.

Ritual Tools

• **Wand** — The wand is a tool that is vital for doing your will. It corresponds to the element of fire. The wand extends your intentions, thoughts, and deeds. A wand is really an extension of your own energy, and a wand has its own energy. Because metal, crystal, and wood have an energy or aura within them, we combine our energy with the energy of the wand. Then you can project whatever it is that you want the wand to do. A Witch can have many wands, with the vibration of the material of each wand being good for different types of majick. While the base substance—be it metal, wood, or stone—is the primary influence of the wand, handcrafted wands can be dressed with crystals, stones, or wire and decorated with paint, markers, wood burning and other methods. Ideally a wand is about two and a half feet long, but some wands are longer and others are shorter. A staff is used much like a wand, as an extension of our will. Many Witches will drill a hole in a wooden wand, add a drop of blood, and seal it with candle wax. Wands and staves can be used as divining rods, for "water witching" or finding water, lost objects, and areas of power.

• **Chalice** — The chalice is representative of the Goddess and her sacred womb. It is the symbol of the element of water, and the Cauldron of Inspiration. Water is our sacrament, taking the imprint of intention and emotions used for majick. In the Cabot Tradition, unlike other Witchcraft Traditions, we do not ever use wine or any representation of blood in our chalice. We use only fresh spring water.

• **Athame** — The athame is a double-sided blade, usually at least four inches in length, though some use crystal "blades" for athames. Traditionally it has a black or dark handle. It is the tool of the element of air and a representation of the God, used to draw the energies of the Universe, the

All, the Moon, the Sun and other forces into the circle during ritual. The athame is used for circle-casting, for protection majick, for charging tools, and for carving candles. Some Witches have only one blade for all of these uses, while others have different blades, each consecrated for a particular use. In many traditions, the athame is never used to cut or carve—instead, a white-handled, single-edged knife known as a boline is used—but in the Cabot Tradition, we believe the blade should be functional as well as majickal. In some states the possession of a double-edged blade is illegal, and it must be transported only with other religious tools such as a chalice, peyton, and wand to be considered a religious tool and not a weapon. Check with your local law enforcement as to what is allowed in your area.

• **Peyton** — The peyton is the ritual "dish" found in the myths of the Holy Grail and the Grail Castle. It is often said to mean "House of Women" and a symbol of the holy blood of humanity. The blood of a man and a woman who wanted to marry would be mixed in this dish, and if they did mix, the couple could marry. If they did not, then no wedding would be allowed. While some Witchcraft traditions use it as a plate for sabbat cakes, our tradition uses it as a flat, five-pointed star, a pentacle, to represent universal light and spirit, though many consider it, like the pentacles of the Tarot deck, a symbol of elemental earth. To manifest something physically on the earthly plane, one needs all five elements, hence the five-pointed star. We use the peyton to call the ancestors and the elemental quarters by holding it up in the air facing the proper direction when in a circle. We can also place items upon it to enhance their majick. When used in a Christian context, it is usually spelled paten.

• **Sword** — Swords are used much like the athame blade, but are larger. In the Third Degree, the sword is the primary tool, as Cabot Witches use the blade and energy of Excalibur due to the association of Excalibur and the Arthurian Mysteries with the Witches of Kent. In our tradition, my own blade was touched by the Light of Excalibur when I was initiated by my teacher, Felicity, one of the Witches of Kent. I pass this blade now into the blades of initiates in the Third Degree. The sword is a symbol of protection, and Excalibur in particular is the symbol of the relationship between the people and the land, through the King and the Goddess, as well as our connection to the Faery world and the realm of Avalon.

• **Cauldron** — The cauldron is a vessel of spirit, combining all the elements, and is used to contain, mix, and release energies and substance. Witches have many cauldrons. Some are used for burning spells. Others are used for cooking and brewing. Small ones can be used like a thurible for burning incense. Many use a cauldron as a vessel for healing, placing the names of people who have requested healing in it and using it as a focus for both sending light and healing candle majick. Traditionally iron cauldrons are used for protection. An iron cauldron will absorb anything you put into it, so if you use it for cooking or brewing, only use it for that, and remember some herbs are poisonous, so don't mix up your cooking edible food cauldron with your overall majick herb cauldron. Many will use brass or copper cauldrons for non-protection majick.

• **Besom** — The besom is also the Witch's broom. Traditionally made with a handle of ash, bristle of birch, and binding of willow, today they come in many forms and woods. In folklore it was reported that Witches used to fly on brooms, but this might come from a misunderstanding of either crop fertility rites or astral travel. Today, the sweeping motion of the broom is used to keep away harm and clear unwanted energy. It is usually stored bristles up, behind doors for protection and blessing.

• **Mortar and Pestle** — The mortar is the cup-like container, while the pestle is the rod used for grinding. The grinding of the mortar and pestle is used to break down substances for our majick. They can be made from wood, stone, ceramic and even metal, and the different substances can influence your majick. Since it can be difficult to remove sticky or oily substances from our mortars, it is best to have different sets for each use. Have one for resins, one for herbs, and one for cooking. Make sure you never put any toxic herbs in your cooking mortar and pestle set.

• **Hand Sickle** — The crescent sickle is used to majickally harvest herbs. They can be made from steel, iron, or ideally from a Faery-friendly metal such as copper. Traditionally one held the sickle in the right hand and the herbs in the left, harvesting at the appropriate astrological day and time for that particular herb.

• **Cord** — The cord is sometimes tied with nine knots and measures four-and-a-half feet long. When held in the center by an athame, it can be used with the wand at the other end to draw a traditional nine-foot circle, as if the tools create a larger compass, making a perfect circle. The cord is a tool of spirit, binding things together and aligning forces. It can be used to join things or to bind. In some traditions of Witchcraft, a cord was worn around the thigh, like a garter, to signify a Witch Queen. In coven-based structures, the Witch Queen would have a buckle upon the garter for every coven that has hived off from her own.

• **Bell** — The bell is used to call spirits, particularly the Great Spirit, Gods, or the Fey. Choose your bell carefully, making sure it has a pleasing tone when rung. The bell's tone should affect your "inner bell." The bell can also be used in larger rituals to call the coven to circle when it is time to begin.

• **Horn** — The horn is a simple tool from an older time. Many have used this hollowed cattle horn in place of the cup, making it a drinking horn. But in the Cabot Tradition, the horn is akin to the cornucopia, the horn of plenty. It is a symbol of majick and abundance and blessings. It can be filled with aromatic resins, flowers, or stalks of grain. For the symbolism, an egg carved from stone or wood can also be used as a symbol of abundance.

• **Gaming Board** — The gaming board is a tool no other tradition uses. While today we relate it to the game of chess, our ancestors related it to the Game of Life. In the Celtic traditions, it was known as *Fidchell* in Irish and said to be the invention of the god Lugh; in the Welsh traditions, it was known as *Gwyddbwyll* and shows up in the myth known as *The Dream of Rhonabwy,* a tale of King Arthur. The gaming board consists of sixty-four black and white squares. We use it as the centerpiece for our altar and set symbols upon it. You can use it for both spellcraft and for divination, though some keep two separate gaming boards for each intention. We place chess pieces, symbols, roots, talismans, and stones upon it when casting spells. In the center of the board, you place a symbol of yourself. Bring things to you from the left, using black squares to help you manifest things. Send things out or away to the right and place them upon white squares. You can speed majick by moving things around your board.

More information about the Game of Life can be found in the Game of Life section on page 193.

Practical Tools

• **Candles/Holders/Snuffers** — Candles are the tool of elemental fire and light. You will match your candle color to its purpose. On a Cabot altar, the Goddess candle on the left side is black, to draw in energy. The candle on the right, for the God, is white, to send out energy. The best candleholders are brass, which is a conductor of electrical energy. Glass can break. We never blow out a candle with a spell or intention in it because your prana will alter the spell. Instead, snuff it out. A snuffer can be as simple as a teaspoon, but it will seal in the spell until you relight it. Never leave a burning candle unattended.

• **Ritual Matches** — Cabot Witches use ritual matches, not lighters, in our rituals. Lighters often have parts made of plastic, which is ruled by Neptune and can create illusions and misunderstandings. We use plain matches that have no writing on them, that have been cleansed and charged for majick. If you find a design with a pentacle or other appropriate majickal symbol, you can use it in your spells.

• **Incense, Charcoal and Incense Burner** — The thurible is the classic name of the traditional incense burner. It is a flameproof vessel, often brass, though small iron cauldrons can also be used. It is filled with sand to distribute the heat. Be careful when using one as it will get quite hot. Many Witches place a trivet or tile beneath it to further protect the altar from the heat. Upon the sand, you place an instant light charcoal disk, or perhaps one fourth or one half of a disc, and sprinkle powdered herbal incense upon the disc. You can use sugar tongs to hold the charcoal as you light it, to prevent yourself from burning your fingers. Keep your charcoal in an airtight container. Incense can help enhance our majick. As it burns, it releases a light energy and vibration. Incense is usually a mix of resins, woods, and herbs.

There are so many mixtures of herbs and roots and resins that produce energy to change things, so it is important that we designate the different formulas of incense to produce an effect. These are the majickal incenses that can be burned. Not only does it contain the herbs, resins and roots, but I also sometimes add the oils or the potions that attribute the same nature of energy. We often use a base of colored wood to add the majick of color to our incense, along with a pinch of colored glitter to reflect the appropriate light frequencies. As you progress, you'll learn how to hand blend your own incense, but these basic ingredients can get you started:

Frankincense and Myrrh: Clears out all incorrectness (corruptive or harmful energies)
Dragon's Blood: For love, power, and protection
Copal: For happiness, fulfillment, and ease — attracts helpful spirits
Benzoin: Increases the psychic atmosphere, making divination and scrying easier
Lavender Flowers: For peace and purification
Pine Needles: For clarity, good fortune, and purification

• **Parchment Paper** — Modern parchment is a fancy, non-recycled paper used for spell work, not the skin of an animal. You should always have parchment on-hand. We use it to write our spells and Full Moon Wish Lists. We also use it for majickal correspondence, aligning colored parchment with our intentions. We do not use recycled paper or lined paper. This interferes with the energy of the spell.

• **Pen and Ink** — Pen and ink can be majickally cleansed and charged, as can pens and markers of various colors. In general, we use black ink for all-purpose majick. You can make liquid inks by adding oils, stones, and herbs, and then using a pen nub to write your spells.

• **Tea Stain** — Tea stain is technically not tea, but emulates the color of tea, and is used to stain the edges of spells and our Book of Shadows, to add color and romance to it. To make a tea stain, start with two cups of spring water. Add one teaspoon of liquid dish soap (like Dial) to prevent fermentation. Add to the mix a heaping tablespoon of brown acrylic paint and one quarter of a teaspoon of black acrylic paint. Place within the mix one clear quartz crystal charged to consecrate all majickal works. Mix well. Keep in a tightly sealed jar. Shake and use with a brush to stain the edges of the pages and papers. Let it dry, and it will "crinkle" like an old page.

• **Ash Pot** — This is a lidded pot that you place burning spells in. Fire-resistant pottery, marble, or metal with sea salt in the bottom to distribute the heat can be used. We save the ashes of our spells and use them in other majick and rituals. A larger cauldron is sometimes used as an ash pot, or ashes from a cauldron can be transferred to an ash pot.

• **Altar Table** — An altar can be any surface, including the top of a bureau, a coffee table, or a small curio shelf in your room. Many Witches have multiple altars throughout their homes. These are often dedicated to specific deities. No candles should be placed on shelf-type altars, as this creates a dangerous fire hazard. Instead, these places should more devotional-style altars, with the likeness of the God or Goddess they honor or some item pertaining to them, like an apple or a harp.

• **Altar Cloth** — Altar cloths are simple strips of fabric used to prevent your altar from being ruined by wax, oil, and heat, and to add vibration by matching the color of the cloth to your majickal intention and working.

• **Salt** — Sometimes salt, as a symbol of elemental earth and protection, is placed upon the altar. At various times in the Cabot Tradition, we've also used black coral or black tourmaline as an earthy substance of protection upon the altar.

Personal Tools

• **Witch's Robe/Cape** — Robes and capes are personal ritual clothing for a Witch, not to be shared. It is usually worn only when doing majick or doing a circle. It is personal as it absorbs the energy of the workings you do and becomes a part of your majick. Charge it in a circle to encompass all of your majick.

• **Witch's Jewelry** — Also known as the "Witch's Jewels," these are majickal pieces of jewelry worn during ritual and sometimes in daily life. The metals, gems, and other substances reflect and refract universal light energy. This jewelry can be expensive fine jewelry or costume jewelry. Each is equally precious to the Witch in the majickal world. We do, however, refrain from using diamonds and rubies, due to the immense violence and injustice associated with their extraction and import. So unless you can find Fair Trade diamonds and rubies, do not use them in your majick. Synthetic diamond and ruby are preferable to those stones that have been associated with harm.

• **Book of Shadows** — This is a lifelong record of your life as a Witch. Some Witches have many Books of Shadow, abbreviated in writing as a BOS. They may have one book for herbs, another for spells, and yet another for religious rituals. Or you could make sections for each in a larger book. You should cleanse and neutralize your BOS before you start writing in it. It is the only book to really bring into your majick circle. Usually the cover is black. Use a protection potion and fix its energy. Further protect it by tea staining each page.

• **Book of Talismans** — Like a Book of Shadows, a book of talismans can be used to contain all your majickal designs and art.

• **Statues** – Many Witches place statues of the Goddess and God for their working altar, or for personal devotional shrines.

Divination Tools

• **Pendulums** — Pendulums are weights hanging from cords or chains. The weight can be made from stone, wood, ceramic or metal. Traditionally a quartz crystal is attached to the chain, and on the opposite end, a charm or another stone. Answers can be given through directional swinging or circling, or through pendulum boards. A good experiment is for someone to get three identical boxes, putting one object in one of the boxes, and leave two empty. Have your dowser return to the room with no conscious knowledge of which box has the object. Use the pendulum to dowse which box has the object.

• **Tarot Cards** — A traditional tarot deck is made up of seventy-eight traditional cards divided into twenty-two Major Arcana cards and fifty-six Minor Arcana cards, further subdivided into four suits, based upon the four elemental tools—cups, swords, wands and coins. The cards are used to help us interpret psychic information, seeing and feeling with the mind's eye according to the images and colors.

• **Runes** — Runes, a system of majickal symbols from the Norse and Saxons, can be used for both divination, and—in the form of talismans and amulets—for majick. They contain an ancient power and intelligence that we can tap into and partner with for our majick.

• **Crystal Ball** — The crystal ball, usually a quartz crystal sphere, is used for scrying. It helps produce visions and can clarify and magnify the mind's eye. Crystal balls are often bathed in potions of mugwort or vervain, and then kept out of the light when not in use, usually covered by silk.

• **Witch's Mirror** — The Witch's mirror, also known as a black mirror or a scrying mirror, is used the same way the crystal ball is used. The Witch gazes into the depths of the black mirror to project the mind's eye and see images. Some are concave, others convex, and many are flat. While some mirrors are carved from obsidian, a natural black glass, we often make our mirrors by painting the inside of the glass from a picture frame with black paint. We then decorate the frames. I use the image of the crown, along with carnelian, citrine, quartz, and moonstone.

Majickal Tools

• **Herbs** — Herbs include most plants, weeds, trees, and even fungi used in majick. All herbs have majickal properties, and some have medicinal properties. Everything has a universal light energy, and we use the roots, leaves, flowers, gums, bark, seeds, sap, and pods of the plants for our majick, to tap into that energy.

• **Quartz Crystal** — Clear quartz is silicon dioxide that has grown into a crystalline matrix instead of being a glass. Crystals refract and reflect light, and absorb and amplify energy. Upon the Cabot altar, one points down (south) on the left side and one points up (north) on the right side to help us bring energy in and send out energy from our circles. Quartz is the most important crystal because it does anything and everything you can ever want. You can project anything through a quartz crystal.

• **Stones and Crystals** — Stones are minerals and gems used in majick according to their colors and astrological influences. People are drawn to certain crystals. They intuitively feel a connection. The chemistry and density influence the energy of stone. For example, a rose quartz is pink, instead of being clear, due to a titanium impurity. Because of this metal and color, it exudes the energies of Venus, giving off the properties of love and self-esteem.

• **Amulets** — Amulets are three-dimensional majickal items charged with a specific intention; they are used in the same way as talismans. A crystal hanging on a cord or a majick charm bag could be considered an amulet.

• **Talismans** — Talismans are flat majickal items; they are used in the same way as amulets. A pentacle or seal printed upon paper is considered a talisman.

• **Pentacles or Seals** — Pentacles can refer not only to a five-pointed star in a circle, but also to a series of seals and symbols found in majickal grimoires. The Cabot Tradition has its own series of majickal seals, evoking the powers we call.

• **Potion Bottles** — Sealable glass bottles are used for our potions, brews, philters, and other herbal mixes. You can use new, recycled, or antique bottles, and ideally we like to use unique and beautiful bottles for our majick. Some Witches prefer simple, utilitarian bottles, like mason jars. They must be sealable with either a tight cork or a tight-fitting lid.

• **Chart of Hours of Planets** — A chart of planetary days and hours, along with an astrological calendar, can be quite helpful in understanding when and how to do spells. Each of the seven days is "ruled" by one of the seven classic planets—Sun, Moon, Mars, Mercury, Jupiter, Venus, and

Saturn. The day is divided into twelve day hours and twelve night hours, each one further ruled by a planet. These are the energies we work with when casting our spells.

• **Witches' Alphabet** — The Witch's alphabet, also known as the Theban script, is used to create talismans and amulets. We translate our intentions into this code to empower them with majick. The universe understands this potent majickal script, but you can hide your intentions from others.

A	B	C	D	E	F	G	H	I	J	K	L	M
౧	౩	౫	౬	౭	౯	౮	౿	౸	౹	౺	౻	౼

N	O	P	Q	R	S	T	U	V	W	X	Y	Z
౽	౾	౿	౦	౧	౨	౩	౪	౫	౬	౭	౮	౯

Theban, the Witch's Alphabet

THE THIRTEEN TREASURES

In the Arthurian lore of our ancestors, Britain is said to have "Thirteen Treasures" guarded by Merlin. In the Cabot Tradition, we work with the correspondences of thirteen celestial bodies and associate a primary tool with each one. Place a special emphasis on understanding these thirteen tools upon your altar and in your own work, and make them your own mystical treasures.

Planet	Treasure
Sun	Candle
Moon	Cauldron or Chalice
Mercury	Wand
Venus	Thurible
Mars	Sword
Jupiter	Cord
Saturn	Athame
Uranus	Cord or Garter

Neptune	Crystal Ball
Pluto	Black Robe or Cape
Vulcan	Peyton or Gold Pentacle
Earth	Animal Horn or Egg
Sparta	Majick Mirror

CHARGING TOOLS

Neutralization clears an item of any unhelpful or imbalanced energies. Charging fills the tool with an intention, thereby consecrating it to a specific purpose. It tells the tool what the purpose is. Neutralize all unwanted, incorrect energies and forces in all your tools prior to using them, and then recharge all your tools. When you do, "fix" your tools so that nothing and no one can interfere with the energy of the tool.

Neutralization can be done through intention while in alpha, wiping away unwanted energies. You can also put a drop of protection potion or oil on the item to clear it, or pass it through a cleansing smoke, such as a blend of frankincense and myrrh, or storax.

To charge the tool, place it in your hand. With your words and through visualization, program the tool for your intention. You can end it with, "It is fixed" and "It is done" to indicate the energy will not be changed.

The first and most important tool to charge is the wand. We charge our wands within the majick circle, so they have the energy of the majick circle and can recreate this sacred space. In that way, we are "passing the torch" of the light of the circle, from wand to wand, though those who are solitary can charge their wands through the use of the Salt Circle.

Charging Your Majick Wand

To charge your wand in the circle, make sure you are in alpha, within the circle, with the wand in your hands. Take one hand and visualize removing, neutralizing, and cleansing anything incorrect from the wand. Pull it out of your wand with your hand and use the prana of your breath to blow it from the palm of your hand into the cosmos. Ask the cosmos, or Divine Mind, to turn the incorrect energy into something correct. Repeat these actions with your other hand on the other side of the wand.

Hold your wand and feel your aura flowing into the wand. Your hands will pulse. Say,

"I charge this wand to catalyze my thoughts, words, and deeds, by my will. So Mote it Be. It Is Fixed."

Give yourself Total Health Clearance and either continue with the circle if in a majick circle, or simply count up from alpha level.

When done, examine the tip of the wand. Check its energy and temperature. You'll find that the wand is now different, willed with a majickal fire and light.

You can use a similar process for any of your majickal tools.

DIFFERENT MAJICK WANDS

Different substances have different vibrations and can be more helpful to particular types of majick. You can use special wands for casting the circle, healing, divination, and even meditation. Simply holding a particular wand while in alpha can confer particular energies to a Witch. Here are some different ideas in terms of wands and wand materials:

Apple — For connection to the Faeries, the ancestors and Avalon; useful for physical healing

Ash — For enhancing astral travel and remote viewing in all realms

Birch — For fertility and health majick

Blackthorn — For protection majick and justice

Elder — For rituals involving the Dark Goddess

Hawthorn — For the High Faery Queen, love, and the heart

Hazel — For divination, communication, and travel majick

Lilac — For finding the truth and aligning with purpose

Maple — For the sweetness of life, and for balance

Oak — For strength and success

Rose — For love and beauty majick

Rowan — For protection and blessings; will also speed up any majick

Willow — Used for lunar and faery majick; also a powerful healer

Yew — Facilitates communication with the dead

Quartz — To amplify all majickal intentions
Amethyst — For mystical pursuits and peaceful, calm majick
Citrine — To energize majick and help things manifest quickly
Rose Quartz — For love majick and self-esteem

Gold — For total success, health and happiness
Silver — For psychic enhancement and intuitive power
Copper — For love and money majick; to relieve pain

THE ALTAR

The altar for a standard Cabot circle is fairly simple. Towards the back of the altar, on the left, is a black candle signifying the Goddess/drawing in/receptive energy. Balanced on the right side is a white candle signifying the God/sending out/active energy. Between these two candles is the working (or astrological) candle of the appropriate color. The color of this candle would be appropriate to the work you will be doing in circle. If you are doing a prosperity working, you might choose a green candle.

In the middle of the altar is your ash pot. A cauldron can also be used for an ash pot. In the north, place your bell; in the east, your cauldron, wand, and athame; in the south, the thurible or incense burner; and in the west, your chalice, filled with water. Your bottle of protection potion will be on the right, along with (perhaps) a clear quartz crystal pointing north, while on the left you would place another clear quartz crystal or any other stone suitable to your workings, pointing south.

For those with painted checkerboards and other designs directly upon the altar, sometimes a silver pentacle, facing downwards, is placed upon the left side of the altar, while a gold pentacle, facing upwards, is placed on the right, serving much the same purpose as the two quartz crystals, creating patterns of receiving and projecting energy.

The altar can be consecrated with saltwater, sea water, or High Altar Oil, moving clockwise around the edge of the altar. This clears and attunes the altar to majickal workings.

High Altar Oil
1/8 Ounce Almond Oil
5 Drops of Frankincense Oil

4 Drops of Myrrh Oil

3 Drops of Benzoin Oil

2 Drops of Storax Oil

3 Drops of Amber Oil

1 Drop of Cinnamon Oil

Pinch of Sea Salt

You can also smudge the altar with incense to help bless and consecrate it.

Altar Incense

1 Tablespoon of Frankincense

1 Tablespoon of Myrrh

1 Teaspoon of Dragon's Blood

1 Teaspoon of Solomon's Seal

1 Teaspoon of Cinnamon

The "test" of the Second Degree training is to set up the Cabot Altar and demonstrate the Majick Circle Ritual correctly. Each student performs the ritual individually to graduate.

The Cabot Altar

While this is the basic Cabot Altar set up and works best for a group ritual, in a solitary setting you can adapt the altar set up in a way that works best in your personal practice. There is a lot more creative leeway in your personal altar to express yourself and adapt as your own practice adapts and changes. The altar is symbolic of the Witch, but when in a group setting, it is the focus for the energies of the group consciousness and the current of the tradition.

The Altar Pentacle

You can craft your own personal altar pentacle out of paper, wood or clay. Ideally craft it one half hour after the new Moon and add your own personal symbols around the circle clockwise, starting at the top. You can make new altar pentacles, with new symbols, as your focus changes each lunar month, or create an all purpose altar pentacle.

Be Careful of Your Fire Alarms

Since we burn many things in our rituals, from spell papers to incense, we have to be particularly careful about our home fire alarms. Many a Witch has set off the fire alarms unintentionally, myself included.

When I lived on Daniel Street in Salem, we had a fire alarm that was not very loud. During a ritual with friends, we must have set it off, but with the music and trance, we didn't hear it. We had smoke billowing out of our little window, and we didn't know it, but from the outside, it looked like the house was on fire. Someone must have called the fire department. We didn't even hear them approach. The firemen were banging on the doors with the back of their axes, just about to use the blade to break down the doors, when we finally opened it. They said, "Are you aware your house is full of smoke?" Our friend Alice said, "Of course. Everything is fine. We're Witches!" The officer said, "Oh, okay. Sorry to interrupt you."

One of my friends and fellow Witches who lived in a nice house in Beverly Farm did this too. Her husband was not too happy about her practicing Witchcraft, so she chose to do her ritual in the front vestibule of the house, which was an open space two stories high and far from where he was in the house that night. She set up her altar while in her black nightgown. She lit the charcoal and put a little too much loose frankincense and myrrh in the thurible. Before she knew it, even in that large space, the smoke had set off her fire alarm. She lived at the end of a long driveway and didn't want the firefighters to disturb her husband as he somehow didn't hear the alarm, so she ran out into the night in only her nightgown, wand in hand, waving it back and forth trying to stop the fire engines from coming. And I guess she was successful as the husband never found out she was doing a ritual!

So the lesson is to be careful with smoke and your fire alarm. Use only a little bit of loose incense. Position your altar as far from the smoke detector as possible. Open a window. Don't put out more smoke than if you were frying something in a pan in your kitchen, and you should be fine.

THE MAJICKAL HOUSEHOLD

Cabot Witches live in majickal households. We charge everything in our homes, even our furniture, with intention so that we are in control of our environment. Visitors will feel the majick within our homes. Everything you have, carry, and do is used for a majickal purpose in your life. Charge your house daily by filling the entire home with pink light.

THE MAJICK CIRCLE

The majick circle creates a sacred space between the worlds, both a temple and a container for our majick, to help focus the power. The majick circle is envisioned as a literal circle, though some perceive it as a sphere, and into the circle, we call the four elemental energies from the four directions, plus spirit. While elemental energies can come from anywhere, we anchor them in the four "corners of the world" as the ancients would say, the four cardinal directions. Each elemental energy has an elemental guardian, an energetic entity guiding the power and flow of energy and helping protect and aid us in our majick. In the basic Cabot Circle of the Second Degree, we call upon the four elemental Dragon guardians.

Element	Plane	Part of Self	Part of Body	Tool	Qualities
Earth	Physical	Body	Feet, Bones	Peyton, Stone, Egg, Horn, Black Mirror	Cold & Dry
Fire	Energetic	Vitality	Head, Nerves, Heart	Wand, Candle	Hot & Dry
Air	Mental	Mind	Chest, Lungs	Athame, Sword, Thurible, Cord	Hot & Wet
Water	Emotional	Heart	Belly, Blood, Tears	Chalice, Cauldron, Crystal Ball, Silver Mirror,	Cold & Wet

Season	Colors	Planets	Signs	Majick
Winter	Black, Green, Brown	Earth, Venus, Saturn, Sparta	Taurus, Virgo, Capricorn	Prosperity, Health, Home
Summer	Red, Orange, Yellow	Sun, Mars, Jupiter, Pluto, Vulcan	Aries, Leo, Sagittarius	Creativity, Passion
Spring	Yellow, Light Blue	Mercury, Uranus, Venus	Gemini, Libra, Aquarius	Communication, Learning
Fall	Blue, Sea Green	Moon, Neptune, Jupiter	Cancer, Scorpio, Pisces	Psychic, Healing, Dreams

Faery Ruler	Animals	Mythic Creature	Plants	Deities
Ghob of the Gnomes	Stag, Bear, Goat, Badger	Unicorn	Oak, Mandrake, Patchouli	Cernunnos, Dagda, Danu
Djinn of the Salamanders	Red Fox, Boar, Horse, Lion	Dragon	Holly, Thistle, Nettles	Lugh, Bel, Brid, Morrighan
Paralda of the Sylphs	Crow, Eagle, Wren	Gryphon	Hazel, Vervain, Scullcap	Gwydion, Tarranis, Macha, Nuada
Nixsa of the Undines	Salmon, Dolphin, Seal, Snake	Mermaid	Willow, Mugwort, Jasmine	Cerridwen, Lyr, Mannanan

In the Cabot Tradition, unlike many other traditions, we call fire in the east, the direction of light, in honor of the fiery Sun that rises in that direction. In the ancient Greek traditions, the primal elements—fire and water—are always placed opposite, leaving the more complex two elements, earth and air, opposing. This dynamic flow helps create an intense energy conducive to majick and change.

Beyond the Second Degree, Cabot Witches studying the Third Degree learn to use the totems of the quarters as allies and guides. These totems are examples of animals found in family crests and shields. Animals such as the Eagle, Salmon, Crow, Stag, Boar, and Unicorn are found on crests, but we begin work with the elemental Dragons.

The sacrament involves calling up the spirit of our ancient homelands in the Otherworld. In Irish myth, the center of Ireland, which was akin to the center of the world, is Tara, surrounded by the four provinces of Ireland, as we in the circle are surrounded by the four directions and elements. The Hill of Tara is a real place and it is also the spiritual heart of the gods of Ireland. We call upon Avalon, the Apple Island of the wise women and ladies of the lake in Arthurian lore, as the realm of Faeries, Witches, and final resting place of the sacred king. Through these evocations of sacred place, we center ourselves in the sacred landscape and declare our sovereignty.

The waters of the cup are blessed as the waters of life, but truly, by taking our thumb to our lips three times, we are evoking the imagery of the Welsh magician-bard Taliesin, who gains all knowledge and majick from consuming three drops of the potion *greal*, from the cauldron of Cerridwen, granting *awen,* or divine inspiration. Cerridwen is the mother of all bards, a dark mother goddess of majick and Witchcraft. Iska Ba are the majickal words meaning "the fire that flows and the water that burns," the blessings of inspiration from the waters of life. It is also an Irish toast!

We call upon the Goddess and God in our ritual as the cosmic, more universal forms of the Mother and the Father, though religiously in the Third Degree, we see the Great Mother as the Goddess Danu, mother of all of the Gods, the Tuatha De Dannan. We see the father as the Great Father god, the Dagda. When we light their candles, we set up a little relay station for energy to enter and leave our circle for our intentions.

Before circle starts, make sure your altar is set up and you have everything you need. Individuals approach the altar and self-anoint with the protection potion, or alternatively, one or more Witches will go around the circle anointing the participants with protection potion. Starting with the left wrist, put a dab of protection oil on, then anoint the right wrist, the forehead, and the back of the neck. While anointing, state aloud:

"I anoint (or consecrate) you (myself) in the names of the God and the Goddess. Blessed Be." While this is going on, the others are centering and grounding themselves.

Protection Potion

2-4 Cups of Spring Water

2 Tablespoons of Sea Salt

2 Tablespoons of Myrrh

2 Tablespoons of Frankincense

1 Tablespoon of Iron Powder (iron shavings)

1 Teaspoon of Vervain

Pinch of Wolf Hair from a live, shedding wolf

Pinch of Graveyard Dirt from someone you revere for courage or bravery (optional)

Protection Oil

1/8 Ounce of Almond Oil

10 Drops of Patchouli Oil

10 Drops of Frankincense Oil

10 Drops of Myrrh Oil

1/4 Teaspoon of Mandrake Root

1/4 Teaspoon of Sea Salt

Pinch of Wolf Hair from a live shedding wolf or a pinch of fur from your familiar

With either of these formulas, make sure you charge all the ingredients and place them in a vessel to mix. The water potion requires heat, but the oil can be quickly passed through the flame for the spark of fire, with no other heat required. Using your Instant Alpha Trigger, make a clockwise motion over the mix, saying,

"I charge this potion to protect me and anyone I designate from all positive or negative forces that may come to do harm. So shall it be!"

The Majick Circle Ritual

Set up your altar with all necessary tools facing the north.

Anoint your wrists, brow, and the back of your neck with protection potion. If you have not yet made a protection potion, use a mix of salt and water. This will help clear you of incorrect energies prior to the ritual, similar to other traditions that use sage to smudge before ritual.

Holding your wand and facing north, visualize a beam of light coming out of the tip of the wand, coming from your own focused energy. With this laser-like light, trace a perfect circle of light around you. With this first circle, say, "I cast this circle to protect us from any and all positive and negative energies and forces that may come to do us harm."

Repeat this step, tracing a second circle of light over the first. Do this in silence.

Repeat this again, tracing a third circle of light over the second. Bless the circle with the words: "This circle is cast, so shall it be."

You will complete the third circle facing north. Bow to the north, acknowledging its power and the sacred circle, and then tap the altar three times with your wand.

We empower the circle calling the four quarters and elements. The guardians of the elements in this ritual are the dragons of the directions, ancient primal powers that can aid us in our majick. Other rituals can call upon animals or elementals. For simple majick, hold out your left hand to invite energies into the circle; use your right hand to release. If you are doing more formal or religious ritual, you can hold up a peyton, a ritual disc or dish with a pentacle upon it, to open to the energies of the four directions.

Hold up your outstretched fingers of your left hand, like a five-pointed star, face the north and say,

"Dragon of the North, powers of Earth, we welcome you to this circle. So Mote it Be."

Turn clockwise, face the east with the outstretched fingers in the left hand and say,

"Dragon of the East, Power of Fire, we welcome you to this circle. So Mote it Be."

Turn clockwise, face the south with the outstretched fingers in the left hand and say,

"Dragon of the South, Power of Air, we welcome you to this circle. So Mote it Be."

Turn clockwise, face the west with the outstretched fingers in the left hand and say,

"Dragon of the West, Power of Water, we welcome you to this circle. So Mote it Be."

Acknowledge Spirit when you return to the front of the altar by saying,

"And Spirit, always with us. So Mote it Be." If you are using a peyton, instead of your outstretched fingers, place it back upon the center of the altar.

The blessing of the circle, considered the sacrament or mystery, is based upon the Celtic concepts of the Otherworld and inspiration. While facing north at the altar, hold your arms up in a receptive position. Say, "This is Tara (lift left hand), this is Avalon (lift right hand). I am Sovereign in this space. We are Sovereign in this space."

Hold your wand or athame with a triangular grasp in both hands. Raise it up and say, "I draw into this circle and water all of the most correct and harmonious energies of the universe."

Keeping your grasp as it is, stir the water clockwise three times. Say, "I bless these waters, the waters of life."

Touch your thumb to the water, then to your lips, three times. Raise the cup and say, "A libation to the Gods and the Ancient Ones. Iska Ba!" Replace the chalice in the west.

Anoint your black candle three times from the top down, saying, "I anoint this candle with the energies of the Goddess." Light the candle saying, "I strike this candle with the light of the Goddess. So Mote it Be."

Anoint the white candle on the right side of the altar three times from top down, saying, "I anoint this candle with the energies of the God." Light the candle saying, "I strike this candle with the light of the God. So Mote it Be."

Anoint and charge your working candle, referencing the attributes of work to be done. Different colored candles are coordinated with different intentions.

Perform your spells and enchantments at this time. Once the working is done, we thank the gods and ancient ones.

"Goddess, thank you for joining us tonight. God, thank you for joining us tonight. We are forever in your service."

Pinch candles or use a snuffer. We never use our breath to extinguish candles with spells on them; always use a snuffer or pinch them out. The reason is your prana, your breath, can defuse or interfere with the spell.

Release the quarters by starting in the North; hold up your right hand (or peyton) and say,

"Dragon of the North, Powers of Earth, thank you for joining us tonight. So Mote it Be."

Move counterclockwise to the west; hold up your right hand (or peyton) and say,

"Dragon of the West, Powers of Water, thank you for joining us tonight. So Mote it Be."

Move counterclockwise to the south; hold up your right hand (or peyton) and say,

"Dragon of the South, Powers of Air, thank you for joining us tonight. So Mote it Be."

Move counterclockwise to the east; hold up your right hand (or peyton) and say,

"Dragon of the East, Powers of Fire, thank you for joining us tonight. So Mote it Be."

Release the circle by moving counterclockwise around the circle with the wand and saying, "The circle is undone and not broken. I send it out into the cosmos to do our bidding."

Return to the altar and tap three times to honor the Triple Goddess.

When you are in a circle with others you may say,

"Merry Meet, Merry Part, and Merry Meet again."

TIPS FOR CASTING THE MAJICK CIRCLE

- Make sure all animals are out of the room so that they will not walk through the circle and break it.
- Make sure you or no one else extends their bodies to break the circle until you have finished your majick.
- Make sure you are in a place where you will not be disturbed. Close the door. Turn off all phones, alarms, and electronic equipment. Place clocks out of view so you will not see the time, which will help you be truly beyond time and space.
- Use a compass and start the circle in the north.
- Count yourself down into alpha with your wand in your hand before you begin, or use your Instant Majick Trigger as you start the circle.
- Dress all in black, if not in your robe and cloak, perhaps with accents of color appropriate to the work at hand.
- Unlike other traditions, Cabot Witches do not open doorways or permit any kind of movement in and out of the circle. Don't ever break the circle once the energy is cast.
- Do not take superfluous things into the circle. Have only your tools and your ritual Book of Shadows. If borrowing from a book, write down what you need on parchment paper. Do not bring an entire book into the circle. An excess of words will confuse and diffuse the majick.
- Circles can be done inside or outside.
- Use your majick and visualization through the Instant Majick Trigger to make sure the environment is cleansed prior to starting. Neutralize any unwanted forces with an "X."

- The circle can be imagined to be a perfect size, going through the walls if necessary, since most rooms don't accommodate a full circle. Be sure to neutralize anything within the walls that might inhibit your majick.

THE SEA SALT CIRCLE

In the Cabot Tradition, the energy of the majick circle is passed from teacher to student, because the student's majick wand is charged in a circle cast by the teacher. In essence, they are passing the light of the circle, like passing a torch. Sometimes we do not have access to a teacher and need that pure sacred space to start. Other times, we might not have access to a charged wand, and therefore need to do this on our own. To effectively create sacred space on your own, you can cast a Sea Salt Circle.

Start by making sure you have your altar set up and enough open space around you for a traditional nine-foot diameter circle. Use your Witch's cord, four-and-a-half feet long, anchoring it in the center of the circle to measure out a nine-foot-wide circle. Use a compass to find magnetic north and begin there, marking the nine-foot circle by sprinkling sea salt to cast your boundary. Once you complete the first circle, cast a second in sea salt, one foot inward from the first. Complete the second circle, and cast your third one foot in from that second circle. Ultimately your working space within the third circle will be five feet in diameter. In that space, you can charge your wand and do your majick as you would in a traditional circle.

Elemental Balance Meditation

Count yourself into alpha using the Crystal Countdown. Envision the area between your feet and groin as Earth; envision your groin to your waist as Water; envision your waist to your neck as Air; envision your neck to the top of your head as Fire.

Allow the four elements to blend. Let them flow through your body and invite the God and Goddess within you to join the flow.

Find your center and balance in this as the elements slow, observing them as they return to their proper places. Fire returns to the top; moving down, Air settles; further down, the Water flows; finally, Earth finds stillness around your feet.

Give yourself Total Health Clearance. Count back up and out of alpha.

THE TALE OF TALIESIN

As the story of Taliesin and Cerridwen forms a key part of the sacrament of the Cabot Majick Circle, you should be familiar with the story of Taliesin and how it influences our understanding of the Waters of Life and the three sacred drops.

There upon an island on Lake Tegid was a giant of a man named Tegid Voel, and his wife, the sorceress known as Cerridwen. The couple had two children, a daughter named Creirwy, the most beautiful girl in all the world, a son named Morfan; and another son named Avagddu, whose name means "utter darkness" for he was the most ugly boy in the world, covered with patches of black hair or feathers. Some believe that Avagddu is simply another name for Morfan. Avagddu could only be admitted among the nobles, the heroes and the like, for some extended knowledge or skill. Otherwise he would be shunned for his frightening looks.

Cerridwen consulted the majickal Book of Fferyllt for the formula of greal, a potion for her ugly son from the Cauldron of Inspiration. He could win his honor if he had knowledge of all the mysteries, and of the future of the world. The recipe called for the cauldron to continue to boil without ceasing for a year and a day, until it distilled down to three drops of awen, of inspiration.

To succeed in this, she took the son of Gwrean of Llanfair, Gwion Bach, as her servant to stir and tend the cauldron for a year and a day, along with the blind man Morda, who would tend the fire beneath the cauldron. By the planetary hours and days, by the sacred alignments of the stars, she set forth across the world to gather the herbs. Upon her return from each trip, she would add them to the brew with the proper incantations.

Towards the end of the year, Cerridwen was out gathering plants, and Morda let the fire get too hot. Three drops of enchanted liquid flew out of the cauldron upon the thumb of poor Gwion Bach. To prevent himself from burning, he brought his thumb to his lips and took the three drops of inspiration and all their majick. He instantly foresaw all that was about to happen and realized Cerridwen would kill him for this, so he knew he had to flee. As he left, the cauldron cracked and burst into two, and all the remaining liquid was poisonous. The poison flowed down from the lake to a stream, and the horses of Gwyddno Garanhir drank the poisoned waters and died.

Cerridwen instantly knew what had happened and returned to her hut upon her island in Lake Tegid. She struck Morda with a wooden log causing one of his blind eyes to fall out, but he protested, telling her he was innocent. She then realized it was Gwion Bach who had robbed both her and her son Avagddu.

Cerridwen chased after Gwion Bach. When he noticed Cerridwen coming after him, he shifted his shape into that of a hare and even more quickly fled from her. But Cerridwen would not be outdone. She transformed herself into a greyhound and almost caught him. The hare made it to a river and became a fish. Cerridwen continued the chase, changing from greyhound to otter. She chased him through the water until he jumped out and transformed himself into a bird. She became a hawk to follow him, giving him no rest in the sky. In fear of his life, Gwion spotted a barn, and upon the threshing room floor, a heap of wheat grains. Just as she was about to catch him, he flew into the barn and transformed into one of the grains. Cerridwen became a high-crested black hen and went into the wheat pile, scratching until she found him and swallowed him. But then she realized her mistake. Rather than destroying him, she was now pregnant with him and bore him nine months later.

Once Cerridwen delivered him, she could not kill this beautiful boy, but she would not keep him because of what he had done. So she wrapped him up, placed him in a leather satchel, and released him out to the sea and the mercy of the gods on the twenty-ninth day of April.

Upon that May Eve, Elphin, the unfortunate son of Gwyddno, was fishing for salmon upon the weir, the watery pool, to see if good luck would finally befall him. Majickal things can happen on Beltane, and he hoped that perhaps his luck could be reversed. The one who had the honor of gathering the fish from the weir would be blessed. Elphin returned the next day to see the catch, along with others. Nothing was found, and one person accused Elphin of destroying the virtue of the weir, for it always yielded fish on this night before. He turned and found a leather bag upon a pole in the weir. He told them there might be treasure in the bag, to make up for the lost fish. They took it, opened it, and saw the forehead of a boy and said, "Behold a radiant brow!"

Elphin took the child and said, "Taliesin be he called," (Taliesin meaning "radiant brow") and carried the boy back to his horse and rode gently towards his home. He lamented his luck until the infant boy began to speak, giving praise to Elphin, prophesying his future honor and good fortune through a poem. Elphin then realized what a remarkable child he had found. And thus began the adventures of Taliesin, the Bard.

So essentially Gwion Bach undergoes three main levels of experience before becoming his majickal self, Taliesin. The three levels can be related to our understanding of the three degrees in Witchcraft:

Degree	Initiation	Learning
First Degree	Hut	Learning Silence, Stillness, Meditation and Control
Second Degree	Chase	Learning to work with the Four Elements, Making Majick
Third Degree	Rebirth	Learning to enter into the World in Service as a majickal being

First he is in the darkness of the hut. Here, he must learn to observe, still the mind, and enter into a meditative state, not unlike the later bards he would inspire, who learned to listen to and tell stories in total darkness as a part of their training. In Witchcraft I, the amount of time we spend with our eyes closed, in alpha, is like being in the hut.

He receives the three drops of *greal,* the brew of *awen*—of inspiration, our waters of life—and is utterly transformed. He can do majick! He can not only transform, but he knows things, just as we can make things happen through spells or through listening to divine answers, all learned in the Second Degree. The majick circle involves the four elements, and he undergoes four transformations, with Cerridwen in pursuit. Each transformation can be corresponded with an element.

Element	Gwion Bach	Cerridwen	Lesson
Fire	Hare	Greyhound	Movement, action, escape, fear
Water	Fish (Salmon)	Otter	Diving deep, exploring the unknown
Air	Bird (Wren)	Hawk	Rising up, seeing the bigger picture
Earth	Grain	Black Hen	Reuniting with the earth, becoming one with the Mother

He then enters the darkness of the womb, the second darkness, before he is born and sent on his way in a leather sack upon the waters. He moves from the personal womb of the Goddess to a more global womb upon the waves of waters in the oceans and rivers. He is then received by the world, renamed, and starts his career of majick, poetry, and service to the land and the Divine.

We could learn a lot by following the path of Taliesin, and in many ways, most Witches already do.

One of my most profound experiences with the gods and spirits came from Taliesin, a memory I treasure to this day. I called upon him and asked to hear one of his songs. I used a special tool to get into a deep trance. I packed a hollowed horn with resins, herbs, and oils, and placed it upon my chest as I lay down upon my bed. I breathed in the scent from the herbs and went in vision to a meadow by a woods to meet with Taliesin. He sang me a love song, a love spell. I was mesmerized and feared I would not get back, but when I woke, I remembered this much, a gift from Taliesin to me.

I am the soft breeze that moves your golden hair.
I am the cool wind that brings color to your face.
I am the spindle that weaves the clothes you wear.
I am the fingers that sew the trim of lace,
that crown your beauty,
that warm your heart.
I am the songbird that sings your love,
that sounds your beauty,
and beats your heart.
I am the moonlight that showers your sleep,
that deepens your beauty,
that rests your heart.
I am the starlight that illumines your dreams.
Love is all that is seems.

If you desire to meet with Taliesin, Cerridwen, or any of the ancient ones in deeper trance, you can create a similar horn of deep peace. Place three polished quartz stones at the bottom, each cleansed and charged for one of the following intentions—deep trance, clear communication, and total remembrance of vision. Fill the horn with a mixture of frankincense, myrrh, copal, dragon's blood, benzoin and storax. Add to it dried flowers and leaves of lavender, jasmine, mugwort, wormwood, rosemary and chamomile. Add drops of oil corresponding to the resins and herbs. Cover, and let it mingle for at least a Moon cycle before you use it. Write down the name of the deity you wish to visit and place the paper beneath your pillow. Uncover the horn opening, breathe deep, and then place it upon your chest. Breathe deep and count down to alpha level, holding the intention of the deity you wish to communicate with. Follow your intuition and seek them out to learn their mysteries. When done, return, count up, and remove the horn; quickly record everything you remember from the experience.

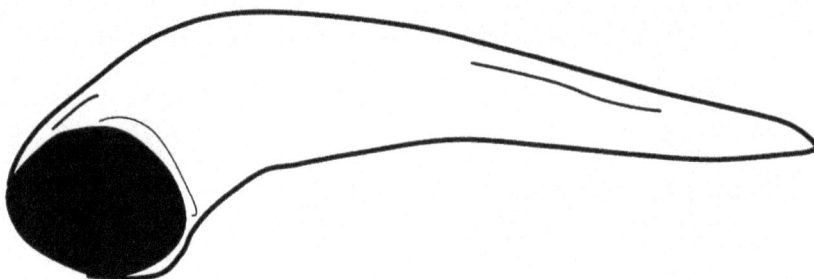

Horn

SPELLS

Spellwork is a Witch's life. It is the heart of the art of our craft, and an essential part of our spiritual development. Spells are often described as "prayers" but they are really intentions done in support of the science of Witchcraft. Your correctly broadcast intentions require the universe to respond to, and manifest them. You can use spells in alpha state, in your Instant Alpha Trigger state, or in a majick circle.

There are many different types of spells and rituals to explore. The most simple is known as a petition spell, written on parchment. Other forms of spellcraft include:

- Candle Spells
- Potions and Philters
- Amulets and Talismans
- Crystal Charms
- Majick Bags
- Spell Bottles
- Majick Cords

Anything in nature can be used to help us cast spells, as everything corresponds to some energy in the universe and Divine Mind. Through experimentation and exploration, we can find new and different methods of spellcasting and learn from nature through the All.

PETITION SPELLS

A petition spell simply states your intention, as clearly worded as possible. Petitions form the basis of other spellcasting, because learning to do such spells helps us formulate a clear intention, and that ability to get a clear intention in thought, word, and visualization will help us with every other kind of spell. Petition spells are written in either black ink, which is all-purpose, or with an appropriately corresponding colored ink matched to your intention. There are even recipes of majickal inks you can use that incorporate stones, herbs, and oils to enchant the ink into alignment with a specific planet or power. Old-fashioned quill or nub pens are then used with that ink.

Petition spells look like this:

I, (state your name), ask in the name of the Goddess and God, to be granted/to remove
_____. I ask this be for the highest good, harming none. I thank the Goddess and God for all. So Mote it Be.

Spell petition papers are wafted through the incense. Then they are usually read aloud in the majick circle. The paper is put to the flame of the black candle and then the flame of the white candle, and then quickly placed into the ash pot or cauldron to burn, releasing the spell's energy.

As you practice your spellcraft, you will learn what works and what does not work through experimentation and trial and error. Record all of your spells in your Book of Shadows. If a spell did not work well for you, cross it out in your book and note why it did not perform as you intended. Since we usually burn our spell papers, it is important to keep a copy and record it in your Book of Shadows.

THE WISDOM OF SYBIL LEEK

Sybil Leek was a famous Witch from Britain who came to America to teach and share her Craft with the world. She appeared on numerous television shows and wrote many books. Her most famous is *Diary of a Witch*. While we never met in person even though she was in the Boston area for a number of years before moving to Florida, she kindly mentored me through letters and phone calls, giving me great advice for being an open and public Witch.

One of her teachings I pass on to my students is a blessing to write on the back of all your petition spell papers.

IN NO WAY
WILL THIS SPELL REVERSE
OR PLACE UPON ME
ANY CURSE

Write this on the back of all your parchment papers when casting a spell. This will make sure no harm comes to you, and that your spell is for your highest good.

WELL-INTENTIONED BUT INEFFECTUAL

The spiritual plane is not one entirely of sweetness; it is not monopolized by the well-intentioned. Such an attitude is ineffectual. While Cabot Witches do majick for the highest good, not all people hold that core value. Many people use energy unconsciously, creating destruction without even intentionally meaning to do so. We must be aware of the consequences of our actions, and particularly in majick and our spells, state in our alpha level that what we are doing by working majick should always be for the good of all.

When we do our spells, we must be specific and focus upon the outcome. Thinking that things work out in your favor no matter what you do or think is not majick. While we work within our karma, we also know majick can change our lives. If everything was "meant to be," then why bother with anything at all? We know majick is real, and we must take responsibility for changing our lives.

TIPS FOR SPELL CASTING

Keep the following in mind when writing petition spells and doing any kind of spellcrafting:

- Take tips from fellow Witches and teachers on the phrasing of spells.
- Be precise. Say what you mean and mean what you say. Don't be too wordy or flowery in your speech.
- Do not make any grammatical mistakes. Make your petition as perfect as you can.
- Do not scratch out, erase, or "white out" on your spell papers. Make them perfect.
- Wear black when casting a spell to draw all colors and light to you for your majick.
- Don't use the word "negative." Use the word "incorrect" instead and use the word "correct" instead of "positive."

- Do not do more than three specific spells per ritual day. It's recommended that you only do one. The only exception to this is the Crystal Moon Wish List.
- Specify what you want, but not how it will come to you. Project your spell for the end result, the final goal, not how it will occur. The universe has a way to make all things happen. Project your spell for the final outcome, not the means to get it there. Focus on the end result. The universe will figure out the details, and it is wiser than you.
- Majick works within a time schedule of its own. Usually you can put a time frame in your spell, but the universe may not want it to happen that way.
- There is nothing wrong with doing spells for financial security, success, or tangible items.
- Not every spell works immediately or all the time because we don't always know what is for our highest good. You can neutralize things used in spellwork before throwing them away: things like candle nubs, unbound wicks, old charms, and herbs. Just go by your feeling regarding each spell.

CRYSTAL MOON WISH LIST

The Crystal Moon Wish List is a specific act of majick in the Cabot Tradition. It is done upon the first Full Moon after your birthday, to harness the power of the personal "new year" astrologically. Make a list of all the material things you desire right now. Leave off intangible things like happiness or satisfaction, or goals like a new job or new relationship. Other majick serves those goals better. Make it a list of needs and desires, including vacations and travel as well as tangible objects. Make it a part of a petition spell, and in the Full Moon Majick Circle, recite your Crystal Moon Wish list, for the highest good, harming none. And within the year, your wishes will manifest.

ASTROLOGY AND MAJICK

The placement of the heavens influences our majick. The most powerful influence upon our majick is the astral tides of the Moon, but other planets influence us greatly as well. You should obtain an astrological calendar or datebook (not a Witch's almanac, which is incomplete astrologically) and take time to study the symbols, glyphs and meanings of the patterns that are occurring. I recommend Jim Maynard's "Celestial Influences" Calendar and the "Llewellyn Astrological Calendar." Both of these calendars can give you a quick lesson in astrology.

To start with, learn about the Moon. When the Moon is waxing, or growing in light, the time is right to do majick to manifest. The closer you are to the Full Moon, the stronger the manifestation will be. When the Moon is waning, or diminishing in light and growing in darkness, the time is used to banish and remove unwanted forces. The closer you are to the Black Moon, the antithesis of the Full Moon, the more powerful the banishing or protection will be. Despite our popular notion of the Triple Goddess of the Moon—its symbolism as maiden, mother and crone—astrologers divide the Moon into four quarters. Two are waxing and two are waning, and different majick is best under these different circumstances.

Quarter	Tide	Appearance	Majick
First	Waxing	Crescent to Half	New beginnings, slow manifestations
Second	Waxing	Half to Full	Powerful and immediate manifestations
Third	Waning	Full to Half Dark	Slow release and diminishment
Fourth	Waning	Half Dark to All Dark	Immediate banishments and removals

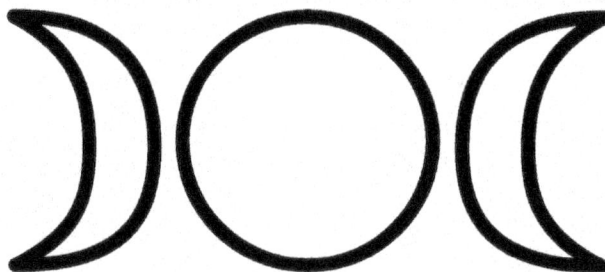

Triple Moon Symbol

All the planets have relationships that build between them, based upon their alignments. Alignments, known as aspects, can be helpful or difficult in our lives, and for our majick. By studying the aspects, we can learn when it is a powerful and good time to do majick involving that planet, or when to wait. A good astrological calendar will note and explain the aspects.

Mercury retrograde is an important time; Witches must be aware of it happening. A retrograde is when a planet appears to be going backwards from our perspective on Earth. While all the planets except the Sun and Moon can go into retrograde, the most important, and most frequent, is Mercury, going into retrograde three to four times every year. As Mercury is the planet of communication and travel, its retrograde affects us greatly. People feel that communication, technology and travel break down. When Mercury is in retrograde, it is a time to absorb, practice, reflect, and write. When the retrograde is over, that is the time when we put it to use, taking action. Don't sign contracts, buy major things, or make any big changes when Mercury is in retrograde, which can last a few weeks. Astrological calendars indicate when planets enter and leave retrograde motion.

PLANETARY DAYS AND HOURS

According to ancient traditions from the Chaldeans, those astrologers connected to the Sumerians and Babylonians, each of the seven days of the week are ruled by one of the seven classic majickal planets.

Day	Glyph	Planet	Majick
Sunday	☉	Sun	Physical Strength, Success, Health, Winning, Creativity, Obtaining Goals, Wealth, Illumination
Monday	☾	Moon	Psychic Ability, Psychological Balance, Beauty, Feminine Force, Dreams, Astral Travel, Protection, Intuition
Tuesday	♂	Mars	Action, Force, Protection, Partnership, Marriage, Passion, Sexual Love, Courage, Clothing, Determination, Furniture
Wednesday	☿	Mercury	Wisdom, Knowledge, Motion, Communication, Travel, Transportation, Speed, Healing, Motivation, Creativity
Thursday	♃	Jupiter	Good Fortune, Wealth, Success, Law, Influence in High Places, Business, Officials, Honors, Expansion, Material Logic
Friday	♀	Venus	Love, Growth, Health, Fertility, New Projects, Beauty, Sensuality, Money, Jewelry, Cosmetics, Pleasure, Friendship, Prosperity

Saturday	♄	Saturn	Testing, Binding, Manifestation, Crystallization, Science, Concentration, Maturity, Discipline, Invention, Pragmatic, Neutralization, Longevity

Likewise, the days are further subdivided into twelve daylight hours, and twelve night-time hours. There are many ways to interpret the calculation of the planetary hours. Some Witches and magicians say that the hours of the "day" begin at sunrise, and the hours of the "night" begin at sunset. To determine the length of each planetary hour, they add the minutes between sunrise and sunset for daytime use, or add the minutes between sunset and sunrise for night-time use, and divide by twelve. For, you can find the exact times of sunrise and sunset in a Farmer's Almanac for your area, the newspaper—or these days—online.

This system, while older, creates a lot of confusion. I prefer to use the method that represents the hours of the day as the AM hours, and the hours of the night as the PM hours. So hour one is not one o'clock to two o'clock. It is the first hour of A.M., twelve o'clock to one o'clock. The second hour is one o'clock to two o'clock and so on through the rest of the hours.

The order of the planetary hours is Saturn, Jupiter, Mars, Sun, Venus, Mercury, Moon, and then back to Saturn. Each day starts daylight hour one with the planet that rules that day, and then follows that order until the next day, where the pattern conveniently starts again on the right planet for that day.

	Sun.	Mon.	Tues.	Wed.	Thurs.	Fri.	Sat.
Day							
Hour 1	☉	☽	♂	☿	♃	♀	♄
Hour 2	♀	♄	☉	☽	♂	☿	♃
Hour 3	☿	♃	♀	♄	☉	☽	♂
Hour 4	☽	♂	☿	♃	♀	♄	☉
Hour 5	♄	☉	☽	♂	☿	♃	♀
Hour 6	♃	♀	♄	☉	☽	♂	☿

	Sun.	Mon.	Tues.	Wed.	Thurs.	Fri.	Sat.
Hour 7	♂	☿	♃	♀	♄	☉	☽
Hour 8	☉	☽	♂	☿	♃	♀	♄
Hour 9	♀	♄	☉	☽	♂	☿	♃
Hour 10	☿	♃	♀	♄	☉	☽	♂
Hour 11	☽	♂	☿	♃	♀	♄	☉
Hour 12	♄	☉	☽	♂	☿	♃	♀
Night							
Hour 1	♃	♀	♄	☉	☽	♂	☿
Hour 2	♂	☿	♃	♀	♄	☉	☽
Hour 3	☉	☽	♂	☿	♃	♀	♄
Hour 4	♀	♄	☉	☽	♂	☿	♃
Hour 5	☿	♃	♀	♄	☉	☽	♂
Hour 6	☽	♂	☿	♃	♀	♄	☉
Hour 7	♄	☉	☽	♂	☿	♃	♀
Hour 8	♃	♀	♄	☉	☽	♂	☿
Hour 9	♂	☿	♃	♀	♄	☉	☽
Hour 10	☉	☽	♂	☿	♃	♀	♄
Hour 11	♀	♄	☉	☽	♂	☿	♃
Hour 12	☿	♃	♀	♄	☉	☽	♂

Use the planetary days and hours, as well as the planetary aspects and the Moon, to determine what kind of spells to do when.

A WITCH'S MAJICKAL CORRESPONDENCES

	SUN		MOON
Day	Sunday	Day	Monday
Rulership	Leo	Rulership	Cancer
Exalted	Aries	Exalted	Taurus
Detriment	Aquarius		Capricorn
Fall	Libra	Fall	Scorpio
Colors	Yellow, Yellow-Gold, Gold	Colors	Silver, Light Silver
Tone	C#	Tone	G#
Tool	Candle	Tool	Cauldron, Chalice
Element	Fire	Element	Ocean Water
Intentions	Physical Strength, Success, Health, Winning, Creativity, Jewels, Obtaining Goals, Wealth Rulership, Ilumination	Intentions	Psychological Balance, Psychic Ability, Beauty, Feminine Forces, Dreams, Astral Travel, Protection, Intuition, Majick
Animals	Bee, Stag, Lion	Animals	Cat, Rabbit, Cow
Metals	Gold	Metals	Silver
Stones	Adventurine, Amber, Ametrine, Cat's Eye, Citrine, Clear Quartz, Herkimer Diamond, Howlite, Peridot, Smokey Quartz, Topaz, Tourmaline Quartz	Stones	Cat's Eye, Clear Quartz, Moonstone, Opal, Pearl, Rainbow Moonstone, Sea Salt, Selenite, Smokey Quartz

Plants	Amber, Ambergris, Bay, Bayberry, Benzoin, Bilberry, Black Walnut, Blessed Thistle, Blue Cohosh, Boldo, Calamus, Calendula, Caraway Seeds, Cat's Claw, Cedar, Chamomile, Chili Peppers, Cloves, Coltsfoot, Dill, Echinacea, Elder, Eucalyptus, Eyebright, Feverfew, Fir, Five Finger Grass, Frankincense, Gum Mastic, Heather, Heliotrope, Hibiscus, Honeysuckle, Juniper, Lavender, Lemon, Lemon Balm, Lemon Verbana, Lemongrass, Lovage, Lucky Hand Root, Marigold, Marjoram, Milk Thistle, Mimosa, Mistletoe, Mustard, Orange, Pumpkin, Rosemary, Solomon's Seal, St. John's Wort, Sunflower, Tansy, Tarragon, Thyme, Tragacanth, Witch Hazel, Wood Betony	**Plants**	All Night Blooming Flowers, Balsam Fir, Benzoin, Bergamot, Bilberry, Birch, Blessed Thistle, Blue Cohosh, Blue Vervain, Boldo, Camphor, Caraway Seeds, Cat's Claw, Cherry, Chickweed, Coltsfoot, Cumin, Dill, Echinacea, Elder, Eucalyptus, Fennel, Feverfew, Fir, Five Finger Grass, Frankincense, Guar, Honeysuckle, Horehound, Jasmine, Lemon, Lemon Balm, Mandrake, Marshmallow, Meadowsweet, Mesquite, Milk Thistle, Mint, Moonwort, Motherwort, Mugwort, Pumpkin, Star Anise, Storax, Tragacanth, Vetiver, Willow, Witch Hazel

---

♂ MARS

			☿ MERCURY	
Day	Tuesday		**Day**	Wednesday
Rulership	Aries, Scorpio		**Rulership**	Gemini, Virgo
Exalted	Capricorn		**Exalted**	Virgo, Aquarius
Detriment	Libra, Taurus		**Detriment**	Sagttarius, Pisces
Fall	Cancer		**Fall**	Leo
Colors	Red		**Colors**	Orange, Gray
Tone	D		**Tone**	D
Tool	Sword		**Tool**	Wand
Element	Fire		**Element**	Ocean Water, Earth, Air
Intentions	Active Force, Partnership, Marriage, Passion, Sexual Love, Courage, Clothing, Determination, Furniture		**Intentions**	Wisdom, All Knowledge, Motion, Communication, Transportation, Speed, Healing, Motivation, Creativity
Animals	Horse, Wolf, Woodpecker		**Animals**	All Birds, Rabbit
Metals	Iron, Steel		**Metals**	Aluminium, Zinc

Stones	Bloodstone, Fire Agate, Garnet, Hematite, Obsidian, Onyx, Pyrite, Rhodocrosite, Ruby, Serpentine, Snowflake Obsidian, Tiger Iron, Tiger's Eye, Zoisite	Stones	Agate, Botswana Agate, Carnelian, Fire Agate, Kyanite, Moss Agate, Opal, Tree Agate, Zebra Jasper
Plants	Bayberry, Black Peppercorn, Bloodroot, Boldo, Broom, Cactus, Caraway Seeds, Cherry, Chili Pepper, Comfrey, Coriander, Cumin, Damiana, Dragon's Blood, Garlic, Hemlock, Horny Goat Weed, Jalapeno, Juniper, Mustard, Nettles, Nutmeg, Parsley, Passion Flower, Pepper, Pine, Spearmint, Sweet Woodruff, Tarragon, Vanilla	Plants	Benzoin, Birch, Blue Vervain, Boldo, Broom, Buckthorn, Calamus, Caraway Seeds, Cinquefoil, Cumin, Dill, Echinacea, Eucalyptus, Eyebright, Fennel, Five Finger Grass, Hazel, Horehound, Hyssop, Lavender, Lemon Verbena, Licorice, Mandrake, Marjoram, Mint, Orchid, Peppermint, Pumpkin, Scullcap, Storax, Tansy, Thyme, Tragacanth, Valerian, Vervain, Vetiver, Witch Hazel

♃ JUPITER   ♀ VENUS

	JUPITER		VENUS
Day	Thursday	Day	Friday
Rulership	Sagittarius, Pisces	Rulership	Taurus, Libra
Exalted	Leo, Cancer	Exalted	Pisces
Detriment	Gemini, Virgo	Detriment	Scoprio, Aries
Fall	Aquarius, Capricorn	Fall	Virgo
Colors	Royal Blue, Turquoise, Purple	Colors	Green, Pink, Copper
Tone	F#	Tone	A
Tool	Witch's Cord	Tool	Thurible
Element	Earth, Fire, Air, Water	Element	Air, Earth
Intentions	Material Logic, Influence of People in High Places, Good Fortune, Wealth, Success, Law, Business, Officials, Honors, Expansion	Intentions	Love, Growth, Health, Fertility, Beginnings, New Projects, Beauty, Sensuality, Money, Jewelry, Cosmetics, Pleasure, Friendship, Prosperity
Animals	Eagle, Horse	Animals	Bee, Cat
Metals	Pewter, Tin	Metals	Copper

Stones	Amethyst, Ametrine, Azurite, Blue Goldstone, Chysocolla, Jasper, Lapis Lazuli, Sapphire, Sodalite, Sugilite, Turquoise
Plants	Balsam Fire, Bay, Beth Root, Blackberry, Blue Malva, Borage, Cedar, Chestnut, Cinnamon, Clover, Clove, Comfrey, Frankincense, Heather, Hemlock (tree), Hibiscus, Honeysuckle, Hyssop, Irish Moss, Jasmine, Juniper, Lavender, Lemon Balm, Lilac, Lucky Hand Root, Milk Thistle, Mustard, Orange, Pine, Saffron, Sage, Tonka Bean, Violet, Wild Yam, Yellow Dock

Stones	Aventurine, Cat's Eye, Chrysocolla, Emerald, Fuchsite, Green Goldstone, Howlite, Lapis Lazuli, Lodestone, Malachite, Opal, Peridot, Pink Shell, Prehnite, Rhodocrosite, Rhodonite, Rose Quartz, Seraphinite, Watermelon Tourmaline, Zoisite
Plants	Adam & Eve Root, Apple, Beth Root, Black Peppercorn, Black Walnut, Blackberry, Bloodroot, Blue Vervain, Caper, Caraway Seed, Catnip, Cherry, Chili Pepper, Clover, Damiana, Feverfew, Frangipani, Heather, Hibiscus, Juniper, Lady's Mantle, Lemongrass, Licorice, Lily of the Valley, Lovage, Lucky Hand Root, Mandrake, Marshmallow, Motherwort, Nettle, Nutmeg, Orange, Orchid, Orris, Primrose, Pumpkin, Spearmint, Star Anise, Strawberry, Sweet Woodruff, Tansy, Tonka Bean, Uva Ursi, Valerian, Vanilla, Violet, Yarrow, Yerba Santa

♄ SATURN

Day	Saturday
Rulership	Capricorn, Aquarius
Exalted	Libra
Detriment	Cancer, Leo
Fall	Aries
Colors	Wine, Magenta, Black
Tone	D
Tool	Athame
Element	Earth (Salt), Water (Fresh), Air, Fire

 # URANUS

Day	Wednesday (Higher Octave of Mercury)
Rulership	Aquarius
Exalted	Scorpio, Virgo
Detriment	Leo
Fall	Taurus, Pisces
Colors	Lavenger, Dazzling White
Tone	G#
Tool	Garter
Element	Air, Water, Fire

Intentions	Testing, Binding, To Inhibit, Manifest, To Crystalize Things, Science, Concentration, Maturity, To Invent, Pragmatism, To Neutralize Evil Intent, Discipline, Longevity
Animals	Snake
Metals	Lead
Stones	Black Onyx, Diamond, Galena, Garnet, Jet, Petrified Wood, Rutilated Smokey Quartz, Snowflake Obsidian
Plants	Bat's Head Root, Beth Root, Bilberry, Black Cohosh, Black Peppercorn, Blue Malva, Blue Vervain, Boldo, Buckthorn, Comfrey, Datura, Elder, Gum Mastic, Hemlock (poisonous plant), Ivy, Mandrake Root, Mashmallow, Meadowsweet, Moss, Musk, Myrrh, Patchouli, Solomon's Seal, Tobaco, Uva Ursi, Wolfsbane

Intentions	Esoteric Ideas, Inventiveness, Publicity, To Reform, To Expand Unusual Ideas, Clear Electrical Energies, Bizarre Happenings, Unexpected Changes
Animals	Eel
Metals	Uranium, White Gold
Stones	Blue Goldstone, Clear Quartz, Fire Opal, Labradorite, Rutilated Quartz, Tektite
Plants	Burdock, Clover, Ebony, Gum Mastic, High John Root, Lavender, Lemongrass, Pomegranate, Rice, Rue, Vetiver

♆ NEPTUNE

Day	Friday (Higher Octave of Venus)
Rulership	Pisces
Exalted	Cancer
Detriment	Virgo
Fall	Capricorn
Colors	All Iridescent Colors, Phosphorous Opaque Colors
Tone	A
Tool	Crystal Ball
Element	Water
Intentions	Visions, Dreams, Ideals, Fantasies, Artistic Abilities, Psychic Awareness, Healing, Imagination, Water, Illusions, Chemical Change

♀ PLUTO

Day	Tuesday (Higher Octave of Mars)
Rulership	Scorpio
Exalted	Aries, Pisces
Detriment	Taurus
Fall	Libra, Virgo
Colors	Black
Tone	D
Tool	Cape or Robe
Element	Water
Intentions	To Bring Order Out of Chaos, Group Ideas, Sudden Manifestation of Spells and Thoughts, Witch's Power, Unification or Disruption

Animals	Abalone	**Animals**	Beetle
Metals	Platium, Pewter	**Metals**	Chrome, Plutonium
Stones	Amethyst, Aquamarine, Azurite, Beryl, Bloodstone, Blue Quartz, Fire Opal, Goldstone, Howlite, Sea Salt, Sea Shell, Sugilite, Unakite	**Stones**	Black Adventurine, Black Coral, Black Quartz, Jet, Labradorite, Obsidian, Snowflake Obsidian, Tektite, Tourmaline Quartz, Zebra Serpentine
Plants	Chili Pepper, Copal, Dulse, Fennel, Fire, Frangipani, Grapes, Kelp, Lotus, Lovage, Myrrh, Seaweed, Water Lily, Watercress	**Plants**	Ambergris, Arrow Root, Bat's Head Root, Bayberry, Birch, Black Cohosh, Bloodroot, Coltsfoot, Dogwood, Foxglove, Ginger Root, Hawthorn, Hemlock (poisonous plant), Horny Goat Weed, Low John Root, Marshmallow, Sweet Woodruff, Vanilla Bean, Wormwood

VULCAN

SPARTA

Day	All Days	**Day**	All Days
Rulership	All Signs	**Rulership**	All Signs
Exalted	All Signs	**Exalted**	All Signs
Detriment	No Signs		No Signs
Fall	No Signs	**Fall**	No Signs
Colors	Spectrum of Colors	**Colors**	Brown
Tone	All Tones	**Tone**	G
Tool	Gold Pentacle	**Tool**	Majick Mirror
Element	Fire	**Element**	Air, Earth, Fire, Water
Intentions	Total Force Into Majick, Jeweler of the Gods	**Intentions**	Grounding, Balance, Pragmatism
Animals	Stag	**Animals**	Snake
Metals	Gold	**Metals**	Bronze
Stones	All Precious Stones, Black Tourmaline, Diamond	**Stones**	Shale, Slate

Plants	Angelica, Bayberry, Black Currant, Blue Cohosh, Clove, Frankincense, Galangal Root, Lemon Balm, Lotus, Mullein, Myrrh, Oak Bark, Solomon's Seal, Tansy, Thyme	Plants	Barley, Betel Nut, Fennel, Ginseng Root, Nutmeg, Potato, Shepherd's Purse, Snakeroot

---

◇ EARTH

Day	All Days		
Rulership	Taurus, Virgo, Capricorn		
Exalted	Pisces, Libra		
Detriment	Scorpio, Pisces, Cancer		
Fall	Virgo, Aries		
Colors	Rust Brown, Brown		
Tone	G		
Tool	Egg, Animal Horn		
Element	Air, Earth, Fire, Water	**Metals**	Brass
Intentions	Action, Force, Passion, Partnership, Building, Gardening, Marriage, Balance, Decisions, Grounding, Nesting, Stability	**Stones**	Andalusite, Aragonite, Clear Quartz, Granite, Howlite, Jasper, Jet, Marble, Mookaite, Moss Agate, Rutilated Quartz, Rutilated Smokey Quartz, Sandstone, Serpentine, Smokey Quartz
Animals	Dog, Chicken, Cow, Sheep, Horse	**Plants**	Adam & Eve Root, Bay, Benzoin, Birch, Black Cohosh, Black Walnut, Borage, Caraway Seed, Copal, Echinacea, Elder, Eucalyptus, Ginseng, Mastic, Meadowsweet, Milk Thistle, Mint, Motherwort, Mushrooms, Musk, Nettle, Nutmeg, Orange Peel, Patchouli, Rose, Rue, Shepherd's Purse, Tarragon, Tragacanth, Wood Betony, Wormwood

PLANETARY INKS

One way to attune to the planets is to write your petition spell using planetary inks. Here are some example formulas of effective planetary inks. Make the inks on the planetary day, on the planetary hour, when the Sun or Moon are in a zodiac sign corresponding to that particular planet, or when that planet is particularly well-aspected. Earth Ink can be made any day and hour, though it is best when the Moon is in Taurus, Virgo, or Capricorn. Use your own judgment for the proportions, based on how much ink you are making in one batch.

Sun Ink

Gold or Yellow Base Ink

Small Piece of Gold Jewelry

Citrine

Rosemary

Sunflower Seeds

Drop of Frankincense Oil

Moon Ink

Silver, Lilac, or Pale Yellow Base Ink

Small Piece of Silver Jewelry

Moonstone

Mugwort

Jasmine Flowers

Drop of Jasmine Oil

Mercury Ink

Orange Base Ink

Agate Stone

Fennel Seeds

Drop of Lavender Oil

Venus Ink

Green or Pink Base Ink

True Copper Coin

Rose Quartz or Raw Emerald
Powdered Rose Petals
Drop of Rose Oil

Mars Ink

Red Base Ink

Ruby

Iron Powder

Powdered Black Peppercorns

Pinch of Dragon's Blood

Jupiter Ink

Blue or Purple Base Ink

Lapis Lazuli

Powdered Cinnamon

Powdered Cloves

Drop of Cinnamon Oil

Saturn Ink

Black Base Ink

Onyx

Patchouli

Myrrh

Drop of Myrrh Oil

Uranus Ink

Light Blue Base Ink

Zinc

Labradorite

Burdock Root

Drop of Lemongrass Oil

Neptune Ink

Sea Green or Sea Blue Ink

Aquamarine
Seaweed
Drop of Ylang Ylang Oil

Pluto Ink
Black or Dark Red Base Ink
Obsidian Stone
Black Cohosh
Vanilla Bean or Drop of Vanilla Extract

Earth Ink
Brown Base Ink
Mushroom
Eggshell
Drop of Patchouli Oil

CANDLE SPELLS

Candle majick is one of the easiest forms of majick to do. You can do specific candle spells, but Witches often have a "working candle" in the center of the altar for the entire majick circle ritual. This working candle is the color of the predominant energy for our majick that night, based upon the corresponding element, planet, or zodiac sign.

Choose the color based on the correspondence of your intention. Candles come in all shapes and sizes, but I tend to prefer the taper candles, or for bigger majick, the seven-day jar candles. You can decorate the glass jar candles by putting symbols and writing on the outside of the glass, combining your candle with forms of symbol majick. You can anoint the candle with a corresponding single oil, or with a blended oil potion that matches your intention. Hold the candle and focus upon your intention. You can write a petition and read it while holding the candle, and place the petition under the candle, or simply speak your intention while visualizing what you want to manifest. Then light the candle from another candle, or a match, and let it burn. If you have to leave the candle unattended before it burns completely, snuff it and relight it when you are home again. Keep burning the candle until it goes out on its own, and the spell will be sent out to manifest.

If you are anointing a candle, we usually anoint from the top of the candle downward to the base, to bring its majick to us, anchoring that majick in the candle for burning.

POTIONS & PHILTERS

Potions are majickal mixtures of herbs, minerals, and sometimes animal hair that carry a specific intention. Potions can store a majickal charge, and can be used later like a perfume on your body, or in other, larger spellworkings. They can be used to anoint candles, talismans, amulets, your home, vehicle, or anything else, and when you do, you bring the energy of that potion, its vibration and light, to the aura of the person or object you are anointing. It traditionally lasts for about four days.

While there are many forms of potions, some linked to medicinal herbology, we will not be making any edible potions in this Book of Shadows. All of these formulas are to be used majickally, to change the energy of a situation, but not specifically as medicine, even though the medicine and the majick have a lot in common. If you are going to consume any herbs, make sure you consult a reputable medical herbal book, to learn what is toxic and what is not, and be careful of any interactions with prescription medicines and other herbs.

Potions can come in several forms. The most basic and common are water-based potions, preserved with sea salt as a fixative. Oil-based potions are usually more popular, as they use wonderful scents from essential oils. Lastly there are "dry" potions, powders, and dusts known as philters.

Herb	Rulership	Properties
Balsam Fir	Moon, Jupiter	Strength, Insight, Power, Love
Bay Leaf	Earth, Sun, Jupiter	Legal Success, Winning in Court, Victory, Psychic Powers
Bat's Head Root	Saturn, Pluto	Wishes, Protection from Evil
Beth Root	Jupiter, Saturn, Venus	Protection, Success, Love, Easing Childbirth
Bilberry	Sun, Moon, Saturn	Getting Benefit from Hard Work, Earth Spirits, Money, Pleasure Happiness, Success, Safety

Herb	Rulership	Properties
Birch Leaves	Mercury, Moon, Earth, Pluto	Healing, Blessing, Beauty, Protection, Stop Gossip
Blackberry	Venus, Jupiter	Goddess Energy, Brid, Healing, Transformation of Bad Luck, Feminine Health, Childbirth, Prosperity, Protection
Black Cohosh	Pluto, Saturn, Earth	Attraction and Repulsion, Safe Home, Happiness, Neutralize Enemies
Black Peppercorn	Venus, Mars, Saturn	Fire, Passion, Sexuality, Intensity, Protection, Aggression
Black Walnut	Venus, Earth, Sun	Protection, Blocking Emotional or Majickal Poisons
Blessed Thistle	Sun, Moon	Power, Blessings, Child Blessings of Love, Beauty and Wisdom
Bloodroot	Venus, Mars	Stir the Heart, Beauty, Warming, Love
Blue Cohosh	Moon, Sun	Ease Pain, Protection of People and Places
Blue Malva	Saturn, Jupiter	Unexpected Good Luck, Money, Fortune, Blessings
Blue Vervain	Saturn, Moon, Venus, Mercury	All Purpose, Protection, Love, Dreams, Money, Healing
Boldo	Mercury, Mars, Moon, Sun, Saturn	Faery Contact, Increase Faery Power, Vision and Faery Sight
Borage	Earth, Jupiter	Courage, Confidence, Ease Pain, Cleansing, Clearing, Intuition
Broom	Mercury, Mars	Cleansing and Clearing, Dispelling Harm
Buckthorn	Mercury, Saturn	God Energy, Balance, Protection from Abuse, Change Destiny
Burdock	Sun, Venus, Mars, Saturn, Uranus	Tenacity, Strength, Healing, Protection
Calamus	Sun, Mercury	Strengthen Any Spell, Binding, Healing, Banishing
Calendula	Sun	Psychic Power, Dreams, Prosperity, Fidelity
Caraway	Sun, Moon, Mercury, Venus, Mars, Earth	Sexuality, Fidelity, Healing, Preventing Theft

Herb	Rulership	Properties
Cat's Claw	Sun, Moon	Protection of Valuables, Health, Vision Quest and Guidance
Catnip	Venus	Relaxation, Dreams, Healing, Humor, Feline Connections
Cedar	Jupiter, Sun	Health, Wealth, Happiness, Protection, New Opportunities
Chamomile	Sun	Healing, Rest, Regeneration, Dreams, Meditation, Success
Cherry	Moon, Venus, Mars	Love, Romance
Chickweed	Moon	Cooling Hot Emotions, Attraction, Friendship
Chili Peppers	Sun, Venus, Mars, Neptune	Love, Lust, Sexual Gratification
Cinnamon	Jupiter	Influence People in High Places, Good Graces, Gambling, Fortune, Success, Luck
Cloves	Sun, Jupiter, Vulcan	Prosperity, Success, Business, Fame, Protection from Hostility
Coltsfoot	Sun, Moon, Pluto	Understanding, Peace, Tranquility, Love, Acceptance, Clairvoyance
Comfrey	Venus, Mars, Saturn	Deep Wisdom, Past Life Memory, Regeneration and Healing, Mend a Broken Heart, Banish Depression, Increase Fidelity
Coriander	Mars	Love, Lust, Peace, Good Will, Energy
Cumin	Moon, Mercury, Mars	Fidelity, Protection
Damiana	Venus, Mars	Aphrodisiac, Love, Lust, Passion, Spirit Guidance
Dill	Sun, Moon, Mercury	Speeding Up Spells, Protection, Prosperity, Fertility, Virility
Dulse	Neptune	Ocean Majick, Sea Creatures, Water Elementals, Psychic Abilities, Dreams
Echinacea	Sun, Moon, Mercury, Earth	Support, Strength, Stop Poisons, Healing
Elder	Saturn, Earth, Sun, Moon	Faery Contact, Protection, Healing, Beauty

Herb	Rulership	Properties
Eucalyptus	Saturn, Pluto, Sun, Moon	Healing, Aids Investigations, Truth, Clarity
Eyebright	Mercury, Sun	Psychic Sight, See Your Path, Beauty
Fennel	Moon, Mercury, Neptune, Sparta	Calming, Soothing, Contentment, Multiplicity, Abundance
Feverfew	Sun, Moon, Venus	Clear Thinking, Clear Anxiety, Prevents Accidents
Five-Finger Grass	Mercury, Sun, Moon	Protection, Undo Harm, Grounding, New Perspectives
Hemlock	Saturn, Mars, Jupiter, Pluto	Protection, Knowledge of the Astral Worlds, Wisdom
Hibiscus	Venus, Jupiter, Sun	Love Spells Over a Distance, Open Heartedness
Horehound	Mercury, Moon	Overall Health, Protection, Banishment, Memory
Horny Goat Weed	Mars, Pluto	Sexuality, Virility, Lust, Passion, Desire
Hyssop	Jupiter, Mercury, Sun	Influence People in Authority, Cleansing, Heals Guilt and Shame
Irish Moss (Sea Weed)	Jupiter, Neptune	Mermaid Majick, Luck, Money, Protection, Sea Travel
Jalapeño	Mars	Lust, Passion, Sex, Power, Majickal Catalyst
Jasmine	Moon, Jupiter	Majick, Mystery, Romance, Success, Prosperity, Love, Attraction, Dream Majick, Psychic Development, Moon Goddess
Juniper	Venus, Mars, Sun, Jupiter	Protection, Hex Breaking, Anti-Theft, Psychic Power, Love, Health, Weight Loss, Purification, Beauty
Kelp (Sea Weed)	Neptune	Water and Ocean Majick, Protection When Over Water
Lady's Mantle	Venus	Mysteries of Nature, Goddess Energy, Love, Alchemy, Beauty
Lavender	Mercury, Jupiter, Uranus, Sun	Peace, Tranquility, Sleep, Dreams, Healing, Sobriety, Cleansing, Psychic Powers, Wisdom

Herb	Rulership	Properties
Lemon Balm (Melissa)	Moon, Jupiter, Vulcan, Sun	All Purpose, Life Force, Brightness, Lightness, Love, Healing, Quick Money, Psychic Power, Success
Lemongrass	Venus, Uranus, Sun	Cleansing, Blessing, Happiness, Success, Attracts Good Business Partners and Friends
Lemon	Sun, Moon	Discovery of True and False Friends, Purification, Health, Longevity, Lifts Mood, Clarify Intentions
Lemon Verbena	Mercury, Vulcan, Sun	Love, Fidelity, Chastity, Dreaming, Sleep, Success, Money, Wealth
Licorice	Mercury, Venus	Clear Speaking, Eloquence, Creativity, Love, Lust, Fidelity, Dreams, Break Addictions
Lovage	Venus, Neptune, Sun	Love Majick, Attraction, Opening the Heart, Beauty
Lucky Hand Root	Venus, Jupiter, Sun	Attraction of Your Desires, Gambling, Dexterity
Mandrake	Saturn, Venus, Mercury, Moon	Majickal Catalyst, Protection, Love, Fertility, Power
Marjoram	Mercury, Sun	Clear Mind, Love, Happiness, Blessings of Marriage, Healing Grief, Peace
Marshmallow	Moon, Venus, Saturn, Pluto	Softening and Soothing, Healing, Comfort, Spiritual Assistance, Blessing, Love, Sex Majick, Remove Blocks to Success
Meadowsweet	Moon, Saturn, Earth	Love, Happiness, Relief of Stress, Merriment, Prevents Theft
Mint	Mercury, Moon,	Communication, Clear the Mind, Ease Pain, Psychic Healing Earth
Milk Thistle	Jupiter, Earth, Sun, Moon	Heals Anger, Increases Strength, Health, Prosperity for Family
Mistletoe	Sun	All Healing, All Majick, Catalyst, Divine Connection, Power, Health, Wealth, Wisdom
Motherwort	Moon, Venus, Earth	Goddess Energy, Aids in Fertility and Childbirth
Mugwort	Moon	Psychic Power, Divination, Euphoria, Protection, Fertility
Mustard	Mars, Jupiter, Sun	Prosperity and Abundance, Wealth, Good Fortune, Gambling, Remove Enemies

Herb	Rulership	Properties
Nettle	Mars, Venus, Earth	Connection and Separation, Love and Marriage, Healing Love Lost
Nutmeg	Venus, Mars, Earth, Sparta	Expands the Aura, Health and Happiness, Good Fortune
Orange	Sun, Venus, Jupiter, Earth	Success, Well-Being, Love, Marriage, Business, Immune System, Divination Success
Orchid	Mercury, Venus	Beauty, Love, Aphrodisiac, Psychic Power
Pumpkin Seeds	Venus, Mars, Sun, Moon	Protection, Invisibility, Prosperity, Healing, Lust, Dreams
Scullcap	Mercury, Moon	Clear Mind, Memory, Academic Success, Perceptions, Sleep, Cleverness in Business
Solomon's Seal	Saturn, Vulcan, Sun	Purification, Protection, Harmony, Divine Wisdom, Spirit Contact, Money, Success, Riches
Spearmint	Venus, Mars	Activates Change in Life, Love, Career
Star Anise	Moon, Venus	Joy, Happiness, Soften a Lover's Heart
St. John's Wort	Sun	Protection, Light, Heals Depression, Heals Trauma, Banishes Nightmares
Sunflower	Sun	Blessings, Joy, Prosperity, Good Luck, Pleasant Dreams, Health, Self-Esteem, Inner Fire
Sweet Woodruff	Mars, Venus, Pluto	Protection Against Evil, Increase Self-Love and Self-Esteem
Tansy	Venus, Mercury, Vulcan, Sun	Funerary Herb, Immortality, Health and Well-Being, Protection
Tarragon	Earth, Sun, Mars	Independence, Strength, Dragon Majick
Thyme	Vulcan, Mercury, Sun	Chivalry, Wishes, Speeds Up Spells, Love, Protection
Tonka	Jupiter, Venus	Luck, Prosperity, Love, Power
Uva Ursi	Saturn	Psychic Power, Personal Strength, Clear Psychic Information, Elf Communication, Spiritual Guidance
Valerian	Venus, Mercury	Dreams, Sleep, Psychic Power, Ancestor Majick, Love, Protection, Purification

Herb	Rulership	Properties
Vanilla	Venus, Mars, Pluto	Love, Lust, Friendship, Mental Powers, Wishes
Vetiver	Uranus, Mercury	Psychic Flight or Astral Travel, Tranquility, Relaxation, Moon, Protection from Thieves, Curses, and Evil
Wild Yam	Jupiter	Aphrodisiac, Love, Healing, Infertility, Vitality, Goodness
Willow	Moon	Healing, Dreams, Psychic Power, Protection
Witch Hazel	Mercury, Moon, Sun	Protection from Psychic Attack, Harmony, Psychic Flight or Astral Travel, Prophetic Dreams
Wood Betony	Sun, Earth	Protect Body and Soul, Manifest Physical Needs, Protection from Nightmares, Purification
Yarrow	Venus	Courage, Power, Love, Psychic Ability, Astral Travel, Friendship, Faery Beings, Boundaries, Protection
Yellow Dock	Jupiter	Healing, Prosperity, Fertility, Abundance
Yerba Santa	Venus	Beauty, Healing, Psychic Power, Protection, Dreams

Animal	Rulership	Properties
Abalone Shell	Neptune	Healing, Release, Protection, Purification
Bee Pollen & Bee's Wax	Sun, Venus	Blessings, Alchemy, Healing, Prophecy, Romance, Protection
Cat Hair	Moon, Venus	Psychic Power, Dreams, Intuition, Otherworld, Invisibility
Dog Hair	Earth	Grounded, Joy, Friendship, Loyalty, Protection
Egg Shell	Earth	Life, Birth, Protection, Catalyst, Purity
Feathers	Mercury	Communication, Travel, Freedom, Messages
Fleece	Earth	Peace, Comfort, Dreams, Guidance, Purity, Help
Horse Hair	Mars, Jupiter, Earth	Power, Freedom, Travel
Rabbit Fur	Mercury, Moon	Speeds Up Spells, Fertility

Animal	Rulership	Properties
Snake Skin	Saturn, Earth, Sparta	Psychic Ability, Change, Transformation, Regeneration
Stag Antlers	Earth, Sun, Vulcan	Strength, Alertness, Independence, Nobility, Regeneration
Wolf Hair	Mars	Protection, Clan, Learning

Water-based potions can be made over a stovetop in a Pyrex or enamel pan. Iron and steel should only be used for protection potions. If you have a vessel that can simmer herbs by candle flame in the circle, you can make a potion anywhere. Potpourri dishes, if large enough, or even fondue sets, are ideal. For every cup of water you are using as a base, dissolve one tablespoon of all-natural sea salt or kosher salt into the water to preserve the potion. Salt is also an excellent ingredient in any protection majick. Resins like frankincense and copal, as well as woods like sandalwood and roots such as orris root, are also great fixatives for potions, but I still recommend the sea salt in the water base to prevent fermentation.

Even if the potion does not call for a crystal in it, you can add a small quartz, small enough to fit into the bottle, to absorb the energy of the potion. That way, if you want to make it again, you can use the same crystal to "carry over" the energy of the original potion, even if the astrological conditions are different.

Love Potion
2 Cups of Spring Water
2 Tablespoons of Sea Salt
Slice of an Apple
1 Teaspoon of Clove
1 Teaspoon of Lovage Root
1 Teaspoon of Red Rose Petals
1 Pinch of Basil
Rose Quartz

Prosperity Potion
1 Cup of Spring Water
1 Tablespoon of Sea Salt

1 Teaspoon of Cinnamon

1 Teaspoon of Calendula

1/2 Teaspoon of Milk Thistle Seeds

1/2 Teaspoon of Yellow Dock Root

Citrine Stone

Psychic Potion

1 Cup of Spring Water

1 Tablespoon of Sea Salt

1 Teaspoon of Mugwort

1 Teaspoon of Jasmine Flowers

3 Star Anise Seedpods, Crushed

Piece of Silver Jewelry to be dipped into the potion

Oils usually blend essential oils, and sometimes fragrance oils, with a base oil for scents that are not easily available in all natural forms. Base oils include:

Oil	Rulership	Properties
Olive	Earth	Most easily available, but has a stronger natural scent and most likely to go rancid quickly. Only use if using all of the potion immediately. Associated with the Greek Goddess Athena.
Sunflower	Sun	Inexpensive, but does not mix well with other oils or absorb into the skin easily. Excellent for any type of Sun majick.
Almond	Sun, Moon	Excellent all-purpose base oil.
Hazelnut	Mercury	Strong nutty aroma preventing it from being a neutral scent base. Excellent oil to evoke the powers of Mercury and the wisdom of the Salmon.
Sesame	Mercury, Earth	Strong natural smell, less useful for blending essential oil. Can be used as a healing oil.
Apricot Kernel	Venus	Excellent oil that blends well with essential oils. Appropriate for any sensual blends, as Apricot evokes the power of Venus.
Coconut, Fractionated	Moon, Saturn	Excellent oil for blending and absorbing essential oils.

Oil	Rulership	Properties
Jojoba	Earth	The most expensive and best option. Jojoba is a liquid wax which is least likely to go rancid, preserving expensive essential oils the longest.

Usually majickal oils are measured in drops and drams. A dram was classically twenty drops, though in modern measurements, we say it is equal to 1/8 fluid ounce. Essential oils are added to a base oil by swirling them in clockwise for waxing majick, and counterclockwise for waning majick. Though we do not "cook" these potions, I like to quickly pass the mixing vessel through a flame to add the energy of fire for creation to the oil. One of the best fixatives, or preservatives, for an oil-based potion is Vitamin E Oil. Add a few drops of it to any blend to help preserve it. Some will add bits of dry herb, hair, or stones to the potion to keep the energy vital and anchored in the oil. You can certainly do that too.

Oil	Rulership	Properties
Amber	Sun	Success, Health, All Majick
Ambergris	Sun, Pluto	To Bind All Majick
Apple	Venus	Protection, Love, Empowerment
Apple Blossom	Venus	Psychic Vision of the Otherworld, Faery Majick
Bayberry	Vulcan, Sun, Pluto, Mars	To Calm Wild Weather, To Bring Blessings of the Winter
Benzoin (Styrax)	Mercury	Peace, Astral Travel, Psychic Ability, Memory, Clarity
Catnip	Venus	To Bring Success in Love, Attractiveness, Seduction
Cherry	Moon, Venus, Mars	Love Spells, Kissing, Romance, Fun
Cinnamon	Jupiter	Success, Money, Fortune, Gambling
Clover	Venus, Jupiter	Plant Spirit Majick, Psychic Travel to Ireland
Dragon's Blood	Mars	Adds Power to Any Majick

Oil	Rulership	Properties
Elder	Saturn, Earth, Sun, Moon	Energy of the Dark Goddess, Faery Majick
Fir	Moon, Neptune, Sun	Eternal life, Freshness, Good Fortune
Frangipani	Venus, Neptune	Sexual and Sensual Majick, Altered States of Awareness
Frankincense	Sun	Good Luck, Career Success, Purification, Protection
Heather	Venus, Sun, Jupiter	The Majick of Scotland. Faery Majick
Heliotrope	Sun	Success, Health, Wealth, Happiness
Honeysuckle	Sun, Moon	The Majick of Wales
Jasmine	Moon	Lunar Majick, Success, Psychic Powers, Speaking with Spirits
Lavender	Mercury, Jupiter, Uranus, Sun	Peace, Tranquility, Good Communication, Faery Contact
Lemon	Sun, Moon	Purification, Love
Lilac	Jupiter	Power, Balance, Truth, Harmony, Childhood
Lily of the Valley	Venus	Faery Power, Healing the Heart
Lotus Blossom	Sun, Moon	Opening Psychic Centers, Vision, Spiritual Awareness
Mimosa	Sun	Enchantment, Glamour, Shapeshifting, Self-Image
Mugwort	Moon	Psychic Power, Visions, Dreams
Musk	Saturn, Earth	Lust, Romance, Stag God of the Wild Wood
Myrrh	Saturn	Purification, Protection, Ancestors, Dark Goddess
Orange	Sun, Venus, Jupiter	Health, Success, Happiness
Orris	Venus	Fixative, Binding Harm

Oil	Rulership	Properties
Patchouli	Saturn, Earth	Love, Protection, Manifestation
Peppermint	Mercury	Clear Communication
Pine	Jupiter	For Merlin and the Morrighan, Leadership, Power
Rose	Venus, Earth	Majick of England, Love, Healing, Dreams
Rosemary	Sun	Increases Memory, Purifies
Sage	Jupiter	Clears and Cleanses, Encourages Wisdom
Strawberry	Venus	Love, To Open to Love's Power
Tonka	Jupiter	Fixative, Money, Success, Power
Vanilla	Pluto	Love, Lust, Power
Vetiver	Uranus, Mercury, Moon	Astral Travel, Protection, Nature Spirits
Violet	Venus, Jupiter	Love, Past Lives, Getting Over Shyness

Public Speaking Oil

1 Dram of Base Oil
5 Drops of Lavender Oil
4 drops of Rosemary Oil
1 drop of Peppermint
1 Blue Lace Agate

Isis Oil

1 Dram of Base Oil
10 Drops of Rose Oil
5 Drops of Amber Oil
5 Drops of Styrax Oil

3 Drops of Lotus Oil

1 Piece of Lapis Lazuli

Black Feather Oil

2 Drams of Base Oil

10 Drops of Heliotrope Oil

5 Drops of Pine Oil

Pinch of Apple Leaves, powdered

Hemlock Tree Cone

1 Crow Feather cut into small pieces

Witch's Lightning Oil

1 Dram of Almond Oil

10 Drops of Myrrh Oil

10 Drops of Sweet Orange Oil

5 Drops of Oakmoss Oil

5 Drops of Apple Oil

3 Drops of Pine Oil

Pinch of Lightning-Struck Oak

Pinch of Wood Betony

Pinch of Rabbit Fur

Piece of Sterling Silver

Use this to speed up your spells, or to bring about success and strength.

Philters are usually a mixture of herbs that are ground up. To use them, they can be scattered, or burned as incense. The best incenses are a mixture of resins, woods, herbs, and oils, which help the incense burn with a more pleasing and consistent smell. Often a wood, or naturally-dyed wood powder, is used as the base of the incense, and various colored glitters are added to the incense to reflect the majickal light of the intention.

Resin or Gum	Rulership	Properties
Amber	Sun	Healing, Balance, Purification

Resin or Gum	Rulership	Properties
Benzoin	Sun, Moon, Earth, Mercury	Prophetic Visions, Divination, Stabilization
Camphor	Moon	Healing, Purification, Awareness, Psychic Lore, Faeries
Copal	Earth, Neptune	Blessings, Invitation to Spirits
Dragon's Blood	Mars	Life Force, Power, Protection, Love, Lust, Banishment, Catalyst
Frankincense	Sun, Moon, Jupiter, Vulcan	Temple Incense, Meditation, Introspection, Peace, Healing, Protection, Neutralization, Binding
Guar Powder	Moon	Wolf Majick, Wild Moon Majick, Fixes Intentions
Gum Mastic	Sun, Saturn, Uranus	Binding Spells, Prevent Harm
Myrrh	Moon, Saturn, Neptune, Vulcan	Protection, Preservation, Neutralization, Purification
Storax	Moon, Mercury	Neutralization of Harm, Deep Trance, Purification
Tragacanth	Sun, Moon, Mercury, Earth	Binding, Calming, Clearing, Faery King Majick

Majick Circle Incense

1 Tablespoon of Frankincense

1 Tablespoon of Myrrh

1 Tablespoon of Benzoin

1 Tablespoon of Storax

Pinch of Rose Petals

5 Drops of Frankincense Oil

5 Drops of Myrrh Oil

Burn to create sacred space.

Triple Goddess Incense

1 Tablespoon of White Sandalwood

1 Tablespoon of Red Sandalwood

1 Tablespoon of Myrrh

1 Tablespoon of Jasmine Flowers

1 Tablespoon of Red Rose Petals

1 Tablespoon of Patchouli

3 Drops of Myrrh Oil

3 Drops of Jasmine Oil

3 Drops of Rose Oil

Burn to call the Goddess who is Maiden, Mother, and Crone.

Horned God Incense

2 Tablespoons of White Oak Bark

2 Tablespoons of Patchouli Leaves

1 Tablespoon of Black Copal

1 Tablespoon of Myrrh

1 Tablespoon of Nettle

1 Tablespoon of Vetiver

1 Teaspoon of Oat Straw

1 Pinch of Powdered Antler

10 Drops of Patchouli Oil

7 Drops of Vetiver Oil

Burn to call the Horned God of Witches.

Witch's Lightning Incense

1 Pinch of Lightning-Struck Oak

1 Tablespoon of Pine Resin

1 Tablespoon of Frankincense

1 Tablespoon of Myrrh

1 Tablespoon of Apple Wood

Pinch of Rabbit Fur

Makes majick manifest lightning fast!

AMULETS AND TALISMANS

Any object can be infused with majickal intention. Everything has some correspondence through their vibration and color. Amulets are three-dimensional charms for majickal intention, while talismans tend to be flat, geometric shapes imprinted upon paper, leather, wood, or metal. They can be brand new designs, or include traditional symbols and sigils. Most Witches learn to create their own symbols for their personal spellwork. They can be carried with you, usually in your left pocket for things you want to attract and right pocket for removal or protection, or in the center as a pendant. They can also be hung or hidden in the environment where you want the majick to work. Protection talismans and amulets for the home are left in the home. They can also be made for the office and car, or carried with you in your pocket or purse. These items can even be used on the board of the Game of Life.

MOON
POWER

MERLIN MERLINA
MAJICK POWER

ANOU ANU
CREATION

SUN
POWER

WATER
MISTLETOE

EPONA
FIXING VERVAIN

EARTH
BALANCE

PLUTO CERNUNNOS
BEING

DAGDA
POWER

FIRE
RED RACE

JUPITER MARS
WIN

RHIANNON
POTION

Cabot Tradition Talismans

CRYSTAL CHARMS

Any crystal can be turned into an amulet by charging the crystal with your intention. You can have many crystals all working for you; you can carry them with you, place them on your altar, or put them around your home and office. To cleanse a crystal, place it in dry sea salt for twelve days. Brush it off with a white cloth. Charge it with your intent by speaking onto it what you want, and then fix the energy. Store them when not in use in a white cloth.

There is a physical power in crystals. Quartz crystals, for example, contain electricity and electromagnetics through the piezoelectric effect. If you are in the bath, and you drop and break a large quartz in the water, it can electrocute you. Think of a quartz watch and how long that tiny chip of quartz keeps the watch running. It's the electrical power from the quartz that does so. They are good to wear around your neck as they can be used for anything. You can trap incorrect energy into a crystal and bind it. You can put your spirit guides into a crystal for ritual for their energy and then set it for them, so when you call on them, their energy is drawn into their crystal.

Stone	Ruler	Properties
Amber	Sun	Healing, Prevent Poison, Energy, Life, Balance
Ametrine	Sun, Jupiter	Balance, Intelligence, Clarity, Healing, Success
Amethyst	Jupiter, Neptune	Courage, Clarity, Peace, Strength, Sobriety, Addictions, Success
Andalusite	Earth	Memory, Balance, Faery Folk, Clarity in Thinking and Intent
Aquamarine	Neptune	Spiritual and Emotional Healing, Mermaids, Voice, Creativity
Aragonite	Earth	Confidence, Relieves Stress, Clears Environment, Grounding
Aventurine	Venus	Money Majick, Gambling, Luck, Prosperity, Healing, Compatibility
Azurite	Jupiter, Neptune	Psychic Ability, Intuition, Vision, Projecting Intention
Bloodstone	Mars, Neptune	Legal Success, Invincibility, Revealing Secrets, Protection, Healing the Blood
Botswana Agate	Mercury	Comfort, Stress Relief, Friendship, Protection, Travel

Stone	Ruler	Properties
Blue Goldstone	Jupiter, Uranus	Wisdom, Energy, Inspiration, Healing, Success, Wisdom
Boulder Opal	Moon, Venus, Uranus	Scatter Energy, Disperse Harm, Protection, Remove Blocks
Calcite	Variable	Healing, Removing Obstacles, Revealing Illusions, Spirituality, Manifestation
Carnelian	Mercury	Energy, Healing, Courage, Sexuality, Blessings
Cat's Eye	Moon, Venus	Beauty, Wealth, Protection, Healing Karma, Projection of Intent
Chrysocolla	Venus	Peace, Wisdom, Love, Clearing, Harmony, Children, Mother, Communication
Citrine	Sun	Health, Wealth, Money, Prosperity, Rest, Success
Emerald	Venus	Healing the Eyes, Love, Immunity, Wisdom, Prophecy, Vision, Prosperity, Health
Fire Agate	Mercury, Mars	Creativity, Energy, Stamina, Pleasure, Speeds Up All Spells, Heals Depression, Increases Motivation
Fuchsite	Venus	Projection of Loving Intentions, Good Fortune, Blessings, Healing, Faeries and Nature Spirits Communication
Garnet	Mars, Saturn	Passion, Sexuality, Creativity, Grounding, Sovereignty
Green Goldstone	Venus	Money, Healing, Grounding, Nature
Hematite	Mars	Healing, Vitality, Grounding, Manifestation
Howlite	Earth, Venus, Neptune, Sun	Adaptability, Healing, Awareness, Clarity, Vision
Jasper	Earth, Jupiter	Beauty, Self-Esteem, Protection, Pain Relief, Weather Majick, Success, Money, Influence
Jet	Earth, Saturn, Pluto	Protection, Power, Luck, Ancestors, Knowledge
Kyanite	Mercury	Tranquility, Peace, Clear Communication, Psychic Ability, Restful Sleep, Dreaming Majick
Labradorite	Uranus, Pluto	Patience, Clarity, Courage, Meditation, Dreams, Psychic Abilities, Connection to Cosmos and Higher Dimensions

Stone	Ruler	Properties
Lapis	Venus, Jupiter	Meditation, Psychic Development, Peace, Success, Loyalty
Lodestone	Venus	Drawing To You, Desires, Unlocking Blessings, Grounding
Malachite	Venus	Love, Attraction, Business, Success, Protective, Nature
Mookaite	Earth	Connection to Mother Nature, Slow and Gentle Healing, Being Present in the Moment, Gentle Protection
Moonstone	Moon	Lunar Power, Dreams, Sleep, Divination, Psychic Power, All Majick Spells, Empathy, Feminine Mysteries
Moss Agate	Earth, Mercury	Healing, Energy, Clearing Skin Ailments, Attraction, Beauty, Confidence
Obsidian	Mars, Pluto	Psychic Power, Divination, Scrying, Wishes, Protection, Ordering Chaos, Instant Manifestation of Intentions
Onyx	Mars, Saturn	Strength, Courage, Exorcisms, Disperse Evil Intent, Healing Grief
Peridot	Venus, Sun	Healing, Restful Sleep, Increase Money, Fame and Luck
Petrified Wood	Saturn	Past Life Recall, Longevity, Healing, Grounding, Stability
Prehnite	Venus	Healing, Unconditional Love, Getting to the Root Issue
Quartz	Sun, Moon, Earth	All-Purpose, Amplification, Healing, Manifestation of Intent
Rainbow Moonstone	Moon	Intuition, Psychic Powers, Dream, Harmony, Balance, All Majick
Rhodocrosite	Mars, Venus	Love, Self-Esteem, Happiness, Loyalty, Patriotism, Lucid Dreams
Rhodonite	Venus	Peace, Balance, Happiness
Rose Quartz	Venus	Love, Compassion, Spirituality, Heart Healing
Rutilated Smoky Quartz	Earth, Saturn	Telepathy, Psychic Ability, Grounding, Protection, Grounding
Rutilated Quartz	Earth, Uranus	Protection, Mental Powers, Weather Majick

Stone	Ruler	Properties
Sapphire	Jupiter	Awareness, Good Fortune, Academic Success, Enhance Talents, Influence People in Power
Sea Salt	Moon, Saturn, Neptune	Protection, Clearing, Purity, Healing
Selenite	Moon	Peace, Clearing, Protection, Meditation, Clear Judgment, Psychic Power, Purity
Seraphinite	Venus	Healing, Cooperation, Communion with Spirit, Psychic Travel, Regeneration, Nature Spirits, Spirit Messengers
Serpentine	Earth, Mars	Double Blessings, Good Fortune, Protection from Bites, Grounding, Attunement to Nature, Serpent Power, Kundalini
Smoky Quartz	Sun, Moon, Saturn	Meditation, Grounding, Clarity, Stability, Protection, Reduces Toxicity
Snowflake Obsidian	Mars, Saturn, Pluto	Protective, Grounding, Balance Polarities, Restore Order, Create Chaos
Sodalite	Jupiter	Transform Anxiety into Success, Business, Clear Communication, Settles Disagreements
Sugilite	Jupiter, Neptune	Third Eye Opening, Psychic Power, Calming Overstimulation, Emotional Clearing, Peace, Restores Health to Brain
Tektite	Uranus, Pluto	Courage, Protection, Extraterrestrial Contact
Tiger's Eye	Mars	Power, Energy, Health, Life Force, Success
Tiger Iron	Mars	Energy, Common Sense, Grounding, Solidity
Tourmaline	Various	All Purposes Depending on Color, Removes Blocks, Energizes
Tourmaline Quartz	Sun, Pluto	All Purpose, Protection, Money, Business, Success, Courage
Tree Agate	Mercury	Gentle Grounding, Attuning to Nature, Friendship, Protection, Healing
Turquoise	Jupiter	Sacredness, Protection, Friendship, Courage, Peace, Time Travel, Past Life Regressions
Unakite	Neptune	Emotional Balance, Clarity, Healthy Pregnancy, Animal Communication

Stone	Ruler	Properties
Zebra Jasper	Mercury	Stamina, Endurance, Balance
Zebra Serpentine	Pluto	Bravery, Courage, Balance Mood Swing and Hormones
Zoisite	Venus, Mars	Love, Happiness, Healing the Heart, Vital Energy

You can charge crystals for specific healings, continuing to send healing light to someone even when you are not in alpha. You can use the different minerals for chakra healing. You can place them upon the body, or carry one with you when you want to heal that specific chakra.

Chakra	Color	Stones
Root	Red	Ruby, Garnet, Red Jasper, Red Quartz
Belly	Orange	Carnelian, Orange Calcite
Solar Plexus	Yellow	Citrine, Yellow Calcite, Yellow Topaz
Heart	Green and Pink	Emerald, Peridot, Rose Quartz, Kunzite, Green Calcite, Pink Calcite, Tourmaline — Green/Pink/Watermelon, Green Fluorite
Throat	Blue	Lapis Lazuli, Turquoise, Blue Lace Agate, Sapphire, Blue Calcite, Blue Fluorite
Brow	Purple	Amethyst, Sugilite, Purple Fluorite
Crown	Violet, White	Quartz, Opal

After you have had a crystal for a long time, you may become aware that you need to give it back to the Earth. Bury it someplace and return it to her.

MAJICK BAGS

Majick bags are a type of talisman. They are usually a mixture of majickal substances, including herbs, resins, stones and animal hair, all formulated for your intention. The color of the bag is chosen to correspond with your spell, and the items placed into the bag. Other traditions call these mojo bags or gris-gris bags, but they are simply majick bags, for they hold the substances of your majick. They can be as simple as a single stone in a bag, or involve complex formulas of pre-made philters or incense.

Protection Charm

1 Tablespoon of Sea Salt

1 Tablespoon of Frankincense

1 Tablespoon of Myrrh

1 Teaspoon of Blue Vervain

1 Teaspoon of St. John's Wort

1 Pinch of Dragon's Blood

3 Iron Nails

1 Obsidian Stone

Carry in a black majick bag.

Healing Charm

1 Tablespoon of Chamomile

1 Tablespoon of Blackberry Leaf

1 Tablespoon of Eucalyptus

1 Tablespoon of Lemon Balm

1 Tablespoon of Peppermint

5 Drops of Eucalyptus Oil

5 Drops of Peppermint Oil

1 Citrine Stone

Carry in a yellow or gold Majick Bag.

RUNE MAJICK

The Norse Runes come in two distinct alphabets, the Elder Futhark and the Younger Futhark. Most modern Witches today tend to favor the Elder Futhark. Runes have many majickal uses. They can be used in divination sets, much like tarot cards, with each sign having a meaning to answer a question. They can be used individually as talismans and also combined, either written in a row left to right, or geometrically combined to create a sigil. They can even be combined with other symbols.

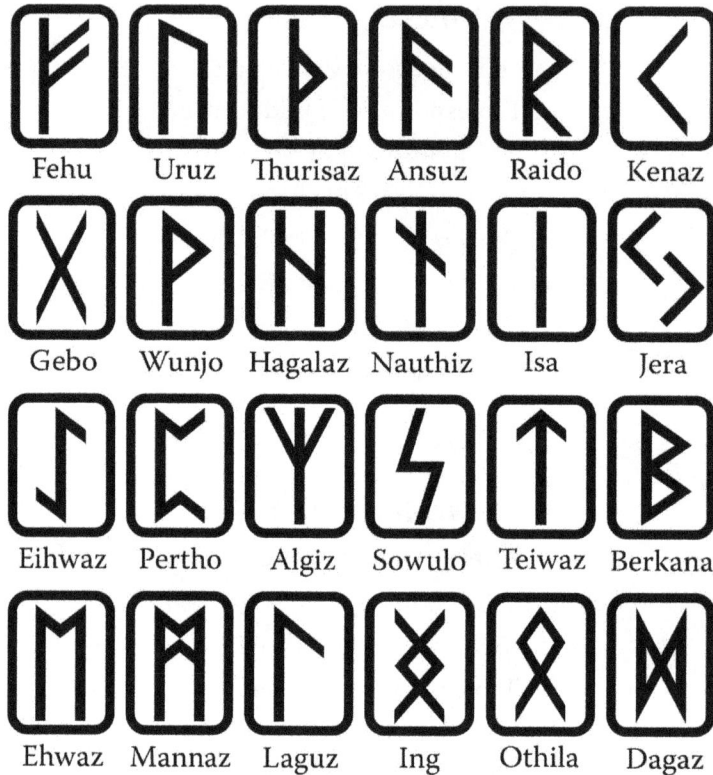

Fehu	Uruz	Thurisaz	Ansuz	Raido	Kenaz
Gebo	Wunjo	Hagalaz	Nauthiz	Isa	Jera
Eihwaz	Pertho	Algiz	Sowulo	Teiwaz	Berkana
Ehwaz	Mannaz	Laguz	Ing	Othila	Dagaz

Elder Futhark Runes

Rune	Letter	Meanings
Fehu	F	Cattle — Prosperity, Property, Money, Riches
Uruz	U	Ox — Health, Strength, Vitality, Healing
Thurisaz	Th	Vexing Thorn/Thor/Giants — Protection, Difficulties to Overcome
Ansuz	A	Aesir Gods, Mouth — Communication, Eloquence, Majick

Rune	Letter	Meanings
Raido	R	Ride, Journey — Travel, Movement
Kenaz	K	Fire, Torch — Illumination, Light, Passion
Gebo	G	Gift — Blessing, Offering, Presents, Talents
Wunjo	W	Joy — Enjoyment, Blessing, Fun, Wishes
Hagalaz	H	Hail — Unforeseen Difficulties, Violent Change
Nauthiz	N	Need — Desire, Want, Requirements
Isa	I	Ice — Slow-down, Frozen, Standstill, No Progress, Rest
Jera	J	Harvest — Good Year, Rewards, Reaping What You Sow
Eihwaz	Ae	Yew Tree — Protection
Pertho	P	Lot Cup — Mystery, Fate
Algiz	Z	Elk — Protection, Life, Opportunity, Higher Self, Valkyries
Sowulo	S	Sun — Success, Victory, Good Fortune, Health
Teiwaz	T	The god Tyr — Warrior, Justice, Balance, Sacrifice, Victory
Berkana	B	Birth — Motherhood, Blessing, Fertility, Rejuvenation
Ehwaz	E	Horse — Spirit Journey, Dreams, Astral Travel
Mannaz	M	Mankind — Humanity, Fellowship, Others
Laguz	L	Lake — Water, Intuition, Reflection, Rebirth, New Starts
Ing	I	The god Ing — Fertility, Increase, Power, Growth
Othila	O	Estate — Inheritance, Ancestry

Rune	Letter	Meanings
Dagaz	D	Day — Increasing in Light or Brightness, Balance, Harmony

For example, the following runes are used together for health:

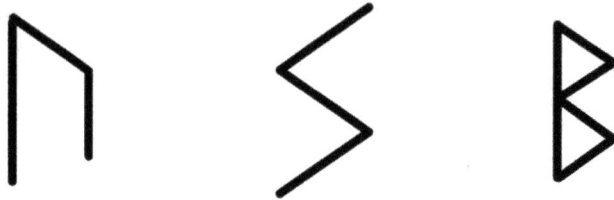

They can also be combined into a sigil:

These runes are used for prosperity:

A combined sigil for prosperity is:

SPELL BOTTLES

Spell bottles are magical amulets where all the ingredients for a spell are placed in a bottle. Spell bottles can either contain unwanted energies and forces, or radiate out a particular power and intention. In many ways, they are similar to the majick bags, but instead of using a bag, the vessel is a bottle.

The Bottle Binding Spell

4 Tablespoons of Sea Salt
4 Tablespoons of Orris Root Powder
2 Tablespoons of Frankincense
2 Tablespoons of Myrrh
4 Tablespoons of Iron Powder
1 White Candle
1 Bottle with a Cork or Lid
Mortar and Pestle
Parchment Paper

Black Ink and Pen
Black Thread

This spell is used to neutralize the harm directed towards you from another. While it doesn't bind the person, it binds the harm, creating a target for the harmful energy that will continue to absorb and neutralize it. This spell should only be used in intense and necessary situations, and never frivolously.

Using black ink, write upon the parchment:

"In the name of the Goddess and God, I neutralize the power of (name your adversary) to do me and my loved one any harm. I ask that this be correct and for the good of all. So be it."

Read the intention in the majick circle, doing this ideally on the Dark Moon. Charge your white candle for protection and neutralization. Roll up the parchment, tie it with a black thread, and place it into the bottle. Then fill the rest of the bottle with the herbs and salt. You can grind them up in the mortar and pestle before you put them in if you desire. Seal the bottle and turn the bottle counterclockwise as you drip white wax upon it, sealing it thoroughly. Do not open the bottle, or you will neutralize the spell. You can bury it somewhere it will not be opened, or you can keep it in your freezer, where many Witches keep their protection bottles.

MAJICK CORDS

Majick cords are amulets made using an old form of majick, infusing intention into braids and knots. They can be used for specific spells, but more often are used to attract general influences like prosperity or hold long-term intentions like protection, and are hung where you wish that influence to manifest.

Choose three cord colors that align with your intention. Decide how long you want the cord, remembering when you braid a cord, it will get shorter, and putting knots will make it shorter still. Tie the three cords together in a knot with a loop at the top, for hanging. Make the knot with a specific intention or wish. Then braid the cords together. Tie at least two more knots, for a three-knotted cord, or if you desire, you can tie as many knots as you wish for your majick, with five, seven, nine, and thirteen being traditional number of knots.

From the cords, you can hang other majickal symbols and talismans appropriate to your intention. I like to hang tarot cards, majick bags, and keys, or glue stones and other charms right onto the cord. Make sure all the items have been properly cleansed and charged for your intention. Then, when done, charge the entire thing in a majick circle. Hang it where you want it to do its majick.

FEATHER MAJICK

One spell my teacher Felicity used was casting intentions upon the wind using feathers. It was both a way to launch your majick into the world, and a test to your relationship with the elements, much like we used healing cases to test our psychic abilities. You must summon the wind by whistling it up, or calling to it.

Start with a handful of feathers, ideally of a type and color appropriate to your majick. Clear them of unwanted incorrect energy and charge them for your spell. Use your Instant Alpha Trigger to enter into a light trance, and call forth the wind. Release the feathers, and your spell, into the wind.

The direction the wind is blowing from can indicate a different use in majick. These winds are particular to my experiences in the Northeast of America. Your own experience of the winds in your area might be different, based on geography and topography.

North Wind — Blows strong from the lands of endurance. Courage and the psychic power of all-knowing. Old north wind calls you to travel and find new places.

East Wind — Comes across the Atlantic as the sun rises. The east wind will clear your thinking and blow away your indecision. The east wind will sweep away doubt.

South Wind — South wind brings a warm loving feeling. Cast a love spell while the south wind brushes your face. With a strong south wind, let your written spell go. The wind will speed its outcome.

West Wind — Walk with the west wind at your back. Casting a spell for success while walking with the west wind at your back will push you towards success.

GRAVE DIRT

Witches have always had a close association with the dead, ancestors, and graves. One thing you will find in many Witchcraft books is the use of graveyard dirt or graveyard dust in a spell.

While sometimes that is a code for herbs like patchouli and mullein, just as names like Bat's Wings are for holly leaves or Eye of Newt for Juniper Berries. But I was taught that Witches do use the actual dirt from graves and graveyard. And we can do majick in graveyards, asking the dead, and the gods of the dead, to help us.

Ideally you want to gather the dirt from someone who you knew and had a relationship with, or someone you did not know but respect. We sometimes use graveyard dirt for our Protection Potion, using a pinch of dirt from the grave of someone you revere for bravery and courage. It should be someone who makes you feel safe and protected.

Many traditions believe when saying thank you to the spirit of the grave, you should leave an offering—like a coin, flower, or a shot of alcohol—as payment.

CRYSTAL SCRYING

Scrying, or crystal gazing, is one of the many forms of divination. Usually done with a crystal ball, you can also use a large crystal point, or even a dark mirror. Once you understand how to project the screen of your mind to a majickal object, you will find that you can scry into anything —including water, fire, smoke, or even the branches of a tree—but reflective surfaces, particularly crystals, tend to help magnify psychic impressions, making them more powerful. Many will "scry" into their tarot cards or runes for additional information.

To scry, go into alpha and gaze into the crystal that has been cleared and charged for scrying. Note what you see on the crystal or in your mind's eye. The images and symbols must be clear. Deflect your eyes. Don't look directly into the stone or mirror. If you do, you'll simply see the crystal itself. Imagine looking past it, or through it, using a soft focus to get your psychic mind active. You may only see symbols as they develop, and the symbols will inform you of their message or answer any questions. Write them down and figure out the meaning later if it is not clear to you. Sometimes it will be clear, and you will simply know the meaning and answer. While research can help you, you can't go to books for all the meanings. Scrying is personal. Ultimately, they are your symbols. As with dreams, you have to figure out what they mean to you.

PSYCHOMETRY

Psychometry is the art of reading the energy of an object, usually in the form of uncovering the past of the object. We like to practice on objects with a rich history that can be sensed by the psychic mind. Psychometry can also refer to reading the past of the person who owns the object, through the energetic connection between the owner and object. Many psychics will ask to hold your keys, watch, or piece of jewelry—using the natural ability of the metal, stone, or wood to attune to your vibrations—and then find the "thread" of your life, reading your past, but also being able to read your future.

To perform psychometry, hold the object in either your left (receptive) hand or using both hands, and then use your Instant Alpha Trigger. Take note of what you see in your mind's eye, and any feelings, thoughts, or words that come to you, regarding this object. Sometimes they seem unrelated but turn out to be quite true. The object might flash images that could be its literal past, or as with crystal scrying, display a symbolic image to de-code later.

DOWSING

Dowsing is a method of divination that usually uses either a pendulum or divining rods. Traditionally "Water Witches" would dowse to find water for well digging, and many people still use these tools to dowse for water today. A pendulum is a weight, such as a crystal, hung by a cord. Dowsing rods are typically metal "L" rods, usually copper, with one held in each hand.

The pendulum is a method to speak with spirits and gain psychic information. In its most simple form, a spirit can influence the movement of a pendulum through you, to give you simple "yes" and "no" answers, or move the pendulum over a board with multiple options. Your own divine psychic mind can answer through the pendulum when you don't ask to work with a specific spirit. Your own response will move the pendulum to answer you truly.

Traditionally a clockwise movement of the pendulum indicates a "yes" while a counterclockwise movement indicates a "no." You must ask the specific spirit you want to connect with to answer through the pendulum; otherwise your yes/no answer will come from your own inner psychic mind. Hold your Instant Alpha Trigger in one hand. Ask the spirit guide to speak with you and show you their yes and no movements, which might be different from the traditional clockwise and counterclockwise. Then with those established, ask your questions. When done, thank and disconnect from the spirit and release your trigger.

Likewise dowsing rods are used in a similar manner. Hold the long end of the L out horizontal to the ground, with the short end in your hands, perpendicular to the ground. Many have a tube that you hold, instead of holding the rod directly, allowing them to swing freely. As you move, searching for something, the rods, starting parallel to each other, will cross, indicating whatever you are searching for. They have been used for water, but can also be used to find lost objects and to find the energy lines of the Earth, also known as ley lines.

Pendulums and dowsing rods, like other ritual objects, should be cleansed and charged to be majickal tools. You can keep the pendulum in a bowl of salt for ten days to clear it, and then simply hold it in your hands while holding your trigger and think, "I charge this pendulum to answer me clearly and truly." Dowsing rods are often too large for a bowl of salt, so you can clean them with a cloth soaked first in salt water and then in clear water. Charge the rods in a similar manner to the pendulum.

AUTOMATIC WRITING

Automatic writing is the process of allowing the psychic mind, or other spirits, to speak to us through the unconscious mind and unconscious movement of a pen. Start with blank sheets of loose paper and a good, flowing pen. I suggest a ballpoint. I charge the pen and paper for accurate psychic information. Enter into an alpha state by either the Crystal Countdown or Instant Alpha Trigger, and ask your questions, either aloud or silently. Then allow your hand to move. Sometimes you will start to doodle with no letters or structure, but given time and the ability to relax and move into it, your pen will begin to answer the questions.

Ideally automatic writing is automatic, with the writer having no idea what is being written until they look down on the paper. Some find that it works well when done more like automatic dictation, that there is a slight delay, and the Witch hears the message and writes as they are hearing it, transcribing a divine directive with a greater flow and speed than their normal writing process.

Return from alpha and make sure you give yourself clearance and balance.

TAROT

Tarot cards are used to stimulate our psychic mind and give us information. We are the psychics doing a reading, so we shuffle the cards and lay them out for ourselves or anyone else we are reading for. We can gaze upon the cards, and see what meanings the symbols reveal to us. Though there are traditional meanings with each card, the most important thing is what the card is saying to you or showing you for that individual reading, which can be different from what the books say the card means. You are almost scrying into each card and letting it tell you a story about what is going on for the reading.

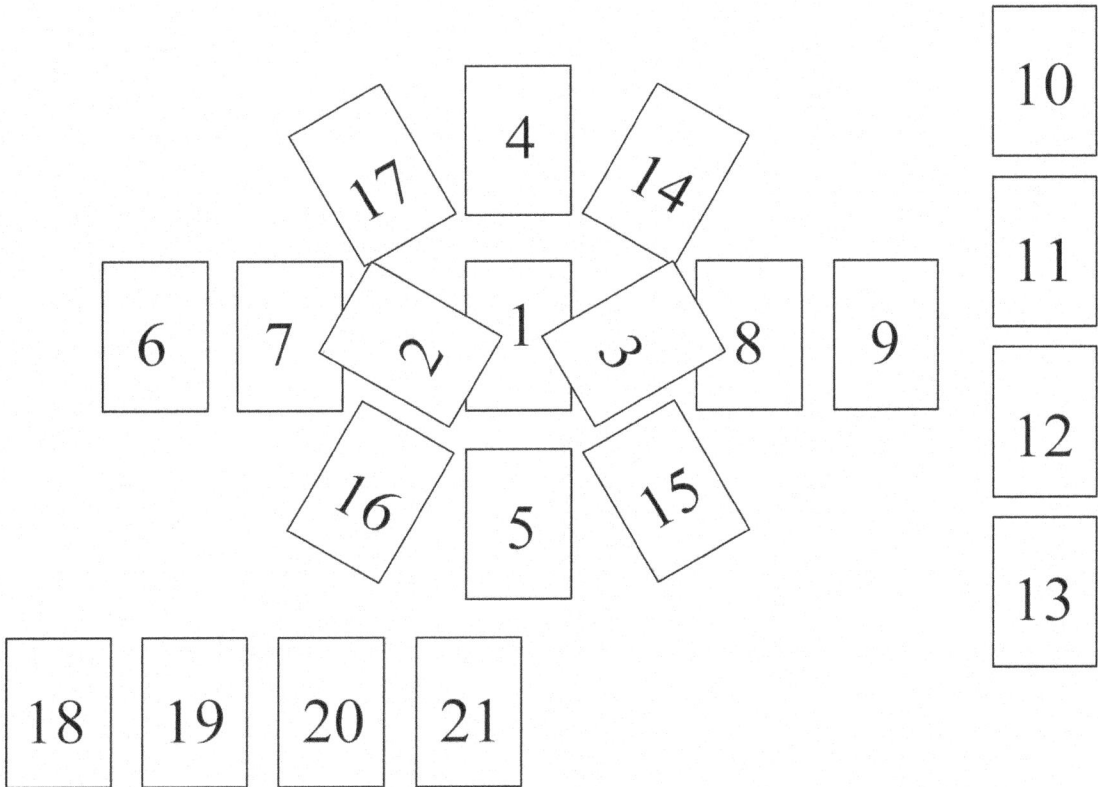

Tarot Layout

1	Subject of the reading, question asked, or what is primary to the reading
2-3	Clarifying the subject
4	What is hanging over the situation, or what has been pushed away or hasn't yet come into the picture
5	Past of that subject, what is under the situation, or the deeper cause
6-7	Far past (three to six months)
8-9	Future (two to six weeks)
10-13	Last three to five years concerning this issue

14	Additional information about cards 3, 4 and 6
15	Additional information about cards 3, 5, and 8
16	Additional information about cards and 2, 5 and 7
17	Additional information about cards 2, 4 and 9
18–21	Three to six months in the future

We read the tarot intuitively in the Cabot Tradition. While each card has a set of symbols on it, and each deck has its own symbol system, we use the psychic mind while in alpha to read the cards. We access divine information through our alpha state, and the cards become doorways to receiving that information. You might see the Eight of Wands, and one of the wand reminds you of a pipe. Your mind moves towards the image and idea of a leaky pipe in your querent's basement, and suddenly your reading is about the broken pipe leaking water in the basement. That meaning won't be found in any tarot book, but you'll find such intuitive leaps are completely accurate when reading for someone.

The layout of the cards can be quite accurate in terms of time frame and the unfolding of events. In 1990, I read for Prince Tidal of Saudi Arabia. In positions 18-21, it was clear, intuitively, that in the next three to six months, his homeland would be going to war. He scoffed at my reading and told me that Saudi Arabia is the most peaceful place on the Earth. Approximately three months later, the first Gulf War broke out in the Middle East and not soon after that, I got a call at my home, from the Prince, wanting to know more since my prediction turned out true for him and his country. Often things that don't make sense or seem plausible in a reading turn out to be totally accurate.

RUNES

The following are some of my personal interpretations of the Runes in divination, to help you explore their meanings in your own readings along with their majick. You can ask a question and pull a single rune from the pouch or cast runes, much like the Game of Life, interpreting the pattern of runes, how and where they fall, and what runes are next to each other.

Rune	Meaning
Algiz	Opportunities and challenges, unwanted influences. A shield. Use it to channel energies appropriately.

Rune	Meaning
Ansuz	Others seek the real you. Find your center, and work from there. Knowing yourself is true wisdom.
Berkano	Stay grounded, allow the roots of your soul to draw energy from the nurturing of Mother Earth.
Daguaz	Trust the Universe, make the leap. An important breakthrough. Have the courage to take action.
Ehwaz	This is the time of transition and change. Pay attention to cooperation and partnership, adapt to change.
Eiwaz	The fortress around the start of a new life. Visualize the possible results of your actions before you act.
Fehu	You are nourished on levels both spiritual and physical. Helping others is a sign of personal well-being.
Hagalaz	Your reality and beliefs have been shaken. Changing your thoughts can change your world.
Gebo	Find the balance in receiving and giving. You will find rewards, but perhaps only after sacrifice.
Ingwaz	You feel a need to belong, you search for kindred spirits. Leave unhealthy relationships.
Isa	Your life is gestation, not stagnation. We create, but are also governed by the ebb and flow of time.
Jera	The seeds you planted are growing fast. Nurture and cultivate your plans, persevere and be patient.
Kenaz	Passion warms your creativity, or burns you obsessively. Harness your inner fire to work for you.
Laguz	Flowing water — intuitions and emotions. Live on the stream of interconnected Universal energy.
Mannaz	Don't judge; all other relationships flow out of the relationship you have with your own ego.
Nauthiz	Your shadow obscures your true path. Wounded creatures attract predators — withdraw and recover.
Othala	Physical actions bring physical results. Take the initiative in new endeavors — you are unlikely to lose.
Perthro	Like the phoenix, fire has cleansed you. Rise above yourself, and gain a wider vision of the world.
Raidho	A coming together, whether in the physical world, or between the divide of your own heart and mind.
Sowilo	Your essential self is the course of your vitality. The fire of your soul forges a new unity.

Rune	Meaning
Thurisaz	Contemplate your past before continuing on to succeed. Review your past closely, bless it and let it go.
Tewaz	The warrior spirit — courage and dedication temper your drive to conquer with honor and devotion.
Uruz	You may have suffered the loss of something dear. This is natural, let go, accept, and awaken your heart.
Wunjo	Safe and secure, you can finally relax. You have the clarity and productivity to rebalance and renew.

THE GAME OF LIFE

The Game of Life can be used for divination as well as spellcraft. Some Cabot Witches keep one checkerboard for the altar for manifestation, while the other is for divination only. But many will use the same board for both. For divination, you will need to create a set of personal symbols and charms to be used on it. Examples include:

New Moon — New Beginnings, Answers Coming on the New Moon.

Full Moon — Manifestation, Might Manifest by the Full Moon

Pentacle — Protection, Wisdom

Crown — Sovereignty, Your Decision, Your Control of the Situation

Scales — Balance, Justice

Ring — Engagement, Majick Circle Ritual

Heart — Love, Relationship

Sword — Excalibur, Sword of Light, Truth

Labyrinth — Find Your Own Way

Cup — Libation, Offering, Love, Relationships, Fulfillment, Birth, Wedding, Good Luck

Apple — Avalon, Passing Into the Otherworld, Message from the Otherworld, Faeries

Coin — Wealth, Prosperity

Ankh — Life, Reincarnation

Gold Chain — Solar Power, Healing, Strength, Links Symbols Together

Silver Chain — Lunar Power, Sensitivity, Psyche, Majick, Links Symbols Together

Picture of Car/Boat/Plane — Travel

Eye of Horus — Power of the Egyptian Gods, Protection, Majick

Black Feather — Someone Doing Evil Who Needs to be Found Out

Planetary Symbols — Found in the Planetary Correspondence Section

Runes — Found in the Rune Correspondence Section

Tumbled Stones — Found in the Correspondence of Stones Section

Chess Pieces — Different pieces, such as King or Queen, represent different forces. I use the King and Queen as the God and Goddess, and the other pieces for the Ancient Ones.

Photo of Yourself as a Child — Inner Child

Photo of Yourself as an Adult — Personal Self, Ego

Various Amulets, Talismans and Other Charms

To gain guidance, grab a handful of the pieces, ask your question, and drop them on the board. Let them fall and scatter. Don't be afraid to let them fall in a random pattern. Those that fall off the board have no significance. Then look to what is left on the board and what is next to each other. Interpret them based upon what pieces fall, and where they fall. Is a particular symbol on a black square, or a white square? Is it on the left side, meaning it is coming towards you? Is it in the center, or presently with you? Is it on the right side and moving away from you? Interpreting the Game of Life is an art in and of itself. Use your intuition.

HEALING WITH MAJICK: TOOLS, WANDS, AND SPELLS

While much of our psychic healing is taught in Witchcraft One, we can enhance our healing majick by learning how to add tools such as the majick wand, as well as healing spells, to our practice. The tools and spells amplify the healing we have already learned through alpha level. Alpha is the key, but these tools supplement our natural psychic healing skills.

Dowsing Diagnosis

You can diagnosis where an illness is in the body by having a client lie down upon a table or the floor. Taking your cleared and charged pendulum, start at the top of the head, asking for the source of the illness to be revealed. Move slowly over the body, looking for areas where the pendulum reacts. When you believe you have found an area of illness, you can ask yes-no questions to discover if this is the right place, and then try to determine the nature of the illness.

You can also place a pendulum over each of the chakras and ask if that chakra is healthy? Balanced? At full energy? If not, you can use the pendulum to help. If a "no" pendulum response is usually a counterclockwise movement, you can ask your healing spirit guides to help you heal, balance, and energize the chakra by then moving the pendulum clockwise. Some Witches simply ask to balance, heal, and energize the chakra and let the pendulum move in whatever manner it does to heal. Then ask the pendulum if that charka is as healed as much as it can be at this time, and move onto the next. You can start at the crown and work your way down, or at the feet and work your way up.

Ideally, the pendulum should be weighted by a crystal; a quartz crystal point is best for this kind of healing work.

Majick Wand Diagnosis and Healing

You can have a majick wand specific for healing and diagnosis. Clear and charge the wand for diagnosis and healing, and like the pendulum, move slowly over the body with a light grip, with the intention of finding the illness within the client. Pass the wand, held horizontally, over the body to look for spots of illness and imbalance. The wand will either dip down as you move, or will feel "stuck" as if moving through a viscous liquid over that part of the body. You can then point the wand at that area, and use the wand to magnify your healing light energy. Hold your Instant Alpha Trigger and focus on that area with the healing wand for as long as you feel it is appropriate.

Ideally such healing wands are tipped with a quartz crystal point to help focus and magnify the healing light.

Healing Spells

Healing spells can be used in conjunction with our psychic healing techniques of sending light and energy. Like other spellwork, these rituals use the art and science of correspondence to bring healing. One of the primary majickal correspondences for physical health is the Sun, bringing vitality and well-being with its golden yellow light. Use and adapt these spells for your own healing needs and to help others.

Healing Oil

1 Dram of Almond Oil
5 Drops of Bergamot Essential Oil
3 Drops of Orange Essential Oil

1 Drop of Chamomile Essential Oil
1 Clear Quartz Stone
1 Piece of Gold

Healing Candle Spell

Metallic Gold Candle (Can Substitute with Orange or Yellow Candle)
Black Candle
Gold Chain
Healing Oil
Carnelian
Photo of the Person to be Healed

This candle spell works well for healing on all levels and many different conditions. While in a majick circle, cleanse and charge all items for healing. Anoint the candles, chain, and stone with Healing Oil. Light the black candle to draw in energy for healing and place it on the left of the photo. Place the gold candle charged for healing on the right of the photo. Connect the two candles with the gold chain, going over the photo. Place the charged carnelian over the photo as well, for healing. Recite this spell three times:

By the Rays of the Sun
And the light of the Moon
Father Sun and Mother Earth will heal you soon!

When the candles have burned away, give the stone to the healing recipient to carry in the left pocket until fully healed.

Healing Cord

7 Feet of Orange Cord
7 Feet of Yellow Cord
7 Feet of Gold (or White) Cord
Various Majick Bags (yellow, orange, gold, green, and white filled with healing herbs such as calendula, chamomile, frankincense, myrrh, and vervain)
Carnelian
Citrine

Emerald

Ribbon

Glue

Sun Tarot Card

Strength Tarot Card

Moon Tarot Card

Any Charms That Symbolize Healing (Caduceus, Equal Arm Cross, Gold Pentacle, Etcetera)

You can do this spell on a Waxing Moon to bring health and increase the healing, or a waning Moon to remove any illness. Ideally it is done on a Sunday, in the hour of the Sun.

Braid the three cords together and make a loop at the top with a knot, to be able to hang your majick cord. When you tie the top knot, tie it with the intention of healing, based upon the phase of the Moon you are working in. Then repeat with a healing knot in the middle of the cord, and a healing knot at the bottom. Punch a hole in the cards to pass a ribbon through, or tape the ribbon to the back of the card to hang each of the three cards, equally spaced, with the Sun at the top, Strength in the Middle, and the Moon at the bottom.

Glue the three stones upon the cord, perhaps on or near the three knots. Then creatively hang the bags of healing herbs and other charms upon the cord, infusing each with the intention of healing. Change the entire cord in a majick circle for the recipient and instruct them to hang it in a prominent place in the home or office, where they will see it every day and be infused with the energy of healing.

BORROWED MAJICK

Borrowed majick refers to any majick that is from an outside culture. With a thorough understanding, Cabot Witches can borrow majick from other systems and cultures successfully, as long as we understanding it and express that it be used for the highest good, harming none. While we see our Witchcraft as Celtic, we can draw upon the system of majick from the Greeks, Romans, Egyptians, Hebrews, Africans, and Native Americans. I myself have had a deep kinship with the Egyptian traditions, and there are historic links between the Egyptians and the Scots, as well as a love of the Voodoun traditions through the Salem Witch Tituba. Once you understand your own majick and its principles, you can successfully and safely borrow majick from other cultures.

THE MOONS OF THE LUNAR YEAR

Witches celebrate each of the Moons, in what is known among some as an esbat, or Moon ceremony. Most lunar majick circles are for the Full Moon, but the Dark or New Moon can also be celebrated. The Full Moon is one of the best times for spellcasting, so Witches tend to gather on that night.

Each of the Moons is associated with a folk name and has a different character. Different traditions use different folk names, based upon their location, weather, and culture. These are the names we use:

Moon	Full Moon Sign	Sun Sign	Usual Month(s)	Majick
Seed Moon	Libra	Aries	March/April	Planting Seeds for Future Goals, Germination of Plans
Hare Moon	Scorpio	Taurus	April/May	Fertility, Prosperity, Shapeshifting, Fast Majick
Rose Moon	Sagittarius	Gemini	May/June	Love, Mysteries, Coming into Bloom/Power
Mead Moon	Capricorn	Cancer	June/July	Celebration of "Honeymoon," Sweetness of Life, Abundance
Wort Moon	Aquarius	Leo	July/August	Healing, Medicine, Creativity, Inspiration
Harvest Moon	Pisces	Virgo	August/September	Manifestations, Results, Abundance, Satisfaction
Blood Moon	Aries	Libra	September/October	Release, Ancestors, Divination, Planning for the Future
Snow Moon	Taurus	Scorpio	October/November	Manifesting our dreams, Stillness, Clarity
Oak Moon	Gemini	Sagittarius	November/December	Strength, Guidance, Straight Talk, Leadership
Wolf Moon	Cancer	Capricorn	December/January	Protection, Learning, Family, Health
Storm Moon	Leo	Aquarius	January/February	Change, Energy, Chaos, Inspiration, Power
Crow Moon	Virgo	Pisces	February/March	Mystery, Majick, Light from Darkness, Psychic, Endings and New Beginnings

Use these associations to plan your own lunar celebrations and majick circles. There is more on calculating your Tree Sign Birth Chart in the Third Degree section.

THE WHEEL OF THE YEAR

Modern Witches celebrate eight holy days, also known as sabbats. Four of the sabbats are known as fire festivals and are traditional Celtic holy days occurring in the center of the seasons. They start with Samhain, considered to be both the start of "winter" and the "New Year" for Witches, and continue onward through Imbolc, Beltane and Lughnassadh. Each of the fire festivals occurs when the Sun is in one of the fixed signs of the zodiac. Between them are the solar holidays; these have more Nordic and Saxon flavor in their practice, having two equinoxes and two solstices. The solar holidays occur when the Sun is moving from a mutable sign in the zodiac to a cardinal sign, initiating a new season. Together, the Wheel of the Year's eight holidays (in order) are Samhain, Yule (Winter Solstice), Imbolc, Ostara (Vernal Equinox), Beltane, Litha (Summer Solstice), Lughnassadh, Mabon (Autumn Equinox) and back to Samhain again.

In the mythos, we see half the year as waxing, or growing in light and life force, from Yule to Litha, and then half the year waning, or diminishing in light and life force, Litha to Yule again. Celtic Tradition tells us the Oak King rules the waxing half of the year, while the Holly King rules the waning half of the year, both in service to the Great Mother Goddess. The two kings are actually both sides of the God, who is born at Yule, unites in ecstasy with the rejuvenated goddess at Beltane, is sacrificed at the harvest of Lughnassadh and returns to the underworld by Samhain, to be born again.

Sabbat	Appox. Date	Zodiac	Themes
Samhain	October 31st	Scorpio	Ancestors, Underworld, Divination
Yule	December 21st	Sagittarius – Capricorn	Rebirth, Light Returning
Imbolc	February 2nd	Aquarius	Awakening, Cleansing
Ostara	March 21st	Pisces – Aries	Rising of Flowers, Return
Beltane	May 1st	Taurus	Ecstasy, Sexuality, Fertility

Sabbat	Appox. Date	Zodiac	Themes
Litha	June 21st	Gemini – Cancer	Peak of Power, Faery Twilight
Lughnassadh	August 1st	Leo	Harvest, Sacrifice, Grain
Mabon	September 22nd	Virgo – Libra	Journey to the Underworld, Fruit

As new priestesses and priests of the Craft, we encourage Witches of the Second Degree to take part in the seasonal celebrations, and to understand the rhythms, cycles, and myths that are a part of our heritage as expressed in the changing seasons.

PRACTICE

To become proficient in our art, you must practice, practice, practice! Much like a musician or artist, you will not improve without practice. While alpha is the keystone for our majickal work and tradition, you should explore all majickal tools and skill. You can't be good at everything right off the bat. Some Witches are great psychics. Others are amazing potion makers. Some are called to do healing work. Others do wonderful readings with the tarot. We all have skills to explore. The more you practice, the more powerful you become to heal yourself, humankind, and the world. Sometimes our bodies are weaker than our majickal power. At these times it doesn't mean we can't use the energy and science of majick. If you don't have it already, move into alpha and pull in the appropriate energy. You can see it with the mind's eye.

THE ASTROLOGICAL NATAL CHART

The natal chart, also known as a birth chart, is the astrological "snapshot" of the sky the moment you were born, as viewed from where you are born. The chart is considered to be a "map" of the lessons of your life, with the placement of the planets and signs in the sky indicating specific challenges, blessings and lessons that will unfold in your life. Wise Witches get their astrological chart done by a qualified astrologer, who then "reads" or explains it to them to so that they may better understand their own lessons and how karma is working in the their lives. A clearer and more conscious understanding of our blessings and challenges helps us face them with more awareness and grace. Certain planets indicate the influence of karma in our lives, including the Moon, Saturn, and the Nodes of the Moon. Lessons are not always "punishment" for mistakes in past lives, but simply the process of working out all issues and experiencing all things, from life to life, so we can become more like the Divine Mind, that encompasses everything. This is our evolution. With each new life, we are given new lessons as indicated by the birth chart. If we are comfortable with the lessons and embrace them, they can empower us. We are here to learn the lessons, because some lessons can only be learned here, in a body, upon the Earth. It's a blessing to be here learning.

Transits show the relationship of the planets in the sky currently to the patterns in your natal chart. Reading the astrological transits can be like a daily reading of the coming changes in your life. Astrologers can prepare a transit chart for a specific period of time. Like a weather report, the transits help us prepare for what is coming, but our own free will can determine how we manifest the lessons, based up on our choices.

If you remember nothing else from your birth chart, commit to memory and understanding three things:

1. **Sun Sign** — This is your natal sign by month which most people know. Remember what element it is — fire, earth, air or water —and what that means, along with what quality it is, meaning cardinal, fixed and mutable. The Sun Sign gives you your areas of strength and weakness, and the parts of the body it rules will be places of gifts as well as illness or injury.
2. **Moon Sign** — The sign the Moon occupied when you were born indicates your emotional self, your inner secret self, and how you approach your majick and intuition. Like your Sun Sign, understand its element and quality.
3. **Rising Sign** — The Rising Sign is also known as the Ascendant, or the Cusp of the First House. It is the sign that was on the eastern horizon when you were born. It influences the relationship we have with ourselves, which is what the First House's area of learning is, but it is also how other people see us. Some call it our comfortable "mask" we wear to the world. If you are born during the night, the energy of the Rising Sign will be more apparent to people.

This is the primary "triad" of our chart that most Witches have memorized about them selves and use it to guide their lives.

If you look closely to my own chart, you can see that my primary triad is:

Sun Sign – Pisces

Moon Sign – Cancer

Rising Sign (Ascendant) – Gemini

My Sun Sign—who I am learning to be in this lifetime and where the core of my energy is—is in the sign of Pisces. Pisces is one of the most psychic signs of the zodiac. Pisces people are often dreamers and artistically creative. Pisces rules the feet within medical astrology and many Pisces, like me, have a love of dance and have been professional dancers. Pisces can have difficulty getting organized and grounded because we have such strong creative visions. It's easy to get lost in some of the romance and dreams. Pisces Sun Signs are empathic and can pick up on the feelings of others quite easily. That's why I need to surround myself with people who are happy and pursuing their own goals, though I tend to try to help out those who are having difficulty because I do empathize with them.

My Moon Sign is in Cancer, another strongly psychic and sensitive sign. The Moon is your inner emotional nature, the side people don't see. Cancer has the fierce goddess energy, as Cancer is the crab ruled by the Ocean Mother where all life arises. Cancer people have strong defenses and boundaries because they are more sensitive than people think. They also love their own homes and like to feel comfortable and safe in their home environment. My home is my sanctuary. I try to make people feel comfortable, loved, and accepted. Because of this, many people see me as a Mother figure, even those who are not my children.

The Rising Sign is the face the world sees, and my rising sign is Gemini. I think and speak quick on my feet, and I can be clever when needed. I tend to have a lot of different projects going on at once and like to do a lot of different things until I lose interest. Gemini rising gives me a lot of energy that I try to put to good use; otherwise I become restless. Thoughts and ideas fascinate me, though people think of me as more social and talkative in big groups and parties than I really am. Gemini rising helps me be an avid reader and eternal student. I always want to know more as I need to know the reasons behind things. That's why I studied the science of Witchcraft. I had to know how and why it worked. The Rising Sign also influences how you get to know yourself, so I get to know myself deeply through the inner dialogue, how I talk with myself. The twins are really about the two voices, the inner and outer.

ACTION VERSUS REACTION

Humankind is ruled by emotions. We often react rather than act. We need to learn to appropriately respond to a situation consciously, rather than react to it automatically and unconsciously. As a Witch you need to learn how to act and not react, especially with your majick. Otherwise you could be creating some difficult lessons.

Learn how to use your emotions and understand them. Keep your self-esteem high with the use of pink light. Everyone, but especially a Witch claiming more majickal power, needs to constantly work on self-esteem and appropriate action. Make sure you are keeping a journal and recording your thoughts and feelings for future reflection. You will notice how greatly you will change over time. Record keeping is vital for a Witch to use majickal power appropriately and understand the consequences of it. We can all change the world, but we have to start with a solid understanding of that greater inner power. Know that you have it, and that you can overcome most anything.

MAKING MISTAKES

Majick as a science includes trial and error. Nothing works 100% of the time. Everybody makes mistakes, both in terms of understanding and in personal behavior. What matters is how we make the mistake. Some mistakes are simply errors of understanding, and our majick does not work. Other mistakes must be owned up to, and we must take personal responsibility for them, correcting any harm we've done to ourselves and anyone else. We must learn from all our mistakes. There are no excuses. If you do something unethical or hurtful, you must understand the nature of it. If you don't understand what is wrong, go to an elder and seek counsel. You will not be judged, but admired for admitting your fault and your desire to fix the mistake and learn from it.

DEALING WITH DRAMA

Sadly in the Witchcraft world, we have to deal with personal drama from those around us in community. Drama happens not just in the Witchcraft and Pagan communities, of course, but in all communities. We must learn how to deal with it.

The way I deal with drama is simple. I usually close my eyes and shut my ears and walk away. I won't participate in the drama because I have better things to do. The problem is some people don't have anything better to do, and they create a dramatic life. Such people like to create controversy. It's almost motivation for them to live. They have no other motivation, unless somebody talks against them or gives them something to fight. It's really awful when you think about it. It's human nature to knee-jerk react to someone speaking against you. However, the best defense is to neutralize it simply by saying, "I can't accept what they're saying. They're really talking about themselves." Then turn around and walk away. Put your mind to something that is productive.

If you don't have something productive in your life, you must be careful because you will make a drama out of every little nuance of someone talking against you or making you feel bad. It's almost your motivation for getting up in the morning, because you don't have another motivation or identity. You don't have a goal in mind for your life. So you get out of bed in the morning, you have your cup of coffee, and you're on the phone with a friend saying, "You know what she said about me?" You see this behavior on television these days, on the so-called reality shows. It's absurd. "The Real Housewives of Hollywood" show is one big example. What a waste of time in their lives. They bicker and harm each other, all to create that drama. Obviously, the people don't have a purpose.

If you have a purpose in this lifetime, you will go towards that goal and ignore everything else. There are always naysayers. There's always one to say "Oh, you can't do that." "Oh yes I can" is my response. I can establish some kind of help for the poor. I can go work and help at an animal shelter. There's nothing to prevent me from doing that. There's always someone that will try to stop you from your goal. Tenacity is what you need. You must say, "No. This is my goal." My goal is not to argue with people every day of my life or to knee-jerk react to people's opinions. Those people also may not have something to do with their lives other than to create disharmony. You need to live your life in harmony, and ignoring those people who do this kind of damage is the best thing you can do.

BEING A WITCH IS 24/7

We do not play at being Witches. This is not something we do only on the weekend or when it is convenient. It's important to realize that to commit to the life of a Witch is to commit to being a Witch twenty-four hours a day, seven days a week. While we are human and have normal lives, loves and issues, we are also majickal and cannot forget our Witch soul at any point.

Majick is in everything we do. How we think and act matters. We are projecting all day, and we must be conscious of it and neutralize that which isn't for the good of all involved. It's a way of life, a way of being. You will integrate these ideas into your life as you continually practice and learn. Be mindful of all that you do.

THE CABOT TRADITION CODE OF ETHICS

One

We abide by the Threefold Law of Return: "An it harm none — do what ye will."

Two

Treat others in our tradition as you would like to be treated. We are Witch sisters and brothers.

Three

We recognize a Cabot Witch of any degree as a part of our tradition.

Four

Integrity, Discipline, and Respect must be self-evident in all our affairs as we represent our tradition.

Five

We practice our craft according to Hermetic Laws, and are accountable to the God/Goddess/All.

Six

We do not accept any outside contributions or any influences that would undermine our authority. We are a sovereign tradition. As such, we do not take part in the inner circles of other traditions.

Seven

Each Cabot Witch is sovereign and accepts the responsibility that this incurs.

Eight

We are committed to our way of life and firmly grounded in the science of our majick. We express our tradition as an Art, a Science, and a Religion.

Nine

We respect and adhere to the wishes of our Council of Elders.

Ten

Our tradition has an interest in issues such as ecology, hunger, and human rights. We seek to heal and protect our Mother Earth and better the lives of the humans and animals around us through majickal and charitable means.

Eleven

Our public relations policy is based on attraction rather than promotion; we do not proselytize. We do not seek to educate anyone who does seek knowledge from us.

Twelve

We place principles before personalities. We abstain from gossip and other behaviors that would undermine our brothers and sisters or our tradition. Our actions reinforce "for the good of all..."

Thirteen

We do not charge money for taking healing cases, but may charge for any type of psychic consulting to the public as a reader (for example, tarot).

— *Courtesy of James Cabot Daly, H.P.* —

BEING PRIESTESSES AND PRIESTS

Completing the Second Degree means you are a priestess or priest in the Cabot Tradition, capable of doing ritual for yourself, casting your own spells, and practicing the art of the Witch. Witches strive to be priests and priestesses, for we need no intermediary. Through our own meditations and rituals, we build relationships with the powers of the universe, and with our ancestors, guides, and deities. The torch of the majick circle, through the wand of the Witch, is passed to you. You now have a responsibility to manifest the life you need and want. You have the skills, the tools of our art. You must take responsibility. It is only through taking responsibility for your own healing, feelings, and ultimately life, that you can then learn to serve the greater good. We must first find balance in ourselves. Then, from this place of balance, we can seek the mysteries of the religion of the Craft, and become High Priestesses and High Priests.

CIRCLES, COVENS, TEMPLES AND TRADITIONS

Witches often practice in groups, and different kinds of groups indicate different kinds of relationships. Cabot Witches form these groups to practice their majick together. A circle is a group of peers and practitioners coming together at certain times. A circle is considered less formal than a coven.

A coven is a group of Witches dedicated to the work of the group and to each other, usually lead by a High Priestess or High Priest, or one of each in tandem. The coven meets regularly to do majick, to study, and to explore the mysteries. My own former coven, the Black Doves of Isis, worked regularly and helped me establish much of the tradition and community of Cabot Witchcraft.

A temple is a publicly recognized community and group, just as the ancient Pagan temples were in days past. The Cabot-Kent Hermetic Temple is a state and federally recognized religious Temple, consisting of the community of Cabot Witches, with the same rights and responsibilities as other religious groups. Prior to this, the Cabot Witchcraft community had been involved in the Temple of Nine Wells, an affiliate of the Aquarian Tabernacle Church.

A tradition is a body of practitioners with a shared body of practices, rituals, mythos, and lineage. The Cabot Tradition comes from the lineage of the Witches of Kent, and is one of the modern traditions of Witchcraft today established fully in the public eye and available to seekers.

THE CABOT ROBE

Cabot Witches have their own style of robes used in ritual. Those who complete the Second Degree are entitled to wear these robes and can put them with the sash of the first degree. The robe is of simple black, and is later "piped" with Royal Steward Plaid at the sleeves upon the completion of the Third Degree, matching the sash, and the inner sleeve is then lined with red. In earlier patterns of the Cabot Tradition, a pentacle ring was also a common sign of the Second Degree, but now the ring is a favored tool for those of the Third Degree.

THE CABOT ACADEMY OF WITCHCRAFT

The Cabot Tradition, prior to the establishment of the Cabot-Kent Hermetic Temple (and still separate from it), created a branch of education for Cabot Witches, helping them explore more deeply topics that are beyond the immediate scope of the First and Second Degrees, that really are introduced but require lifelong study. Cabot Academy classes provide education in these areas from trained Cabot priestesses and priests, as well as honored guests. You can use the topics as a guide in your own exploration and training.

- Astrology
- Tarot
- Green Environmental Ministry
- Women's Spirituality
- Healing
- Psychic Readings & Mediumship
- Faery Lore
- Celtic Studies
- Numerology
- Herbology
- Crafting
- Ministerial Skills

THE CABOT TRADITION CREST

In Britain and parts of Europe, there is a tradition of the family or clan shields, a heraldic coat of arms consisting of the family "motto" and animal "supporters" distinguishing the family or clan by demonstrating its mythic history, lore, and support.

The Cabot Crest—or the Cat, Crow and Crown shield design—embodies many of the elements important in the Cabot "Clan" and tradition. As many High Priestesses and High Priests take Cabot as their middle name upon initiation, it is important to understanding the meaning and culture of our tradition.

Cabot Crest

The shield itself is half checkerboard, indicating the Game of Life. The other half is a gold pentacle upon a red background, the symbols of majick, power, and success. At the top of the shield is the Triple Moon sign of the waxing crescent, Full Moon circle, and waning crescent. Flanking the shield are the familiars of the crow and the cat, each known for their association with majick and Witchcraft. The crow is the keeper of the sacred law and the inner mysteries. Within its claw is the pentacle, a sign of the Witch and our majick. The cat is the psychic companion and sacred to the ancients for their Otherworldly insight and intuition. At the top of the whole design is the crown, a symbol of sovereignty, the right to "reign" in our own individual lives and majick.

PREPARATION FOR THE THIRD DEGREE

We expect a Witch to be proficient in the Art of the Craft, as well as practicing alpha regularly, if not daily, and developing a meditation practice and psychic skills. The bridge one must cross between Witchcraft II and Witchcraft III is the development of our science and art into a deeper spirituality of self-introspection and a desire to serve a greater good.

To help facilitate that bridge, we have several teachings and rituals helpful in making that transformation. They are:

- The Mystery of the Cracked Cauldron
- The Teachings of the Elemental Dragons
- The Brew of *Awen* Ritual

The Mystery of the Cracked Cauldron

One of the mysteries in the tale of Taleisin is to ask, after he took the three drops of *awen,* why did the cauldron crack in two? Why did the remaining potion become poisonous? Why did the horses of Gwyddno, who is the father of Elphin, die? And why was Elphin the one to find the newly born Taliesin?

There are all powerful questions, worthy of reflection. In essence, the tale teaches us about what we might call karma, the consequences of our actions, and how all things move to bring balance to our actions. Through the initiation of the three drops, Gwion is released from much of his old life. But the energies of the life must go somewhere. They go into the cauldron, and being too much, they crack the cauldron and potentially poison the land and animals. As a greater initiate into the mysteries, Gwion, now Taliesin, must take responsibility for what his past self has done, even unintentionally. He had no malice towards the horses. But their death was the consequence of his three drops. Before he went on to further greatness, he must rectify things with the house of Gwyddno, and to do this, helps elevate Elphin.

As those seeking initiation into the mysteries, into our tradition, we too must take responsibility to clear and heal ourselves so we can better serve. Through some simple additions to the Waters of Life sacrament, we can add a further dimension to it and help prepare ourselves and continue to clear and heal as we become High Priestesses and High Priests.

Once you have taken your three drops from the thumb to the lips, pour out a small amount of water in a libation offering bowl, or if outside, directly upon the ground, as a libation to the Gods and Ancient Ones, silently giving thanks for all blessings, people, and lessons in your life. Make sure to leave some water still in the chalice.

Then take a pinch of salt or a small stone and think about all that must be released, healed, and transformed within you. Sprinkle the salt or drop the stone into the chalice with the remaining water. Hold it in both hands, and imagine filling the chalice with all that does not serve your highest good inside you. The salt or the stone is holding and neutralizing it.

Replace the chalice on the left side of the altar.

When done your ritual, pour your libation bowl out to the land for the Gods and Ancient Ones.

Pour the remaining chalice water in a different place, and ask the Earth to transform what doesn't serve within you anymore as this water is transformed.

In essence, this addition expands the sacrament and gives it a three-fold purpose:

- **Drinking** — Rejuvenation and Inspiration with the Three Drops enters into you. This will continue to revitalize you and bring you greater levels of creativity and majick.
- **Libation** — Gratitude and Thanks to the Gods and Ancient Ones. Gratitude and thanks is a powerful key to the deeper mysteries and to self healing.
- **Release** — The transmutation and pouring out of the poisons, with the dregs returned to the Earth.

Make this a part of every majick circle you cast as you prepare for the Third Degree.

Elemental Dragon Meditation

Start by deciding which of the four dragons you wish to visit. When you decide, sit facing the appropriate direction of that dragon.

Direction	Element	Lair	Gem	Metals	Teaching
North	Earth	Cave Deep within a Mountain	Emerald	Copper & Lead	Sovereignty
East	Fire	Cave within a Volcano Crater	Ruby	Gold & Iron	Destiny
South	Air	Cloudy Castle High upon a Cliff	Yellow Topaz	Liquid Quicksilver	Truth
West	Water	Hidden Grotto by the Sea	Aquamarine	Silver & Tin	Compassion

Enter into alpha level through the use of the Crystal Countdown. Start by using the Crystal Door meditation to travel in the direction you are facing. Go far outward, and when you open the door, find yourself before that dragon's lair. It will be in the appropriate environment for that dragon's element.

You will feel yourself welcomed in to this place. Respectfully explore and seek out the dragon master of the element you have chosen.

You will find the dragon resting in its cavern deep within the lair. The dragon is upon a pile of metallic treasure appropriate for its element. The dragon will be clutching a rather large gem.

Introduce yourself to this dragon, and ask to learn about the lessons of its element. The dragon will speak and show you more about its own teaching and how it relates to the element. The dragon might show you one of the four elemental tools— the wand, cup, blade or stone, the one appropriate for its teaching.

The dragon might shine the light of its gem upon you, granting you an attunement to that elemental power and blessing, or even, if you are fortunate, place a small part of the gem within you, not unlike your Emerald Tablet of the left hand. The dragon might even offer you a part of its metallic horde, something to take with you and meditate upon in your majick room. If you are offered a gift, you should also reach within yourself and make an offering to the dragon as a thank you.

When your experience is complete, return through the Crystal Door, coming back to your awareness in your body. Give yourself clearance and balance and count up from alpha to beta level. Over the next few days and weeks, repeat this exercise with each of the dragons, and go back to the dragons to visit them, ask for advice and counsel, and get deeper teaching on elemental majick and personal development.

Brew of Awen Ritual

Brew a potion of *awen* from safe, ingestible herbs. Consult a medical herbal, or health care professional, to make sure you choose herbs safe and effective for your own health and well-being, particularly if you have any health problems, injuries, or are on any prescription medicines. If you want to be especially cautious, stick to culinary herbs, popular herbal teas, and kitchen spices. You will only be having three drops of the brew, so there is little chance any nontoxic herb will harm you at that dose, unless you suffer from an allergy.

Your only requirement is that the potion requires twelve edible ingredients, one ruled by each sign of the zodiac, for Cerridwen spent a year and a day collecting her herbs and flowers at the proper time. Choosing the herbs is part of the test of this ritual. Will your formula be balanced and work? Put just a pinch of salt, for the salty sea foam said to be used in the brew, along with honey and malted grains. Brew the mix like you would a water-based potion. Use this potion in your chalice.

Cast a majick circle, and for the four quarter guardians, use the totems of Gwion Bach, Cerridwen's servant. Write your own poetic quarter calls for each direction. Note one totem is not an animal, but a plant eaten by an animal—wheat.

Earth	Wheat
Fire	Hare
Air	Wren
Water	Salmon

Perform the Waters of Life Sacrament and the Cracked Cauldron. Taste the potion with the three drops. Go deeper into alpha, and go to each of the quarter guardians, starting with the Hare in the east, then Wren in the south, Salmon in the west, and Grain in the north, asking each in turn for wisdom and blessings. What do they say or do with you? In the center, you might even encounter the bard Taliesin, or the goddess Cerridwen. Dwell as long as needed in this meditation.

When done, close the circle normally. Do any other spells or projections, thank the gods, release the quarters, and release the circle.

* * *

The following are the requirements for those seeking to go on from Witchcraft II to take Witchcraft III in the Cabot Tradition. Prerequisites need to be completed and will be monitored before petitioning for WCIII. The work needed in order to petition will take six to twelve months to complete. All tasks must be done in the order listed. In other words, do not submit a petition for WCIII before you have done the work and have a recommendation from a small selection of Cabot Elders. Proof of the work done must be sent to all five Mentors/Elders monitoring you by submitting your work to our private emails provided. Evidence of your work would be pictures of your finished product and a write-up of the majick information that was gathered to complete the task. Tasks are from Rev. Laurie as listed here, and from your chosen Mentor/Elder that you'll be working with. Simple examples are provided below the task assigned by Rev. Mother, but it's up to the student to research and do the work.

All tasks need to have an explanation of use of color, number, herbs, oils, god/dess, date and time done, plus a description of astrological influences, include the phase of the Moon, used. Most importantly, the student must explain why all these aspects were chosen for the work done.

- Make a Talisman or Charm Bag
- Make a Witches Cord of Nine Knots
- Make Three Potions (potions can be made with oil or water as a base)
- Simple Candle Spell
- Pick an approved Mentor to mentor you.

- Write an essay on the story of the Cracked Cauldron of Cerridwen and Taliesin. Explain how this story pertains to our ritual today from calling quarters to the waters of life. Make sure this is in your own words and not copied from any source.
- Write and perform eight sabbats, one Full Moon and one New Moon esbat in the Cabot tradition style from beginning to end by yourself. Record it for Elders' viewing. Again, provide an explanation of your correspondences, timing, and imagery.
- Attend a minimum of four Cabot public rituals. Absolutely no one will be accepted in WCIII without this being done.
- Commit to a community service whether it's once a week, bi-weekly, or a commitment to take on a several Temple tasks (for example, setting up for rituals or storage, creating decorations, fundraising, writing for newsletter, etcetera).
- Complete all tasks assigned by your chosen Elder in the manner and timing in which they require it.
- Read ten required books (your choice) and write a four-paragraph essay pertaining to the basis of each book, so we know it was read and generally understood.

When all your tasks are completed, you may give them to all Elders associated with WCIII for review. These Elders will not alter your work or grade you, but merely review and reflect. Your chosen Elder will then choose to either write a letter of recommendation, or pass it on to another Elder for further review. This means you may receive tasks from a second, not chosen Elder, in order to receive a recommendation. All marks and comments by Elders will be noted.

After all work is done and a recommendation letter from an Elder is completed, only then do you submit a petition letter stating your desire for the Third Degree Class. All petitions submitted before this is complete are voided.

CABOT TRADITION WITCHCRAFT III RELIGION CLASS PETITION

Full Legal Name:

Address:

Phone:

Email:

Date of Graduation from Witchcraft II:

Teacher of Witchcraft II:

Location of Class:

Requirement Check List

- Pick an approved Mentor. Complete all tasks assigned by your chosen Elder in the manner and time in which they require it
- Keep a regular practice of alpha meditation, self-esteem work and psychic development
- Keep a regular journal and majickal Book of Shadows
- Write and perform eight sabbats, one Full Moon and one New Moon esbat in the Cabot tradition style from beginning to end by yourself. Record it for Elders' viewing.
- Attend a minimum of four Cabot public rituals.
- Perform a successful Candle Spell
- Make a Witches Cord of Nine Knots
- Make a Talisman or Charm Bag
- Make Three Different Potions (water or oil based)
- Write an essay on the story of the Cracked Cauldron of Cerridwen and Taliesin. Explain how this story pertains to our ritual today from calling quarters to the waters of life.
- Meditate with the Four Elemental Dragons. Ask them for help in your life.

- Complete the Cerridwen Cauldron Brew of *Awen* Ritual
- Complete and Submit Petition for Witchcraft III to the Cabot Council of Elders
- Commit to a community service whether its once a week, bi-weekly, or taking on Temple task.
- Reading list. Read ten required books of your choice from the list and write a four-paragraph essay on each pertaining to the basis of the book, so we know it was read and understood.

Questions

1. In one thousand words or less, describe why you want to take The Cabot Tradition Witchcraft III Religion Class.

2. Describe your experiences with the Witchcraft I alpha meditation and psychic development work.

3. Describe your experiences with The Witchcraft II spellwork.

WITCHCRAFT II: WITCHCRAFT AS AN ART
RECOMMENDED READING LIST

Power of the Witch by Laurie Cabot*

Love Magic by Laurie Cabot*

Laurie Cabot's Book of Spells & Enchantments by Laurie Cabot with Penny Cabot & Christopher Penczak*

Herbal Magic by Laurie Cabot*

The Outer Temple of Witchcraft by Christopher Penczak*

The Witch's Heart by Christopher Penczak

The Witch's Coin by Christopher Penczak

True Magick by Amber K

The Master Book of Herbalism by Paul Beyerl*

Gem and Mineral Lore by Paul V. Beyerl

A Compendium of Herbal Magic by Paul Beyerl

The Symbols and Magick of Tarot by Paul V. Beyerl

Painless Astrology by Rev. Paul V. Beyerl

Encyclopedia of Magical Herbs by Scott Cunningham*

Cunningham's Encyclopedia of Crystal, Gem & Metal Magic by Scott Cunningham *

The Complete Book of Incense, Oils and Brews by Scott Cunningham

The Magic in Food by Scott Cunningham

The Magical Household by Scott Cunningham

The Art of Divination by Scott Cunningham

Culpepper's Complete Herbal by Nicholas Culpeper

Egyptian Magic by E.A. Wallis Budge

Tarot for Your Self by Mary K. Greer

Witchcraft for Tomorrow by Doreen Valiente

Dictionary of Symbols by Juan Eduardo Cirlot

Rune Lore by Edred Thorsson

The Complete Book of Witchcraft by Raymond Buckland

Practical Candleburning Rituals by Raymond Buckland

Scottish Witchcraft by Raymond Buckland

Everyday Magic by Dorothy Morrison

The Encyclopedia of 5,000 Spells by Judika Illes

Moon Magick by D.J. Conway

Rosemary Gladstar's Medicinal Herbs by Rosemary Gladstar

The World Atlas of Divination by J. Mathews

* Required Reading for the Second Degree

Third Degree: Witchcraft as a Religion

Becoming a High Priestess or High Priest

Receiving the Sword and Questing for Mystery

Serving through the Grail

Witchcraft is a Science, Art, and Religion, and the Cabot Tradition culminates in the religious training of the Witch. All Witches are priestesses and priests of their own art. To take the Third Degree means to serve not only as clergy for oneself, but to answer a higher calling to serve the land, the planet, the gods, and our people.

The knowledge a High Priestess and High Priest must learn, and the wisdom such a minister must embody, is vast. The changing nature of the Third Degree over the last thirty or more years has reflected the scope of these needs. Currently, we divide the Third Degree into three separate "rings" or teaching cycles. Each teaching cycle is important, and some people attempt to do all three in the year and a day, but the separation gives students a chance to rest and reflect before petitioning for initiation. The three cycles are:

- Twelve Lessons in the Religion of Witchcraft
- Nine Lessons on the Mystery and Myths of the Wheel of the Year
- Guidelines in Clergy Training from a Six-Lesson Clergy Course

The first cycle is what many have learned, more or less, in the Cabot Third Degree in the past. We emphasized the importance of the Wheel of the Year and providing rituals for the community at large. Exploring both cycles at once, fully, is an immense task. And to these two cycles, we've added further training on the role of public ministry, from rites of passage rituals to more active care and aid to fellow Witches and the community at large.

The three-cycle approach is broken down even further into three sections. We approach these teachings much like we approach the Craft itself—as a science, art, and religion.

- **Academics and Research:** This is the science of our training. We expect Witches to be well-educated and to understand the origins and meanings of the topics presented, and when a question arises, to be able to research the understandings and conclusions of academics past and present, then make their own decisions based upon their research. Because we have these requirements, Witchcraft III students are required to complete homework and research papers.

- **Ritual Construction and Prose:** This is the art of our training. We must be able to use what we learn academically, to bring it alive and make it vital for what we are doing here and now. It must inspire our majick. Students are expected to perform rituals on their own, in class, and as a ministry to the public.

- **Meditations to Learn, Honor, and Transform:** This constitutes our religious training in each cycle. We use the science of alpha to contact and communicate with the higher and deeper powers, and learn to travel to different dimensions of consciousness and points in time, each to illuminate our understanding of our majick and path. Students will perform meditations in class, as well as be expected to keep a regular practice of alpha in their daily life.

Potential students must be self-motivated, as there is no hand-holding here. The scope and time commitment of these trainings together is akin to a college-level program. With a thorough understanding of all three cycles, on all three levels, you can be prepared for initiation and the role of ordained clergy.

I.
The Religion of Witchcraft

One:

Introduction to the Powers, Patterns, and Purpose of the Cabot Tradition

Exercise: Introduction to the Spiritual Powers of the Cabot Tradition in Majick Circle, Advanced Apple Meditation, and the Silver Branch

Tools for Class: Athame for Students, Sword for Teacher

Two:

The Chase of the Four Elements

Exercise: The Chase of Gwion Bach

Tools for Class: Four Elemental Tools, Cauldron in the Center

Three:

The Gods of Witchcraft

Exercise: God and Goddess Meditation

Tools for Class: Deity Altar

Four:

The Expanded Science of Witchcraft

Exercise: Astral Exploration of the Solar System and Galaxy

Tools for Class: Yellow Gold Candle, Stone for Each of the Planets

Five:

The Religion of Witchcraft

Exercise: Time Travel to the Ancient Past

Tools for Class: Quartz Crystal

Six:

The Powers of the Earth

Exercises: Stone Consecration and Land Homecoming Meditation

Tools for Class: Personal Altar Stone for Students, Cabot Lia Fal from Teacher in Majick Circle

Seven:

Faery Majick

Exercise: Faery Contact Meditation

Tools for Class: Wooden Wand for Students in Majick Circle, Faery Offerings

Eight:

Ancestral Realm and Past Lives

Exercise: Ancestral Memory Meditation

Tools for Class: Cup for Students, Lancets from Teacher in Majick Circle, Cauldron, Herbs, Stones, Sea Salt

Nine:

The Creation of the Cosmos

Exercise: Root Races Meditation

Tools for Class: Cauldron, Symbols of Our Ancient Past

Ten:

Rebirth of the Witch

Exercise: Taliesin Rebirth Ritual

Tools for Class: Veil of Black or Dark Cloth in Majick Circle, Chalice

Eleven:

Preparation for the Grail Quest

Exercise: Time of Silence

Tools for Class: Veil of Black or Dark Cloth, or Hooded Robe In Majick Circle

Twelve:

Whom Does the Grail Serve?

Exercise: Grail Castle Ritual in Majick Circle

Tools for Class: Ashes from the Grail Quest Journal from Students, Cauldron for Ashes from Teacher

Notice four of the lessons—classes one, five, seven and eight—make use of the classic tools of the Witch (the blade, stone, wand and cup respectively), culminating with a mystery of the Holy Grail.

ONE: INTRODUCTION TO THE POWERS, PATTERNS, AND PURPOSE OF THE CABOT TRADITION AND THE BLADE

Knowest thou aught of Mabon son of Modron,
who was taken away from his mother when three nights old?
— Culhwch and Olwen from *The Mabinogion*

POWERS OF THE CABOT TRADITION

In the religion of Witchcraft, we work with the spiritual powers of our tradition. The Cabot Tradition focuses on the Indo-European connections of the Witch, but specifically looks to Celtic myth and majick as our guide. We work with the goddesses and gods of the Celtic people, and the best known surviving myths of the major goddesses and gods are the Irish, Welsh and Scottish myths, with guidance from Gaulish sources. We work with the heroes, the enlightened and Mighty Ones of the Arthurian Tradition. The tales of Arthur encode vast secrets of the lands and Faery beings. We work with the Faery folk, the Good People, and believe that all Witches carry the Faery blood. We are family to the People of Peace. I was taught this by my teacher, as part of our lineage to the Witches of Kent. We look to the spirits of our ancestors, of blood and tradition, and in particular to the ancient Witches who have come before us. We look to all of nature, and to the spirits of nature—the animal powers, plant spirits, land spirits, star spirits, and guides—as our allies. We look to evoke the spiritual reality of Tara in Ireland and Avalon in Arthurian myth within our hearts, minds, and bodies.

TOTEMS OF THE CABOT TRADITION

Every majickal tradition has the powers aligned with it. Each tradition is unique because it is a unique alignment of spiritual powers. It draws from a current of energy from its ancestors, culture, and sacred sites. It has guardians in the form of deities, spirits, and totemic powers. The totems, or power allies, are the ones that help guide and guard the tradition, becoming inner teachers, healers ,and messengers.

While we work with many different animals, three prominent animal spirits for us are the Cat, the Crow, and the Wolf.

Cat

The Cat is the Witch's familiar, the keeper of the psychic mysteries and the one to help us tune into our own intuitive and majickal nature.

Crow

The Crow is the teacher of sacred wisdom and the mysteries of majick. The Crow is the harbinger of justice and sovereignty.

Wolf

The Wolf is the protector of the clan of the pack, and the teacher of the ancient ways.

Likewise, we see the plants to be wise spirits, and the two prominent tree spirits of the Cabot Clan are the Apple and the Oak. And from the plants themselves, the Rose is the prominent plant spirit teacher.

Apple

The Apple Tree is the Faery tree of Avalon, associated with the Fortunate Isles of the Otherworld. Apple is a healer of the body and soul, and teaches us how to love, protect, and open to the spirits of the Otherworld. Within the Apple is hidden the pentagram, formed by its seeds.

Oak

Oak is the tree of the Druids, and is the world tree of our people. It connects the Heavens, Earth, and Underworld. It is a tree of great wisdom and power. It grants strength and attracts lightning. Mistletoe growing upon it is the most holy plant, a gift from the gods.

Rose

Rose is the flower of the Goddess, coming in many shades and hues, though Red Rose, for the power of life and majick, is the most important of them all. Rose, at its heart, is five-petaled like the Tudor Rose, a symbol of the pentagram and of the Witch. The thorns and fruits show us the dangers and blessings of our majick.

And lastly from the mineral realm, powerful allies for us are Clear and Rose Quartz, as well as Lapis and Carnelian.

Clear Quartz

Clear Quartz, the stone that can refract the rainbow of the Crystal Countdown and serves as the stone of our Crystal Wheel, is the primary stone of the Cabot Tradition. Etheric Quartz points and spheres can be placed into the body for healing and empowerment, much like the Emerald Tablet.

Rose Quartz

Rose Quartz is the stone of the Pink Star, and of self-esteem and self-love. A titanium impurity in the quartz makes the formation of points difficult, but grants the rose quartz its beautiful and healing pink hue.

Lapis Lazuli

Lapis is the blessings of the Goddess, and also the blessings of Jupiter. The blue stone flecked with gold pyrite helps us evolve and enlighten with peace and prosperity.

Carnelian

Carnelian is a powerful healing stone, said to be the blood of the Goddess. Use it to help give you energy and vitality.

Work with these correspondences not only in spells and rituals, but also in your meditations and dreams. Call them to you in the Majick Room. Let them guide you and heal you. Find peace and power in their wisdom.

The Advanced Apple Meditation and the Silver Branch

Part of our work in the Third Degree of the Cabot Tradition is to go deeper. To do that, we work with guiding spirits of our clan. We review and continue to practice the basics, such as the seemingly simple Apple Meditation from Witchcraft I. To advance this exercise, we are going to work with the spirit of the Apple and one of its most powerful images from Celtic myth, the Silver Branch.

Like the Golden Bough of Greek myth, the Silver Branch is the Celtic "key" to the Otherworld. Nine bell-like silver apples hung from an apple branch, an apple wand, and the shaking of these apple bells would help open up the way to the spirit world, facilitating communion with the gods, faeries, and ancestors.

One day, in the neighborhood of his stronghold, Bran went about alone, when he heard music behind him. As often as he looked back, 'twas still behind him the music was. At last he fell asleep at the music, such was its sweetness. When he awoke from his sleep, he saw close by him a branch of silver with white blossoms, nor was it easy to distinguish its bloom from that branch. Then Bran took the branch in his hand to his royal house. When the hosts were in the royal house, they saw a woman in strange raiment on the floor of the house. 'Twas then she sang the fifty quatrains to Bran, while the host heard her, and all beheld the woman.

And she said:

A branch of the apple-tree from Emain
I bring, like those one knows;
Twigs of white silver are on it,
Crystal brows with blossoms.

– From The Voyage of Bran

Perform the Crystal Countdown to enter into alpha state. Upon your screen, call the energy and aura of the Apple. Allow the image to expand, and then perceive the entire tree. Step through the screen of your mind, and be there, with the entire spirit of the Apple Tree, with the fruit you drew to you hanging upon it.

Talk to the spirit of the Apple Tree. Commune with its wisdom. Ask to be able to enter in and out of the spirit world.

Visualize yourself taking the fruit and cutting it in half, revealing the five-pointed seed star. The pentagram is also a gateway. You take the seed star and fruit and press them into your heart, to link your heart with the spirit of the Apple Tree. You might even perceive of the tree "giving" you a branch with nine silver-red apples, ringing like a bell.

You can take that silver branch within you, and then later put it in your Majick Room, or keep it within you as an inner spiritual tool, like the Emerald Tablet.

When done, step back from the Apple Tree and thank its wise spirit. Step back and wipe the Apple Tree from the screen of your mind. Give yourself clearance and balance. Count yourself up from alpha.

This can be a powerful exercise to repeat with an actual apple tree fruit if possible. You can make a charm out of the seeds and hang it from your neck at heart level or carry it in your pocket. Many students of the Celtic mysteries obtain a physical apple branch and fasten nine bells to it to use as a form of rattle when doing ritual and meditation, blessing it with the power of the Silver Branch.

THE CABOT FORMULA FOR INITIATION AND TRANSFORMATION

While some traditions have multiple initiations or elevations in the Craft, the Cabot Tradition, like many forms of Traditional Witchcraft, has only one true initiation ceremony. Everything leads to this ritual, but the process leading us to it is the formula for true initiation. Anything that alters your worldview can be an initiation, and for many, the first psychic diagnosis healing case or the first successful spell is as much an initiation as any ritual, as long as it was approached in a clear and conscious way.

Degree	Key	Function	Task	Result
1st Degree	Science	Self-Esteem	Psychic Development	Becoming a Witch
2nd Degree	Art	Responsibility	Spell Manifestation	Becoming Priest/ess
3rd Degree	Religion	Study	Questing for Mystery	Becoming HP/S
	Celebration	Service	Turning the Wheel	Becoming Celebrant
	Initiation	Ministry	Successful Petition for Initiation	Ordination

THE QUEST AND ATTAINMENT

Something found in many of the Celtic myths—and in fact, world myth—is the sacred quest. In our traditions it is portrayed best as the Quest for the Holy Grail, but we also see it as the Quest for the Child of Light and even the search for the Goddess herself. We are really seeking the ineffable. The Grail, Child, and Goddess are really portals to something greater, a mystery that cannot be spoken, but must be experienced by us individually.

Attaining that mystery becomes a sign of greater self-mastery and self-control. Going beyond self-esteem and health, we are then able to serve when we understand ourselves better, and act from that understanding. There are three signs of attainment of this mystery. They correspond to the three levels of the Cabot Tradition.

• **Healing of Past Wounds and Reconnection:** In Witchcraft I, we experience self-esteem, hopefully learning to heal the past wounding through self-love. Meditation can center us, to see ourselves as we truly our in the majick mirror. Psychic development empowers us, reconnecting us to our majickal selves that have always been within us.

• **Needs being met on the Earthly Plane:** In Witchcraft II, we learn to manifest and banish, and we are able to take a greater level of control and partnership in our daily lives. It is hard to be spiritual, to serve, when we feel we are lacking, when our basic needs and wants are not being met, or when we are out of alignment with ourselves. So we learn majick and much of our majick seems material, not spiritual, but we realize taking care of ourselves is the key to then being spiritual, and taking care of others.

• **Service to a Higher Cause Selflessly:** In Witchcraft III, we learn to dedicate the skills we have learned in the previous degrees to go deeper, and to serve a higher and deeper power than ourselves and our own lives. We learn to be in the moment, to do what is necessary, and to be unattached to the reward of our action. We quest and we find the ineffable.

PATTERNS AND MYTHS FOR THE QUEST

The patterns of the mysteries are found in the myths and legends of our people. In the Cabot Tradition, we have three main ways these mysteries of the religion of Witchcraft are expressed.

Chase-Rebirth	Hanes Taliesin	Cerridwen and Taliesin
Search	The Search for the Lost Child	Mabon/Pryderi
Quest	Arthurian Quest	Grail Knight, King, Queen, Magician, Sorceress

The first is the one most familiar to us—the Chase and Rebirth myth found in the story of Taliesin. The ordinary mortal is transformed through the majick and then rebirth through the Goddess. The transformation leads to the majickal self, the rebirth as bard and Druid, in essence, Witch. The teachings come to us through cycles of darkness and rebirth, from the hut, the womb, and then the leather bag adrift on the waters.

The second is found in a lot of our seasonal myths, with the idea that the God of Light, embodying the Sun, is lost in the darkness of the Underworld and must be returned to renew the land. But beyond the seasonal metaphor, it is also the search for the child within, the Child of Promise that dwells within us, and within all things. The tales of Mabon relate to this mystery, as do the stories of Rhiannon's son, Pryderi, among others. Both are lost and must be found again.

The third and final pattern is that of the knight's quest, and the best embodiment of the story for us is the Arthurian Quest for the Holy Grail. A knight, acting as the agent of the King and Kingdom, must prove his work through all types of terrestrial and Otherworldly challenges to claim the Holy Grail, be it the cauldron of the Goddess, or the Cup of Immortality, to renew and heal the land that has become a Wasteland. In many ways, we are living in the Wasteland and constantly on a quest for healing, but the healing for all is only found through service. The Cup is the balance to the Sword of Excalibur.

LIGHT OF EXCALIBUR FROM THE WITCHES OF KENT

Upon initiation, Felicity passed to me the Light of Excalibur, from her blade to my blade. I do the same upon initiation of new Witches. The Witches of Kent tell us they have held the Light of Excalibur in blades since the time of Arthur, Merlin, and Camelot. They have been the guardians and keepers of the light. As they shared it with me, I share it with you. The Light of Excalibur is the intelligence, the "current" of the Tradition. It has an awareness. For this reason, in a new tradition, we can pass the light from sword to athame for the beginning student, to pass this awareness into a tool that will help guide you, heal you, empower you, and teach you when you meditate with it and commune with the light. You will not be able to pass that light onward until it is embodied by the Excalibur Sword after you are initiated, but for now, it is a valuable ally.

Once you have received the light into your athame, meditate with it regularly. Reflect the light of candles off the metal as a focus. Enter into alpha and hold it in your hands. Listen to the still voice within the Light of Excalibur. Let it guide your dreams and visions to understand your role with us better.

THE MAJICK CIRCLE IN THE THIRD DEGREE

In the Third Degree, there are several additional ways to cast a majick circle and call the quarters.

Athame or Sword Casting: While the circle is cast with a wand in Witchcraft II, in Witchcraft III it can be cast with a wand or a blade.

Kent Casting Method: The Kent Method of casting the circle uses the compass directions with Excalibur swords. It requires four swords or athames, and four people. Instead of making a circle, the four start by putting their blade points to the altar, lifting the blade upward to the sky and walking to the perimeter of the circle, placing the sword on the ground at the perimeter of the circle, pointing clockwise. This method is usually done only after initiation, once swords have been consecrated with the Light of Excalibur.

Circle of Swords: This method is used for initiation rituals only. All the initiated Cabot Witches gather in a circle facing inward, with the hilt of their Excalibur sword in the right hand, pointing clockwise to the left hand, touching the hilt of the sword to the person on the left. The initiator and new initiates are in the center of the circle of swords, while the rest of the Third Degree initiates stand outside of the swords, as witnesses holding the space.

Great Animal Quarters: The quarters can be called with the Great Animal Powers, rather than solely the elemental dragons. The Great Animals are teachers and healers on our path, not just guardians of the circle and the directions—Wolf or Bear in the north for Earth; Red Fox or Horse in the east for Fire; Crow, Owl, or Falcon in the south for Air; and the Salmon in the west for Water.

Elemental Faery Quarters: The four elemental Faery "rulers" or "kings" can be called upon to guide us in the four directions of the circle. Ghob is the king of Earth. Djinn is the king of Fire. Paralda is the king of Air, and Niska is the king of Water.

Circle to the Powers of the Cabot Tradition

Perform a Majick Circle as you would in the Second Degree, though the instructor of this degree can cast it with the Excalibur Sword.

Call upon the Four Elemental Dragons.

Perform the Waters of Life Sacrament and offerings.

Recite the Student Vow (given only at the class)

Instructor shall pass the Light of Excalibur to athames, but letting each student strike their blade to the sword. Students will then take seats and hold their own athame, getting into a comfortable meditation position.

Count into alpha using the Crystal Countdown.

Feel the energy of the athame that you hold. Feel the Light of Excalibur shine forth from it, filling you with its brightness.

On your left side, feel the presence of Tara. Tara is the sacred center of Ireland, which is the sacred center of all. It is the home of the gods, where they dwell and rule.

On your right side, feel the presence of Avalon. Avalon is the Apple Island of the Wise Women, the resting place of Arthur, which dwells beyond the mist everywhere and nowhere.

Feel the two sides of our heritage come together in you. Tara becomes one with your heart. Avalon becomes one with your heart. You are in the center. You are everywhere. You are nowhere. And there are all the powers of the tradition.

You find yourself surrounded by shadows, silhouettes, outlines of people in a circle, a ring, around you. These are the gods and goddesses. They are the heroes. These are the Faery folk, the Ancient Witches, the ancestors and allies. All have gathered to be here with you.

Some may step forward, out of the shadows, to commune with you. They are attracted by the light of the blade within your hands. Take this time to communicate with them. Ask their names and purpose. Ask if you have any work to do together.

When done, thank them. The figures shall step back, and the whole circle will begin to fade from your mind's eye.

Give yourself Total Health Clearance. Count up from alpha.

Release the quarters.

Release the circle.

TWO: THE CHASE OF THE FOUR ELEMENTS

There are four cities that no mortal eye has seen but that the soul knows; these are Gorias, that is in the east; and Finias, that is in the south; and Murias, that is in the west; and Falias that is in the north. And the symbol of Falias is the stone of death, which is crowned with pale fire. And the symbol of Gorias is the dividing sword. And the symbol of Finias is a spear. And the symbol of Murias is a hollow that is filled with water and fading light.
– *The Little Book of Great Enchantment* by Fiona Macleod/William Sharp

THE FOUR FOLD PATTERNS: EARTH, FIRE, AIR, WATER

Traditions of majick hold that the world is made of four elements, known as Earth, Air, Fire, and Water. They come from the fifth element, Spirit, also known as Akasha or Quintessence, and they shall return to this fifth element. All things in existence take part of these elements. They stand for the Physical Plane (Earth), the Emotional Plane (Water), the Mental Plane (Air) and the Energetic Plane (Fire). Within you, these elements are the physical body, the emotions or heart, the mind, and the energy. Spirit, the fifth element, is our consciousness. Our understanding of the elements comes from the ancient Greeks, but has parallels in Ayurvedic, or Traditional Indian Medicine, so there is a common Indo-European root. Alone, they form the equal armed cross, a symbol of balance and the Earth. With spirit, they form the Pentacle of the Witches.

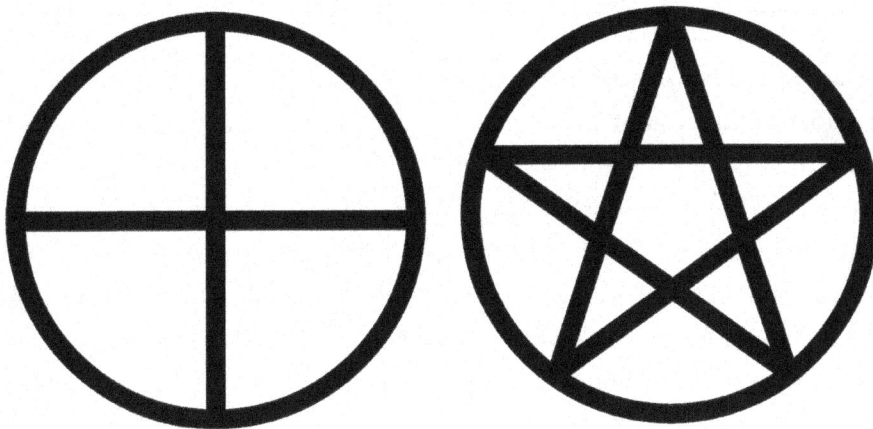

Equal Arm Cross and Pentacle

While the Celtic systems of majick did not use the term "elements" in the same way as we do, modern Celtic systems of majick include elements such as clouds and flowers into their systems. The basic fourfold division, as found in the Witch's Majick Circle, is found in the Celtic traditions through the landscape and mythology, and has played an important role in what we think of as the tools of the magician. Along with alpha, the science of Witchcraft, they form an important understanding of how both majick and human beings work in the universe.

THE FOURFOLD PATTERN IN CELTICA

The most well known division of the four powers is found in the very landscape of Ireland. The four major counties are associated with the four cardinal directions. Based upon the lore of the people and the history of the place, the elements line up quite nicely, though they don't line up with any of the standard Witchcraft or majickal traditions pairing up elements with directions. They also align with the archetypes of the four traditional levels of Celtic society, found in many forms of Indo-European society.

County	Direction	Element	Quality	Celtic "Caste"
Ulster	North	Fire	Warriors, Battle	Warrior-Chieftain
Leinster	East	Earth	Prosperity, Commerce	Farmer and Laborers
Munster	South	Water	Creativity, Music	Artisan and Skilled Workers
Connacht	West	Air	Learning, Education	Priests—Bard, Ovate, Druid

The fifth area, the center, corresponds to Meath and the legendary hill of Tara, home of the gods and central focus in the Cabot Tradition. There is the element of spirit, and the realm of both the gods and the sovereign queens and kings.

In the mythology of the Irish gods known as the Tuatha De Dannan, or Children of the goddess Danu, we have four mythic cities with the four treasures of the Tuatha De Dannan, the Treasures of Ireland, which bear a striking resemblance to both the Witch's and magician's tools and the four tarot suits—stone, spear, sword and cauldron. Today we think of them as the stone/coin/pentacle/peyton, wand/staff, athame/sword and the cup. And we use them in our rituals.

These cities are said to be ruled over by four great wizards, whom we can see as elemental teachers and allies. The great wizards were the teachers of the Tuatha De Dannan, so they must be wise and mighty indeed.

City	Direction	Element	Wizard	Treasure
Falias	North	Earth	Morfessa	Stone of Fal/Stone of Death
Gorias	East	Fire/Air*	Esras	Spear of Lugh/Dividing Sword
Finias	South	Air/Fire*	Uiscias	Sword of Nuada/Spear
Murias	West	Water	Semias	Cauldron of Dagda/Hollow

There is some confusion on the modern elemental associations and the tools, as there are some discrepancies between the original source material, the later popular and inspired work of the poet Fiona MacLeod, and modern interpretations on the correspondences of fire and air.

In the ancient Greek, we learn that each element has two qualities. It is either hot or cold, and it is either wet or dry. Placing the elements around the circle as we do in the Cabot Tradition, we are able to transform the elements, as the Greek philosopher Emedocles taught, by changing one of the qualities.

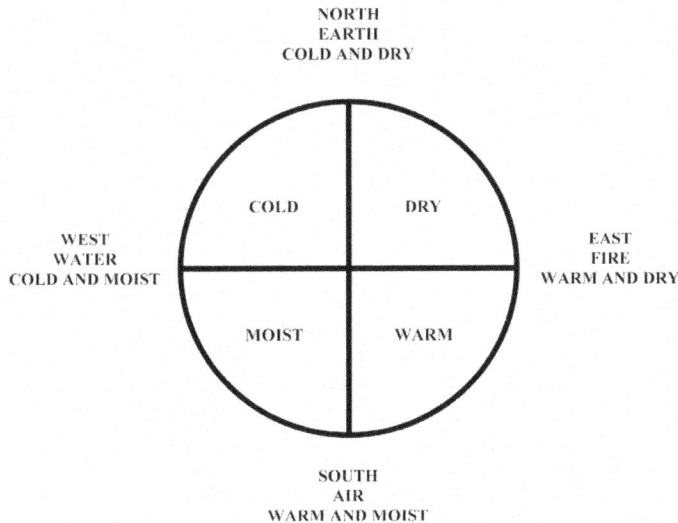

NORTH
EARTH
COLD AND DRY

WEST
WATER
COLD AND MOIST

EAST
FIRE
WARM AND DRY

COLD DRY

MOIST WARM

SOUTH
AIR
WARM AND MOIST

Elemental Circle

Direction	Element	Temperature	Quality	Widdershins (anticlockwise)	Deosil (clockwise)
North	Earth	Cold	Dry	Earth becomes moist. Salts dissolve and soon become a solution.	Earth becomes warm. Gives energy and becomes tinder.
East	Fire	Warm	Dry	Fire becomes cold. Embers go out. Dry ash of salt and minerals left.	Fire releases smoke, becomes moist and goes out, adding to air.
South	Air	Warm	Wet	Air becomes dry. Feeds the fire. Oxygen absorbed by fire.	Air becomes cool. Water precipitates out and causes rain water.
West	Water	Cold	Wet	Water becomes warm. Evaporates. Adds to atmosphere as vapor.	Water becomes dry. Leaves salts behind. Becomes earth.

So not only does the Sun, a symbol of fire, rise in the east, but it also helps our transformation as Witches to put fire and water opposing, and earth and air opposing.

The power and responsibility of transformation, of self and of the world, is at the heart of our majick. And the story of Taliesin, as we learned in the Second Degree, helps us understand that better. The four transformations of Gwion Bach, and the four transformations of Cerridwen, are powerful introductions to the nature of the elements.

Element	Gwion Back's Totems	Cerridwen's Totems
Fire	Hare	Greyhound
Water	Fish (Salmon)	Otter
Air	Bird (Wren)	Hawk
Earth	Wheat Grain	Black Hen

Notice how the elements shift from the axis of fire-water, to then air-earth, landing in the element of manifestation. Rather than going around the wheel, Gwion is confronted with the elemental powers directly.

The Chase of Gwion Bach Ritual

Cast a Majick Circle with these Quarter Calls:

To the north, I call upon the element of Earth.
I call to the wisdom of the Hen and the Seed.
So Mote it Be!

To the east, I call upon the element of Fire.
I call to the wisdom of the Greyhound and the Hare.
So Mote it Be!

To the south, I call upon the element of Air.
I call upon the wisdom of the Hawk and the Wren.
So Mote it Be!

To the west, I call upon the element of Water.
I call upon the wisdom of the Otter and the Salmon
So Mote it Be!

Perform the Waters of Life Sacrament; everyone shall take three drops. You can use the Potion of Awen formula, if you so desire.

Get seated and relaxed for meditation. Enter deeper into alpha level with the Crystal Countdown. The teacher can also use a drum to help with this vision.

Reflect on the Potion of Awen you created, and the herbs and substances you used to introduce yourself to this powerful teaching.

Feel the three drops of wisdom within your belly now, like a fire and light burning bright within you.

Feel them strike up a primal terror within you, as you intuitively know the Goddess is hunting you, seeking you. She desires those three drops back now. Run. Run faster than you've ever run.

Feel yourself transform into the body of a hare, a type of rabbit, as you run. Experience this fear from the point of view of the hare. What does it feel like to be the hare?

Feel the Goddess behind you, as the faster greyhound. Feel her breathing down your neck. She almost has you.

You reach the shores of a river and jump in, shifting your shape into a fish. Become a fish and dive deep. How does it feel to be the fish?

Feel the Goddess behind you, as she has become the Otter. Feel her chasing you.

You jump up and transform into a bird to fly away. But the Goddess transforms into a large and fast hawk, to come after you. You try to outrun her. How does it feel to be the bird?

Soon you see an open barn, and spy the pile of wheat grain. You make a swift descent downward, transforming into a wheat grain, hiding in the pile from the Goddess. What is it like to be the grain?

She lands in the barn too, upon the threshing room floor, and becomes a black crested hen. She kicks and scratches at the wheat until she finds you. And then she eats you.

Enter into the dark womb of the Goddess. Be consumed by the Goddess of Initiation.

There you will remain for the next nine months, awaiting to be reborn.

Return to waking consciousness.

Release your circle with these Quarter Releases:

To the north, I thank the element of Earth.
I thank the wisdom of the Hen and the Seed for joining us tonight.
So Mote it Be!

To the east, I thank the element of Fire.
I thank the wisdom of the Greyhound and the Hare for joining us tonight.
So Mote it Be!

To the south, I thank the element of Air.

I thank the wisdom of the Hawk and the Wren for joining us tonight.

So Mote it Be!

To the west, I thank the element of Water.

I thank the wisdom of the Otter and the Salmon for joining us tonight.

So Mote it Be!

Ground and journal.

Be aware that you have entered into the womb of initiation through this ritual, and will be reborn through the Goddess nine months from now, in the tenth lesson.

GRIEVANCES, CONFLICT RESOLUTION, AND FORGIVENESS

A fourfold approach to conflict resolution can be helpful in difficult times, within our family, coven, temples, or greater community. The teachings of the Celts and the wisdom found in the Arthurian stories are very helpful in letting us resolve conflict.

Restitutions (Earth): Often one who was in the wrong had to make a payment to the person or family who was wronged. Such restitutions would mark the matter as resolved and closed.

Challenges/Games (Fire): The honorable "winner" of a conflict could be determined by a game of skill or chance, to allow the gods and spirits to show who was correct in the conflict.

Arbitration by an Ovate (Air): Ovates were a class of judge within the Druidic class, along with the bards and religious priests. They determined laws and could be called upon to resolve conflict.

Forgiveness (Water): In both the Arthurian myths of the Holy Grail and the stories of the goddess Rhiannon, forgiveness of one's enemies can go a long way in resolving the conflict within us.

In our modern day, we can look at the elements a little differently as a guide in resolving conflict honorably and peacefully, yet still find resonance with our Celtic Wisdom.

Fire: Allow the situation to cool. Do not let anger rule your actions. Wait at least twenty-four hours before taking an action or responding.

Air: Truly listen and speak your truth. Truly listening means not thinking about what you are going to say next, but really understanding what is being said to you, and responding to what is actually said to you. Sometimes an outside mediator trained in communication facilitation can be a great help.

Water: Empathy and forgiveness. Try to understand the other person's view and experience, and have compassion. Once it is resolved, let go of it, not just for others, but also for your own highest good.

Earth: Address wrongs by taking responsibility for what you have contributed, and find a path to go forward.

Earth
Salt
Smokey Quartz, Black Tourmaline, Jasper, Emerald
Patchouli, Mandrake, Mushroom

Air
Incense Smoke
Sapphire, Agate, Turquoise
Lavender, Lobelia, Dill

Fire
Candle Flame
Garnet, Ruby, Fire Opal
Nettle, Chili, Dragon's Blood

Water
Ocean or Spring Water
Aquamarine, Moonstone, Amethyst
Mugwort, Jasmine, Seaweed

Elemental Balance Incense

1 Part Dragon's Blood

1 Part Lavender Flowers

1 Part Mugwort

1 Part Patchouli Leaf

Elemental Balance Potion

1 Cup of Spring Water

1 Tablespoon of Sea Salt

1 Teaspoon of Nettles

1 Teaspoon of Dill

1 Teaspoon of Jasmine Flowers

1 Teaspoon of Mandrake

Use these elemental correspondences alone to attune and understand the energy of individual elements, particularly with the four elemental teachers in the meditation below, and use these formulas to help find elemental balance in your life, harmonizing, your body, mind, emotions, and soul.

ELEMENTAL TEACHERS

Perform the Majick Room exercise from Witchcraft I. While there, call to your spirit guides, but specifically ask for one of the four elemental wizards: Morfessa, Esras, Uiscias, or Semias. Ask them to teach you about their treasure and area of expertise in the elements. They might even take you to their city in one of the four corners of the world, to learn directly about the elements. The elemental teachers are particularly helpful in learning to balance the elements in ourselves, particularly when they are in conflict with one another.

Three: The Gods of Witchcraft

So that they were the Tuatha De Danann who came to Ireland.
In this wise they came, in dark clouds.
They landed on the mountains of Conmaicne Rein in Connachta;
and they brought a darkness over the Sun for three days and three nights.
– Lebor Gabála Érenn: The Book of Invasions

In the Cabot Tradition, we primarily focus upon the Celtic Pantheons of gods. As there is limited information on the Celtic gods compared to some mythologies—as the Celts wrote very little down themselves, preferring a memorized oral tradition—and considering the fact that anything "Celtic" is really a mix of several related languages, people, cultures, and customs, we're "Pan-Celtic," meaning we embrace all Celtic traditions while creating our own. Primarily, we look to the gods of Ireland and Scotland which are very similar, yet more written versions of the Irish myths remain. We also look to Welsh mythology, knowing it went on to influence the Arthurian romances and English Faery traditions. We further look to the oldest surviving lore, found in the art and inscriptions of Gaul, and writings about the Gaulish Celts from the Romans. The Gaulish traditions are most likely similar to those of other continental Celts as they migrated west towards the British Isles.

You can find some interesting cross relationships between the names and functions of the Welsh, Irish, Scottish, and Gaulish deities, helping us understand these figures were most likely one pantheon in an earlier time. Sometimes looking all the way back to the Hindu deities, as they too come from a common Indo-European root source, can help us understand our own Celtic gods.

Welsh	Irish	Gaulish
Modron*	Morrighan*	Matronae
Don*	Danu* Cailleach Eiru, Banba, Folda	
Mabon* Pryderi*	Angus*	Maponus
Rhiannon*	Macha*	Epona

Welsh	Irish	Gaulish
Bran*	Dagda*	Sucellus
	Turren	Tarranis
Cerridwen*		
	Bridget*	Sirona
Taliesin*	Beli Bawr	Belanos*
Branwen*		
Llud/Nudd*	Nuada*	Nodens Esus
Lleu Llaw Gyffes*	Lugh Lámhfhada*	Lug/Lugus*
Arianrhod*	Tailitui	
	Medb	
Pywll		Cernunnos*
Arawn		
	Badb Catha	
	Nemain	
Gofannon	Gobinnu*	Gobannis
	Ogma*	Ogmois
Lyr*		Lir*
Manawydan fab Llyr*		Manannán mac Lir*
Gwydion*		
Math*		
Dylan		
Blodeuwedd*		
	Dian Cetch	
	Airmid	
	Miach	
	Cúchulainn	

Welsh	Irish	Gaulish
	Sckathach*	

* Celtic deities central to the Cabot Tradition. Research these gods and goddesses, and read their stories to better understand and align with them.

Some of the primary deities we work with include:

Danu — Danu is the Great Mother of the Tuatha De Dannan, the source of life, and one of the names used in the Cabot tradition to denote the Goddess, the primal mother. She can be seen as a river and water goddess, giving us the name of the Danube River; as an Earth Mother, akin to Gaea; or really as a cosmic goddess of all. Some associated her also with Modron and Don, as another name for the Great Mother.

Dagda — Though myths associated Dagda with the Morrighan as lover and Bridget as daughter, we see the Dagda, the elder giant good god, as the match to Danu, her consort as the Great God. He is the keeper of the majick cauldron known as the Undry. He plays a harp that changes the seasons. He holds a club that will kill you with one blow and resurrect you with the next. Due to his titanic proportions, Dagda is believed to have a mythic connection to the giant Bran, brother to Branwen, and a sacred king in *The Mabinogion*. His cauldron was one of resurrection, and after his death his severed head continued to advise and protect Britain.

Morrighan — The Morrighan is the dark Triple Goddess of the Irish Celts, associated with battle, sorcery, justice and sexuality. She is triple in nature, being a triad entity with either Anu (Danu), Badb, and Macha, or with Badb Catha, Macha and Nemain. She is a primal giant like the Dagda, yet is more actively engaged with the wars and conflicts of the gods than Danu.

Brid — Brid, known later as Bridget, is an Irish Triple Goddess with her two sisters, also named Bridget, ruling over healing, poetry and smithcraft. Her sacred feast is Imbolc. She can be called upon for inspiration and creativity, for healing and for manifesting something tangible. Some would connect her with other goddesses of light, life, and spring renewal, such as the Teutonic goddess Ostara, celebrated at the Vernal Equinox, which is often named after her.

Mabon — Mabon is considered the young child of light, son of Modron, and although *The Mabinogion* is named for him, he doesn't have a starring role in the myths. He is a minor character in some, but the elements of the story point to a stronger and important folk tradition. He is often equated with other child gods who are mischievous or who get lost, like Pryderi and Angus. The autumnal equinox takes its Neo-pagan name from him, being the Feast of Mabon. The theme of the child of light being lost in the underworld of darkness is central to his mystery, as we each must find that child of light within.

Bel — Bel is the Celtic god of light and fire who gives his name to our spring Beltane celebration. There is not a lot of information on Bel or specific stories, but many relate him to figures like Mabon, Angus, and the Green Man.

Lugh — Lugh is the Irish name of the many-skilled Celtic god. His stories are similar in theme to the Welsh Lleu, and the earliest form we have of his name is Lug, from the Gauls. The Romans most likely equated him with their Mercury due to his many skills. He is associated with light, lightning, and is seen in modern traditions as a Sun and grain god.

Taliesin — Taliesin is the poet, bard, and magician who started life as the servant boy Gwion Bach, who is reborn through Cerridwen's magick and womb as Taliesin, the greatest of bards.

Arianrhod — Arianrhod is the mother to Lleu and sister to Gwydion. She is the goddess of the starry castle, and associated with the heavens and sometimes the Moon. Taliesin is also said to have spent time in her prison and in her chair, seeing the revolving cosmos.

Blodeuwedd — The flower maiden, brought to life by the wizards Gwydion and Math using meadowsweet, oak, and broom flowers, to be the wife of Lleu. She eventually betrays him for her lover Gronw, and for this betrayal, is cursed by Gwydion to take the form of an owl. She is called "flower face" or "owl face."

Gwydion — Gwydion is the brother of Arianrhod and nephew to the wizard king Math. He adopts his sister's abandoned son, Lleu, and raises him as his own, helping him break the curses his mother has placed upon him. Gwydion is a Druidic or Wizard figure, a master of majick and a trickster, with similarities to Merlin and Taliesin.

Math — Math is a wizard king in the Welsh myths, uncle to Gwydion and Arianrhod, among others. The actions of his nephews Gilfaethwy and Gwyidion led to a war between Math's kingdom and the kingdom of Pryderi. He later punished his nephews with transformations into animals. It is said that in times of peace, his feet must be held by a pure or virgin maiden while he is upon the throne, or he will die. His requirement of a pure maiden to hold his feet revealed Arianrhod's pregnancy with Dylan and Lleu. Gwydion suggested Arianrhod, though he knew her to not be a virgin. Some speculate that Lleu is actually his son, as well as his nephew. He later helped Gwydion create Blodeuwedd.

Gobinnu — Goginnu is the Irish smith god, with cognates to the Welsh Gofannon and Gaulish Gobannis. He is a master smith and crafter of weapons and complex items, making him similar to the Roman Vulcan.

Ogma — Ogma is an Irish god of eloquence and poetry. His honey tongue was said to affix chains from his tongue to the ears of his listeners, showing his ability to convince and lead. The Irish Ogham script was said to be invented by him, and he also appeared to have great strength in either body or words that drew comparisons to the Greco-Roman Hercules. Ogmois is his Gaulish counterpart.

Lir — Lyr is the Irish sea king, finding kinship in his Welsh counterpart, Lyr.

Manannán mac Lir — The Irish Manannán and his Welsh counterpart, Manawydan fab Llyr, are the sons of the sea gods Lir and Lyr. Though they are associated with water and boats, they have more of a Mercurial archetype, being travelers upon the water and helping others get to the islands of the Otherworld, rather than embodying the ocean themselves.

Cerridwen — Though never directly stated to be a goddess, Cerridwen lived with her giant husband upon an island in a lake and brewed a majick potion to initiate Taliesin, the first of the bards, so we think of her as a primal deity as well. She is considered the "Mother of All Bards" and giver of inspiration. Call upon her for a greater understanding of majick, herbs, and bardic skill.

Cernunnos — Cernunnos is believed to be the Gaulish form of the stag-horned god, or "horned one" as his name and inscription read. Many see him as a lord of life and death, lord of animals, or god of all of nature. Through little information is available on him, he has become one of the most beloved gods of modern Witchcraft.

Celi — Celi is a Welsh form of the light and Sun god as found in the controversial works of the Druidic revivalist and Welsh nationalist Iolo Morganwg. He is often paired with a form of the goddess Cerridwen, in the joint image of Celiced.

Nuada — Nuada is the Irish king of the Tuatha de Dannan when they land in Ireland. As the king must be perfect, he abdicates his throne when he loses his hand in combat. After rulership under an oppressive half-Fomorian King Bres, the oppressed Tuatha help Nuada reclaim the throne, with the physician god Dian Cetch crafting a silver hand for Nuada, and later Dian Cetch's son Miach creating a flesh and blood hand for Nuada. He later abdicated again, this time in favor of Lugh. Nuada holds one of the four treasures, the Sword of Nuada.

Rhiannon — An Otherworld queen associated with the horse totem, similar to Macha and Epona, she seeks out Pywll, prince of the land of Dyfed, to be her husband even though she is betrothed to another. Their son is the hero Pryderi. Rhiannon is accused of devouring her child Pryderi after his birth, and is punished by carrying people in and out of the castle like a horse, while being forced to tell her shameful tale. Pryderi is later found, and she is exonerated. Pywll passes and Pryderi assumes rulership of the kingdom. Rhiannon's adventures continue when she marries Manawydan.

Oak King — The Oak King is the young lord of the growing season. He is the embodiment and manifestation of the Light Half of the Year. He can manifest as the Green Man, Sun Child or Lord of the Harvest. He is born at the Winter Solstice, and grows in power as the light grows, until he is defeated by the dark Holly King at the Summer Solstice.

Holly King — The Holly King is the lord of the winter, the embodiment of the Dark Half of the Year. He is connected to much of our winter holiday lore and celebrations. He is said to also be one of the riders of the Wild Hunt. Though a "winter" god, he takes his power at the Summer Solstice when the Sun wanes, and he prepares the way for the new Oak King.

THE CABOT CALL OF THE GODDESS

by Dana Burke, HP and Candy-Jean Burke, HPS

Gather together and call me this night,
I will answer your call and bathe you in light.
The moon waxes full and then wanes till there's none,
Whenever you call, I will come, we are one.

Sixty-four squares has the game board of stone,
The choices you make, are yours, alone.
Keep wise your choices, in the moves that you make,
There is always a lesson, there are no mistakes.

I gave you a sword on the day you were born,
Take it with you everywhere, it was meant to be worn.
Your sovereignty is sacred, which you must never yield.
The sword you were given, you must learn to wield.

Exercise caution, like with a spear before hurled,
Your gifts once you've found them, you must share with the world.
Expression and actions must be sent with good aim.
For a spear thrown carelessly can result in great pain.

It lies here within you, the Grail that you seek.
It's the knowledge of the old ways, of which I speak.
Knowledge to wisdom is a rebirth from within.
You are one with the universe, we are all akin.

I am the goddess of life, death and rebirth.
I am the great mother of Moon and the Earth.
By Water, by Earth, by Air and Fire,
I am sought by the God to quench his desire.

You will find me in all, whether awake or in dream.
I am She. I am You. I am the Red Queen.

THE CABOT CALL OF THE GOD

by Dana Burke, HP and Candy-Jean Burke, HPS

Child of Redemption, young and bright.
Promise and hope, Lord of the Light.

Young and playful, witty and jolly.
The trickster, the prankster, The Lord of Folly.

Jack in the green, virile and good,
The father and protector, The Lord of the Wood.

Old and Wise, the call we all must hark.
The Magi, The Reaper, The Lord of the Dark.

Learn well the lessons of his life and his stories.
Use them and your tools, to create your own glories.

His life is a cycle, like yours and mine.
The dance that goes on throughout all time.

Know well the secret, it is truly a key.
The god lives in all, that includes You and Me.

Goddess Oil
1 Dram of Base Oil

5 Drops of Myrrh Oil

1 Drop of Rose Oil

Pinch of Dragon's Blood Resin

God Oil
1 Dram of Base Oil

4 Drops Frankincense Oil

2 Drops of Pine Oil

1 Drop of Orange Oil

Pinch of Ground Cinnamon

Along with the Celtic pantheon, we also look to many of the Egyptian traditions. One of the first goddesses I called upon, who is still beloved in my life and teachings, is the Egyptian mother goddess Isis. Many of the main Egyptian gods, such as her husband-brother Osiris, son Horus, as well as Bast, Hathor, Thoth, Ra, Sekhmet and Nephthys, play a role in the Cabot Tradition. We honor the deities of the Egypt for their connection to the ancient mysteries.

SCOTA, EGYPTIAN PRINCESS

Did you know there is a link between Egypt and the British Isles? Folkloric history tells us that Princess Scota, an Egyptian Princess, was the daughter of the Pharaoh in the time of Moses, or perhaps at the time of the Tower of Babel. Her husband was a Scythian prince. She and her family along with a group of followers escaped Egypt or Scythia, before any of the plagues and dangers, taking treasures and cultural artifacts with them upon the open sea. They followed the guidance of the gods, and eventually went on to the British Isles. They settled there, merging with local Irish tribes, and as princess, she gave her name to their land, Scotland. In 1320 A.D., through the Declaration of Arbroath, Scotland announced their Egyptian and Scythian heritage to the world at large.

So we see a direct link between the Egyptian Mysteries and those of the Celtic traditions of Scotland, and honor the heritage of Scota by also honoring the main deities of Egypt.

HEROES AND ANCIENT ONES

Beyond those recognized as specific deities are those whom the ancient Greeks called heroes, existing somewhere between the humans and the gods. We think of them as the Ancient Ones, the ancient ancestors who help guide us as they no longer have to reincarnate. Some Witches call them the Mighty Dead.

Most specifically, we look to the ancients of the Arthurian myths. Many of these "heroes" were either fey-blooded, or of the fey themselves, like Morgan. They built bridges between the Otherworld and the human world, through an alliance between Avalon and Camelot. While the myths change with the human storytellers, their energy is always available to us. Look to the names and myths of such legends as King Arthur, Merlin, Guinevere, Morgan Le Fey, Lancelot, Nimue, Vivian, Gwain, Galahad, Bors, Perceval, the Fisher King, and even Modred, the villain named as the downfall of Camelot.

Arthur	Bear King, successor to the Dragon Kings
Guinevere	Queen, possible Faery Queen
Merlin	Prophet, bard, magician, dragon priest, advisor to the king
Morgan	Lady of the Lake, Priestess of Avalon, Faery Queen, Arthur's "Sister" and sometime nemesis
Lancelot	Son of the Lady of the Lake, Tarnished Knight, Lover of Gwenievere
Nimue/Vivian	Lady of the Lake or Lady of the Lake in training, Merlin's lover
Gwain	One of the great knights of the Round Table. Quest involves the Green Knight. Is said to have a Pentagram upon his shield
Galahad	Son of Lancelot, Grail Knight who attains the Grail
Bors	Bors the Younger becomes one of the Grail Knights from the Round Table
Perceval	Grail Knight who fails to ask the right question of the Holy Grail
Fisher King	Wounded King who keeps the Holy Grail in the Grail Castle
Modred	Son of Arthur and possibly Morgan, Nemesis of Camelot

Some see all the characters of Arthurian lore as humanized Faery and land spirits, or humans with Faery blood so strong, they have become mythic. Many others see them as human ancestors that have been mythologized. Another occult tradition tells us the roles of Camelot are sacred orders hailing from the west, from the shores of Atlantis, continuing a line of the Dragon Kings, Pendragons, through the sacred sites of the landscape to maintain order on Earth after the cataclysm. There have been many Merlins, Morgans, Arthurs and Guineveres. They keep the cosmic order in their age.

Merlin Oil
1 Dram of Hazelnut Oil
1 Dram of Fir Oil
1 Pebble from a location sacred to Merlin,
such as Tintagel (Merlin's Cave) or Dinas Emrys (Merlin's First Prophecy)
1 Sprig of Oak, Lightning Struck if Possible

Along with the familiar Arthurian heroes, we look to the mythic ancestors and heroes of all the Celtic traditions. We look to the Irish, Welsh, and Scots, as well as the British, Manx, and those of Brittany. We even look to an earlier time, to the "tribes of Witches" known as the pre-Christian, Iron Age people called the Dobunni, and the early medieval Hwicca, where we might get the original word "Wicca."

THE NINE LADIES

Some of the most important of these Otherworldly heroes are the Ladies of the Lake. There are nine ladies from the Otherworld that show up time and again in Celtic and Arthurian lore, most mysteriously.

There are nine "Witches" of the Cauldron of Annwn that show up in *Preiddeu Annwfn*, attributed to Taliesin. Their breath warms the pearl-rimmed cauldron. We have the nine sisters of Avalon, all named but with no further information given, from *The History of the Kings of Britain* by Geoffrey of Monmouth. In further Grail myth, we have the nine maidens of the well, from The Elucidation, prologue to Perceval, *The Story of the Grail* by Chrétien de Troyes. The rape of the maidens and defilement of their wells is what creates the Wasteland in one story. There are also nine Witches of Gloucester, or of Caer Loyw, from *Peredur son of Efrawg,* one of the Three Romances in *The Mabinogion* collection.

The concept of Nine Sisters or Nine Maidens is found in many traditions, and most detailed in the tradition of the Greek Muses. Occultists have associated them with the planets, musical notes, and areas on the zodiac, though the correspondences between these occult correspondences and their original Greek functions are not always clear.

While the Witches of Gloucester, Well Maidens, and Maidens of Annwn are never named, the nine sisters of Avalon are named in *The History of the Kings of Britain,* though no other imagery or detail is given beyond their name. Kathy Jones, in her *Priestess of Avalon, Priestess of the Goddess,* explores these figures through an unusual and unorthodox Wheel of the Year mandala. They are often related to the Muses, connected to King Arthur, often depicted as a solar king, much in the same way the Muses are associated with Apollo.

In Caitlin Matthews' *The Ladies of the Lake,* she works with three triads of women in Arthurian lore. While majickal, they have more human qualities in the later Arthurian Romances. First there are those who are kin to King Arthur, including Morgana, Igraine, and Guinevere. Next are the Otherworldly ladies of the sovereign Sisterhood. While earlier versions of Morgan would certainly be chief of this triad, in Matthews' work, it is Argante, with Nimue and Enid. The last triad includes the Grail Maidens—Kundry, Dindraine and Ragnell.

This chart can help relate some of these sets of Nine Ladies who act as teaching spirits in our traditions. The Zodiac degrees and dates can help you find the one that rules your own birthdate as a personal ally, and which one is functioning strongly at any moment in the year in this system. Use it to inspire your own relationship to go deeper with the nine.

Avalon Sister	Lady of the Lake	Muse	Planet	Note	Astrology	Dates
Gliton	Igraine	Thalia	Earth	Silent	1 Aries–10 Taurus	March 21–April 30
Thetis	Nimue	Clio	Moon	A	11 Taurus–20 Gemini	May 1–June 6
Gliten	Enid	Calliope	Mercury	B	21 Gemini–0 Leo	June 10–July 22
Gitonea	Guinevere	Terpsichore	Venus	c	1 Leo–10 Virgo	July 23–September 1

Avalon Sister	Lady of the Lake	Muse	Planet	Note	Astrology	Dates
Monroe	Argante	Melpomene	Sun	d	11 Virgo–20 Libra	September 2–October 12
Mazoe	Kundry	Erato	Mars	e	21 Libra—0 Sagittarius	October 13–November 21
Tyronoe	Dindraine	Euterpe	Jupiter	f	1 Sagittarius—10 Capricorn	Nov 22–December 31
Thiten	Ragnell	Polyhymnia	Saturn	g	11 Capricorn—20 Aries	Jan 1–February 8
Morgen	Morgana	Urania	Fixed Stars	–	21 Aquarius—0 Aries	February 9–March 20

Morgan Le Fey Oil

3 Drams of Almond Oil

1 Dram of Apple Oil

1 Dram of Amber Oil

10 Drops of Rose Oil

1 Black Feather

1 Jet Stone, Small

1 Garnet, Small

1 Quartz Crystal, Small

Avalon Incense

3 Tablespoons of Willow Bark

9 Applewood Twigs

1 Tablespoon of Amber Resin

3 Tablespoons of Lavender

1 Tablespoon of Hawthorn Berries

1 Tablespoon of Red Rose Petals

9 Drops of Lavender Oil

5 Drops of Rose Oil

3 Drops of Storax Oil

Nine Ladies Meditation

Before you start, use your own birthdate to determine which of the nine ladies is your ally and guide. What is her name as a sister of Avalon? As a Lady? As a Muse?

Cast a circle and create a sacred space. Wear Morgan Le Fey Oil and burn Avalon Incense. Enter into an alpha state using the Crystal Countdown. Close your eyes, and hold the intention of visiting with the nine ladies of the Fortunate Isles, who are also the nine maidens and nine witches.

Call forth the mist, and soon find yourself surrounded by a cool, white mist, as if it were rising up off a lake.

You are walking, almost blind, in the mist, feeling the rounded pebbles beneath your feet. You are walking on a winding path, which takes you deeper.

As the mist begins to clear, you find yourself entering into a cave. You enter the dark opening of the cave, and in the distance, you see the flickering light of some sort of fire.

As you get closer, you realize the fire is beneath a cauldron, a pearl-rimmed cauldron, and there are nine ladies, all dressed in black, all priestesses, around the cauldron, tending to it and mixing in it. Ask for your ally, your guiding sister-lady-muse, and see who comes forward. Take this time to explain you are here seeking deeper wisdom and majick, and let this ally teach and show you the deeper majick.

When done, thank your ally and say farewell. You can always come back, or invite this priestess to your own majick room as a spirit guide. Make your way out of the cave, coming back the way you came, and enter into the mist. Follow the mist back to your body in this world. Give yourself clearance and balance, and count yourself back from alpha.

THE CABOT ALTAR FOR THE THIRD DEGREE

More and more in the Third Degree, we look at the sacred gaming board as both a majickal tool and altar. Read the tale known as *The Dream of Rhonabwy* in *The Mabinogion* to understand the significance of the game board of life. Use it in your divination. Use it in your majick. Use it to connect with the gods of Witchcraft, placing pieces and statues of the gods directly upon the board, to help you go deeper in your relationship with them.

INVOCATION OF THE DEITIES

Keep the gods in your heart and mind as you practice the religion of Witchcraft. To do so, work with the following:

Education: Learn all you can about the gods you wish to know personally in your life. Read their stories. Learn their history. Find any imagery and icons associated with them.

Build Deity Altars: Honor the gods with whom you wish to build a relationship.

Making Offerings: Light candles in the gods' names and make offerings of incense, oils, food, and drink that are appropriate to the gods you seek. One can see the faces of the gods in the smoke of incense, especially when making a lot of smoke outdoors.

Art: Making art to honor the gods—drawings, music, dance—all of which serve to bring us closer to the deities of our Craft.

Invitation: Make a formal invitation, asking a god to be a part of your life.

Conversation: Speak with the gods aloud before their altar and in the majick circle as you would a beloved friend or honored teacher. Ask them questions and know that sometimes they will answer directly, psychically, and other times they will answer in dreams, meditations, and through synchronicity.

Meditation: Meditate with the gods and call them to be with you in your majick room.

Invocation: Ask to move and speak for the gods that you have a strong relationship with while in ceremony. During the sabbats, we often enact mystery plays, like passion plays, but invoked in the presence of the gods. We offer our hands and voice to them to manifest in the world.

Though Witchcraft is a religion, I would say we do not worship our gods. We honor and respect them, but we do not grovel or beg. We know they are divine beings, and we seek to be like them, so we honor and learn from them. They help us, teach us, and guide us. But they also expect us to do work on our own. They are not going to hand everything to us. They are not our cosmic parents. We may work with them, but they are not here to do our bidding. They are not here at the whim of our ego. They have their own lives to lead and are simply allies to us, and we are allies to them.

High Priestesses and High Priests will sometimes dedicate themselves at some point in their path to a Matron Goddess or Patron God, a particular deity that shares similar work with that priestesses or priest. We see ourselves as a daughter or son of that god, and much of our spiritual path is about the lessons and expertise that god or goddess has to offer. Be careful in picking a matron or patron relationship. Unlike most human relationships, they can last lifetimes, and they carry deep spiritual responsibilities and consequences.

God and Goddess Meditation

Cast a circle and create a sacred space. Wear God Oil on your right wrist and Goddess Oil on your left wrist. Recite the Cabot Call of the Goddess and the Cabot Call of the God as a part of your ritual.

Enter into an alpha state using the Crystal Countdown. Close your eyes, and hold the intention of visiting with your Goddess and God. You can ask to visit with specific deities or simply allow the one that is most favorable to you at this time to appear.

Call forth the mist, and soon you find yourself surrounded by a cool white mist, as if it were rising up off a lake. You are walking, almost blind in the mist, feeling the rounded pebbles beneath your feet. You are walking on a winding path which takes you deeper into the realm of the gods and spirits.

As the mist begins to clear, you see the rolling green grass beneath your feet. The cloudy sky overhead is still illuminated by light from beyond, and in the distance there is a hill. As you look closer, upon the hill there is a building, perhaps a castle or tower. Your path leads you winding up the hill and towards the building. You know what you seek is inside.

Take notice of any plants or animals you see along the way. They could be future allies for you on the path of the Witch.

You come to the castle gate, but a moat separates you from the entrance. As if sensing your desire to cross, the drawbridge is lowered, yet there is no one there. You are able to cross the moat and enter into the castle.

You make your way forward, to the center, to find the throne room of the Goddess and God. There they sit before you, waiting for your arrival. How do they appear to you? Often the Goddess appears as the most beautiful and powerful woman you have ever seen, while the God's face shimmers and shifts, like quicksilver. Commune with your Goddess and God. Explore your relationship together and the work you have to do in the world as an aspiring High Priestess or High Priest. The gods will teach you how to work with them, and how to call upon them in the future.

When your work is done, thank the Goddess and God. Reach within your heart and pull out something to offer to each of them. In turn, they might offer a gift to you, to seal this connection and continue it at a future time. They will tell you how to return and when. Say farewell and depart, back the way you came across the drawbridge. Follow the path down the hill, and as you do, soon you'll be enveloped by mist again. Enter the mist. Follow the mist back to your body in this world. Give yourself clearance and balance, and count yourself back from alpha. Release your circle.

Four: The Expanded Science of Witchcraft

"We don't have Soul, but it's other way around, Souls have us."
"The Soul is repository of information that we gather during a lifetime."
— "From Atom To Cosmos" video with Itzhak Bentov

New Paradigm Science

In New Paradigm Science, the universe is often described through the working model of the hologram. A hologram is a three-dimensional sculpture of light created by shining a laser through a holographic plate. If you divide the plate, rather than getting half an image, you get two smaller but complete images, indicating that information in the hologram is stored "non-locally" and you will theoretically continue to divide and shrink the images until the plate can no longer hold an image. Each part contains all of the information of the whole.

A holographic photo is taken by splitting the laser into two beams, and the plate records the interference pattern of the two overlapping beams upon an object. The polarity of two patterns, overlapping, is the source of the information. Many see this as corresponding to the Hermetic philosophy of *The Kybalion.* Many believe our understanding of the physical universe, what the Hindus call the illusion of maya, is really like a hologram, an image we interpret as real, resulting from two overlapping patterns, akin to Goddess and God coming together.

Within the theories of modern scientific paradigms, such as quantum physics, is the concept of parallel universes. Such models theorize the existence of different universes, existing side by side with our own, in what we might consider a different dimension, where the differences between our universe and this other universe could be miniscule or great. Everything that could have possibly happened in our past, but didn't in our universe, did in another universe, along with all appropriate changes based upon that different happening. This is sometimes known as alternative time lines.

Many Witches believe that the different orders of spiritual beings are simply those entities that exist in different dimensional realms and parallel universes very different from our own, and some have advanced enough to know how to communicate and even traverse into our universe. Tales of the different types of Faery beings through the centuries, such as the races of majickal people in the Arthurian myths, came from these different dimensions.

I believe in parallel universes myself. I had an experience taking the train from Boston into New York. Someone had given me a book on time travel, and I was reading it on the train. Just as soon as we were nearing Montauk—a place famous for strange reality-warping stories though I didn't know it at the time—I opened to a page in the book with the heading "Montauk." I started to get this really weird feeling. We headed into Penn Station and the station was much darker than usual. It was as if the bulbs in the station lights were from the 1930s or 40s. Everything had a yellow tinge to it. A gentleman in a uniform, looking strangely out of place with his little cap and mustache, greeted me; my friends and host who usually greeted me at the train door were not there. There was not the hustle and bustle of all the people exiting the train, just me and the family before me. The uniformed gentleman led me upstairs and it was strangely empty for two in the afternoon. Outside looked as if it were night-time. Everyone seemed to move in slow motion, and at one point, the people all stared directly at me. Then the lights flickered and flashed, and suddenly the room was filled with people and everything was "normal." I called my host in New York to see where she was, and she told me she had gone to Penn Station and hadn't been able to find me. I asked her if she had been there when the lights went out, and she informed me that the lights had not gone out in Penn Station that day. I know that the reading and passage through Montauk triggered a slip into another dimension like our own, but not quite our own. I'm lucky I was able to slip back again.

Parallel Universe Meditation

Start by focusing on a decision that you have made, one that makes you wonder if you have missed out by not choosing something different. Through this meditation, we can gather the insight and energy of the path not chosen. Many believe that every choice we make leads to the creation of a different parallel universe, unfolding as if we had made the alternative choice. Through the majick of the quantum field, we can explore that parallel wisdom.

Once you have chosen your decision point, enter into an alpha state using the Crystal Countdown. Use the Crystal Door meditation to take yourself back to the point of the decision, and decide on the other choice in this instant. Explore your life as if you had made that other choice. Look and feel how your life will be different. Explore it. Feel it. Understand it.

Imagine stepping out of the life and looking at it on the screen of your mind, like a movie. Ask to absorb the lessons and energy of this life choice in a manner that is correct and for your highest good. Feel that energy entering into you.

When done, wipe away the screen of your mind. Use the Crystal Door to return to this place and time, and then return to your body. Give yourself clearance and balance and count up from your alpha state.

ENERGY OF THE BODY AND PSYCHIC ANATOMY

While most Witches are familiar with the seven chakras, we also like to use the Celtic version of the chakras, a simple model known as the Three Cauldrons. Information on the Three Cauldrons is found in an Irish text called *The Cauldron of Poesy:*

"What then is the root of poetry and every other wisdom? Not hard; three cauldrons are born in every person, i.e., the Cauldron of Incubation, the Cauldron of Motion and the Cauldron of Wisdom."

– The Cauldron of Poesy

Location	Traditional Name	English Translations	Powers
Belly	Coire Goiriath	Cauldron of Incubation/Warming	Life Force and Vitality
Heart	Coire Ermae	Cauldron of Motion	Heart, Emotions, and Blessings
Head	Coire Sois	Cauldron of Wisdom	Enlightenment and Inspiration

Location	Traditional Chakras	Colors	Stones
Belly	Root, Belly, Solar Plexus	Red, Orange, Yellow	Garnet, Carnelian, Citrine
Heart	Heart	Green	Emerald, Peridot, Azurite,
Head	Throat, Brow, Crown	Blue, Purple, White	Clear Quartz, Topaz, Opal

The first cauldron supports life, and is upright in everyone. The second cauldron is tilted on its side and requires great joy or great sadness to turn it upright to take its fill, showing emotion is the key to the heart center opening. The third cauldron is turned over, and it requires the work of the other two, plus inspiration, to turn it upright.

To the Celts, the concept of inspiration—Awen in Welsh, and Imbas in Irish—is central to the mysteries. We must be like the gods, inspired with "Fire in the Head." Inspiration descends from above, and we must be ready with our cauldrons to hold it, just as in the Eastern traditions, the Kundalini, the fire serpent, rises from below. Our pathways must be clear. The inspiration and life force are the keys to expanding psychic power and understanding the mysteries.

Three Cauldron Meditation

Enter into an alpha state using the Crystal Countdown method. Be aware of the energy of your body, and perceive the three main centers, the three main cauldrons of your body. Scan your body, dropping all your awareness to your belly first. Feel the cauldron of life. Is it full of life? Or is it depleted? Scan the heart cauldron. Is it on its side? Is it upright? Is it full of any energy, or does it still need filling? Is your heart center not fully enlivened and awake? Then to your head cauldron; is it overturned, on its side, or upright? Do you have access to your inspiration and divine awareness? Or do you need to adjust this center and fill it? Take stock of your entire energy system.

As you inhale, breathe in the energy of the Earth beneath you, into the cauldron of belly. Take deep breaths through the nose, and fill the belly with the life force of the Earth. Feel the Cauldron of Warming growing warm and energizing the entire physical body. Keep breathing until you feel the cauldron is full and at peak physical energy, peak vitality for your own unique body.

Then draw the energy up with your breath to the heart center, to the Cauldron of Motion. Allow yourself to feel great emotion. Think back on deeply emotional times, either times of great sadness or great joy. In fact, thinking of both great sadness and great joy, back and forth, helps "tip" the cauldron right side up, allowing you to feel compassion for yourself and for others. Then allow this cauldron to fill and revitalize your emotional body, your astral or star body, used for journeying. Fill the heart cauldron up.

Then draw the energy up with your breath into the cauldron of the head, the Cauldron of Wisdom and Inspiration. Let all the creative energy, the creative heat, build and flow. You might have difficulty determining the position of the cauldron, but allow the energy to build and in time, it will be upright, and it will be able to catch the three rays of inspiration, of awen, from the heavens. This revitalizes your divine body. This divine body, through the upper cauldron, has all the information of your soul, all the creativity of your soul. Tap into it to access anything you need to know for yourself, or for the inspiration, the vision and energy, to do anything you wish to do.

EASTERN ENERGY SYSTEMS

Our understanding of energy is incomplete in the West. We look to the knowledge of Eastern systems, which hold complete systems on energy, and arts such as Tai Chi and acupuncture. Witches use these systems today, as part of the traditions of borrowed majick, to deepen our own understanding on topics that our ancestors did not record for us to discover today. We believe ancient Witches had an understanding of life energy and how it flows in the body, akin to those in India and Asia, but like the Druids, they did not write down their secrets. We learned the basic Hindu understanding of the seven chakras in the first degree, but now we look to the complex traditions of Asia.

Eastern traditions hold that chi, known as ki in Japan, or life force, flows through very specific pathways that link the subtle systems to the nerves, glands, and organs in the body. In China, these complex pathways, called meridians, are mapped out upon the body. Stimulating certain points on the pathways stimulates the flow of energy and can revitalize specific organs and systems seemingly unconnected to that specific body point, ultimately revitalizing the whole system. Modern practitioners think of it in terms of bio-electricity moving through the body, but it is simply another way to look at the movement of life force. The art of acupuncture, using needles upon the points, should only to be done by a professional licensed acupuncturist. Acupressure, however, is a system one can safely learn and practice on their own, as well as with a professional. Tai Chi is a form of martial art that focuses upon the direction of chi, and has enormous health benefits. Understanding this system of energy creates the foundation for the modern use of energy points known as the Emotional Freedom Technique.

right			left	
Head/Brain		Pituitary		Head/Brain
Teeth/Sinuses		Throat		Teeth/Sinuses
Eye		Nose		Eye
Ear		Neck		Ear
Trapezius		Cervical Spine		Trapezius
Armpit		Thyroid/Bronchia		Armpit
Lung/Chest		Esophagus		Lung/Chest
Arm		Solar Plexus		Heart
Shoulder		Diaphragm		Arm
Liver		Stomach		Shoulder
Gall Bladder		Adrenals		Liver
Kidney		Pancreas		Spleen
Elbow		Duodenum		Elbow
Hip Joint		Lumbar Vertebrae		Kidney
Ascending Colon		Ureter		Hip Joint
Small Intensine		Bladder		Descending Colon
Appendix		Rectum		Small Intensine
Sciatic Nerve		Sacrum		Sciatic Nerve
Knee		Lower Back/Gluteal Area		Knee

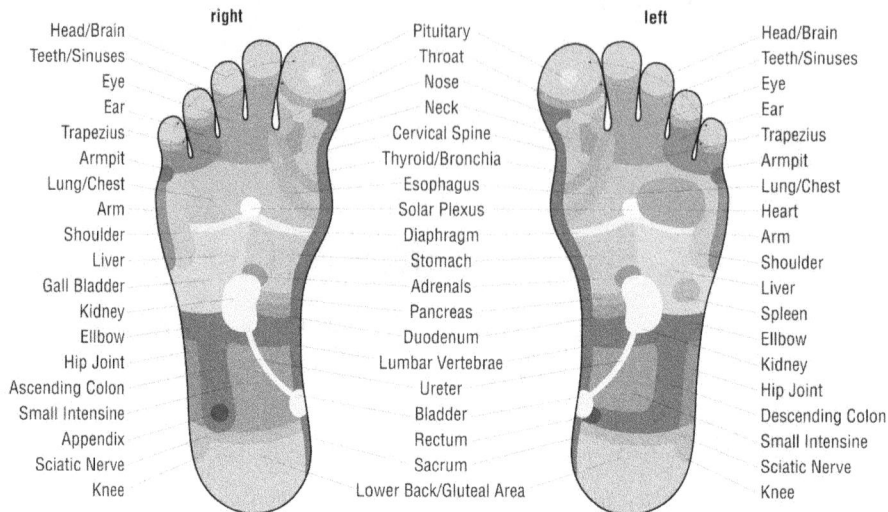

Foot Reflexology Chart

EMOTIONAL FREEDOM TECHNIQUE

An innovative and easy way to incorporate the meridians into your own healing work is EFT, or the Emotional Freedom Technique. During a period of deep depression in my life, a therapist introduced me to it, and it had an immediate effect on my depression. The technique was created and popularized by Garry Craig, but has been embraced by a number of healers, both traditional and non-traditional. It's used a lot in innovative therapy sessions and with energy healers looking to empower their clients.

The theory behind it is that distressing experiences and the memory of such experiences creates a disruption in the body's energy system, and that creates a "negative" emotion which can lead to stress and ill health. This system helps reset and reprogram the energy system around any issue, neutralizing it. People can have profound emotional and even physical healings once cleared. This is an excellent complement to the healing techniques of the Cabot Tradition of Witchcraft.

Basic instructions and variations on the basic instructions can be found in many books and videos, but these are the basics you need to know to effectively try the technique. First, become familiar with the main points involved:

	Point	Meridian	Location
KC	Karate Chop	Small Intensive	Fleshy part of the non-dominant hand, where one would "break" a board if giving a karate chop to it.
EB	Eye Brow	Bladder	Just at the start of the eyebrow, near the center of the brow
SE	Side of the Eye	Gall Bladder	Just outside of the eye
UE	Under the Eye	Stomach	Just beneath the eye, on the bone ridge
UN	Under Nose	Governing	Beneath nose, above lip, centered
Ch	Chin	Central	Beneath lip, centered
CB	Collarbone Sore Spot	Kidney	Just beneath the collarbone where it feels "sore"
UA	Under Arm	Spleen	Parallel to nipple, under the arm
BN	Beneath Nipple	Liver	One inch beneath nipple
Th	Thumb	Lung	Side of thumbnail, outside of thumb
IF	Index Finger	Large intestine	Side of index fingernail, side closest to thumb
MF	Middle Finger	Heart	Side of middle fingernail, side closest to thumb
BF	Baby Finger	Heart	Side of little fingernail, side closest to thumb
9GP	9 Gamut Point	Triple Warmer	Either hand, ½ inch below the middle point between the knuckles of the ring and little fingers.
TH	Top of Head	Hundred Point Meeting	Crown point

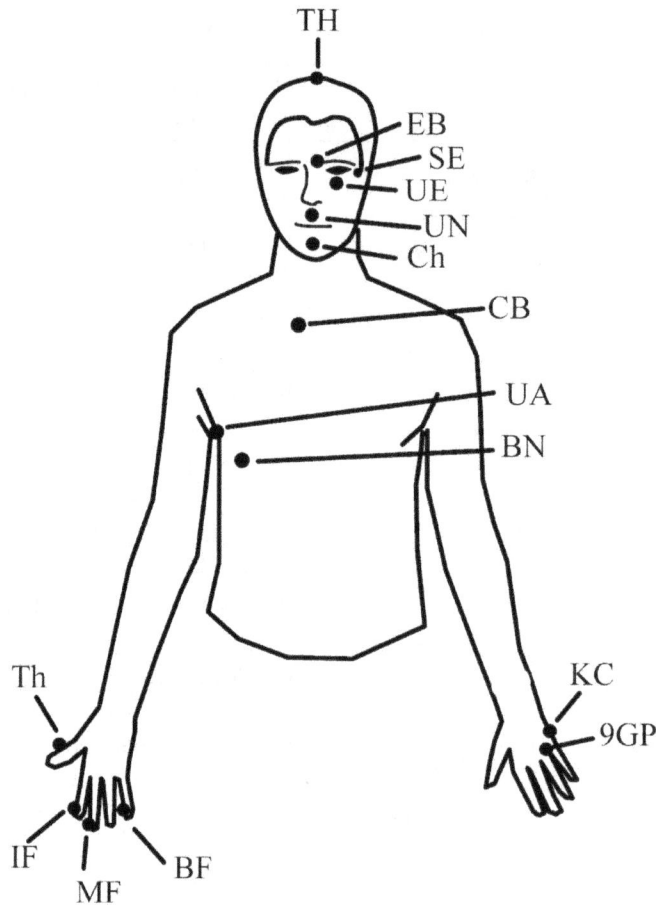

EFT Points on the Body

Set Up — First you have to set up the session. We set things up by reversing our polarity regarding an issue with an affirmation, something like "Even though I have _____, I still love and accept myself unconditionally." Fill in the blank with your issue, emotion, or illness while reciting that affirmation at least three times. The blank in the affirmation is often considered the reminder phrase, used below.

You could say, "Even though I have this anger at my job, I still love and accept myself unconditionally." "Anger at my job" becomes the reminder phrase.

Sequence — Tap seven to ten times on each point with the index and middle finger in the following sequence of points. It doesn't matter which side you do, but only one side is necessary EB, SE, UE, UN, Ch, CB, UA, BN, Th, IF, MF, BF, KC. While tapping, you can repeat the "reminder phrase" continuously. For many, the set-up and sequence is the entire process, but Garry Craig suggests the following additions.

Nine Gamut Point Reprogramming — Tap the gamut point repeatedly while doing these nine actions. This stimulates the Triple Warmer meridian as well as stimulates both hemispheres of the brain.

- Close your eyes
- Open your eyes
- Stare hard down to the right
- Stare hard down to the left
- Roll eyes in a circle clockwise
- Roll eyes in a circle counterclockwise
- Hum a song for two seconds
- Count from one to five
- Hum a song again for two seconds

Then repeat the Sequence section again, and your basic session is complete.

Now some start the sequence tapping the crown of the head. Others add the Below Nipple point after the Under Arm point. Some omit the fingers entirely.

Gauge if you feel some relief. It can be helpful to rank your issue on a scale of one to ten, and then reevaluate after a few sessions. Many experience immediate relief. If your ranking lowers on the scale, you can adjust your affirmation to recognize the relief. You can say, "Even though I have some of _____, I still love and accept myself unconditionally."

Focus on one issue at a time, and repeat EFT sessions three to ten times a day until you feel the problem has been resolved. While this is wonderful for illnesses, pain and long-term issues, it is also excellent when we are in crisis or trapped in any form of obsessive thinking or unhealthy actions. It literally resets our energy system and allows other forms of majick, like sending light, to have greater effect.

EMPOWERMENT, HEALING, AND THE HEALING OF OTHERS

Witches have long been known as the wise women and men, the healers and cunning folk people come to when they are in need. This is still true today, though whenever we can, we try to empower those who come to us, sharing the knowledge of how to heal, as well as lending our majick to their success.

Long ago, I had a surprise knock on my door to remind me that when people are in need, they will find you. Most people don't know where I live. I'm cautious. I was sitting having a cup of tea in my kitchen when there was a loud knock at the door. I answered it and there was a very well-groomed man there. He told me that he had heard I was a Witch and could do healing. I invited him in and said, "Well, let's talk about it." I made him a cup of tea, and we began our consultation at the kitchen table. This man told me about his painful case of tennis elbow and his lack of relief from traditional doctors. Come to find out, not only did he play tennis, but he was a professional in tournaments. I don't follow tennis, so I had no idea who he was or how successful, but he was desperate to save his career. Tennis was the most important thing to him.

My comfrey plants hadn't yet flowered, but they were three feet tall. I knew as he spoke to me that the comfrey was the key. Comfrey is a great herb for regenerating tissue and getting deep to the source of pain. I had been using fresh comfrey leaves for bruises, and overnight it healed any bruises my daughters or I had overnight and they were gone. Fresh comfrey can reach the bone, right through the body.

We went out to the garden, and I began to cut the comfrey leaves. Back in the kitchen we crushed them, placed them in a Pyrex dish, and covered them with boiling water. With soaked gauze, I wrapped his entire arm from his bicep to his wrist with the warm leaves. We then wrapped it in plastic wrap and then a towel. I told him to leave it on overnight. The next day he came back to visit me and told me that it was completely healed. It was the first time in months he was without pain. He was elated. I was concerned it was temporary relief, not a complete cure, but he called me a month later to tell me that he still had no pain and could move it completely. He didn't slide back into pain. Even though I had some doubt, the cure worked and worked permanently on his injury.

I used the same technique on a cross-country skier for an injury of the Achilles heel. He injured it, but it wasn't broken, just painful. We used the same technique, and he too was healed. Both were strangers who knocked on the door unexpectedly, just like with the Witches of old in their huts at the edge of the village.

Keep this in mind as you become clergy in the Witchcraft traditions. It can also help to have some understanding of first aid and basic herbal healing to use in situations like this, to augment your psychic healing and spellcraft.

Please keep in mind this is a list of herbal home remedies, not medical advice for anyone, and when facing illness, consult a doctor. Modern medicine and Witchcraft can work well hand in hand.

List of Healing and Medicinal Uses of Herbs

Arnica — Arnica is a powerful aid to soothe aches, pains, and swellings. It can be used as a poultice, though many creams are made using arnica. It is also very effective as a homeopathic medicine taken whenever there has been trauma or bruising. Homeopathic medicines are available at many health-food stores in pellet form, labeled with a number to indicate how many times and in what system it has been diluted. Take three pellets of Arnica Montana 30c when experiencing trauma or physical bruising.

Chickweed — Also known as starweed, this simple garden herb is nutritious, used in salad, and can be a powerful support in many different bodily systems, internally as a tea, or externally to reduce inflammation, pain, or burns as a poultice. I knew someone who used it as a poison ivy remedy as well. Most importantly, taking chickweed internally helps deal with food cravings and diet management.

Cinnamon — Warming herb that aids in recovery from a cold, as well as eases the pain from rheumatism and arthritis. You can add a pinch of it in tea, coffee, or hot cider, and it can also go into ice tea. A full infusion is made by placing a tablespoon of the powdered bark in a cup of boiling water and drinking to relieve symptoms. Cinnamon can reduce blood pressure too, which is great if you have high blood pressure but should be avoided in excess if you have normal blood pressure.

Dandelion — Dandelion root helps treat jaundice and is a great all-around liver herb. Tea or tincture of it can be taken in the spring for liver cleanse support. It is also a remedy for rheumatism. Dandelion is also a natural diuretic without a lot of mineral loss, as the root and leaf is very nutritious. Make sure if harvesting dandelion, you do not mistake it for several other similar looking, yet very different plants, such as hawkweed.

Fennel — Remedy for stomachaches and digestive issues. Make a tea of fennel seeds by putting a teaspoon of seeds in one cup of boiling water to soothe stomach problems. I learned this when I was unemployed, and both of my daughters had painful stomachaches with vomiting. I was out of money and out of ideas, and this information came directly from the Divine Mind psychically. Their pain was relieved almost instantly, and it works well for many others I've shared it with over the years.

Ginger — Ginger root tea soothes the stomach and aids in digestion. It can also increase metabolism and aid in fighting off colds and flu, particularly if there is a fever involved.

Honey — Natural wildflower honey, local to you, is one of the best medicines and sources of nutrition. It helps boost the immune system. It provides a healthy energy to you, while at the same time being antimicrobial, helping combat all sorts of infections.

Lavender — Lavender essential oil can be used for many problems. It is a sure fire cure for insect stings, burns, and bruises. The scent of it soothes the nerves, and it aids in sleep. It clears the skin and is also an insect repellent. Lavender is antiseptic and can kill off harmful bacteria when inhaled frequently. Christopher Penczak recommends it in a mix of other oils when traveling by plane, to prevent illness from the stale air within the airplane.

Lemon — Lemon is a wonderful, safe and effective all-purpose plant. Lemon juice in water, warm or cold, is a great tonic, and the peel can be made into tea. Lemon helps with indigestion and constipation, aids in weight loss, relieves respiratory issues, combats fever, helps heal colds, flu, sore throat, and high blood pressure. It may also be used topically on the skin for burns and rashes, muscle relaxation, and hair and scalp treatment, and orally as a mouthwash and oral antiseptic.

Licorice Root — Licorice root can help you manage your sugar levels and prevent cravings for sweets. It is also a great remedy for other cravings, such as the craving for nicotine. While tea and tincture are effective, many get the raw "sticks" of licorice root and chew on them to satisfy the oral fixation of any craving or addiction. As a tea it soothes the throat, and it is also a support for fatigued adrenal glands. Like many other herbs, licorice can interact with medications, so check with a health care provider before using it if on prescription medication.

Nettles — Nettles, also known as stinging nettles, can be painful to have in your garden if you are not careful. The little hairs can sting you like a bee. Some people lie down in patches of nettles, for even though the stinging is painful in the moment, it can give relief to arthritis and joint pain for many weeks to months afterwards. When dried, the stingers fall out, and it can be taken as a tea, which is a great source of iron, but also a natural antihistamine to help reduce allergies.

Parsley — Remedy for kidney issues. I took parsley tea regularly; it and practically cured kidney problems induced by my diabetes. My daughter Penny suggested it as a safe remedy for me. Though it doesn't sound pleasant, it wasn't that bad. It's a very earthy and green taste. Once I was on it for a good two weeks, my previously extremely elevated kidney tests went back down to normal.

Red Clover — Red Clover leaf and blossoms are great for all issues of feminine menstrual cycles and reproductive health. It is known as a "blood cleanser," helping normalize and nourish the blood, and it is rich with iron.

Salt — A simple solution of salt water is a remedy for many things. Make a dilute solution of salt and water. You can use it as a rinse for your sinuses for sinus problems and infections. Today, we use pots from India known as Neti pots to help administer it, which are available at many health food and drug stores these days. Salt water baths are also an excellent remedy for hemorrhoids.

Valerian — While it tastes awful to most people, valerian root tea is an excellent sedative, calming the nerves and the mind and allowing a deep sleep. Try taking a cup of tea—with one tablespoon of chopped root to a cup of hot water—before bed. Test it out on yourself, as in a small portion of the population, it acts like a stimulant, not a sedative. Cats think it's better than catnip, showing us that herbs have different effects on animals than they do on people.

Yarrow — Yarrow leaves are used to treat cuts and wounds. The yarrow's natural chemical action causes the wounds to close, and it's also antiseptic, preventing infection in the wound. Yarrow tea is also powerful remedy for the flu and the prevention of flu, but if taken in excess, can be toxic to the liver.

ASTROLOGY

Astrology is a sacred science that guides a Witch upon the path. It helps us understand ourselves, each other, and those who seek us out for aid. By understanding the patterns unfolding in your own chart, you can better prepare and make decisions for your highest good.

Beyond your Sun Sign, Moon Sign ,and Rising Sign, as reviewed in the Second Degree, well-educated Witches should have a basic understanding of their own birth charts. This includes:

Planets and Signs — Each planet occupies a particular sign in the astrological chart. Planets are often described as actors, parts of yourself in the chart, taking on one of twelve different roles. Understanding what part of you is acting, and in what way it is acting, is an important piece of self knowledge.

Sun — Personal Self, Healthy Identity, Ego Development, Who you are learning to be in this life
Moon — Emotional Self, Karma you are earning in this lifetime, Reaction, Emotional Memory
Mercury — Mental Self, Personal Mind, Memory, Education, Communication
Venus — Social Self, Friendships, Romance, Ability to Attract
Mars — Action Self, Will, Power, Energy, Ability to Act
Jupiter — Higher Self, Benevolence, Good Fortune, Big Picture, Also Excesses
Saturn — Taskmaster, Judge, Responsibilities, Consequences
Uranus — Higher Mind, Inspiration, Sudden and Unexpected Changes
Neptune — Higher Love, Unconditional Love, Creativity, Dreams
Pluto — Higher Will, Destruction and Death, Forces that inhibit Higher Will, Transformation, Rebirth

Houses and Signs — If planets are the actors, and signs are the roles, then the houses are the scenes, the "where" the action takes place in our life. Every house, one of the twelve divisions of the sky, is "ruled" by one of the twelve signs. Every planet occupies a house.

First House — House of Self Identity, Relationship to your inner personal self

Second House — House of Resources, Wealth, Possessions, Skills to earn money

Third House — House of Daily Communication, Siblings, Learning

Fourth House — House of Home, Mother, Nurturing, Childhood

Fifth House — House of Children and Lovers, Creativity, Ego Development

Sixth House — House of Daily Work, Healing, Service

Seventh House — House of Partnership and Marriage

Eighth House — House of Sex, Death, and Taxes; Transformation, Things we cannot control

Ninth House — House of Higher Education, Philosophy, Travel

Tenth House — House of Career and Vocation

Eleventh House — House of Social Consciousness, Friendships, Society

Twelfth House — House of Merging, Undoing, Hidden Enemies

Aspects — Aspects are special angles between planets, to denote the relationship between two planets as being particularly easy and supportive, or difficult. In spell casting, they tell us when to use or not use a particular planet's energy; in the birth chart, they represent more complex relationships and networks of energy. They are the "building blocks" of our character.

PLANETARY INFLUENCES UPON YOU

Within the science of astrology, there are some basic influences the planets and signs can place upon you. These influences are based upon your birth, or natal, chart.

Transit — Transits are the study of the relationships between the current positions of the planets and the positions of the planets when you were born. The places in the sky that were occupied by planets when you were born become "sensitive areas" in the sky for you now. Planets that pass over those points, or make other aspects to them, such as oppositions (180 degree angle), trines (120 degree angle), and squares (90 degree angle), will trigger issues involving both the current planets and the planet that occupied that space when you were born. The Uranus Opposition is a famous transit, named for when Uranus is halfway in its cycle, at the opposite point of where it was when you were born, occurring near age forty-two.

Return — Returns are transits that occur when a planet returns to the place it occupied when you were born, indicating an end of a cycle for that planet. Some transits are easier and more frequent than others, like the Mars cycle which is a little over two years. Witches look out for the Jupiter return, which happens every twelve years, and the Saturn return, which happens every twenty-nine and a half years.

Progression — Progression is a system of predicting your life cycle by advancing your birth chart a day for every year of your life. To predict the forces unfolding at age twenty, an astrologer would "progress" your chart twenty days from your birth date, for a snapshot of your life. Progressed planetary signs can differ from their birth signs. Anyone over thirty will have their Sun sign progress at least into the next sign. The natal chart is not obsolete—it is the template—but this progressed chart gives you many areas of understanding.

Composite — Astrologers combine the charts of any two people in relationship to understand the composite energy of the relationship. When you enter into any relationship with another— whether for romance, business or friendship—you now have a composite chart ruling over that relationship and informing the "life" of the relationship.

THE "MYTHIC" PLANETS

Several planets are not found in traditional astrology, but can be useful to Witches. In the Cabot Tradition, we work with—through my own psychic experience of—the planets Vulcan, Sparta, and the Earth herself. Modern astrologers also have quite a few "new" heavenly bodies to influence us. Many of these unproved "hypothetical" planets may not exist in our dimension, but as in the teaching of esoteric astrology, influence us from an etheric realm.

Vulcan — Vulcan is speculated to be an inter-mercurial planet too close to the Sun to really be detected. It played a role in the teaching of *Esoteric Astrology* by Alice Bailey and some astrologers speculated an ephemeris for this planet. Vulcan is the "jeweler or craftsman of the gods" and puts total power into any majick.

Sparta — Sparta is said to be a twin to the Earth, unspoiled paradise, on the opposite side of the Earth's orbit. It helps us connect to the pure spirit of nature.

Earth — Earth is no hypothetical planet, but is often forgotten in the astrological chart and in astrological magick. The Earth is said to be in the opposite sign of the Sun, though technically it can be found in the center of the astrological chart. Earth rules over all aspects of earthly life and incarnation.

Transpluto — Transpluto is a hypothetical planet beyond the orbit of Pluto. Even though we've identified many transplutonian masses, esoteric astrologers are still holding out for a larger planet mass. It has been sometimes referred to as Persephone or Proserpine, Pan, or Niburu. It is said to rule over the outer darkness, and often has a feminine, dark queen quality to it, as well as rulership over fear, shadows, and justice.

Chiron — Chiron is a "planetoid" orbiting elliptically between Saturn and Uranus. It rules over where we are wounded physically and emotionally, how we heal, and how we share that healing with others. All forms of holistic treatments are influenced and ruled by Chiron.

Asteroids — The asteroid belt is found between Mars and Jupiter, and many believe it was either a destroyed planet, or a planet that never formed. Some refer to this planet as Tiamat or Maldek. It has a strong goddess association, with many of the asteroids named after goddesses, balancing out the predominantly male planets. Four main asteroids—Ceres, Pallas, Vesta and Juno—are said to embody the archetypes of Mother, Daughter, Sister, and Wife respectively.

Dark Moon Lilith — The Dark Moon Lilith has been considered a hypothetical natural satellite, but is most likely the point in the "void" between the Earth and the Moon's apogee, being a shadow sister to the Earth, and representing a lot of the repressed and suppressed feminine powers.

ASTROLOGICAL AGES AND THE PROCESSION OF THE EQUINOXES

We often say we are entering into the "New Age" meaning we are leaving the Age of Pisces and entering into the Age of Aquarius. Due to a wobble in the Earth's axis, where we spin like a very slow top, the area of the heavens where the axis points changes, making a large cosmic cycle known a the Great Year. Within the great year are twelve great "months" or ages, following the Zodiac signs backwards.

In western astrology, we measure the Zodiac by the space around the Earth, marked by the seasons. At the Vernal Equinox, the Sun enters the first degree of what astrologers call Tropical Aries. The Tropical Zodiac is the zodiac of the seasons and space around the Earth. The Sidereal

Zodiac refers to the actual star constellations, and is used in Hindu, or Vedic, Astrology. At one point in our history, the first degree of Tropical Aries and Sidereal Aries were the same. Due to the wobble, they are proceeding out of phase with each other until the cycle is complete. While the Vernal Equinox is always the first degree of Tropical Aries, the Sidereal sign indicates what cosmic month we are currently in, and we are said to be entering the cosmic month of Aquarius, the sign of science, technology, equality, utopia, revolution, inspiration, non-hierarchy, and cosmic consciousness. Pisces was the age of hierarchy, duality, sacrifice, unconditional love, martyrdom, art, and creativity. Much of the best and worst of that age was in the embodiment of the Christian Church. Now, we are making new spiritual expressions and returning to old wisdoms in the Age of Aquarius, prophesized by many as either a golden age and utopia, or a time of great disaster.

The wobbling pole of the Earth presents another mystery teaching. The North Star changes, rotating through several bright stars, though not with the regularity of the cosmic months or ages. We feel this myth plays out in the Arthurian Myths, with the change from Uther Pendragon to Arthur. Uther represents the time of the Dragon Kings, when the pole star was Thuban, in the constellation Draco the Dragon. King Arthur is the Bear King, as Arthur means bear, and our current North Star, Polaris, is in Ursa Minor, or the Little Bear constellation.

Power of the Witch Incense

Sometime the Witch Power just wells up inside you and you don't know why. You might feel an urge to make something powerful, or do some big majick. You might feel it rise up from your solar plexus, or get a powerful tingling in your fingers. This feeling rises up and tells us 'tis time to make something powerful.' For me, it would happen at the oddest times, but I would follow my gut and reach for the herbs and oils. Each time, I found I would need it later for myself or someone else. So follow those urges.

When you feel it next and are unsure what to do, try making the Power of the Witch formula. My Power of the Witch formulas are based upon one simple premise—an ingredient for each of the twelve zodiac signs. Over the years I've designed a number of Power of the Witch perfumes, potions, and oils, and each one had twelve ingredients. Make your own personal formula for a Power of the Witch incense, oil, or potion. Pick one ingredient for each of the twelve zodiac signs. As the power rises up in you, charge the entire mixture and power will exude from it. Do anything that empowers you as a part of the process. Crush a stone with a hammer to add it to the formula. Use food coloring to make your power color. I like purple, and would mix red and blue together to make a potion purple. Use what ever empowers you, but make sure to use twelve items, one for each zodiac. Then your Power of the Witch mix can be used for anything, at any time. The zodiac formula gives it access to all the powers of the stars. Power of the Witch can be used in all forms of majick, for any intention.

CELTIC TREE "ASTROLOGY"

The traditional three hundred and sixty degrees of the zodiac has been altered in a system primarily popularized by Helena Patterson, to reflect a thirteen-sign division. Using the chart below, you can convert your entire astrological chart into its Celtic Tree Astrology equivalent, and gain a new perspective on the placement of your planets. Each of your planets is marked in your traditional astrological chart by a sign, which is divided into thirty degrees. Each degree is divided into sixty "minutes." The chart below divides the signs by Tree Ogham. Calculate what sign each of your planets is in by Tree sign, as well as your Rising Sign. For more guidance in interpretation, please look to resources such as *The Celtic Astrology Handbook* by Helena Patterson.

Tree	Ogham	Degrees	Qualities
Birch	Beth	2°00` – 29°59` Capricorn	Ambitious, successful, Family responsibility
Rowan	Luis	0°00` – 27°59` Aquarius	Visionary, Humanitarian, Controversial, Opinionated
Ash	Nion	28°00` Aquarius – 25°59` Pisces	Artistic, Sensitive, Compassionate, Realistic
Alder	Fearn	26°00` Pisces – 23°59` Aries	Warrior, Leader, Competitive, Impatient
Willow	Saille	24°00` Aries – 20°59` Taurus	Psychic, Mystical, Hidden, Mysterious, Emotional
Hawthorn	Uath	21°00` Taurus – 17°59` Gemini	Charisma, Craftsmanship, Strategy, Leadership
Oak	Duir	18°00` Gemini – 14°59` Cancer	Optimistic, Charming, Successful, Sacrifice
Holly	Tinne	15°00` Cancer – 11°59` Leo	Strong Will, Values, Loyal, Historical, Pretentious

Tree	Ogham	Degrees	Qualities
Hazel	Coll	12°00` Leo – 8°59` Virgo	Communication, Wisdom, Good Memory, Challenging
Vine	Muin	9°00` Virgo – 6°59` Libra	High Emotions, Restless, Gentle, Angry, Sad, Gentle
Ivy	Gort	7°00` Libra – 4°59` Scorpio	Justice, Responsibility, Shrewd, Manipulative
Reed	Ngetal	5°00` Scorpio – 2°59` Sagittarius	Personal Power, Magnetism, Imaginative, Obsessive
Elder	Ruis	3°00` Sagittarius – 1°59` Capricorn	Transformative, powerful, Disciplined, Adventurous

If you convert my own astrology chart, you can see my planets by their Tree Sign. So my Sun Tree Sign would be Ash, my Moon Sign Oak, and my Rising Sign Oak.

Rising Sign	22 Degrees	Gemini	Oak	Duir
Sun	15 Degrees	Pisces	Ash	Nion
Moon	11 Degrees	Cancer	Oak	Duir
Mercury	03 Degrees	Aries	Alder	Fearn
Venus	04 Degrees	Pisces	Ash	Nion
Mars	08 Degrees	Virgo	Hazel	Coll
Jupiter	18 Degrees	Virgo	Vine	Muin
Saturn	11 Degrees	Aquarius	Rowan	Luis
Uranus	21 Degrees	Aries	Alder	Fearn
Neptune	08 Degrees	Virgo	Hazel	Coll
Pluto	21 Degrees	Cancer	Holly	Tinne

Astral Exploration of the Solar System and Galaxy

Burn Power of the Witch incense to attune to the entire solar system and all the stars of the zodiac. Enter into your alpha brainwave state through the use of the Crystal Countdown. You are going to use the same technique we have used in the Past Life Regression meditation. Allow yourself to leave your physical body and exit through a door that leads outside. Using your psychic light and will, affix a blazing white pentacle to the door as you leave. Then, allow yourself to rise up, to ascend above the building. Notice the features as you go higher. Look down, and fix a glowing white pentacle to the rooftop beneath you. This will be your guide to return.

Rise up, higher and higher into the atmosphere, and beyond. State your intention to "safely explore the solar system, and then galaxy, and return safely when I wish."

Find yourself traveling outward, beyond the Moon. Take notice of the Moon, and how it looks up close, which is probably much more different from what you might expect. Look to the Sun, almost too bright, white, holding the center of the solar system together, and gaze out into the orbits of the inner planets first, such as Venus, Mercury and even Vulcan. The proportions might be very different from what you are expecting from textbooks. Then look outward to the planets beyond Earth's orbit, to Mars, the asteroids, and the more massive Jupiter and Venus, with their many moons as well.

You go beyond Saturn, into the orbits of Uranus, Neptune. and the tilted orbit of Pluto. Beyond that are many rocky bodies in a cloud of smaller celestial objects. You head outward, toward the stars, and begin your exploration now.

Look into the many systems of our galaxy, never losing the internal sense of "home" with your white light pentacles.

When you feel you are done, turn your attention behind you, and think of home. State your intention "return, return, return" and feel the pull of the white light pentacles on the roof and door guiding you home. Travel swiftly through space to return to our solar system, making your way from the outer planets to the inner planets, with our brilliant white Sun at the center of it. Some believe our soul must make its way through each of these planets before incarnation into the Earthly sphere, so you have done this before. Make your way back to Earth and our Moon, and begin your descent through the atmosphere. Return, return, return, finding the white pentacle down from where you are now. Land safely on the white roof pentacle. Descend down in front of the door, and find the other white light pentacle. Enter the building and find yourself returning to your physical body. Wiggle your fingers and toes to make sure you are back. Give yourself total health clearance and the count yourself back up from alpha level.

FIVE: THE RELIGION OF WITCHCRAFT

"Generally speaking, there are three uniquely honored groups among the Gauls: Bards, Votes, and Druids. The Bards are singers and poets, while the Votes oversee sacred rites and examine natural phenomena. The Druids also study the ways of nature, but apply themselves to laws of morality as well. The Gauls consider the Druids the most just of people and so are entrusted with judging both public and private disputes. In the past, they even stopped battles which were about to begin and brought an end to wars. Murder cases especially are handed over to the Druids for judgment. They believe that when there are many condemned criminals available for sacrifice, then the land will prosper. Both the Druids and others say that the human soul and the universe as well are indestructible, but that at some time, both fire and water will prevail."

— Strabo

WITCHCRAFT AS A RELIGION

We believe that what we call Witchcraft was an ancient religion that was suppressed and forgotten. Those whom we call Witches and Druids were the priestesses and priests of this ancient religion. Through the persecution and suppression by the Christian Church of those indigenous European practices, we have lost the holy spiritual roots of our culture. It is important to understand the history of this persecution, what some call the Burning Times. I suggest all Witches read *The Witch's Hammer,* the handbook for persecuting Witches.

Modern Witchcraft, borrowing much in an effort to reconstruct what was lost, is the revival of those practices. Today, we are still very misunderstood, as our religion is different in scope from the mainstream religions of today.

In our modern Witchcraft and Pagan culture, there are many expressions of the ancient religions:

British Traditional Wicca — British Traditional Wicca, sometimes also referred to as British Traditional Witchcraft, refers to specific lines of teachings originating with Gerald Gardner, who gives us Gardnerian Wicca, and Alex and Maxine Sanders, who give us Alexandrian Wicca. One must be initiated into the tradition by a recognized group or High Priest/ess to be a member, though much of the Wicca material has become public and forms the basis of Eclectic Wicca. A variety of other traditions with either direct links, or imitations of British Traditional Wicca-style teachings, also continue the traditions. It is important to realize the founders never called themselves "Wiccan" or what they practiced "Wicca"; it was Witchcraft.

Eclectic Wicca — A modern, freeform style of Wicca focusing upon self-dedication and self-initiation, as well as an eclectic myth and ritual practice. Though popularized by Scott Cunningham, it really began with Raymond Buckland's Seax Wicca tradition.

British Traditional Witchcraft — Those who use this name differently from British Traditional Wicca refer to a pre-Gardnerian form of Witchcraft, more deeply rooted in the folk ways and customs of the British people without the same ceremonial and masonic influences found in Wicca. Witches are usually not sky clad; they have a stronger link to the myths and landscape of Britain, but can also embrace the Medieval sabbatic imagery of the Witch found in the Witchcraft trial transcripts. Some, but not all, refer to themselves as Luciferian. The Kent tradition would be considered British Traditional Witchcraft.

Modern Witchcraft — Modern Witchcraft can be inspired by, or an amalgam of, any form of Wicca or Witchcraft styled to suit the life of the modern practitioner.

Ceremonial Magicians — Ceremonial Magicians are those who continue the traditions of the medieval grimoire traditions—the Hermeticist, Theurgists, and Alchemists, and most recently those in the vein of the Golden Dawn, Aleister Crowley's Thelema, and the teachings of Dion Fortune. Many modern magicians self-identify as Pagan or Witch along with their practices as ceremonial magicians.

Neopaganism and Paganism — Neopaganism, or new paganism, and those self identified as Pagans, belong to a wider category of Earth-based spiritual traditions looking for inspiration from the ancient customs of the Western World. Some are Pagans philosophically, or in lifestyle. Others practice the majick and religions of Paganism.

Reconstructionism — Reconstructionists are Pagans who focus on a specific culture and time period, or use the available historical information to reconstruct the religion of that time and place to the best of their abilities. Historical accuracy and verified information tend to be more important than personal inspiration. Reconstructionists can be found in the Celtic, Norse, Greek, Roman, and Egyptian traditions.

Heathenism — Heathen is the northern term that is usually equated with Pagan, meaning "people of the heath." Teutonic-based Pagans, including those following German, Norse, and Saxon practices, will often refer to themselves as Heathen, not Pagan, Wiccan, or Witch. Within the Heathen traditions, a specific popular branch is known as Asatru, meaning followers of the sky gods known as the Aesir.

Shamanism — Today shamanism refers to a wide range of tribal-influenced healing and spirit-based practices. Mostly commonly associated with Native American religions, technically the word "shaman" comes from the Tuguska region of Siberia and refers to medicine practitioners from that culture. It has been later applied to the spirit healing practices of all indigenous people and separated into the "core shamanism" practices found globally. Many think of Witchcraft as a European form of "shamanism."

New Age Traditions — New Age Traditions fit any and all seekers in the modern age who mix and blend religious practices and who seek healing, meditation, and the secrets of the ancient world. Though often forgotten, the roots of the New Age movement are found in Spiritualism and Theosophy, serious esoteric studies that also influenced modern Witchcraft.

The Cabot Tradition considers itself Modern American Traditional Witchcraft. We draw from the Kent Tradition, considered British Traditional Witchcraft, but have developed here in America, amid the folk and occult teaching in America, in the environment of Salem, Massachusetts. We are modern people, infusing the newest ideas of quantum science with our majick, as well as an understanding of Hermetic philosophy and metaphysical lore. When I began, there was not all of this information available as there is today. We used what we had. We borrowed and adapted from books. We found our own way.

RELIGIOUS THEOLOGY AND "BELIEFS"

Unlike other religions, Witches don't believe. We know. At least we know what is right for us. There is no required belief in anything. We experience things, and we know them to be true for us. No one has to "convert" through a statement of beliefs.

We often frame our experiences and systems to understand them in the ways our ancestors did, and make connections to the same spirits and gods that our spiritual ancestors connected with, to continue the traditions. But no one is required to believe anything without experiencing it. An open mind and a willingness to experience are the only two requirements.

But when talking with others, those experiences, techniques and systems lead us to some core statements about Witchcraft that we agree upon, that many might see as beliefs. They include:

- Witchcraft is a Nature-based Religion.
- Witchcraft is a Mystery Tradition from the Stars.
- Witches celebrate eight sabbats marking the turning of the Wheel of the Year.
- Witches celebrate the thirteen moons of the lunar year as times of majick.
- Witches believe in the immortality of the soul and consciousness after death.
- Witches believe in the existence of spirits and psychic communication with spirits. Spirits can include former humans now deceased, and non-human spirits.
- Witches believe in the return of the soul to a new body through reincarnation.
- Witches believe in a multitude of goddesses and gods alive in another world, the oldest of the ancestral spirits. Other expressions of deity as Goddess and God are aspects of the Divine Mind in polarity and gender.
- Witches believe in majick, the ability to create change in both inner and outer worlds.
- Witches use divination to gain non-linear information about the past, present, and future.

COMPARISONS OF WITCHCRAFT AS A RELIGION TO OTHER RELIGIONS

Modern Witches should be thoroughly educated in other religious traditions, the better to understand their own belief systems and theologies, particularly how they differ and are the same as our own. Familiarizing yourself with the following traditions is a good start to this global religious survey:

- Judaism
- Christianity (including Catholicism, Protestantism, and Orthodox Christianity)
- Islam
- Hinduism
- Buddhism
- Sikhism

- Jainism
- Baha'i
- Zoroastrianism
- Daoism
- Shinto
- Voudou
- Native American Religions

Time Travel to the Ancient Past

I have always found turquoise to be an excellent stone for time travel. You can hold a cleared turquoise stone programmed for that intention when doing this work. Hold it in your left hand. Rhodochrosite placed upon the brow also helps. Use the Crystal Countdown to enter into a trance state. Call forth the mists of the Earth, and feel a cool otherworldy mist rise, like breath upon the cold air, until it surrounds you in an opaque white glow. Feel as if you have become untethered to the Earth, that you are floating in the mist with the Earth somewhere beneath you. The Earth is turning, but you are turning away from the modern day and floating towards the past, to the deep memories of the Earth and of our ancestors. You are moving in time, and in space, to a time when the Ancient Ones ruled, when the ancient Witches and Priestesses shaped the world.

You will feel yourself reconnect with the Earth, and feel as if you are stepping down upon the Earth. The mist begins to fade, and you appear like a ghost in the space and time, with no substance, only as an observer. Where are you? When are you? Who and what do you see?

Wander about, exploring this past time. Look for our ancestors and see what work they are doing. What are their rituals? What are their spells? What can you learn from their practice?

Observe them interacting with their community and with each other. Observe them in their daily lives. You might feel as if you are watching this time go by at an accelerated pace, showing you what you need to see and hear in this journey.

When your time here is done and you've learned all you can at this point, the mists will begin to rise again. You'll feel yourself floating up a bit off the ground as the white mist surrounds you, and you'll be turning towards the present time and place, back to your physical body here and now. Give yourself clearance and balance, and count yourself up from alpha level.

Advanced Majick Mirror

We study the stars and cosmos to better known ourselves. As above, so below. As we use the stars and astrology to be more reflective and aware, we can use the techniques of the "mirror" to be more aware about ourselves and the High Priestess or High Priest we wish to be. The heavens are said to be mirrored on Earth. Now that you have some deeper introspective tools from the last lesson, Lesson Four, you can explore your personal development and growth. This will help you go deeper when you have to focus on your rebirth in Lesson Ten.

Hopefully, you have been continuing your affirmations and majick mirror exercises, looking to align yourself with the three keys of esteem, confidence, and love. But sometimes we need to face what is not changing, then name it, claim it, and take responsibility for transforming it.

Start by facing a mirror, ideally a mirror hanging on a wall where you can sit before it and really look at yourself and talk to yourself. Have a notebook with you, and divide the notebook into two columns. Choose one side to present helpful and healing aspects of yourself. The other side is for harmful, detrimental aspects of yourself.

Look at yourself, and write down the "good" things about yourself that you see, feel, and hear. Be honest. Claim who and what you are truly are and appreciate yourself.

Then look at yourself, and write down all the "bad" things about yourself that you don't like, things that are harming or holding you back. Do not punish yourself, but simply be objectively honest with yourself, as if looking at yourself through the eyes of a neutral person.

Review the "good" list and divide it into traits you have naturally and traits you have "earned" through doing work and making conscious choices.

Review the "bad" list and divide it into things that are inherent and you feel cannot change, and those that you feel you can take responsibility for and change. This is a tough list, as we often feel we can't change something, but often the real reason is that we have chosen to think of something as permanent because we've chosen not to change it.

Evaluate these lists in the mirror. Look at yourself and forgive yourself for things that are truly beyond your control. Thank yourself for the good things you have been given. Praise yourself for the things you have truly earned. And promise yourself to change the things you have power to change.

Record this in your journal. Repeat this exercise at least one or twice more during the course of your training year, and occasionally as you progress as a High Priestess or High Priest, taking a majick mirror inventory. Use the techniques you've learned, including meditation, spirit guides, healing, spells, energy work of the cauldrons/chakras, EFT, and astrology to help create strategies to make better choices, change your thinking, and keep your promise to yourself.

Six: The Powers of the Earth and the Stone

"City wisdom became almost entirely centered on the problems of human relationships,
in contrast to the wisdom of any natural tribal group, where relationships with the rest of the
animate and inanimate world are still given due place."
— *Gaia: A New Look at Life on Earth* by James E. Lovelock

Planetary Consciousness

Our planet is alive. Our planet is living, thinking and feeling. Did you know that? Biologist James E. Lovelock pointed the way to remembering what the ancient people knew all along in his Gaia Hypothesis. While he didn't necessarily say that the world was thinking and emotional, he did say that the biosphere behaved like a living organism, and that all things in it were part of a greater system. We are part of that greater system, like cells within the biosphere of Mother Nature.

The ancients have always taught that the world was alive. We still call her Mother Nature today. She is the Goddess of the Earth. A wide variety of goddesses were said to be the "Soul of the World" including the Greek Gaea and Hecate, Egyptian Isis, and even the Christian Holy Sophia, Goddess of Wisdom.

Many believe she is the basis of our collective consciousness, currently a collective unconsciousness. Together, we dream the dream of the world. Witches learn to awaken to their relationship with nature, with Mother Earth, with sacred land. As Witches, we must hear the call of the Goddess of the Earth, and live our lives in harmony with her as much as we possibly can.

Brain Wave States and The Planet Earth

Just as we shift between brainwave states, the Earth herself has different zones associated with those brainwave states. When we attune our brainwaves to those frequencies, we attain a level of connection to the Earth. Some would say that the natural state of those on the surface of the Earth is alpha, but we've created a culture that values beta wave lengths, missing out on our natural state of being. Perhaps our "Garden of Eden" is really to be upon the Earth in our aware and connected alpha state.

Iron Core of the Earth	40 Hz	High Beta, Inspiration, Creative Flashes, Deep Focus
Layers Within the Earth	40-7 Hz	Relaxation from Inspiration, to Beta, to Alpha
Earth's Crust	7.5 Hz	Transition Between Alpha and Theta
Inner Van Allen Belt	7-4 Hz	Theta
Outer Van Allen Belt	4-1 Hz	Delta

(Chart adapted from *The Mayan Calendar and the Transformation of Consciousness* by Carl Johann Callerman)

THE SACRED LANDSCAPE

To our tradition, our sacred homeland is the British Isles. The sacred sites of our mythos are tied deeply to the land of England, Ireland, Scotland, and Wales. Ireland herself is divided into the four sacred provinces around the spiritual center. Britain itself can also be divided from the sacred center, the Isle of Man, sacred to the sea god Manannan.

The center of Ireland is very sacred to us, with Tara the holy center and the mythic city of the Tuatha De Dannan central to our rites. The Hill of Tara still has the sacred king stone. Tara is near the Stone Age sacred site of New Grange, located in County Meath, the modern center, known for its ancient spiral patterns and for being a tomb and birthing chamber of the goddess, allowing the light in on the Winter Solstice.

Along with Tara, our next pivotal sacred site is found in Glastonbury, England. Glastonbury is said to be the mythic isle of Avalon, with the Glastonbury Tor towering over the landscape and both the Red and White Wells near its base. This is holy isle of priestesses in the Otherworld, and today, Glastonbury is still an interface for such powers, being a land of sacred ancient oaks such as Gog and Magog, apple trees, and holy hawthorn. Many believe Glastonbury is the heart chakra of Mother Earth. Not far from Glastonbury is Cadbury Castle, the supposed site of Camelot, as well as the famous Stonehenge and Avebury circles.

The Chalice Well

Along with these most popular sites, we also hold sacred the sites of Scotland and Wales, particularly those sacred to Merlin, such as Dinas Emrys, where Merlin gave his first prophecy as a child in the mountains of Snowdonia, Wales. Merlin's Cave in Tintagel, England is also a sacred site.

Less well known are the Sacred Sites and forests of Kent, England, where our ancestors in the Kent Tradition of Witches come from. The standing stones of Kits Coty, of the Medway Megaliths, is probably the most famous of these.

Egypt plays a strong role in our majick, due to the connections to the ancient world, and to Scotland. We look to the ancient temples there, particularly the pyramid chambers of Giza.

While perhaps not a traditional sacred site—more of an infamous site—Salem, Massachusetts, is a place where we honor the souls of those who gave their lives in Witchcraft's name, even if they were not necessarily Witches themselves. With all the Witches, psychics, covens, and rituals here, along with the Crystal Wheel, Salem has developed quite an energy to it, and opens the doors to Witchcraft for many seekers starting on the path.

LEY LINES AND VORTICES

Sacred sites are considered to be special majickal places, standing between the worlds. The energy is higher there. They are said to each be a vortex of power, where two or more ley lines, or energy lines, cross. Ley lines are considered to be the meridians of the Earth, and where they meet are like chakras of the Earth. Some are major chakra points, like our seven main points, while others are minor, like those on our fingers and toes. Each gives us access to the entire planetary grid of the Earth. Ceremony and majick at a vortex are considered to be stronger, more energized, and more immediately global in scope.

While there are major ley lines in famous sacred places, there are a whole host of minor ley lines all around. They are probably in your town, and even in your own yard. You can dowse for ley lines with L-shaped dowsing rods. Cleanse and charge the rods. Move with the L-shape rods, asking to find a ley line. Where they cross, there is a ley line. Move to find where that ley line is coming from, and what direction it is heading in. Most ley lines are considered to be fairly straight, but some ley lines are spiraling out of vortices.

Ley lines have been associated with several different spiritual phenomena:

Faery Paths — Often the lines of force are associated with "trouping faeries" that rise from the ground, revivify or protect an area, and then return below the surface. To block one of these paths is to invite disaster from the Faery realm.

Ghost Roads and Dead Man's Tracks — Some believe that ghosts, or at least spirits that have not yet crossed over first, can only travel upon these lines and will gather at vortices. Some may even find their way to cross into new realms through the vortex.

Witch's Paths — The flight of the medieval Witches off to the sabbat in the woods was said to follow the paths of the ley lines, as they wandered with the Wild Hunt along with ghosts, faeries, and gods.

Dragon Line — The ley lines are most popularly associated with the power of dragons, or at least ancient reptilian forces circling the Earth.

UFOs — In the modern age, there is a higher percentage of UFO sightings near sacred sites and along known ley line paths, making many speculate that the UFOs follow the ley lines as we would follow highway roads.

All of the mysteries of the ley lines are associated with strange lights, natural trance states, unexplained time loss, healing, illness, and contact from unseen races.

EARTH DRAGON ENERGY

In the planetary grids around Mother Earth, the ley lines are described as male and female, or red and white. Just as the chakras have the Ida (lunar) and Pingala (solar) channels, the Earth has energies described as red and white channels, referring to the red and white dragons of mythology. When a sacred site or a ley line is desecrated, it is sometimes called a black dragon.

In *The Mabinogion*, the tale of Lludd and Llefelys has a red and white dragon in it. They are the manifestation of the "second plague" and Lludd must put them to sleep with mead and bury them in stone caskets. Many made comparisons between the figures of Llud and Llefelys and Lugh and Nuada in *The Second Battle of Mag Tuired* in the Irish traditions. More importantly, the two sleeping dragons appear again in *The Prophecies of Merlin* as told in *The Histories of the Kings of Britain.* In his first prophecy, he correctly predicts the source of the falling tower being two dragons, red and white, stuck in stones, and attempting to fight. They are released and his prophecies continue. Many believe the dragons are not physical entities, but metaphors for telluric powers, akin to the popular "Mary" and "Michael" ley lines that run through Somerset.

One form of dragon we can work with is the living life force of the Earth. Though it's from a popular movie, the authors of Excalibur perceived a similar truth, with the stories of Merlin's "dragon" being the life of the planet itself, and his Charm of Making a way to direct the Dragon's Breath and energy to make majick and change.

Dragon's Mist Oil

1 Dram of Heather Oil
1 Dram of Oak Moss Oil
1 Dram of Pine Oil
3 Drams of Witchhazel Extract
1 Sprig of Broom, chopped fine

1 Piece of Irish Moss, chopped fine
2 Pinches of Vervain
½ Teaspoon of Sea Salt

The Dragon's Mist: Calling forth the Dragon's Breath

Wind among the boughs did song,
and the dragon's wing did move
across the Midnight sky.
Trails of mist on Earth so long,
and the dragon's breath did prove,
Merlin did not lie.

THE CABOT CRYSTAL WHEEL AND THE PLANETARY GRID

Go to the Crystal Wheel above Salem, Massachusetts, and with your new understanding of the energy grids around the Earth, look out from the Crystal Wheel, and see how it is connected to the greater planetary grids. Understand how the Crystal Wheel is a majickally constructed sacred vortex intersecting with the energies of the town of Salem and its connection to the greater grids around the world.

If you are studying with a Cabot teacher, both of the following exercises can be done together in the Majick Circle with the class.

Attuning Your Stone to the King Stone of the Cabot Tradition

Clear your own altar stone of any unwanted energies using protection potion or incense. Make sure you have chosen a special stone from someplace meaningful for you. This will become a talisman for your own Lia Fal, your own King Stone.

Gently tap your own stone nine times upon the Cabot Tradition Lia Fal Stone, or the attuned Lia Fal of the instructor. This will transfer the resonance between the two.

Enter into alpha using the Crystal Countdown and meditate with your stone, feeling both the energies unique to your own stone, and the energies connecting you to the Cabot Tradition.

Those not studying with a Cabot Tradition teacher can tap their own stone to a stone from a sacred space, famous or hidden, to attune to that sacred place. It should instill a feeling of sovereignty to you, and connect you to your majickal roots. This is a good reason to make pilgrimage to a holy site for Witches.

Land Homecoming Meditation

This ritual is an attempt to create in you something profound that naturally occurred to me, one of my most majickal life experiences, when I first visited England. It didn't happen in a ritual or when casting a spell, but unexpectedly when I stepped out of the car and onto the grounds of the manor house where I was staying in Preston on Stour. Without warning, it felt like my feet had grown enormous roots deep into the land. My energy was rooting deep beneath me. I was overwhelmed, but also had to prepare to meet my host who was coming out of the house to greet me. The countryside of the British Isle literally rose up to greet me, and I dug down deep to reciprocate. I bonded my physical and energetic being to the land. While there, my majick was amazing. Anything seemed possible. Everything I tried manifested! Psychic work, profound healings, and manifestations all came true. And I think I brought back a lot of that sacredness home with me.

Enter into an alpha state through the Crystal Countdown. State your intention to connect with the deep powers of the sacred land. With each exhale, extend the energy of your feet down into the land, as if they were roots. Build your roots to be strong and thick, then dig deeper into the land. Keep going until you feel you have made contact with the primal powers that dwell there, like striking a reserve of deep energy. Then let that energy shoot up the roots and into you, filling you with prana or chi, with life force. Awaken to, and then attune to, the powers of the land. You might feel like your inner "note" is changing to match the land. This is good. When done, give yourself clearance and balance and count yourself up.

You should repeat this again when outside, away from any commotion, someplace in nature that is sacred to you, and really see what this attunement is like.

Seven: Faery Majick and the Wand

"THESE Siths, or FAIRIES, they call Sleagh Maith, or the Good People, it would seem, to prevent the Dint of their ill Attempts, (for the Irish use to bless all they fear Harme of;) and are said to be of a middle Nature betwixt Man and Angel, as were Dæmons thought to be of old; of intelligent fluidious Spirits, and light changeable Bodies, (like those called Astral,) somewhat of the Nature of a condensed Cloud, and best seen in Twilight."
— *The Secret Commonwealth of Elves, Fauns and Fairie*s by Robert Kirk

Theories About Faeries

Faeries are a race of non-human beings that are older, wiser, and usually more powerful than humanity. Faery is a term that can apply to a wide range of beings, all intimately connected to nature. Some are described as the little people. Others are giants. Many are like the elves of popular mythology.

Witches believe the world was once ruled by faeries, who then withdrew from the world to allow humanity to develop. They might have been strictly an elder race of noble spirits or our oldest and deepest human ancestors. Some of the most ancient branches of humanity are considered to be the little people of legend, like the Picts. As the faeries are the "People Under the Hills," and the ancient hills in England are often ancient burial mounds, perhaps they are our human ancestors from a time past. Some see the Pagan gods, the Tuatha de Dannan, as faeries, and while we believe they have a kinship, we believe faeries are separate from the gods. Elementals and nature spirits are also called faeries. Some look to the dryads, nymphs, satyrs, and nereids of Greek myth as faeries as well.

The World of Enchantment

The Faery beings live in a world of enchantment that is also called Faery. The Scottish traditions have referred to it as a "Secret Commonwealth." It is also known as the Hidden Country. British folklore, corrupting the Norse realm of the elves known as Alfheim, refer to it as Elphame, and often the Witch Goddess and Witch God were ruling there as Queen of the Faeries and King of the Faeries.

The enchanted realm is said to exist either parallel with ours, on a different frequency, or beneath ours, in the Underworld. There, time is often distorted, either in an eternal twilight, or an experience of the opposite day, time, and season. If it's daylight here, it's night in Faery. If it's summer here, then it's winter there. The still surfaces of lakes and ponds, perfect opposite reflections, are access points to this realm, along with the hollowed holes in trees and burrows within the ground. One can also experience a few moments there, and have a much longer time pass in the realm of humanity.

KINDS OF FAERIES

Three of the most prominent names for faeries is the overall understanding come from the Irish, Scottish, and Welsh. The word Faery itself relates to the Latin *fata*, concerned with the fates. The capricious nature of these beings can be seen as a form of fate, or aid to the goddesses of the fates. But in the Irish traditions, they are known as the *Sidhe*, pronounced "she," as in Banshee. The Scottish use the word *Sith*, while the Welsh use *Tylwyth Teg*. Within these overall names for the race of beings, we have specific kinds of entities from different Celtic cultures:

Knockers — The Knockers are faeries who will warn you of upcoming danger and difficulties by knocking on your walls or doors if you ask them to warn you.

Pixies — Small, playful and mischievous faeries, strongly associated with Cornwall.

Brownies — Household elves or house Faery spirits, known for helping around the house and protecting the house. Families feed the brownie by pouring offerings onto a stone.

Banshees — Banshees, or Bean-Sidhe, are Irish faeries associated with specific families. They are said to wail or howl when a family member is near death, associating these beings with death, though they do not kill, nor do they guide. They just wail to warn us the death is coming.

Redcaps — Redcaps are a form of harmful or malevolent Faery, taking the appearance of an old man with red eyes, and their red caps are said to be dyed with blood. They are one of the few Faery races unharmed by iron or steel, as their pikes are made of iron, as well as their boots. They exist in areas where humans should not be, and should be avoided at all costs.

Leprechauns — An Irish form of Faery associated with the green hills, rainbows, treasures, and the making of shoes and granting wishes. Leprechauns usually appear as small, bearded men who wear green, or in some cases, red. They are strongly linked with the Irish gods the Tuatha de Dannan and many consider them to be the only aspects of the Faery gods still in touch with human consciousness, diminished in size as our awareness of them is diminished.

Boggarts — Folklore tells us the boggart is a more malevolent form of the house spirit, or genus loci, appearing in some cases in a beneficent form as a brownie or house elf. Boggarts are human looking, and can be small to human size, but often unkempt and bestial, and all together not friendly-looking to humans. They seek to cause mischief, and in some cases, do harm to others by leading them into danger.

Nixies — Nixies, or the Nicks, are shapeshifting water spirits found in many European traditions. They can appear as beautiful women, mermaids, serpents, or white horses. They can be helpful and healing or lead people to death by drowning.

Trolls — Trolls are larger Faery beings, often more like small giants than tiny fey, existing in the hills and rocks. They are usually not very friendly to humans.

Fauns — Fauns are another name for satyrs from the Greek tradition. They are often male, with the hindquarters of a goat or ram and the upper body of a human, with either animal horns or a horned animal head. They are spirits of the woods and deep forests.

Elves — Elves are the high faeries, or arch-faeries, the most human in stature, the most ancient and wise of the faeries, and the ones who guided the Earth before us.

Faery Queens and Faery Courts — Faery Queens are usually of the elvish race, and are beings that express themselves in a court, mimicking queen, king, knight, page, jester, and court attendants. They are really like the queen bee of a hive, a collective consciousness, very different from our normal understanding of spirits, and any of the faeries we talk about can be an expression of a Faery court.

Faery Animals — While we tend to focus upon humanoid faeries, small and large, we often forget that everything has a parallel to the Faery world. There are a multitude of Faery animals in the land of enchantment, appearing in ways that mimic traditional animals we are familiar with, though some are fantastical beings beyond our human experience. Often Faery animals are bright white or tinged with pink.

ELEMENTAL FAERIES AND FAERY COURTS

Faeries and elementals are often treated as the same beings, though many would say they are quite different. While elves and faeries are more complex beings, elemental faeries are quite simple, having only one elemental body. Like more traditional faeries and elves, they can appear to us as if they are in courts or kingdoms, with one elemental ruling over the others as "king."

Element	Elemental	Ruler	Form
Earth	Gnomes, Dwarves, Goblins	Ghob	Gnome King upon a throne
Fire	Salamanders, Drakes	Djinn	King usually made from fire
Air	Sylphs	Paralda	King appearing as empty suit of armor
Water	Undines, Mer-folk (Merrows)	Nixsa	King or Queen appearing as a mer-person

Mermaid (Merrow) Song: Calling Forth the Mermaid of the Ninth Wave

The blue wave feathers white;
her green hair lays spread on the water bright.
Misty, not meant to drink,
sprinkled with starlight falls from the link
of her shelled arm.

In the realm of the elves and faeries, in the Scottish traditions of the Sith, equivalent to the Irish Sidhe, the course of the fey take two major divisions: the Seelie Courts and the Unseelie Courts. The Seelie Courts comprise the faeries that are helpful to humanity and offer blessings and healings. The Unseelie Court are those who do not like humanity, and who might bring illness or injury. Many Faery Witches believe they are one in the same, depending on the day, time, and circumstance.

FAERY OFFERINGS

Faery offerings can be anything from nature that has then been shaped by human hands, showing human energy has been put into it. Traditional offerings include milk, cheese, cream, yogurt, whisky, bread, and pastries. Miniature furniture and items can be offered to the fey, like votive token offerings. Herbs mixed and blessed in love can be a wonderful offering. Some faeries like tea. Anything shining and sparkling is appreciated by the faeries. They shun cold iron and steel, so use only Faery-friendly metals such as copper, brass, bronze, gold and silver.

Faery Fire Oil

1 Garnet
1 Dram of Dragon's Blood Oil
1 Dram of Almond Oil
1 Pinch of Coriander Seeds

Faery Incense

2 Tablespoons of Patchouli
1 Tablespoon of Storax
1 Tablespoon of White Willow Bark
2 Teaspoons of Lavender
1 Teaspoon of Heather
1 Teaspoon of Yarrow
Pinch of Fern Leaf
Pinch of Foxglove
1 Dried Mushroom, Powdered
9 Drops of Lavender Oil
9 Drops of Lily of the Valley Oil
5 Drops of Patchouli Oil

FAERY ENCHANTMENT AND FAERY ILLNESS

In the old folklore traditions, illness was often believed to be a part of people's experiences with the Faery folk. To trespass on their land or to desecrate, intentionally or otherwise, one of their sites is to invite imbalance and harm. Even today, roads in Ireland are built around Faery tracks, and highways built around sacred trees, stones, and wells.

In many cases, the person was considered to be enchanted, as if part of them no longer resided in the mortal world and was instead living in the world of Faery. This might have something to do with the myths of children being stolen by the faeries. Some harm was called Faery illness or even "elf shot." It would lead to physical illness. It would require what was known in Christian times as a Faery Doctor, but earlier was most likely the Witch or Druid to help make peace with the faeries and obtain the necessary remedy to dispel the illness. Today, those who even recognize this form of spiritual illness would call it illness induced by geopathic stress, places where the Earth energy is toxic to humans, making our relationship with nature more mechanical than a living symbiosis. We know geopathic blessings and stress are guided by the faeries, elementals, and nature spirits.

In your work with the Faeries, those that can harm can also heal. You can find a healing ally amongst the fey folk, who will help you heal not only Faery illnesses, but illness in general, and the illness found in humanities broken relationship with nature. If you are a natural healer, seek out a Faery healing guide. Once you do, they will help you in all areas of healing.

Faery Contact Meditation

Before you begin, you prepare by holding any bright and shining stone to help attune to the faeries, though both Andalusite, or Faery Cross, and Botswana Agate are good for Faery connections. The stone known as Merlinite is also great for Faery, elemental, and nature spirit contact. You will be doing this in a majick circle, so ideally have prepared offerings for the Faery Folk, and you can burn Faery incense as well. Make sure you have a wooden wand to work with to help attune to the inner energies of nature, and thus the realm of enchantment. Make sure the wand was previously cleared and charged in a majick circle. Today you will only be adding to its vibration.

Once you have cast your circle and declared Tara and Avalon with your libation to the Ancient Ones, enter into a deeper state of alpha with the Crystal Countdown. Prepare to go deep, deep within the Earth. Hold any crystal you wish to help you connect with the vibration of the faeries in one hand, and your wooden wand, to attune to the spirits of the green world and the Good

Folk, in the other. Make the intention to safely visit the land of Faery, and to meet a Faery that is for your highest good, harming none.

Rather than rise up into the sky as we often do, we are going to sink deep into the Earth, for the land of enchantment is the land beneath our feet. Feel yourself sinking into the floor. Feel yourself sinking down below the floor into the land beneath us. Move through the soil—the minerals, metals and crystals—until you feel as if the Earth is opening up into a new land, a land of twilight. Enter into the realm of Faery.

Cautiously explore. Look around. Take notice of the plants and animals you see. The light here appears strange and otherworldly. There might be a path for you. Follow the path.

The path leads you to a garden, a meeting place, and there in the garden, wait for a Faery being, an ally from one of the races and realms of the fair folk. Open your heart and mind, and attract the ally that is correct for you.

There, in the shadowy twilight, comes a form. It is your ally. Who is it? What does this being look like to you? Commune with it in words or feelings. Ask its name, and introduce yourself. Commune with this potential ally. Be cautious but open-hearted, as the faeries can often be tricksters.

When you feel this time is done, ask the Faery ally if you may call upon him or her again, or return to this place. If yes, ask the ally if it likes any particular kinds of offerings to help build a relationship. Then say your farewells, and return back the way you came. Rise up through the realm into the Earth above. Rise up through the layers of the land, coming back to your corporeal body. Rise up. Return your awareness to your body. Feel the wand within your hand. Take the energy of this experience and imprint it upon your wand. Charge it with this additional energy. Now that wand will help you connect to the spirits of the deep Earth, and guide your will with Faery majick and wisdom. Only then give yourself clearance and balance and count up. When ready, release the circle and make sure you pour the offering and leave the food offering out in nature, to be reclaimed by the Faery folk. Use your experience to help build your relationship with them.

Eight: Ancestral Realm, Past Lives and the Cup

"Then the Irish kindled a fire under the cauldron of renovation, and they cast the dead bodies into the cauldron until it was full, and the next day they came forth fighting-men as good as before, except that they were not able to speak."
— from Branwen the Daughter of Llyr, *The Mabinogion*

In the Cabot Tradition, we teach that those who have passed have three choices: to go to the Otherworld paradise known as the Summerlands; to stay in this world with family and loved ones; or to return from the Summerlands for reincarnation, to start another life.

Since the realm beyond the physical is also beyond time and space, it doesn't matter which of these options a spirit takes, as we still honor all of our ancestors. At Samhain in particular, we honor the spirits of the dead and commune with them from their Otherworldly perspective to help guide us. We look at many entities, such as faeries and even gods, as our most ancient of ancestors available to help and guide us.

Reincarnation: Soul and Blood

Many majickal cultures with a mystical teaching have a belief in reincarnation, or the return of the soul. In our most simple understanding, the material that goes into us get absorbed by the world and universe, and eventually gets used up in making other forms. But we also believe the energy of our consciousness, or soul, gets returned to new form. Most believe it occurs as a discrete and unified packet of awareness that makes us uniquely "us" on this soul level. Belief in reincarnation can be found among many Indo-European traditions, starting with the most popularized concepts form the Hindus of India, but also in the traditions of the Greek Mystery schools, including the philosophies of Pythagorus and Plato, as well as Celtic belief in reincarnation along tribal lines. Buddhist traditions of the East vary in their teaching on the soul and reincarnation, but the concept of return in some form is also found in these religions.

One of the key myths on reincarnation for the Celtic Witch comes from the Myth of Fintan in *The Book of Invasions*. He survives the mythic flood by shapeshifting and preserves the ancient memories of Ireland for us.

Fintan is known as Fintan the Wise, though his formal name is Fintan mac Bóchra. His wisdom was that of a magician, akin to a Druid and seer who lived in the age of the Great Flood.

In a mix with Christianity, he accompanied Noah's granddaughter before the deluge. Three men traveled with fifty women; each man had many wives. They arrived in Ireland in the First Invasion —or then, first settlement—but were all drowned in the flood, all except for Fintan. He survived by shapeshifting into a salmon and lives in a watery cave called Fintan's Grave. He lived for 5500 years after the flood, surviving as a salmon, then an eagle, and later a hawk, before again becoming human and an advisor to the kings of Ireland. He was there with the Fir Bolgs, and later the invasion of the Tuatha de Dannan, and even into the time of Cúchulainn. Though some see him as immortal, others would interpret each shapeshifting as a new incarnation, yet retaining his human memories of the first age and time of Ireland.

He lives until the time of Fionn mac Cumhail, or Fin MacCool, who also has interesting adventures involving a Salmon of Wisdom, though this Salmon was not Fintan. He later befriends Fin MacCool, and they trade stories before leaving the mortal world together for the realm of enchantment.

Interestingly enough, so much of our past life mythology involves water, the ocean and the flood, and these are all symbols for the primordial ancestral pools of wisdom from which we all evolved. The sea and the blood are often compared quite readily.

Irish esotericism has an unusual theory called tuirgin, and many believe the myth of Fintan is more about tuirgin than traditional reincarnation, as his identity remains the same through the lives. Others would see that he has awoken to his "twice born" or initiated nature that remembers past incarnations.

Cormac's Glossary defines tuirgin, or transmigration, as "a birth that passes from every nature into another... a transitory birth which has traversed all nature from Adam and goes through every wonderful time down to the world's doom." Rather than linear reincarnation, the teachings of tuirgin state that everything is in a constant state of becoming everything else, with no linear progression. Perhaps that is more true, but we often experience and remember past lives in a more linear fashion.

One of the big questions involving reincarnation is the separation of Soul Memories from Genetic, or Blood, Memories. We have two strains of lineage: karma, which we deal with when in the body, and that which we carry with our soul, with a more global point of view. These are the memories of lives and times unconnected to your family and tribe. I have memories of ancient Egypt prominent in my mind. But we also have memories and majick we inherit through the blood. Both the soul and blood can bring us gifts, but they give us things we have to figure out and work out too.

KARMA AND SOUL DEVELOPMENT

Karma is a big part of our understanding of past lives. Karma means action, and it's the consequence of what we do, what our actions create. Karma is the life lessons and the lessons we are creating for our next lifetime when we choose to come back. Karma is not punishment or reward, even though many people see it that way. Karma is working out all the things that allow you to fully embrace and be one with the Divine. Every time you think you've learned all that you can, you will get another lesson. I always thought that as you got older, you might not have to learn any more, but that's not true. It just keeps going.

We seek to learn all, and become more and more like the Divine Mind. The Divine Mind has all experiences, so to truly learn, we need to experience everything. We need to experience all sides of all relationships and polarities. It is not good or bad, but simply the result of our quest for seeking divinity, and we engineer our experiences based upon the Principle of Cause and Effect. We are all evolving towards the Divine Mind.

Speak to the Dead Incense
3 Tablespoons of Comfrey Leaf

2 Tablespoons of Myrrh

2 Tablespoons of Mullien Leaf

1 Tablespoon of Black Copal

1 Tablespoon of Tobacco Leaves

1 Teaspoon of Yew Needles

1 Pinch of Coffee

1 Pinch of Graveyard Dirt

Speaking to the Dead Oil
1 Dram of Almond Oil

10 Drops of Myrrh Oil

5 Drops of Storax Oil

3 Drops of Rosemary Oil

1 Drop of Peppermint Oil
1 Pinch of Black Sea Salt
1 Pinch of Graveyard Dirt

Ancestral Memory Ritual

Prepare yourself by having a large iron cauldron full of blessed water on the center of your altar with a ladle or spoon. All students should have their own chalices as well, cleared and charged. Medical lancets, to prick the finger and draw a drop of blood, are the best additional tools for this work, though the old fashioned method used a pin sterilized with fire to prick the thumb. Some Witches keep parchment paper that has a drop of their blood on it, saved anytime their finger is accidentally pricked or cut. We try to save blood for future spells all the time. It can also be helpful to have a stone that helps us access past lives and ancestral memory, like turquoise or petrified wood, or a stone that represents the blood powers themselves, like bloodstone. Herbs that can also help include cat's claw, mistletoe, and comfrey. Sea salt should also be added to the cauldron water, to make it taste salty like the sea, the womb of the Goddess. You can also use Speaking to the Dead incense and Speaking to the Dead oil, or other ancestral and Samhain correspondences, even if the time of the year is not near Samhain.

Create sacred space through the majick circle ritual. Light your incense. Wear your oils. Rather than do the libation of the chalice now, drop your charged stones, salt, and herbs into the cauldron water, with the intention of aligning with ancestral wisdom. Ladle out the water into everyone's chalice. Then instruct them to prick their thumb and place a drop of blood into their own chalice, if they so choose. Stir the chalice with their thumb counterclockwise, stirring awake the memories and powers of the Witch blood, of the Faery blood of our ancient ancestors. Perform the rite of Avalon and Tara, taking three drops to the lips.

Sit down and enter into a deeper state of alpha. On the screen of your mind, visualize the swirling waters of the chalice, and feel the waters within the body, within the heart, veins and arteries. Feel the pumping of the blood, like rivers within you. This is your blood. This is the blood of your ancestors. This has been handed down to you.

Visualize yourself shrinking down smaller and smaller, until you are entering into the flow of this blood. You are being carried away by the whirlpool, by the currents and tides of your own ancestral blood. The flowing blood within your body is also carrying you back into the past, into the past of your ancestry, to a lifetime when your ancestor had the power of the Witch, and knew the Craft.

You immerse yourself in the blood, as if you were diving into it, and soon, in a haze, begin to feel as if you are becoming someone or something different. As you start to grow larger and larger with each breath, you are growing into the body of your ancestor, becoming your ancestor. You feel the feelings of your ancestor. You know your ancestor's thoughts and ideas, even if in different language and time. You have access to the memories, the powers, and the wisdom of this ancestor.

Look around. Where are you? Who are you? What is your gender? What is your age? Do you know your name? Go with the flow and pattern of what the ancestor is already doing, as if you are right there with the ancestor.

What do you understand about what they are doing? Are they a Witch? A priest or priestess? A sorcerer or healer? What is their practice and work like?

Ask to learn the wisdom of this ancestor, and to awaken the ancestor's power. As you ask this, feel something catch on fire within you, within your blood, awakening the ancient power and knowledge.

As you bring your attention and awareness to the sensations in your blood, you return your awareness to the blood of your physical body, not your ancestor's blood in the past. You carry forward the blessings of this ancestor, awaking your own DNA. From this point forward, the ancestor might be a spirit guide, or simply and subtly guide you through your own thoughts and perceptions now that you've awoken the ancestor in your own blood.

Give yourself clearance and balance, and return your awareness back to the circle. Release the circle in the usual manner and return.

Pour out the remainder of the fluid in the chalice and cauldron into nature as an offering to the ancestors and Earth.

NINE: THE CREATION OF THE COSMOS

"Now in this island of Atlantis there was a great and wonderful empire which had rule over the whole island and several others, and over parts of the continent, and, furthermore, the men of Atlantis had subjected the parts of Libya within the columns of Heracles as far as Egypt, and of Europe as far as Tyrrhenia. ... But afterwards there occurred violent earthquakes and floods; and in a single day and night of misfortune all your warlike men in a body sank into the earth, and the island of Atlantis in like manner disappeared in the depths of the sea. For which reason the sea in those parts is impassable and impenetrable, because there is a shoal of mud in the way; and this was caused by the subsidence of the island."
— Timaeus by Plato

COSMOLOGY

Cosmology is the study of the ordering of the universe. How do all the parts fit together? For a Witch, cosmology is the study of not only this world, but also other worlds. Many Witches simply divide our cosmos into the material realm and the Otherworld, or Summerland, but most have a more complex cosmology than that. We look to our ancient and our fairly recent ancestors to understand how they saw the worlds ordered. We have all been influenced by the occult movements, the Rosicrucians, the Hermeticists, and the Neoplatonists, but we strive to work in a cosmology appropriate for Witches.

In the Irish cosmology, we can look to the oak tree as being the World Tree, with a heavenly realm in the branches, an underworld in the roots, and the world we know around the trunk. Around this tree are the four sacred lands of the four directions, the four elemental realms:

Upper World	Over	Sky	Stars	Gods
Middle World	Around	Land	Stones	Faery Folk (Gentry)
Lower World	Under	Sea	Darkness	Ancestors and Primal Beings

In the Welsh traditions—particularly those preserved, or perhaps creatively interpreted by Iolo Morganwg—we see the cosmology in concentric rings:

Annwn	Underworld	Center	Cauldron of Rebirth, Summerland
Abred	Middle World	Middle	Physical World, Four Elements
Gwynvid	Upper World	Outer	Gods and Enlightened Ones
Ceugant	Divinity	Surrounding	Divine Mind, God/dess

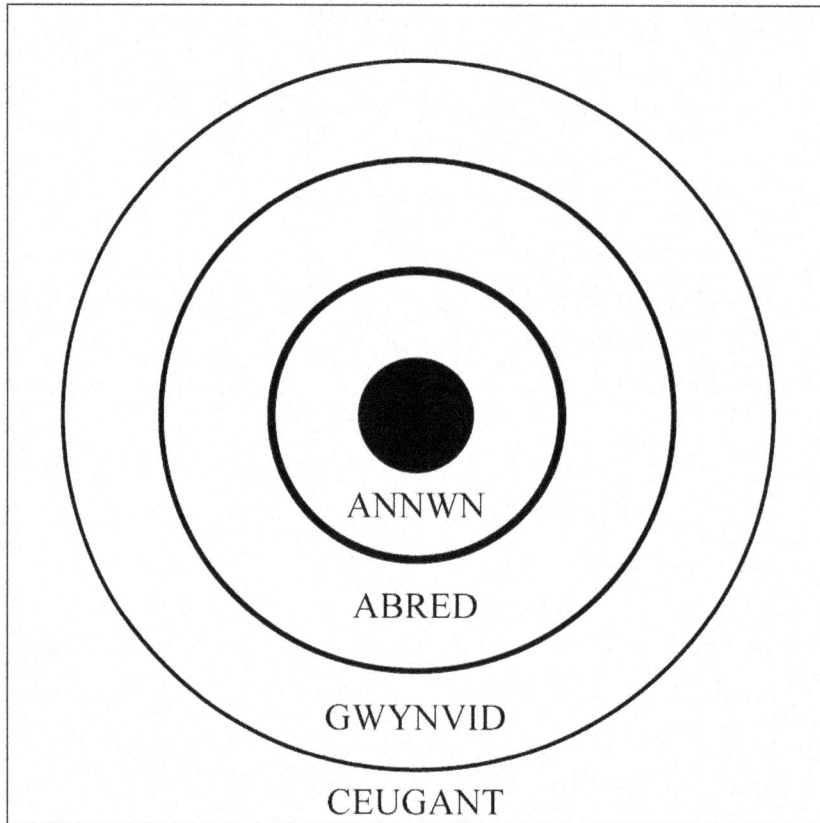

ANNWN

ABRED

GWYNVID

CEUGANT

Welsh Cosmology

CREATION MYTHS

Creation myths are the way we understand how the world came to be, how the cosmology was created, and what has happened since it was created for us to be here now.

One of the more esoteric creation myths, but least religious, comes from the supposed author (at least according to some) of *The Kybalion.* William Walker Atkinson wrote under many names, including Magus Incognito, and has left many to believe that despite the use of the "Three Initiates" pseudonym, he is the sole author of The Kybalion. In his work *The Secret Doctrine of the Rosicrucians,* he outlines a creation story and cosmos quite in line with the principles outlined in *The Kybalion.* The cosmology is divided into seven aphorisms, much like the seven Hermetic Principles, which form an addendum to his *Secret Doctrine,* along with other information on the ancient ages, the evolution of the soul, psychic powers, and the majick of colors.

I.

The Eternal Parent was wrapped in the Sleep of the Cosmic Night. Light there was not: for the Flame of Spirit was not yet rekindled. Time there was not: for Change had not re-begun. Things there were not: for Form had not re-presented itself. Action there was not: for there were no Things to act. The Pairs of Opposites there were not: for there were no Things to manifest Polarity. The Eternal Parent, causeless, indivisible, changeless, infinite, rested in unconscious, dreamless sleep. Other than the Eternal Parent there was Naught, either Real or Apparent.

II.

The Germ within the Cosmic Egg takes unto itself Form. The Flame is re-kindled. Time begins. A Thing exists. Action begins. The Pairs of Opposites spring into being. The World Soul is born, and awakens into manifestation. The first rays of the new Cosmic Day break over the horizon.

III.

The One became Two. The Neuter became Bi-Sexual. Male and Female—the Two in One— evolved from the Neuter. And the work of Generation began.

IV.

The One becomes Many. The Unity becomes Diversity. The Identical becomes Variety. Yet the Many remains One; the Diversity remains Unity; and the Variety remains Identical.

V.

The One is the Flame of Life. The Many are the Sparks in the Flame. The Flame once lighted kindles everything within its sphere. The Fire is in everything and everywhere; there is nothing dark or cold within its sphere.

VI.

As Life is the Essence of Spirit, so is Consciousness the Essence of Life. Spirit is One, yet it manifests in many forms of Life. Life is One, yet it manifests in many forms of Consciousness. While the forms of manifested Consciousness are innumerable, yet the wise know Consciousness to manifest on Seven Planes: and these Planes of Consciousness are known to the wise as (1) The Plane of the Elements; (2) The Plane of the Minerals; (3) The Plane of the Plants; (4) The Plane of the Animals; (5) The Plane of the Human; (6) The Plane of the Demi-Gods; (7) The Plane of the Gods.

VII.

The Soul of Man is Sevenfold, yet but One in essence; Man's Spiritual Unfoldment has as its end the Discovery of Himself beneath the Sevenfold Veil.

One of the most popular Irish myths of creation (or at least, population) comes from *The Book of Invasions*. It describes the different invasions of Ireland in the Irish Mythological Cycle. These invasions are described and interpreted in several ways:

Mythology — These invasions detail mythic figures, goddesses, gods, and heroes with no tangible base in physical reality. They are an understanding of a spiritual truth to the people who live in Ireland, and who later practice Irish spirituality.

Literal Inhabitants — These invasions describe a folk memory, a mythic history connected to a literal history, of the people who invaded Ireland from the Stone Age to the current age. Each mythic name refers to a potentially literal people who once lived upon the isle of Ireland.

Esoteric — In the most esoteric interpretations, Ireland is a metaphor for the world. Each invasion is an invasion of a "race" of consciousness, like the root races of the Theosophists and the great ages found in the myths of Hindus, Egyptians, Greeks, Romans, Mayans, Aztecs, and Native Americans. The invasion cycle follows this pattern:

People of Cessair — Cessair was said to be Noah's granddaughter, who led three men and fifty women to Ireland to escape the Flood, though the Deluge still ended up killing them all but Fintan the Wise, who escaped by becoming a salmon. Cessair was of the pre-Flood age of beings.

People of Partholon — Partholon led the first invasion after the Great Deluge. His people established themselves in Ireland and thrived for a long time. They were all eventually killed by a plague, and thirty years after their death, the Nemedians arrived.

Nemedians — Lead by Nemed, a name for a holy or sacred place in the Celtic culture, suggests the first Druidic inhabitants of the island. While they entered Ireland and established themselves, they fought with a race of beings known as the Fomorians who were also using Ireland at the time as their home base of operations. They conquered the Fomorians, who only returned after Nemed's death to impose rule and taxes upon the Nemedians, eventually driving the Nemedians out. Descendants of the Nemedians were said to create the Fir Bolgs, Tuatha, and later Britons.

Fir Bolgs — The Fir Bolgs arrived in Ireland and were the first to divide it into five counties, or five kingdoms. They were considered great warriors but primitive, preferring spears as weapons. While they appeared to have no problems with the Formorians, they had power in Ireland for less than forty years before the invasion of the next race.

Tuatha De Dannan — The Tuatha De Dannan are the Irish Gods, the Children of the Goddess Danu. They came by ship to the shores of Ireland and brought with them four sacred objects from the ancient world, from the cities in the four corners of the globe. They brought the Stone, the Cauldron, the Sword, and the Spear. They fought with the Formorians and the Fir Bolgs until eventually gaining control over the land. They are beautiful and wise.

Milesians — The Milesians are equated with the modern day Irish people, prior to the conversion to Christianity. They were led to Ireland in their adventures, and the Tuatha De Dannan, not wanting to fight a noble race, eventually decided to withdraw into the land, creating a realm of perfect duplication of the surface world, and retreated within it in peace. Led in part by the bard Amergin, the rulers of the Milesians wed the three goddesses of the land of Ireland—Eiru, Banba, and Folda,—and started a new tradition of sacred kingship.

Christians — Though not clearly expressed in The Book of Invasions, the last of the "invasions" was by Christianity, first establishing the more balanced Celtic Christian Church, and then an invasion by the Roman Catholic Church. While there have been no true invasions since then, the ancient Pagans are making themselves known again, for they never truly left.

A modern telling of the Irish creation stories come in the form of "The Earth Shapers," a story in the book *Celtic Wonder Tales* by Ella Young, published in 1910. This creation story involves primarily Angus, Bridget, Ogma, Midyir, Nuanda, Gobniu, and the Dagda in the "making" of the Earth, particularly with Bridget putting down her mantle in creation. It involves the classic four tools of the Tuatha De Dannan. You also see similarly inspired re-envisioning of the old tales through the Scottish poet and author William Sharp, writing under his majickal identity and Faery muse, Fionna MacLeod.

In the Welsh myths, one of the telltale signs of the ages of creation, a more esoteric view of the cycle, is found in the story of Mabon, within the tale of *Cuhlwch and Olwen* from *The Mabinogion*. In it, the heroes consult the oldest of the animals, each associated with one of the ancient ages:

Animal	Location	Marker of Time	Age
Blackbird	Cilgwri (kil-GOOR-ee)	Anvil Worn Away	Current Age
Stag	Rhedynfre (reh-DEN-vray)	Oak Stump	Fourth Age
Owl	Cwm Cawlwyd (coom COWL-id)	Three Forests	Third Age
Eagle	Gwernabwy (gwer-NAH-bwee)	Stone Mount Worn	Second Age
Salmon	Llyn Llyw (shlin shloo)	Hears Mabon Cry	First Age

NEW PARADIGM SCIENCE AND HISTORY

Witches, occultists, and esotericists don't always accept things that the mainstream status quo tells us is true. We look at the cracks in our history, to see that things are not always what they seem. When you look at the span of human history, along with accepted ancient myths and teachings, a lot of strange data cannot be accounted for in our current world view. New Paradigm

Science and fringe history theories present a number of ideas that don't fit our current models, but can be useful for a Witch to reflect on. I know my first experience reading Erich von Däniken's book, *Chariot of the Gods,* was that there was something true in it, even if not perhaps the exact way he presented it. It aligned with some of my own experiences in time travel and past life journeys. Later it was followed up by the work of Zecheria Sitchen in *The Twelfth Planet.* Together, along with other researchers, they began the concept of the Ancient Astronaut Theory of Civilization. Essentially this theory explores the possibility that humanity has been visited by extraterrestrial beings who helped the advancement and evolution of our species. They may have provided the roots of our understanding of religion, art, culture, science, and medicine. The Bible refers to them as fallen angels, the Watchers. They are also intimately linked to our sacred sites and erection of stone monuments.

This concept often goes hand in hand with an understanding that human civilization is much older than modern history accepts, with periods of flourishing and falling. "New" cultures—seemingly springing up from nowhere, like Sumer and Egypt—are really the result of seeding from these ancient cultures, often after a catastrophe or cataclysm. They came with their technology, art, and religion.

The ancients talk about our going through periods of evolution, or currently a devolution, through a Gold Age, Silver Age, Bronze Age, and Iron Age, referring to levels of human consciousness and perception. This is found in both the ancient Greeks and Hindus. Plato spoke about ancient Atlantis in the Age of Heroes, between the Bronze Age and our current Iron Age. In the Age of Heroes, strange and marvelous creatures roamed the Earth, and many humans came closer to the gods.

While science does not recognize the reality of Atlantis or other mythic lost lands, we are now talking about the possibility of what New Paradigm Science calls a Global Maritime Civilization that was lost under the waves as sea levels rose. Perhaps they are the source of our Atlantean myths.

In the traditions of Theosophy—the mother of the New Age metaphysical movement, started by Madame Helena Blavatsky—the different ages are linked to different ancient lost lands. The immediate future age is centered upon America, though the current modern age was scattered around the globe, broken into five "root races". Previous to this, the fourth age was centered around Atlantis, the third age on Lemuria (also known as Mu), the second age upon the realm of

Hybornea, taken from Greek myth as the land of the Sun God, and the first age upon Pangea, the primordial continent where all life began.

ROOT RACES

Many years ago I was in the company of several Witches one evening, and we were discussing the origin of human life and all the possibilities. I wanted to go back to learn how human beings came to be on Earth, to see the beginnings of our race via time travel. The group counted me down into a very deep trace. And there, I went back to an ancient land more suited for what I would believe to be mythology than anthropology.

I saw a different landscape, with advanced civilizations upon island nations. There was a civilization stretching from Egypt and Greece all the way to the Bimini Islands. There I was shown a story of various entities, seemingly alien gods, created races of brightly colored people. There were five main temple pyramids upon five islands, each with its own god. I was shown that each god came from a different star system, and Earth was a collaborative project. The five solar systems are represented in the five points of the pentagram.

Bright red humans were made in the image of the goddess Isis. Blue people were made by a figure akin to Hermes. The remaining three races were jet black, peach, orange, and a lime green bordering on yellow. The gods associated with these remaining three were not clear to me.

The temples were also schools where the newly engineered brightly colored humans would be shown large sheets of metals etched with strange writing. The writing was their programming, giving them everything they needed to survive. The gods then paired different couples of differing colors and placed them in various areas of the world, to start the human race as we know it today. The various combinations created the seeds for the races and tribes we know today, as the colors became more "muted" skin tones we are familiar with today.

I know this sounds fantastic. I was surprised as you, and often hesitated to share this in my Witchcraft classes. The idea of humans descending from aliens seems strange to me, but also there was something very true to it. At the time I was not familiar with the "Ancient Astronaut" theory, or the work of the author Erich von Däniken and his book Chariot of the Gods. I was familiar with the Barney and Betty Hill alien abduction story from New Hampshire, but had no idea about ancient aliens. Soon I would be introduced to these ideas, and they would bring greater clarity to my vision.

Yet what do we do in an age where we know scientifically that race as we know it is simply physical and cultural adaptations to various regions? There are no races. We are all of the human race. The Theosophical idea of root races came from a prejudiced time and age, looking at some of the modern ethnic groups as superior in some way to others. We don't believe that today. So what do we do with information that guides us to such a wild concept of race, both human and alien?

I think the bright and vivid color imagery speaks more to a majickal reality than a genetic, ethnic, or regional one. The bright colors of my vision speak of auras, energy, and otherworldly awareness. Exploring your root race explores the energy line from which your soul first incarnated here upon the Earth.

I do share it in our Witchcraft classes as a mind-expanding idea, and the meditation to go with it helps break down our expectations and assumptions. It helps us understand what the ancients knew—that our race is from the stars, and our ultimate mystery is found in the cosmos.

Root Races Meditation

Get into a comfortable position for meditation, and count yourself down into a deep state of alpha. Hold the intention to visit the origin of humanity, and the root race of your soul. Draw in white light a flaming pentagram upon the floor, as an anchor to return to this place and time, and rise up. Rise up from this place through the ceiling of the building you are in, into the sky and clouds, until you are high above the Earth, looking down. Look down, and let the Earth turn backwards in time, back to the dawn of humanity.

Descend downward and fly over the ocean, looking down upon it. In the Atlantic Ocean, you will see several large islands, with pyramids of varying shapes and sizes, and the islands are connected by magnificent bridges. In fact, from a distance, the islands almost appear to be a path of gigantic stepping stones leading towards a vastly different shaped continent.

You notice there are five larger main islands, with a large pyramid complex upon each. Which of the five islands calls to your soul? Project yourself towards it, entering the temple. There within the temple structure, upon a large throne, is an alien god. Before the god are humanoid figures, lined up as if in a classroom or school. What color are the figures? Are they red, blue, black, lime green, or peach? Which of the figures calls to your soul? Join with this figure, and experience the events through the eyes of this ancestor.

You are shown a large sheet of metal with esoteric writing upon it. One slab of metal rises up, and immediately you absorb and process the information instantly. It is taken down and other slab is raised. Perhaps the Emerald Tablet of Thoth originated here, and there were other mysterious tablets of majick and teaching to be found. The god upon the throne oversaw this process of education.

As you read this information, you are told everything you need to know. You understand these five beings come from five solar systems, and you were made in the likeness of the god before you. You understand this group came from the Pleiades originally, but their origin was from beyond the Pleiades where they intermingled. They chose Earth as a remote planet so no one would interfere with their experiment. They did not want aliens outside of their pact to interfere with the development of humanity. You see an image of the pentagram, and see how the five join together in unity, and why the pentagram is such a powerful symbol for us today.

Once this information is within you, the gods begin to pair up with others from the different temples or perhaps one from the same temple. Who are you paired up with? From which root race do they come? The gods then begin populating the world with differently matched couples. Feel them take you across the world. Where do they place you? You are not afraid, as you realize you have all the knowledge necessary to not only survive, but to thrive in your new environment.

Find your awareness slipping out of this body, and observe the evolution of the entire world. See the development of the people, the mingling of the different root races creating people closer to what we know today. Each of the root races had specialized knowledge including topics of language, survival, food, shelter, clothing, mechanics, masonry, music, culture, and art. Many focused their efforts on technological achievements while others focused upon more artistic pursuits. Some were masters of majick.

See the ancient aliens destroy some of their temple bases, including the bridge system. They leave the colonies, and the new humans imitate the old temples through the pyramid system across the world. Some created great buildings and temples, and others did not.

Rise up and return to the heavens. Look at the Earth below. Allow it to turn and turn until we return to our current time. Let the white light pentacle guide you back down to the earth, back down to where you began, and reunite your awareness with your body.

TEN: REBIRTH OF THE WITCH

"And, as the story says, she bore him nine months,
and when she was delivered of him,
she could not find it in her heart to kill him, by reason of his beauty.
So she wrapped him in a leathern bag,
and cast him into the sea to the mercy of God,
on the twenty-ninth day of April."
— Hanes Taliesin

BIRTH, LIFE, DEATH, AND REBIRTH

Part of our work to prepare for spiritual initiation and religious ordination is to understand who we are, who we were, and who we wish to be. Do you want to be a High Priestess or High Priest? If so, what are the qualities you believe a High Priestess and High Priest should possess? Do you possess them now? What must you do to get them? Are you truly ready?

QUALITIES OF A WITCH

In your journal, make a list of the qualities you wish to have as a part of your rebirth. Reflect on these qualities, and how you can bring them into your daily life and persona. Think of the codes of medieval chivalry associated with the Arthurian Age in myth, if not in history. Chivalry is a system encoding moral, social, and religious principles for the knights, nobles, and horsemen, but the ideal is for all, including Witches who are a form of spiritual warrior and knight. Chivalry is a blend of qualities, including courage, honor, justice, courtesy, and a willingness to help those in need.

Part of our work in preparing for our second birth is to learn to accept the circumstances of our past, of our first birth, and to forgive our parents, siblings, family, and all those of our first life. They brought you to where you are today, even if the journey was not pleasant. Gwion Bach's life with Cerridwen before his rebirth was not pleasant. Lleu's life with Arianrhod as his mother was not pleasant, but he had to remake himself with his uncle Gwydion's help. He was cursed to not have a name, not bear arms, and not have a wife, and found ways around each of those curses. Many heroes and leaders have difficult circumstances involving their childhood and parents. Use it as fuel to be a better person and accomplish your goals. If you need to, perform a ritual to forgive your parents and family for any problems you had growing up. This will empower your future work, as you won't be draining time and thought on your past once you are at peace with it.

Forgiveness

In your journal, make a list of the things you still hold onto, that you need to forgive, starting with your parents and family. List anyone, or any situation, that is need of forgiveness so you can move onto the next phase of your life.

Part of our work as Witches, as the inheritors of the Druids and the Bards, is to undergo a second birth, to be reborn through the Goddess. She becomes our Mother. The God becomes our Father. We become the eternal Child of Light, but our child-like nature is one of innocence and eternal spirit, not one of immaturity. We must learn how to retain our child-like love and majickal nature, but enter into an adult relationship with our gods and with our community if we seek to serve. While we might take on other spiritual names and take on titles and roles, we know those are only tools to help us do our work, and retain our sense of deep connection, love, healing, and majick while we do it. That is what some traditions call being an "adept" of majick.

Like Taliesin, even though we are reborn, we have to take responsibility for all of our old actions, our karma. We cannot divorce ourselves from the consequences, even if we feel reborn. Gwion Bach accidentally poisons the horses of Gwyddno Garanhir. He didn't mean to do it. He had no idea the cauldron would crack, or the remaining potion would be poison, or that it would go into the lake and river, or that horses would be drinking at that time and place. But that doesn't matter. That is the result. And he must take responsibility for the results of his actions. So in his rebirth, he is found by Elphin, son of Gwyddno, and enters into the service of that family until he has made amends.

While our own responsibilities might not include entering into servitude, we do have to take responsibility in ways that are appropriate for the society we are born into. Sometimes admitting fault and consequence, rather than trying to defend or justify, and simply apologizing is the first step in this process. When we can really handle the consequences of this life consciously, we begin to resolve and free ourselves from the karma of past lives, and can move more fully into our role as the reborn Child of Light, new and clear in all that we do.

Taking Responsibility

In your journal, make a list of all the things unresolved because you have not taken responsibility for your part in them. What must you do to resolve them? This list might echo your list on forgiveness.

Once Taliesin repays his debt, it becomes clear that his calling goes beyond Gwyddno's family, and out into the world. He is able to work with the likes of King Arthur and Merlin. He recognizes in his poetry his lineage to a consciousness that pre-dates Arthurian mythos, and will outlast incarnation in Camelot.

Though not intimately tied to the Grail Quest, being in the company of Arthur and Merlin does link Taliesin to the mystery of the Holy Grail, the Cauldron of the Underworld, and the selfless service it embodies. We must ask, "Whom does the Grail serve?" in these mysteries. We must seek to do what our true purpose is in this world without attachment to the outcome, to how it manifests, to the glory or credit. We must simply do what we are here to do. It is the difference in understanding the consequences of action, karma, and our right action, or majickal will, our dharma.

Taliesin Rebirth Ritual

For this ritual, make sure that along with the traditional tools for the majick circle, you have a veil or blindfold of dark cloth to block out all light during your meditation. The veil symbolizes both the birth caul of those who are considered seers and sorcerers, and the darkness of the womb and the leather sack cast upon the dark sea. You could also use a robe or cloak with an appropriately large and dark enough hood to cover your eyes and block out the light completely.

Everyone can have their own chalice to perform the sacrament of Tara and Avalon, or share a communal chalice.

Prepare this spell upon parchment, in black ink, prior to the circle.

I (state your name) ask in the name of the Goddess and God, to be reborn through the Goddess and God, to take full responsibility for my own actions, balance myself, and serve the Greater Good. I ask this be for my highest good, harming none. So Mote it Be!

Cast your majick circle. Perform the sacrament, and as you take the three drops, remember Taliesin. Think about how your first and second degrees were like time in the hut leading to the womb. Think about your own chase through the four elements. Think about the Goddess consuming you. You are in the womb of the Goddess all this time, waiting to be reborn. Look at all this time studying, learning, and growing as your incubation period, your nine months in the womb. Reflect on all you have learned and all you have done. Take the three drops. With these three drops, feel yourself being reborn to the Goddess. She is of you and you are of her, and you can be reborn now.

Prepare for meditation; sit if you are not already sitting. Place the veil upon your head, covering your eyes, or wear a blindfold. Enter into a deeper state of alpha through the Crystal Countdown. Enter into pure darkness. You are now placed within the leather satchel and cast upon the sea, floating in the dream of darkness, upon the watery abyss, you go. Float. Dream. Be in the darkness.

Take this time to reflect upon your birth parents, your own mother and father. Is there anything unresolved between you? Take this time to truly forgive and let go of everything that might harm you and your evolution.

Rejoice in your rebirth Mother, the Goddess, your Divine Mother.

Rejoice in your rebirth Father, the God, your Divine Father.

Know you are supported by these Divine Parents, Goddess and God. They are always near. They will always love you. You must start your life as a spiritual adult, but you always have their support, even when you must act on your own.

Take this time to reflect on things that you must take responsibility for, even if any harm was unintentional, or not your fault. You still must rectify your past mistakes and harms. You must clear them before your life as a High Priest/ess can start. Just like Taliesin facing the responsibility for the death of the horses of Gwyddno Garanhir, we must face our karma. Let the Divine Mind show you and tell you what you must do next to achieve balance. Let the darkness speak to you.

When ready, take off the veil, like the leather sack being opened. Feel the light upon your eyes and brow. Become bright and illuminated. Prepare to present yourself to others and to the world at large. Affirm to remember and enact the wisdom you found in the darkness.

Give yourself clearance and balance. Count up from alpha.

Recite your spell and burn your parchment in the ash pot or cauldron.

Release the majick circle.

Eleven: Preparation for the Grail Quest

Am I not a candidate for fame, if a song is heard?
In Caer Pedryfan, four its revolutions;
In the first word from the cauldron when spoken,
From the breath of nine maidens it was gently warmed.
Is it not the cauldron of the chief of Annwn? What is its intention?
A ridge about its edge and pearls.
It will not boil the food of a coward, that has not been sworn,
A sword bright gleaming to him was raised,
And in the hand of Lleminawg it was left.
And before the door of the gate of Uffern the lamp was burning.
And when we went with Arthur; a splendid labour,
Except seven, none returned from Caer Vedwyd
— The Spoils of Annwn

As Cabot Witches, we look to the time of the Arthurian Mysteries to guide us, as they occurred at a time of transition that perhaps did not go for the better, as Christianity was on the rise in Europe. The natural indigenous beliefs of the people of the British Isles would soon be overrun with a new religion. The Avalonian Mysteries, the Druidic Schools, the ways of the Witch, would be lost for a time.

We too live in a time of transition. The old ways are returning, with the new ways. The union of the old mysteries with the new sciences will lead our people into the light, but we can learn quite a bit from the mysteries of a past age, so we look to those of Camelot to be our guides, allies, and teachers on the path.

The Golden Age of Camelot

The creation of Camelot by Arthur and inspired by Merlin is the restoration of order and civility upon a time of wildness. Britain, like Ireland in her invasions, is a metaphor for the world, a time when we had only petty tyrants, no true sacred king. We had the rise of Christianity against the native traditions, and the invading Saxons invited by traitorous kings. The king and the land were not one, and it took a vision of Merlin as prophet to guide us to the reign of Arthur.

Though not yet the Age of Aquarius, the Round Table, the heart of Camelot represented an Aquarian ideal—a union of peers rather than a solitary head. It was about brotherhood and service, and ideally worked against ego and control. The Round Table is the Wheel of the Zodiac, or the Wheel of the North Stars. It was said that two knights sat at every zodiac sign, making it a table of twenty-four.

Many believe the Round Table is the dowry of Queen Guinevere. She may have been a human queen, and she may have been a Christian queen, but some believe she was a Faery queen, and her Round Table a promise exchanged between the human world and Faery world. Author Wendy Berg, in her books *Red Tree, White Tree* and *Gwenevere and the Round Table*, makes a good argument for this interpretation. In any case, as the representative of the land, of the Goddess and of the Fey, Guinevere is the queen of union.

In this union, there is a peace between the Pagans and the Christians, the Druids and Witches and the Priests, Nuns, and Monks. In the realms of Camelot, a mystical side of Christianity compatible with the old ways flourished, as it did in the early era of Glastonbury, the land thought to once be Avalon.

Through the powers of the sacred king, the land is safe from invasions. If it is invaded, a force will help repel those who would do harm. Sadly, Arthur, in his arrogance, digs up the head of Bran the Blessed, buried facing the east, to repel invaders. Arthur opens a door to invasion, and then must hold the line to prevent it from coming further.

One can say with the establishment of Camelot, divine order upon Earth is restored. The land prospers and is fertile. Order and peace are established. The code of chivalry, of honoring the feminine and those in need, is established, exemplifying the code of honor, bravery, justice, and courtesy. It is not unlike a nod to the priest-kings of ancient Egypt, the pharaohs, performing the appropriate rituals spiritually, as well as leading socially and politically. The pharaohs were hoping to emulate the first time, the Zep Tepi, when the gods walked the Earth with the humans and animals, in a time of the Golden Age. Camelot reminds us of that Golden Age and our desire to recreate its balance here on Earth again.

THE CREATION OF THE WASTELAND

The Creation of the Wasteland is often called The Dolorous Blow in the mythology. And there have been several different events called the Dolorous Blow, creating different lessons and myths.

But in essence, it is when the sacred contract between humanity and the enchanted world is broken. It is when we strike and injure, in some way, the land and all of nature. It is an echo of the mythologies that have a fall in them. We can compare it to the Christian fall from grace in Eden, the ending of the Zep Tepi time before time in Egypt, or the sinking of Atlantis.

Three main events are said to be the reason for the Wasteland's creation:

The Dolorous Blow of the Fisher King — The Fisher King is a mysterious figure. Christians see him as an incarnation of Jesus Christ. Witches might see him as an older King, before Arthur, or a mystical King on the inner planes, where Arthur is focused in the outer political world for a time. The King is wounded in the groin or genitals with a spear, or gored by the totem of the boar. Without the potential to procreate, the king is considered imperfect, yet without having a son, none can take his place. His wound will not heal, and as he wastes away, so too does the land. He lives in the Grail Castle but on his own, he cannot work the majick of the Grail. He requires an outside agent, a knight from Camelot. He is only the guardian, living in a spectral castle that appears to move from place to place. He spends his time fishing, which has allegories to both Jesus as the Fisher of Men, and the quest for the Salmon of Wisdom in Celtic myth. Injured, he cannot truly hunt. Until a worthy questing knight makes it to the castle and asks the right question, his wound will not be healed, and the land will not be restored.

Rape and Theft of the Nine Well Maidens by King Amangon — King Amangon, a figure not so famous in Arthurian lore for most of us, but important nonetheless, is out questing with his knights. He comes upon Nine Well Maidens who would serve visitors food and drink from golden majick cups. They were the guardians of a grove with at least one, if not nine, wells to it. For some reason, King Amangon and his men took food and drink, but also stole the cups and raped the maidens. They were majickal Faery women, and this act of sacrilege caused the well to dry up and in that drought, the life force of the land was withdrawn and things began to waste away. Later heroes encounter the descendants of the maidens—seven guardians along with maidens, some of whom were possible products of the rape—who must be healed as a part of the Wasteland's curse. The Fisher King's castle disappears at this time, so it is unclear if this un-kingly action by Amangon corresponds to the wounding of the Fisher King.

Betrayal of the King by the Queen and Champion — In the most famous of the Arthurian Tales, the biggest wound comes from the damage between the King and Queen, Arthur and

Guinevere. Though most modern retellings account the tale as Lancelot the most noble Knight of the Round Table having an affair with the Queen, it speaks of a deeper wounding between the King and Queen for that to happen. Arthur focused on the outer world too much, his politics and his realm, and not the inner duties of the Priest-king to the Priestess-Queen, to ensure the ancients ways were kept and the land would be rejuvenated continuously. This break between them caused the Wasteland in modern lore, but not necessarily in the more ancient story cycles.

The effect of the Dolorous Blow, in any form, teaches us some important lessons about our sacred contract with the land and the realm of enchantment. Perhaps it happened because humanity forgot these important lessons. Lessons we can take from the wounding of our relationship and the breaking of the contract include:

The Divine Feminine

The Divine Feminine must be honored by humanity. Failure to do so leads to an imbalance in the world.

Injury of Others

We are all connected through the Divine Feminine. To injure another is to ultimately injure yourself and the whole. To harm one is to harm yourself and all others. To harm yourself is to harm the world. All are wounded.

Poison to All

Wounds unhealed linger and become toxic. These wounds will poison all with a wasting away disease. To not heal is to do a disservice to not only yourself, but to all beings. The Healing Path is necessary for us all.

King and the Land

The King and the Land are one, meaning the appointed representative, the Priest-King, mediates the relationship between the people of a kingdom and the land, the spirits and the Goddess. When the relationship is right, all is right. When the relationship is ill, all is ill. This is an extension of honoring of the Divine Feminine.

When you really look closely at the world, it seems as if we are still living in the Wasteland. With the rise of dogmatic religions that tell us we are spiritually separate, sinful and fallen, with the loss of the feminine mysteries and majick, political and ethnic conflicts and war, the creation of harmful forms of industrialization and technology, and the ravages against nature and our planet, how can we decide we are in anything but the Wasteland? These stories are still important to use today because they still tell our story. We have been wounded and wounded others, like the Fisher King. Our lack of healing continues to poison the world. We have raped and pillaged the Well Maidens, as we have raped and pillaged the Earth herself. We have betrayed the fidelity we have to each other as a community, a society, and the fidelity we have with the land and nature. We are all collectively responsible for the Dolorous Blow, and must take our part in healing it. We must write the new stories and live the new myths to restore paradise from the Wasteland. We must build new Camelots in our hearts, minds, and communities.

We live in the time of the Return of Arthur, but rather than one King returning from Avalon, the meaning of his return is that we all must be kings. We all must bear the Light of Excalibur. We all must assume our sovereignty and rule our lives. We all must be one with the Land as Queens and Kings. When all people can do this, we can heal the Dolorous Blow all across the world and move into our next destiny.

QUEST FOR THE HOLY GRAIL

The quest begins in the classic lore, with a vision of the Grail above the Round Table. The possibility of healing, the possible solution to the Wasteland, is presented. Christian knights would see it as the cup of Jesus from the Last Supper, but Pagan Knights would know it as the majickal cup, the Cauldron of the Underworld.

The quest itself is as important as attaining the Grail, for the quest's challenges change and prepare the knight. The Knight is an emissary of the King and Queen, sent forth from the castle. Knights are extensions of humanity, champions for us all. Usually in the quest, one must enter the wilderness, going away from the broken perfection of Camelot. We must enter the unknown to be truly challenged. This is part of encountering the "other" in initiation. There is a variety of guardians and challenges to the quest, including wild beasts and seeming monsters. Some will turn to friends and teachers, though some remain foes.

The goal of the quest is to seek the Grail Castle and encounter the Fisher King, who is the guardian of the Grail. The wounded Fisher King is preceded by a procession of maidens and his court, and each one has a blessing, gift, or challenge for those who understand.

WITHDRAWAL TO MERLIN'S ENCLOSURE

Merlin was not able to guide Arthur and the Knights of the Round Table when the Wasteland was upon them. He had disappeared from the tales by that point. But what happened to him? As there are many stories of the Holy Grail and the knights, there are many tales of Merlin, and in fact, many Merlins. In one version of his story, he withdrew from the world to the forest, along with a small group that included his sister, living in a glass observatory she had built for him so that he could prophesize until the end times. This tower was the first version of his enclosure.

Though many think of all of the British Isles as Merlin's Enclosure or Merlin's Fortress, it usually refers to his place of withdrawal. Did he willingly go back into nature, into a grove, a tree, a tower of glass, or a cave? Was he tricked by Nimue, his apprentice? Even if Nimue had a hand in it, did he know his time was over, and go with her to withdraw himself from the world, knowing humanity alone must restore the land? Who knows?

In his enclosure, he drew to him the thirteen sacred Treasures of Britain. They are to be saved until the next age, when the true and rightful king shall have use of them.

The Thirteen Treasures of Britain
The White Hilt Sword of Rhydderch the Generous
The Hamper of Gwyddno Long-Shank
The Horn of Bran from the North
The Chariot of Morgan the Wealthy
The Halter of Clyno Eiddyn
The Knife of Llawfronedd the Horseman
The Cauldron of Diwrnach the Giant
The Whetstone of Tudwal Tudglyd
The Coat of Padarn Red-Coat
The Crock of Rhygenydd the Cleric
The Dish of Rhygenydd the Cleric
The Chessboard of Gwenddolau ap Ceidio

The Mantle of Arthur

Modern Witches come up with their own list of thirteen treasures, or sacred tools. In the Cabot Tradition, we associate a different majickal tool with a different planet, as described in the Second Degree teachings. Our sacred tools are the Candle (Sun), Cauldron/Chalice (Moon), Wand (Mercury), Thurible/Censer (Venus), Sword (Mars), Cord (Jupiter), Athame (Saturn), Garter (Uranus), Crystal Ball (Neptune), Black Robe/Cape (Pluto), Gold Pentacle (Vulcan), Animal Horn/Egg (Earth), and Majick Mirror (Sparta).

Merlin's withdrawal reminds us that at times, we too must withdraw, find the inspiration and mystery in the silence, and renew ourselves before continuing onward to the next phase.

Meditation Time of Silence and Mystery

For this ritual, you will need a veil of black or dark cloth, or a robe or cloak with a hood large enough to cover your eyes and block out the light. You will also need to find and prepare a section from one of the primary sources of the Grail myths, or another primary source of Celtic myth you feel is appropriate for this working, that will confer wisdom upon reflection.

Prepare your usual altar to cast a circle. Cast your circle. Call your quarters. Perform your sacrament and make your offerings to the Ancient Ones.

Read your passage from the sacred text, slowly and ritualistically. Contemplate and feel the essence of each word, image, and idea.

When done, place the veil upon your head. If leading others, they can already have donned their veils, hoods, or cloaks and lowered them over their eyes. Ideally, everyone would already be in an alpha state.

Sit in silent, contemplative meditation, reflecting upon the passage, and all you have learned thus far, and all that is before you. Go beyond the thoughts and images. Find the deep inner stillness of the void.

Spend a long time in this space, and when done, release your circle in the traditional way. Ground, reflect and record your experience in your journal.

In times past in the Cabot Tradition, this would also be a time for facing our fears in the most primal way, as we would hold snakes, spiders, and hissing cockroaches. You may do this as well.

GRAIL CASTLE PREPARATION JOURNAL

Obtain a notebook for this work separate from all your other notebooks because it will be destroyed. Each week of this month, three times a week, make five lists or journal entries. The first list will deal with all your unresolved wounds and issues on a personal level, particularly things you perceive as things that were "done" to you by others. The second list involves all the mistakes you have made and all the wrongs you've done to others. The third list is acts of good service you have done for others and the world. The fourth list involves all your gratitude. The fifth and final list each time is a list of things you fear.

When you make each list or journal entry, turn the page and do not look back. When you repeat the exercise, do not look at old lists first. Approach each one fresh, and use what comes to you that day. Your lists will change over time. Some will grow longer. Some will grow shorter. Use it like a creative writing brainstorming exercise. Write quickly what first comes to mind without censoring yourself. You might surprise yourself with what shows up. Dig deep into yourself, but also follow your own intuition on how long or short the lists will be. You will not be showing them to anyone, so bare your heart and soul in them.

Wounds of the Wasteland
Unhealed Personal Issues, Unresolved Complexes, Angers, Problems, Unfortunate Circumstances
List of Wrongs Done to You Intentionally and Unintentionally

Wrongs to Others
Issues Others Have with You, Unresolved Conflicts, Mistakes, Shame, Guilt, Jealousy, Grief
List of Wrongs You Have Done unto Others

Service to the Greater Good
Acts of Compassion, Blessing, Service to Others and the World
List of "Good Deeds" You Have Done Selflessly With No Thought of Reward

Counting Your Blessings
Gratitude for Little and Big Things in your Life
List of "Good Deeds" You Have Received from Others and the Universe

Talking Stock of your Fears
Things Beyond Your Control, Terrors, Nightmares
List of All the Things You Fear

Again, do all five lists, three times a week, for all four weeks. You will make all five lists for a total of twelve times.

On the third week, expand your lists to a regional world as well as the personal. Add to the wounds of the Wasteland a list of the wounds to the regional Wasteland—issues of your family, tribe, community, town/city, state, country or other regional geographic area division that have wounded an area or group of people to which you belong. Think about such things as social injustice, civil rights, slavery, and societal violence.

On the fourth week, add to the wounds of the Wasteland, a list of the wounds to the planetary Wasteland—issues of inter-country, environmental, historic, or global consequence that have caused collective global wounds. Think of issues around environmental problems and ecocide, world trade economics, world wars, and global conflicts. In the Fear List, make sure you include any global, worldwide, or historic fears.

Prior to Class Twelve, review the lists in a majick circle. Read each list and burn them in a cauldron. You can burn them outside of the majick circle and outside of your home, as that amount of paper will create a lot of smoke indoors. Let the ashes cool and save them in a bottle. Bring the ashes to Class Twelve.

Make sure you have been practicing alpha meditations long enough to enter into an extended guided meditation without losing focus, snapping out of it, or falling asleep. The vision work of the twelfth class is long and intense, requiring us to be in peak mental condition.

Twelve: Whom Does the Grail Serve?

*"Only those who have the heart of a child, the courage of a warrior,
and the wisdom of the animals will find the Grail and ask the question."*
— Anonymous

The Mystery of the Grail

The Holy Grail is a mysterious thing, which—contrary to popular images—does not always appear as a cup. The Grail has many forms as a part of its mystery. The Grail moves through Five Miraculous Changes. Each one expresses a different mystery and understanding of the Grail. Each one exemplifies one of the elemental hallows, or treasures, yet the Cup is often the most prevalent form for healing the Wasteland.

Holy Cup

The Cup of The Goddess, or in Christian Mysticism, the Cup of Christ. It is the Cup of Healing and Forgiveness.

Bleeding Spear

The Bleeding Spear or Weeping Lance weeps for the maimed Fisher King.

Plate with the Severed Head

The oracular head speaking prophecy and wisdom from the holy plate in the holy tongue for all to hear. The head of Bran the Blessed in Pagan tradition, or John the Baptist in Christian tradition.

The Fallen Stone

The emerald that fell from heaven, the green meteorite, the alchemist's Philosopher's Stone from which the Emerald Tablet was carved. The stone becomes the king's stone and the living heart of the Faery land.

The Cauldron

The Cauldron of Cerridwen, of Bran, of Dagda, of Gwernach the Giant, of Annwn. The mysterious cauldron of the Otherworld.

The only hallow the Grail does not usually become is the Sword, for the Knight holds the sword in the quest for truth and service. This is one of the reasons why the sword is such a prominent tool and symbol for the Cabot High Priestess or High Priest.

PURPOSE OF THE GRAIL

There are many seeming purposes to the Holy Grail. In myth, each of these purposes is associated with a specific manifestation in mythology and one of the Five Miraculous changes of the Grail.

Abundance
Land Thrives with Food, Drink and Riches. No Hunger
The Cauldron of Dagda — Undry
Miraculous Change: The Fallen Stone

Healing
Healing and Forgiveness of Self, Others and the World
The Holy Grail — San Greal
Miraculous Change: Holy Cup

Wisdom
Grants insight into the True Nature of Reality. Resurrection. Initiation.
The Cauldron of Bran – Pair Dadeni
Miraculous Change: The Plate with the Severed Head

Inspiration
Allows us to Co-Create with Divinity
The Cauldron of Cerridwen — Cauldron of Awen
Miraculous Change: The Cauldron

Restoration of Sovereignty
Right Relationship with the Land, Gods, and Spirits. Renewal of Sacred Contract
The Alchemical Crucible
Miraculous Change: The Bleeding/Weeping Spear or Lance

The restoration of the sacred contract, of sovereignty is key. Each of the other Grail needs show many of the layers required to get to the place of true sovereignty. To have sovereignty, one must:

- *Have Basic Needs Met* — Physical and Spiritual Sustenance, Shelter, Tribe
- *Have Healing* — Take responsibility for Wounds of Self/Others, Release and Forgive
- *Have Service* — Selfless Service to Higher Good, Stewardship, and Caretaking of the Realm

One of the reasons why the cup and cauldron are so prevalent in the Grail mythos is that each of the types of drinks can help us understand a different aspect of the mystery. The three drinks of sovereignty are quite powerful expressions of these ideas in ritual.

White Drink — The White Drink, or milk, is the drink of fostering and adoption, and sustenance for its nutritional value. It is the drink of our basic needs.

Red Drink — The Red Drink, often seen as wine or juice, is the drink of lordship and stewardship. It is the drink of our service to the greater good.

Dark Drink — The Dark Drink is the most mysterious of them all, as it is the drink of forgetfulness and healing. It helps us release our past wounds and let go of what doesn't serve. It is the drink for us on the self-healing path, so our wounds do not overwhelm us.

Sovereignty is the key to the Cabot Tradition of Witchcraft. We wear ritual crowns or crown rings to remind us that we are sovereign. You need to put a crown on your head, pull it down tight. You need to understand your boundaries, your roles, and responsibilities in the life as a sovereign being. You must say, "I will do this" and "I will not do that" in measure with your purpose. You should recognize, regardless of the path, that every person is sovereign in their own right. You must take care of yourself, and that in turn will lead you to your work in the world. Once you realize that it is your power, your knowledge and your goodness, your right action within the laws of the Craft will manifest your sovereignty. They give you power. Power is not a dirty word. You must know how to use it well. You're not going to use it to do harm. You're going to use it to do the exact opposite. You're going to neutralize harm and catalyze change and project good in all that you do. You are going to do your work in the world. So to be sovereign, you need to be stronger than the average bear. Arthur was the Bear King. That's the way Witches work. And that's what people were afraid of. They were afraid of people who were powerful, who were independent, who could manifest their lives, who could heal themselves and heal other people's spirits, bodies and minds. We have returned. You are capable of doing all of this and more for yourself and others.

THE QUEST FOR THE GRAIL CASTLE

The quest for the Grail has five major points found in the mythology: Wildness of the Wasteland, Questing Beast, Crossing the Bridge, the Guardians of the Gate, and the Grail Procession. Each one represents an area of learning and spiritual attainment. Each one has its perils. We look to the ancient myths and the otherworldly patterns they present to us to prepare us in body, mind and spirit, for the mysteries of the Grail, in order to better serve our own needs, our healing, the greater community and kingdom, and therefore the world.

Wilderness of the Wasteland — Once we leave the confines of civilization, of Camelot, of what is known and safe, we must go out into the wilderness. Our own wilderness is when we become lost in our thoughts, feelings, and personal situations. We get overwhelmed. We start to be unable, as the saying goes, to "tell the forest from the trees." Our modern life, in many ways, can be a wilderness of distractions, dangers, and daily stress.

Questing Beast — The questing beast is a collective totem, a mix and blend of many animals and forms, sometimes monstrous and sometimes beautiful. It is the guardian of our fears and chaos. The beast is our animal nature gone wild within us and our society. It is the embodiment of our shame, including sexual shame, our repressed violence, fears, and the overall chaos of our world. These are all forces we feel we have no control over, so rather than embrace that lack of control, we try to hide these things. The Questing Beast must be tamed rather than slain, or a new beast will simply grow and take its place. How you tame the Beast says as much about your quest as simply succeeding. We must be creative in our healing and problem solving.

Crossing the Sword Bridge of the Abyss — To get entry into the Grail Castle, there is a secret passageway, a bridge or tunnel, that is dangerous. In many forms of the myth, the bridge is a sword bridge, with the polished sharp edge of the sword being the way across. On the other side are lions and other animals guarding the edge. To safely cross, a knight must take off his armor, removing his protection, his earthly identity, and identify with the light spirit of self, with the soul. Only then can he walk successfully in balance to the otherworld. Can you release your sense of self enough to cross the gate? Can you stand without your armor? Can you shed your old skin and the unnecessary parts of yourself?

Guardians of the Gates — In the myths, many guardians take form, often in the shape of a knight of various colors. Some show in the Grail Castle, and others outside in the Wilderness. For our work here in the Cabot Tradition, we shall look to the guardians as the Red Knight, the Black Knight, and the Green Knight. The Red Knight is the Guardian of Good Deeds Done and Service. The Black Night is the Guardian of our Wrongs To Others. The Green Knight is the Guardian of Good Deeds Received and Blessings. One has to face what we have done that is good, what we have done that has caused harm, and what good had been done to us.

The Chapel of the Castle — Within the Grail Castle is the Chapel of the Grail, and the Grail Procession made from the Court of the Fisher King. He is the guardian of the wounds of the Wasteland. His procession consists of many of the characters, in new form, that the questing knight has met before, including forms of the nine maiden guardians and their seven protectors at the Well. The nine maidens take many forms, and through our surviving lore, there are five sets of nine maidens, forming forty-five different aspects of these goddesses. Numerologically, forty-five reduces back down to nine again.

Nine Maidens of the Well	Regeneration and Wasteland
Nine Sisters of Avalon	Healing and Hexing
Nine Maidens of the Cauldron of Annwn	Warmth and Gentleness
Nine Witches of Gloucester	Testing and Battle
Nine Ladies of the Lake	Guidance and Passage

There in the Chapel of the Grail Castle, one must ask the Question: Whom Does the Grail Serve?

Grail Castle Ritual and Vision Working

Create a traditional altar with a large cup filled with Holy Water and a medium-sized cauldron to hold the ashes.

Cast the majick circle. Call the quarters. Call upon the Goddess, God, Ancestors, and the Keepers of the Holy Grail.

All students pour their collected ashes from the preparatory work journals into the cauldron together. We are healing not only ourselves, but our people and the world. We share that work together as a community. Mix the ashes together and mark the third eye with the ashes.

Count down into Alpha and prepare for a guided visionary ritual.

You seek the Grail Castle known as Corbenic, where the Fisher King resides and keeps the sacred mystery.

Enter into the forest, the wilderness. While normally you love the forest, there is something wild, something sinister about it now. The branches and thorns seem to obscure the path. You hear the sounds of animals, but don't see them. You begin to feel as if you are wandering aimlessly, and as you do, you get stuck in your own thoughts and feelings. You wander in the darkness, doubting yourself, your decisions and relationships, the path of your life.

You start to hear a haunting music, and in the distance, you catch an image of a glowing parade of people, otherworldly figures illuminated from within, walking in a procession. They sing a haunting melody, but you cannot make out the words. You go towards them, and they disappear from your sight, but put you back on the path. You feel you can find your way again to the Grail Castle.

While you are still on the path, you hear a strange, disturbing animal noise amid the forest, and look to your left to see bent down by the stream, a strange awful beast unlike any you've ever seen before.

The creature is the size of a giraffe. Its head and neck look like the head and neck of a large snake. Its body is the body of a leopard with the hindquarters of a lion. The feet of the creature are those of a hart, a stag. While the snake's mouth makes no noise, you can hear the yips and barks of a pack of dogs from within its belly. The very sight of it unnerves you. It's monstrous.

This is the Questing Beast, the guardian of our primal wild fears. It is the embodiment of animal nature gone wild. The beast is the beast of shame, violence, fear, and the chaos of the unknown. Just looking at it causes you to feel overwhelmed. It is a creature from nightmares and childhood terror. You fear it will turn its attention to you and harm you.

Will you stand and face it, or will you run away?

Though gruesome, it doesn't appear violent. Will you welcome it? Can you tame it? If so, how?

Will you forgive it for embodying these terrors?

Can you befriend it, rather than tame it?

When you look at it closely, you start to realize how ridiculous it really is. It is something to frighten a child, but other than being very different, when you really look at it, the Questing Beast is not so frightening.

As you make friends with it, the Beast transforms, taking the shape of a small white fox. The fox is still pregnant with numerous children within, threatening to tear the fox apart from the inside as she hopes to care for and give birth to the offspring.

Can you offer her compassion?

Can the Beast become your ally?

If so, the Questing Beast will guide you, despite its own difficulties, along the path and upward toward a cliff. In the distance you see what is most likely the Grail Castle, but you have come upon the top of the cliff that is the edge of a chasm. It is there the Questing Beast leaves you to face the abyss alone.

* * *

The chasm separates the land where you stand from the land of the Grail Castle. What at first appears to be a wicked black stream of flowing water is really the Abyss, raging in black with white speckled stars of light. This chasm of the Abyss is bottomless, and all who fall into it are lost forever in a broken land. The chasm is bridged by a large sword, larger than two lances held from end to end, with its edge up and the hilt of the blade closest to your end and the tip of the blade thrust into a tree at the other side. Tied to the trees at the other side are two lions of the King, looking quite ferocious. To walk the blade, one would require uncanny balance, and the sharpness of the blade would maim the feet, knees, and hands in the crossing.

You also see, as you gaze below, a tunnel that goes into or under the water, forming a sort of Water Bridge, possibly to the other side of the Grail Castle. But to get there, you would have to climb down the cliff face and risk falling into the Abyss. You reflect long upon the two choices, but feel called to go the Way of the Sword, reminded of the Light of Excalibur.

To cross the Sword Bridge, one must divest themselves of all armor, including all pretense, all disguise, all that is not the essential self. One must strip away not only the clothes, but also the personality, the likes and dislikes, the human identity, and become one with that which truly is, in all lifetimes, the immortal self.

Strip away yourself, your clothes or armor. Strip away the things that appear to be you in this lifetime—your physical looks, your labels and titles, your names, your likes and dislikes, your stories and beliefs, your accomplishments. You might even feel as if your flesh is falling off your body and your bones are crumbling, revealing pure spirit. You still have all of those things, but it doesn't matter.

Cross the edge of the Sword Bridge with grace and beauty. The lions leave you alone, barely noticing your ephemeral self. As you cross this threshold and begin walking the path again, you start to become "you" again, but more pure, more true, more yourself. You have gotten rid of a lot of things that no longer serve your own highest good.

As you view the castle coming closer from the distance, you realize it is circular, made in three concentric rings, with a central tower in the heart of it. You come to the first gate, and the door is opened by a fearsome Red Knight.

The Red Knight is the guardian of your Good Deeds Done and your Service. He asks you, what have you done that makes you worthy of entering the Grail Castle? What do you say?

If he lets you pass, you are brought into another realm within the castle. The people and place are surreal and ghostly. They barely seem to notice you at all.

You follow your way to the next gate at the second wall. There guarding the gate is the Black Knight, possibly more fearsome than the Red.

The Black Night is the guardian of your Wrongs to Others. The Knight asks you, what you have done that makes you unworthy to enter the castle? What is the worst thing you have done in your life? Can you take responsibility for it, and name it?

If he believes you are truthful, and lets you pass, you enter another world. This one is darker, gritty, and more "real" than the last. You see people tattered and in rags, suffering, and soon realize that this world is populated by people you have wronged, people you have had conflict with or done harm. You must navigate your way through them, blessing them, and make your way to the third and final gate.

The third gate is guarded by the bright verdant Green Knight, as if the Green Man has taken on a knightly form. The Green Knight is the Guardian of Good Deeds we have Received and all Blessings we are grateful to have. The Green Knight asks you to name five things you are thankful to have in your life. What blessings have you received?

If the Green Knight feels this gratitude is sufficient, he opens the gate for you, and you enter into the proper Grail Castle.

* * *

There the familiar procession from the woods is making its way up a spiral staircase. A parade of enchanted women and men carrying strange objects goes before you. The procession is led by two people each holding a ten-candled candelabra, making twenty small flames in all leading the procession. Five more figures follow the two leaders.

They sing in a haunting tune of the Glory and Power, of everlasting Joy and to the Destroyer of Death. It echoes through the tower as they ascend. Though at first you might think it was a Christian hymn, you realize they are chanting in praise of the Goddess and her Child of Light.

You make your way to the top chamber, lit with torches, and find the procession surrounding you.

The first figure shows you a lance, and the lance is dripping with something. It is water, perhaps tears, or even blood dripping upon the ground. It is a hallow that restores sovereignty through sacrifice.

The second figure holds a stone, which appears dark at first, but when the light of the candles and torches hits it just right, a beautiful green stone, like an emerald, is revealed. It is a talisman of the abundance of the land, when embodying the secret wisdom.

The third figure presents a plate or dish with a covering upon it. The covering is lifted to reveal a severed head, the oracular head of the ancients. It is an oracle of wisdom and the mysteries of life and death. It can answer any question and solve any mystery.

The fourth figure holds forward a large cauldron, bubbling with a strange brew. It is a vessel of inspiration, of awen. It contains all the knowledge of the world, all the majick.

And the fifth figure holds the heart the Holy Cup, the Sacred Chalice and Holy Grail of Immortality. It is a vessel of healing. It forgives all that is unforgiven.

The five seem to morph and shapeshift within each guardian's hands. One becomes another and again, until you realize all are one, and one is all.

The guardians of the Grail Procession part and reveal the Fisher King upon his throne. He is wounded upon the thigh, or more accurately, the groin, with a wound that will never heal. He is the guardian of the wounds of the Wasteland. He guards our personal wound, the wounds of our people, and the wounds of the planet. He knows why his own wounds will not heal, and asks, why have your own wounds not healed?

He reveals to you the Nine who truly hold the Heart of the Grail.

You know them as the Nine Well Maidens who were raped by King Amangon and his men.

They have been raped and stolen from many times since then, by many people.

They bring regeneration to restore Paradise when honored, and the Wasteland when dishonored.

You know them as the Nine Sisters of Avalon who live on the Fortunate Isle.

They seek to restore humanity's relationship with Avalon, Tara, and all of the Otherworld.

They bring healing for allies when honored, and hexing for enemies when dishonored.

You know them as the Nine Maidens of Annwn, who tend the Underworld Cauldron.

They seek to keep the cauldron brew for those who are successful in the quest.

Their breath brings warmth and gentleness to the fires of the pearl-rimmed cauldron.

You known them as the Nine Witches of Gloucester.

Those who offer hospitality to the seeker,

Yet they bring testing and battle.

And you know them as the Nine Ladies of the Lake, the Nine "Queens" of the Arthurian Court

Who bring Guidance and Passage,

Accompanying the King to his final resting place to rise again.

Will you ask the Questions?

Whom Does the Grail Serve?

Why does the Lance bleed?

What do these wonders mean?

And will you listen to the answer deep within you?

* * *

They offer you to drink from the chalice three times. What color is the liquid—white, red, or dark?

Drink from the Grail and heal your own wounds.

Drink from the Grail and heal the wounds of your people

Drink from the Grail and heal the wounds of the planet, the Wasteland
Restore Camelot and enchant the World!

Does the cup change form once you drink from it, transforming into one of the other four miraculous changes? Or to something else entirely?

After you drink you start to fall into a slumber and find yourself falling into a bed.
You find yourself healing, and integrating these changes within yourself.
You are majickally transported from the Grail Castle back to the here and now, as if you were never there at all.

Count up out of alpha

Stand in the majick circle

High Priest/ess:

Drink from the Grail and heal your own wounds.
Drink from the Grail and heal the wounds of your people
Drink from the Grail and heal the wounds of the planet, the Wasteland
Restore Camelot and enchant the world!

Pass the chalice, with each Witch drinking from it three times,

Raise the Cone of Power with the Intention to bless and heal all people of the World.

Ground to the Earth to bless and heal Mother Earth and all life.

Release the majick circle. Ground.

Note the color of the liquid in your journal and take stock of what level of the Grail you are working with right now. You can repeat this ritual again and again, to work with the other two levels, when you are prepared for it.

RECOMMENDED READING LIST FOR THE RELIGION OF WITCHCRAFT

Books marked with * are required reading. Out-of-print books can be found through keyword searches at Bibliofind.com.

Astrological Calendar

All 3rd Degree students are required to have Jim Maynard's *Celestial Guide,* an astrological week-at-a-glance engagement calendar, for the calendar year of the class. You could also use *Llewellyn's Astrological Calendar.* You need to bring this to every class and gathering for your class.

Cabot Tradition

Power of the Witch by Laurie Cabot*
The Witch in Every Woman by Laurie Cabot *
Love Magic by Laurie Cabot*
Celebrate the Earth by Laurie Cabot*
A Salem Witch's Herbal Majick by Laurie Cabot*
Laurie Cabot's Book of Spells and Enchantments by Laurie Cabot with Penny Cabot and Christopher Penczak *

Mythology

Voice of the Goddess by Caitlin Matthews
The Divine Feminine in Ancient Europe by Sharon Paice MacLeod
The Power of Myth by Joseph Campbell with Bill Moyers*
Myths to Live By by Joseph Campbell
Bullfinch's Mythology by Thomas Bullfinch
The White Goddess by Robert Graves
The Golden Bough by James Frazer

Celtic Mythology and Spirituality

The Complete Idiot's Guide to Celtic Wisdom by Carl McColman*
Women in Celtic Myth by Mora Caldecott*
Celtic Myth and Magick by Edain McCoy*

Red Haired Girl from the Bog by Patricia Monaghan*

Celtic Myth and Religion by Sharon Paice Macleod*

A Dictionary of Irish Mythology by Peter Ellis

Dictionary of Celtic Mythology by James MacKillop

The Aquarian Guide to British and Irish Mythology by John and Caitlin Matthews

A Celtic Reader by John Matthews*

Mabon and the Mysteries of Britain by John and Caitlin Matthews*

Queen of the Night: Rediscovering the Celtic Moon Goddess by Sharynne MacLeod NicMhacha

The Feast of the Morrighan by Christopher Penczak

The Guises of the Morrigan – The Irish Goddess of Sex and Battle by David Rankine and Sorita d'Este

Visions of the Cailleach by David Rankine and Sorita d'Este

Brigit: Sun of Womanhood by Patricia Monaghan and Michael McDermott (Editors)

The Encyclopedia of Celtic Mythology and Folklore by Patricia Monaghan

The Encyclopedia of Celtic Wisdom by John and Caitlin Mathews

Taliesin by John and Caitlin Matthews*

Celtic Myths, Celtic Legends by R.J. Stewart

Celtic Gods, Celtic Goddesses by R.J. Stewart

Celtic Bards, Celtic Druids by R.J. Stewart and Robin Williams

Awen: The Quest of the Celtic Mysteries by Mike Harris

From the Cauldron Born: Exploring the Magic of Welsh Legend and Lore by Kristoffer Hughes

The Sin Eater's Last Confessions: Lost Traditions of Celtic Shamanism by Ross Heaven

Walking with the Sin Eater: A Celtic Pilgrimage on the Dragon Path by Ross Heaven

The Spiral of Memory and Belonging: A Celtic Path of Soul and Kinship by Frank MacEowen

Arthurian Lore

Hallowquest: The Arthurian Tarot Course by John and Caitlin Matthews*

Ladies of the Lake by Caitlin Matthews*

Merlin: The Prophetic Vision and the Mystic Life by R.J. Stewart*

Arthur and the Sovereignty of Britain by Caitlin Matthews*

The Secret Tradition in Arthurian Legend by Gareth Knight

The Arthurian Formula by Dion Fortune, Margaret Lumley Brown, and Gareth Knight

Warriors of Arthur by R.J. Stewart and John Matthews

The Arthurian Quest by Amber Wolfe

Merlin by John and Caitlin Matthews

Gwenevere and the Round Table by Wendy Berg

Priestess of Avalon, Priestess of the Goddess by Kathy Jones

Avalon Within by Jhenah Telyndru

Faery Faith Traditions

Earthlight by R.J. Stewart

The Power within the Land by R.J. Stewart

The Living World of Faery by R.J. Stewart*

The Faery Teachings by Orion Foxwood*

Red Tree, White Tree: Faeries and Humans in Partnership by Wendy Berg

A Witch's Guide to Faery Folk by Edain McCoy

The Commonwealth of Elves, Fauns and Faires by Robert Kirk

The Fairy-Faith in Celtic Countries by W. Y. Evans-Wentz

Faery Healing: The Lore and the Legacy by Margie McArthur

The Sidhe: Wisdom from the Celtic Otherworld by John Matthews

Faery Mysticism: A Practical Guide to Initiation by Ari Devi

Paganism, Witchcraft, and Majick

Wheel of the Year by Pauline and Dan Campanelli*

Ancient Ways by Pauline and Dan Campanelli

Scottish Witchcraft by Raymond Buckland

The Druidry Handbook: Spiritual Practice Rooted in the Living Earth by John Michael Greer

Portal Book: Teachings and Works of Celtic Witchcraft by Ian Corrigan

Sacred Fire, Holy Well: A Druid's Grimoire by Ian Corrigan

The Sacred Cauldron by T. MacCrossan

Runelore by Edred Thorson

Taking Up The Runes by Diana L. Paxson

ABC of Witchcraft by Doreen Valiente

Witchcraft Today by Gerald Gardner

Diary of a Witch by Sybil Leek
The Wisdom of the Elements: The Sacred Wheel of Earth, Air, Fire and Water by Margie Mcarthur*
Wiccacraft for Families by Margie McArthur
The Cauldron of Memory: Retrieving Ancestral Knowledge and Wisdom by Raven Grimassi*
The Mighty Dead by Christopher Penczak
Deep Ancestors: Practicing the Religion of the Proto-Indo-Europeans by Ceisiwr Serith
To Walk a Pagan Path: Practical Spirituality for Every Day by Alaric Albertsson
Witches, Werewolves, and Fairies by Claude Lecouteux
The Return of the Dead by Claude Lecouteux
Witchcraft Medicine by Claudia Müller-Ebeling, Christian Rätsch and Storl, Wolf-Dieter, Ph.D.
The Encyclopedia of Witches, Witchcraft, and Wicca by Rosemary Ellen Guiley
The Element Encyclopedia of Witchcraft by Judika Illes
The Witches' Book of the Dead by Christian Day

Astrology

The Inner Sky: How to Make Wiser Choices for a More Fulfilling Life by Steven Forrest*
The Only Astrology Book You'll Ever Need by Joanna Martine Woolfolk
Astrology For Dummies by Rae Orion*
Astrology, A Cosmic Science by Isabel M. Hickey and Stephen Arroyo*
Astrology of Fate by Liz Greene
The Changing Sky by Steven Forrest
Astrology, Karma and Transformation: The Inner Dimensions of the Birth Chart by Stephen Arroyo
The Book of Pluto: Finding Wisdom in Darkness with Astrology by Steven Forrest
The Celtic Lunar Zodiac: How to Interpret Your Moon Sign by Helena Paterson*
The Handbook of Celtic Astrology by Helena Paterson

Occultism

The Secret Teachings of All Ages by Manly P. Hall*
The Secret Doctrine of the Rosicrucians by Magus Incognito*
Isis Unveiled by Madame H.P. Blavatsky
The Secret Doctrine by Madame H.P. Blavatsky

An Encyclopedia of Occultism by Lewis Spence
Atlantis: The Antediluvian World by Ignatius Donnelly
Sane Occultism by Dion Fortune
Real Magic by Isaac Bonewitz
The Mystic Foundation by Christopher Penczak
Polarity Magic: The Secret History of Western Religion by Wendy Berg and Mike Harris
The New Encyclopedia of the Occult by John Michael Greer

History

Pagan Britain by Ronald Hutton*
America BC by Barry Fell*
The Stones of Time by Marion Brennan
A History of Pagan Europe by Prudence Jones and Nigel Pennick
The Celts by Jean Markale*
The Celts by T.G.E. Powell*
The Holy Grail by Malcolm Godwin*
The Speech of the Grail by Linda Sussman
The Tribe of Witches: The Religion of the Dobunni and Hwicce by Stephen James Yeates*
A Dreaming for the Witches: The Reconstruction of the Dobunni Primal Myth by Stephen James Yeates
Malleus Malificarum (Hammer of the Witches) by Henrich Kramer and Jakob Sprenger*
The War Against Women by Marilyn French
Triumph of The Moon by Ronald Hutton
Modern Wicca: A History From Gerald Gardner to the Present by Michael Howard
Children of Cain: A Study of Modern Traditional Witchcraft by Michael Howard

New Paradigm Science and Ancient Wisdom

The Quantum Self by Danah Zohar*
The Holographic Universe by Michael Talbot*
Forbidden Archeology: The Hidden History of the Human Race by Michael A. Cremo
Chariots of the Gods by Erich von Däniken
The 12th Planet by Zecharia Sitchin

UFOs Are Here by Brad Steiger
Communion by Whitley Streiber
Gaia: A New Look at Life on Earth by James Lovelock
Earthmind: Communicating with the Living World of Gaia by Paul Devereux,
Shamanism and the Mystery Lines by Paul Devereux
Earth Memory: Sacred Sites – Doorways into Earth's Mysteries by Paul Devereux
The Elements of Earth Mysteries by Philip Heselton
The Camino: A Journey of the Spirit by Shirley MacLaine
The Cosmic Serpent: DNA and the Origins of Knowledge by Jeremy Narby
The EFT Manual by Gary Craig
Acupressure and Reflexology For Dummies by Synthia Andrews and Bobbi Dempsey
Acupressure's Potent Points: A Guide to Self-Care for Common Ailments by Michael Reed Gach, PhD

Environmentalism

Green Wizardry: Conservation, Solar Power, Organic Gardening, and Other Hands-On Skills From the Appropriate Tech Toolkit by John Michael Greer
Pagan Visions for a Sustainable Future by Ly de Angeles, Emma Restall Orr, et al.
Dark Green Religion: Nature Spirituality and the Planetary Future by Bron Taylor

Movies

Practical Magic
The Butcher's Wife
Bell, Book and Candle
Excalibur
Mists of Avalon
Harry Potter Series
Bedknobs and Broomsticks

II.
The Mysteries and Myths of the Wheel of the Year

In the second cycle of the Third Degree, we use the Wheel of the Year as a teaching pattern to understand the deeper mysteries in the seasons. We use it to understand the sacred lands where our traditions come from, as a pattern to explore the myth cycles from those lands.

One: Samhain
Two: Yule
Three: Imbolc
Four: Ostara
Five: Beltane
Six: Litha
Seven: Lughnassadh
Eight: Mabon
Nine: The Center

We divide the Wheel of the Year into two major sections—fire festivals and solar holidays, totaling eight Wheel of the Year sabbats with a ninth sacred center. In our studies, we associate each point upon the Wheel of the Year with a series of correspondences. Some of the correspondences work with all eight sabbat rituals. Others are based in sets of four, with some sets of four focused upon the fire festivals and other sets of four focused upon the solar holidays.

Students are expected to study and explore these correspondences, to anchor themselves in both the landscape of our Celtic motherlands and the mythos of our tradition. Study includes reading primary and secondary texts, and the use of meditation and ritual to have personal experiences of these places, myths, and deities while exploring this section of the year.

FIRE FESTIVALS: SAMHAIN, IMBOLC, BELTANE AND LUGHNASSADH

The fire festivals are classically considered "Celtic" and the most popular surviving lore is rooted in the Irish and Scottish traditions. During the seasons of the fire festivals, we will study:

- The Four Irish Counties and Sacred Landscape
- The Four Elements, Mythic Cities, and Sacred Hallows
- Goddesses of the Irish Landscape
- Irish Myth Cycles
- Irish Gods and Goddesses

SOLAR HOLIDAYS: YULE, OSTARA, LITHA AND MABON

The solar holidays are celebrated all over the world, though much of our Wheel of the Year associations are more rooted in Teutonic myth, particularly the Saxon and Norse, though we've overlaid some Celtic associations. During the seasons of the solar holidays, we will study primarily the Welsh majickal associations, including:

- The Four Branches of *The Mabinogion*
- Welsh Deities
- Totems from the tale of Mabon in *Culhwch and Olwen*

For all eight of the Sabbats, we look to the traditions of England. We focus on the Arthurian-Avalonian myth cycle, for while it has Welsh influence, it spans a greater reach. We divide the different regions of England up into four major sections, and suggest you research the myth, majick, and history of each section. We will look to the nine sisters of Avalon as guides and teachers, as well as other heroes and allies of the Arthurian tradition and majickal totems. We will also emphasize goddesses and gods important in the Cabot Tradition of Witchcraft. We culminate with the "center" of the Wheel, and the creation cycles of the Celts.

The main bodies of primary source lore are from the Welsh, Irish/Scottish, and Arthurian Romance traditions. Here is a list of all the traditional names, in English, of the stories associated with each myth cycle or working. Many texts and translations can be found on *www.sacred-texts.com* and other online sources, as well as in the recommended readings of primary sources listed. Some of the most important are marked by a (*). There are several ways to approach the myths:

- Reading accounts by occultists to understand the esoteric meaning of the texts
- Reading accounts by scholars to understand the historic context and language of the text
- Reading accounts by reconstructionists to understand how to apply the work today
- Reading re-tellings of the myth in clear English
- Reading direct translations of primary source text.

The Mabinogion

The Four Branches of the Mabinogi
Pwyll, Prince of Dyfed*
Branwen, daughter of Llŷr*
Manawydan, son of Llŷr*
Math, son of Mathonwy*

The Native Tales
The Dream of Macsen Wledig
Lludd and Llefelys*
Culhwch and Olwen*
The Dream of Rhonabwy
The Tale of Taliesin*

The Three Romances
Owain, or the Countess of the Fountain
Peredur, son of Efrawg
Geraint and Enid

Four Main Cycles of Irish Myth

Mythological Cycle
The Book of Invasions*
The Book of the Kings*
The Book of Britain*

The Book of Nemed*

The First Battle of Magh Tueredh*

The Second Battle of Magh Turedh*

The Jewels of the Tuahta De Dannan*

The Satire of Caipre Upon Bres

The Fate of the Children of Turenn

The Progress of the Sons of Mil from Spain to Ireland

How the Dagda Got His Magic Staff*

How Oengus Won the Brugh*

The Wooing of Etain*

The Destruction of Da Derga's Hostel

The Dream of Oengus

The House of Oengus mac Og

The Fate of the Children of Lir

The Fosterage of the House of Two Milk-pails

The Tale of Tuan mac Carill

The Settling of the Manor of Tara

The Adventures of Leithin

The Hawk of Achill: selected verses

Who Were the First Doctors in Ireland?

The Fitness of Names

The Founding of Emain Macha*

Bodleian Dinnshenchas (translation)

Edinburgh Dindsenchas

Rennes Dindsenchas I – IV

The Lore of Places (vol. 1–4)

The Lore of Women

The Battle of Partholon's Sons

Ulster Cycle

The Recovery of the Tale of the Cattle Raid of Cooley*

How Oengus Won the Brugh

The Quarrel of the Pigkeepers

The Dream of Oengus*

The Tidings of Conchobar, Son of Ness*

The Birth of Conchobhar*

The Battle of the Assembly of Macha*

Medb's Men, or, the Battle of the Boyne*

Does Greth Eat Curds?

How Amorgen became Athirne's Pupil*

Athirne the Unsociable

Athirne the Stingy

The Wooing of Luaine and the Death of Athirne

The Battle of Cumar

The Birth of Cú Chulainn

The Boyhood Deeds of Cú Chulainn

The Wooing of Emer

The Elopement Of Emer With Tuir Glesta, Son Of The King Of Norway

The Training of Cú Chulainn*

The Words of Scáthach*

Cú Chulainn's Shield*

The Death of Derbforgaill*

The Pursuit of Gruaidh Ghriansholus

The combat of Cuchulaind with Senbecc, grandson of Ebrecc*

The Destruction of Síd Truim*

The Tragic Death of Connla, or, the Death of Aoife's Only Son*

The Wasting Sickness of Cú Chulainn, and the Only Jealousy of Emer*

The Tale of Mac Datho's Pig *

The Siege of Howth*

The Affliction of the Ulstermen*

The Debility of the Ulstermen*

The Cattle-Raid of Fraech*

The Cattle-Raid of Regamon*

The Cattle-Raid of Dartaid*

The Driving of Flidais' Cattle*

The Cattle-Raid of Regamna*

The Intoxication of the Ulstermen*

The Exile of the Sons of Usench*

The Cause of the Exile of Fergus mac Roig

The Wooing of Ferb

The Battle of Ruis na Ríg

The Battle of Findchorad

The Violent Deaths of Goll and Garb

The Adventures of Nera, or, the Cattle-Raid of Angen

Bricriu's Feast George Henderson trans, 1899

The Feast of Bricriu and the Exile of the Sons of Doél Dermait

The Wooing of Treblann

The Cattle-Raid of Cooley*

The Death of Cu Roi mac Dairi *

The Colloquy of the Two Sages*

The Death of Celtchar*

The Death of Loegaire Buadach*

The Death of Cuchulain*

The Great Defeat on the Plain of Muirthemne

The Death of Conchobar

Da Chocha's Hostel

The Battle of Airtech

The Death of Cet mac Magach

The Death of Fergus mac Roich

The Death of Ailill and Connal Cernach*

The Death of Medb*

The Phantom Chariot of Cú Chulainn*

The Genealogy of Cú Chulainn*

Fenian/Ossianic Cycle

The Cause of the Battle of Cnucha*

The Boyhood Deeds of Fionn*

How Find Found Knowledge and the Slaying of Cul Dub*

Finn and the Man in the Tree*

The Enumeration of Finn's People*

The Hostel (or Fight) of the Ford*

The Little Brawl at the Hill of Allen*

Finn and the Phantoms*

The Enchanted Cave of Keshcorran*

Red-haired Eochaid's Enchanted Hall

The Lay of the King of Greece's Son

The Wooing of Ailbe

The Fairy-Palace of the Rowan Trees

The Battle of Ventry

The Adventure of the Churlish Clown in the Grey-Drab Coat

The Battle of Sléphe Cáin

The Pursuit of the Hard Gilly

The Feast at Conan's House*

Finn and Grainne*

The Pursuit of Diarmuid and Grainne

The Hiding of the Hill of Howth

The Battle of Gabhra

The Battle of Ventry and the Death of Finn*

The Chase of Sid na mBan Finn and the Death of Finn*

The Death of Finn*

The Panegyric of Cormac mac Airt and the Death of Finn

The Colloquy of the Old Men

The Poem-book of Fionn*

The Poems of Oisín*

How It Was Learned that Mongan was Fionn reincarnated*

For the fire festivals, focusing on the Irish lore, please take note:

The Two Main Myth Cycles, the Ulter and Finian, will be repeated on two fire festival Lessons. You don't have to read all of the myth cycles in one single sabbat cycle, but you should read the majority of the myths in a cycle by the end of the year. You should also read parts of the Mythological Cycle, dealing with the Invasions and establishment of Ireland. In many ways, the Mythological Cycle is the foundation for the others.

Elemental Associations

The elemental associations in Modern Witchcraft, the Cabot Tradition, the Celtic Four Mythic Cities, and the physical landscapes found in the counties of Ireland, do not all directly correspond. Do not feel you have to make them fit together, but appreciate the diverseness of how the same tradition manifests in different places and with different people.

For example, in most traditions, the direction of the north is associated with the element of Earth and the tool of the Stone. In the counties of Ireland, north is the province of Macha, containing her sacred site of Armagh. While Macha can be seen as an earthly goddess of sovereignty, the county's lore is based in warriors, bloodshed, and conflict, all the way to our current age with the "Troubles" of North Ireland. In the four counties, the realm of Ulster can most easily be associated with the element of fire when we associate each with an element due to this bloodshed, even though their flag of the warrior's shield and a hand can be associated with the pentagram (five fingers) and coin of the element of earth.

Likewise, the west is universally associated with water in Western Majick traditions, including the Cabot Tradition of Witchcraft, but the Western Irish county of Connacht is known as a land of learning, eloquence, and majick, usually associated with the element of air. Likewise, the flag of Connacht is a Griffon, Dagger, and Hand, with two of three of these symbols having an obvious majickal association with air, not water. Even the fabled Salmon of Wisdom, placed in the West, shows connections to intelligence and history in Celtic myth rather than the traditional emotions and dreams of the water element in occultism. It shows that sometimes the Celtic myths diverge from our modern understandings of the elements and occult theory, and we work to reconcile these things in our practice and see the separate systems for what they are.

Use the following correspondences to guide your studies, and the rituals to help inspire your own sabbat rituals. This cycle of eight was mainly crafted by Christopher Penczak as a part of his own Witchcraft III training and represent in-depth community rituals. Often our Cabot rituals involve passion plays, enacting the roles and stories of our gods, and focus on community healing. If you are not in community, you can also craft Sabbat rituals for solitary or small group participation. Use all of this for inspiration, and for another perspective on the Wheel of the Year, please look to my book, *Celebrate the Earth,* for more lore, customs, recipes and rituals.

Samhain

Mythic City: Falias
Wizard: Morfesa
Hallow Tool: Stone of Fal/Stone of Death
"Celtic" Element: Earth
"Celtic" Direction: North
Cabot Element: Earth
Cabot Direction: North

Irish Kingdom: Ulster
"Irish" Direction: North
"Irish" Element: Fire
Flag: Shield and Hand
Qualities: Warrior, Battle
People: Warriors
Irish Goddess: Macha
Sacred Site: Armagh
Irish Myth Cycle: Ulster Cycle

Flag of Ulster

Morgan of Avalon: Mazoe
Arthurian Guide: Merlin
Areas of England: Northwest

Rite of Passage: Funeral
Totems: Crow, Raven
Primary Goddesses: Morrighan, Danu
Primary Gods: Dagda, Cernunnos

Samhain is often equated with Halloween, but Halloween is a Christian holiday. It really has nothing at all to do with Witches and their celebration of life or their majickal path. However, Halloween falls on our own holiday, Samhain, which is a pre-Christian holiday. Today we celebrate it as a three-day celebration, starting with the 30th of October, with the High Holy Day being on the 31st of October and then ending on the 1st of November. Samhain is celebrated as our new year, as it was the start of the Celtic year. The Celtic culture began things as our modern culture ends things. The day began with sunset, not sunrise. So the year began with winter, not spring, and in the earliest forms of the Celtic calendar, the start of winter began on Samhain, as the start of spring began on Beltane.

Because it is our new year, this is why we dress up, to use your majick to become what we want to be for the coming year. We invoke our future by wearing what we want to create for ourselves. We don't dress in horrific costumes or any form of ugliness. We dress in the way we want our community to see us. We are casting a spell about who we are and what we are going to become in the new year. Most witches dress in their finery, wearing their jewelry and best magical clothing. Some people do it in a comical, fun way. They may dress in a suit if they want to have a lot of money and stick money coming out of their pockets. Another may dress in a beautiful butterfly costume to represent transformation into beauty.

Samhain is a grand celebration. This is one of the most important of our eight sabbats. In Salem, Massachusetts, we cast a majick circle and the whole community comes together. We honor those who died for our freedom. We always honor our ancestors because our ancestors are our gods and goddesses. We honor those in our families who have died also, as we are very aware of the passing of our loved ones at this time. At this point in the year the veil between our two worlds, the human and the ancestors, is very thin. The gates are open. You can hear your beloved dead clear at this time. They can talk to us. I think that's how the day got misconstrued by other religions and other people as only the day of the dead.

We view the skull as a good majickal symbol. The skull is a symbol of the housing of the brain and the spirit. It's not a symbol of just death. It is a symbol of the passing of spirit, because we know we are alive in another world once we pass from this one. So a skull might be something used at Samhain. However, when we put on the Witches Ball, as we've done here in Salem with the first Witches Ball in America in 1970, all sorts of costumes came. But when people come with fangs and other horrors, we ask them to remove them. We had a basket little full of them at the door at our first ball. A gentleman came in red long underwear with red horns, a tail and a pitchfork. Had painted his hands and face red. I said, "Give me the tail, give me the pitchfork, and let me have those horns. Go wash your face and hands." And of course then he came to the ball in his underwear. But that was better than the devil image. We don't want to invoke a devil image we don't even believe in on our new year.

Samhain is a delightful celebration. It's so wonderful to look forward to the coming year and casting a spell to have things come to be better in the world, better for ourselves and better for others. Looking in the past is also a good and glorious thing because we see our ancestors and all they've accomplished. Our gods and goddesses are our ancestors and our family. We hope you celebrate your Halloween or your Samhain in a most proper way. Projecting evil and harm is not the thing to do on this holy day. You don't want to live with that energy for the rest of the year. You don't want to create any more horror than there already is in our world. So dress as something powerful and wonderful and create a happy life for yourself for the coming year.

Samhain: Wisdom of the Dark Goddess Ritual

Items Needed:

Traditional Altar

1-3 Oracular Seats

Samhain Incense

Samhain Candle

Protection Potion

People Needed:

High Priest/ess

1-3 Oracular Priestesses

The theme of this ritual is seeking the wisdom of the Goddess. In one Irish legend, the chief of the gods, Dagda, seeks out the wisdom of the war goddess Morrighan. He seeks her advice on the coming battle between his people, the Tuatha De Dannan and their enemies, the Fomorians. On Samhain, he finds her at the river; they mate, and she gives him advice and blessing for success in his battle against the Fomorians. We are seeking her advice and blessing on this Samhain day through the world of oracular priestesses. If the ritual is small, then we call for one priestess. If a larger community, then three priestesses for the triple aspect of the Goddess can be called upon to do oracular trance.

Cleansing and Purification of the Space and People
Smudged with Samhain Incense as they come into the ritual space.

Anointed with Protection Potion.

Place potion and incense back on altar.

Samhain Incense
2 Tablespoons of Myrrh
2 Tablespoons of Patchouli Leaf
1 Tablespoon of Mullien Leaf
1 Teaspoon of Tobacco
1 Pinch of Dragon's Blood
9 Drops of Myrrh Essential Oil
3 Drops of Patchouli Essential Oil

Casting of the Circle Thrice
Cast with a wand or sword starting in the North

First Circle: *I cast this circle to protect us from any and all positive and negative energies that may come to do us harm.*

Second Circle: Silent.

Third Circle: *This circle is cast, So Mote it Be!*

Bow to the North.

Return to the altar and tap the wand three times on the altar.

Calling of the Quarters

Take the peyton in your left hand, face North, and hold up the peyton. Say,

To the powers of the North, we call upon the element of Earth and the Stag. We welcome you to this circle. So Mote it Be!

Face East and hold up the peyton in your left hand. Say,

To the powers of the East, we call upon the element of Fire and the Horse. We welcome you to this circle. So Mote it Be!

Face South and hold up the peyton in your left hand. Say,

To the powers of the South, we call upon the element of Air and the Crow. We welcome you to this circle. So Mote it Be!

Face West and hold up the peyton in your left hand. Say,

To the powers of the West, we call upon the element of Water and the Snake. We welcome you to this circle. So Mote it Be!

Complete the circle, returning to the North. Circle back to the front of the altar; acknowledge Spirit by saying,

And Spirit, always with us, So Mote it Be!

Evocation of the Gods and Spirits

Anoint your Goddess and God candle with protection potion three times, from top to bottom, saying,

I anoint this candle with the energies of the Goddess/God.

Light the candle saying,

I strike this candle with the light of the Goddess/God. So Mote it Be!

I call upon the Great Mother, Danu, Mother of All and Flowing Source of Life.
I call upon the Great Father, Dagda, Master of Seasons and Keeper of Life and Death.
I call upon the Morrighan, Phantom Queen Betwixt the Worlds, Washer at the Forge

I call upon the Triple Morrighan:

I call upon Babd Catha, Boiling, Crow
I call upon Macha of the Red Tresses
And I call upon Nemain, Dark Goddess.
I call upon the Three Who are One, The Morriggu
I call upon the Three Who are Nine, the Sisters of Appleland and Keepers of Wisdom, Avalon.

Anoint and charge the Samhain candle:

We charge this candle for the Dark Mother, Goddess of Earth, Goddess of War, Goddess of the Deepest of Mysteries. We light this candle to attract the Seeking Wisdom of the God, of the Dagda, who desires to know the Mystery of the Goddess and put her wisdom to use in the world of shape and form to turn the Wheel of the Year.

We call upon those who have come before us, ancestors of blood and ancestors of spirit as the veil between the worlds is thin.

Sacrament of Tara and Avalon
Place the peyton in the center of the altar. Place the chalice upon the peyton. While facing North, place your arms out in a receptive position, palms up. Say,

This is Tara (lift left hand), this is Avalon (lift right hand). I am Sovereign in this space. We are Sovereign in this space.

Take your wand or athame, and hold it with a triangular grasp. Raise it up and say,

I draw into this circle and water all of the most correct and harmonious energies of the universe.

Keeping the grasp as it is, stir the water in a clockwise direction three times. Say,

I bless these waters, the waters of life.

Touch thumb to water then to lips three times for the three drops of awen. Raise the cup and say,

By Ancient Memories of the Earth
By the blessings of the Ancestors
We bring the majick of Samhain
By the three rays of inspiration, awen, I bless these waters.
Brewed to Perfection in the Sacred Cauldron, the Sacred Grail
Warmed by the Breaths of Nine Witches
A libation to the Gods and the Ancient Ones. Iska Ba!

Offering to the Ancestors

Community members place offerings, food, wine, candles, and mementos onto a specially prepared ancestor altar.

Invocation of the Goddess into the Priestesses

Take the wand to the Priestesses' brow, down to her left foot, right shoulder, left shoulder, right foot, and back to the brow.

I invoke you by the Endless Knot, Shield of the Morrighan
I ask the Dark Goddess to rise up to this place
I ask the Dark Goddess to rise up to this flesh, this blood, this breath and this bone.
I ask the Dark Goddess to speak through this priestess, bringing your wisdom, your fire and light to our sacred circle. Come across the rivers of blood and forgetfulness. Come to your daughters and sons between.

Veil is placed on her head covering her face. Repeat with each of the priestesses.

Toning

Soft and Simple Tone on a half tone — Oooo (on the note C) — Aaaah (on the note B) — Oooo (on the note C) to help the priestesses' trance.

Guided Meditation for the Priestesses for Oracular Trance

Crystal Countdown

Envision the mists growing up all around you, connecting you to all worlds, all places. You are within Tara. You are within Avalon. You are between the worlds. Soon a dark figure approaches you in the mist, one of the three aspects of the Morrighan. Speak with the Goddess. Ask for her help. Ask her to speak through you to the community. Feel her merge with you. Feel her spirit enter your brow and down into your left foot, up to your right shoulder, your left shoulder and right foot, completing the pentagram to the brow. You are an embodiment of the Goddess. Be between the worlds, like She who straddles the river, part in the spirit world, and part in the physical. You can hear me speak. You can speak. You can move your body, yet you do not lose your link to Her. You are Her and She is you. Your people, like the Dagda, come to you with questions. They seek your advice, your blessing.

Questions from the Community
Individually or as a Group

Release of the Priestesses from Invocation
Thank the Goddess of the River, of the Dark Underworld, and feel her presence leave you. From the brow to the right foot, to the left shoulder to the right shoulder, to the left foot and back out the brow, by the endless knot, she leaves you, moving to the depths of the mist. You feel yourself once more. The mist begins to part and fade and you feel yourself returning to this body, place and time. Come back to this world. Come back to the circle.

Count up. Give yourself clearance and balance.

Any majick for the community or individuals.

Cone of Power
Priest/ess brings the group to attention and together we raise the cone of power. With that, all raise their hands upward to the sky, release the energy, and kneel to the ground to touch the sacred Earth, grounding and blessing the land.

Circle of Healing Light
Name the people you wish to send healing light to in the community, and as a group, do so together.

Release the Gods and Spirits
Devocation of Gods and Spirits from the Circle and the Priestesses

Thanks to the Ancestors

Thank and release the Goddess and God as Morrighan and Dagda

Release the Quarters
Take the peyton in your left hand, face North, and hold up the peyton. Say,

To the powers of the North, we thank and release the element of Earth and the Stag. So Mote it Be!

Face West and hold up the peyton in your left hand. Say,

To the powers of the West, we thank and release the element of Water and the Snake. So Mote it Be!

Face South and hold up the peyton in your left hand. Say,

To the powers of the South, we thank and release the element of Air and the Crow. So Mote it Be!

Face East and hold up the peyton in your left hand. Say,

To the powers of the East, we thank and release the element of Fire and the Horse. So Mote it Be!

Complete the circle, returning to the North. Circle back to the front of the altar widdershins, and acknowledge Spirit by saying,

And we thank Spirit, always with us, So Mote it Be!

Release the circle in the traditional way.

Work:
- Write your own Samhain ritual.
- Read from the Ulster Myth Cycle and the Creation Myth Cycle.
- Work more closely with the element of Earth and the Stone. Call upon Morfesa, the Teacher of Falias, to help you gain greater mastery of elemental Earth.

- Learn about and possibly seek out with your meditations and majick the Goddess Macha, and the Morrighan, Danu, Dagda, Cernunnos, Merlin, and the Avalonian Sister Mazoe.
- Work with the animal spirits of Raven and Crow in majick and meditation.

YULE

Mabinogion Branch: Pywll, Prince of Dyfed
Welsh Gods and Goddesses: Pywll, Arawn, Hafgan, Rhiannon, Pryderi
Mystery of the Branch: Forgiveness of Wrongs

Culhwch and Olwen Totem: Stag
Morgans of Avalon: Tyronoe
Arthurian Guides: Arthur
Areas of England: Northeast

Rite of Passage: Birth
Totem: Horse
Primary Goddess: Rhiannon
Primary God: Pryderi

The traditions of Yule, of course, are ancient and speak to our primal ancestral past. The ancient ancestors brought greenery into their home because they wanted to bring the light and life of nature back into their houses. The Sun's light is the furthest from the Earth at this time, causing things to be so cold. The greenery still present is symbolic of the promise of renewal, as evergreens retain their color in the winter when other leaves have fallen. Evergreens are brought into the house ritually and often in the form of a tree.

All our current holiday tree traditions come from the Pagans, from those we would see as Witches. We brought the tree into the home and celebrated the light with whatever foods were there that were cherished and wonderful because with the long winter you don't always have a harvest. You have already had your harvest and are prepared, hopefully, for the winter. You need to know how to provide for your family, for your friends and your community. Therefore we use gift giving as a holiday tradition, to treasure what we have and share. At that time of year, the darkest time, you give majickal gifts to sustain your spirit until the springtime. Some of these majickal gifts were food, including breads, sweets, dried fruits, and other homemade goods and crafts. So gift-giving came from our ancestors.

Yule is a wonderful time of year and the meaning, the majick, should be about returning our awareness to the Sun. The Sun is coming back to the Earth, reincarnating into a new cycle. The Sun needs to return to us to bring springtime, growth, and change. This is our observance. We light candles. We have a Yule log, a log which we collected the year before. We keep its majick so that we can put it into the fireplace and burn it and bring the fire and light back through our Yuletide ritual. Then we gather another log and we put it into our majick circle. We charge that one for the coming year and save it.

We dress in the colors that bring back the Sun. Witches dress in the green, in the colors of the flora, the bright red, the gold, and the silver, and we honor the Snow Queen and Father Winter. Father Winter sometimes helps us bring gifts and the Snow Queen as well. She gifts us with beauty; all the snowflakes falling down are the most beautiful things you've ever seen in your entire life. They are new. Every Yule they become new again, different and powerful.

Yule: Birth of the Child of Light, The Transformation of Taliesin

Items Needed:
Altar
Yule Incense
Yule Candle
Awen Brew
Protection Potion

People Needed:
Celebrant
Four Quarters

The theme of this ritual is the initiation of Gwion Bach and his transformation into Taliesin as the Child of Light. Rather than focus on the traditional Holly King and Oak King mythos, though important, we decided to work with a more initiatory theme sacred to the Cabot Tradition. The two kings are still invoked, but a different journey is taken, through the four transformations into the manifestation of the initiate.

Cleansing and Purification of the Space and People

Smudged with Yule Incense as they come in.

Anointed with protection potion.

Place potion and incense back on altar.

Yule Incense

2 Tablespoons of Pine Needles
2 Tablespoons of Frankincense
1 Tablespoon of Myrrh
1 Tablespoon of Oak Bark
1 Teaspoon of Cinnamon
1/2 Teaspoon of Holly Leaves
1 Pinch of Mistletoe
5 Drops of Pine Essential Oil
3 Drops of Frankincense Essential Oil
1 Drop of Myrrh Essential Oil
3 Drops of Wintergreen Essential Oil

Casting of the Circle
Thrice with a wand or sword starting in the North:

First Circle: *I cast this circle to protect us from any and all positive and negative energies that may come to do us harm.*

Second Circle: Silent.

Third Circle: *This circle is cast, So Mote it Be!*

Bow to the North.

Return to the altar and tap the wand three times on the altar.

Calling of the Quarters
Take the peyton in your left hand, face North, and hold up the peyton. Say,

To the powers of the North, we call upon the element of Earth and the Hare and Greyhound. We welcome you to this circle. So Mote it Be!

Face East and hold up the peyton in your left hand. Say,

To the powers of the East, we call upon the element of Fire and the Grain and Black and Red-Crested Hen. We welcome you to this circle. So Mote it Be!

Face South and hold up the peyton in your left hand. Say,

To the powers of the South, we call upon the element of Air and the Wren and Hawk. We welcome you to this circle. So Mote it Be!

Face West and hold up the peyton in your left hand. Say,

To the powers of the West, we call upon the element of Water and the Salmon and Otter. We welcome you to this circle. So Mote it Be!

Complete the circle, returning to the North. Circle back to the front of the altar, and acknowledge Spirit by saying,

And Spirit, with the Black Hen, always with us, So Mote it Be!

Evocation of the Gods and Spirits

Anoint your Goddess and God candle with protection potion three times, from top to bottom, saying,

I anoint this candle with the energies of the Goddess/God.

Light the candle saying,

I strike this candle with the light of the Goddess/God. So Mote it Be!

I call upon the Great Mother Danu, Mother of All and Flowing Source of Life.
I call upon the Great Father, Dagda, Master of Seasons and Keeper of Life and Death.
I call upon the Gods as Oak and Holly, turning the Wheel in their constant Tide of Life.
We call upon the Witch Goddess Cerridwen, Wisest of the Women of the West.
Keeper of the Cauldron of Awen,
the Cauldron of Rebirth,

the Cauldron of Transformation.
We call upon her husband, the giant Tegid Foel, Guardian of the Lake and Cauldron.
We call upon their kith and kin.

Crearwy, the Most Beautiful Girl of the World, Daughter of the Land,
Morvran, The Sea Raven, known as Avagadu, Utter Darkness.
Morda, Blind Servant, keeper of the fire,
And Gwion Bach, servant child reborn in the light as the Shining Brow Taleisin. So Mote it Be!

Anoint and charge your Yule candle:

We charge this candle for the Child of Light, the Child of Hope and Promise to be reborn from the Depths of the Mother and the Cauldron of Mystery. We light this candle by the power of the Goddess. Hers is the power. Hers is the mystery of rebirth through the elements and nature. Like Gwion Bach, she offers to us the year and a day apprenticeship, the drink of transformation, and rebirth through her womb, but all gifts have a price. May we all safely pay that price, pass the tests, and travel through gates of rebirth and light the fire in the head as we turn the Wheel of the Year.

We call upon those who have come before us, ancestors of blood and ancestors of spirit.

Sacrament of Tara and Avalon

Chalice filled with Brew (use previously prepared Brew of Awen as part of your work between the Second and Third Degrees.) The following stanza recites some of the "traditional" ingredients and offerings in making the Brew of Awen:

Traditionally before we make the Brew of Awen,
We make offerings of Frankincense, Myrrh and Aloe.
We make offerings of Silver and of the Red Gem.
Into the Cauldron of Cerridwen we brew
Foam from the Waters of the Ocean
St. John's Wort, light of the Sun
Vervain, five-fold blossom of enchanters
Watercress, Wisdom of the Deep
Juniper Berries, Protection and Blessing

To this brew we add wine, honey, water and malt.
This is the Brew of Awen.

Place the peyton in the center of the altar. Place the chalice upon the peyton. While facing North, place your arms out in a receptive position, palms up. Say,

This is Tara (lift left hand), this is Avalon (lift right hand). I am Sovereign in this space. We are Sovereign in this space.

Take your wand or athame, and hold it with a triangular grasp. Raise it up and say,

I draw into this circle and water all of the most correct and harmonious energies of the universe.

Keeping the grasp as it is, stir the water in a clockwise direction three times. Say,

I bless these waters, the waters of life.

Touch thumb to water then to lips three times for the three drops of awen. Raise the cup and say,

By the Light of Wisdom and Peace
We bring the blessings of Yule
Brewed to Perfection in the Sacred Cauldron, the Sacred Grail
Warmed by the Breaths of Nine Witches
A libation to the Gods and the Ancient Ones. Iska Ba!

Journey to Cerridwen with Slow and Steady Drum Beat

Journey to the land of the silver waters. Journey to the Lake of Wisdom and Cunning. Enter the mists. Pierce the veil to the Sunless lands within. And within that lake, through the mists, you shall find the island. Here, today, it is the Island of Cerridwen and Tegid Foel, Witch Goddess and Giant Protector. Here on this island they guard the Cauldron of Awen, of Inspiration and Immortality.

Here is the Holy Family of Witchcraft, and they rule over parts of your own soul. Here is the Holy Family of Wisdom, and they guide you in the work of the initiate. Cerridwen, Master, Teacher, Keeper of Lore, bids you to enter her hut for a year and a day, like the boy Gwion Bach, to learn her Craft of Plant Lore, of Majick of the Cauldron. She is your teacher and initiator, and her husband Tegid is the guardian of the Mysteries.

You see with her the Holy Family that also rules your soul. Her daughter Crearwy is the most beautiful one in the world. She is like an angel, and you aspire to be as beautiful as she, but you feel distant from her beauty.

Morvran is black like the raven, hungry like the sea. He is loved but feels unloved, ugly and dark, frightened and frightening. He is the Avagadu, Utter Darkness.

With them is Morda, blind yet working onward toward the goal, keeper of the flame. May our inner flame of work and discipline never go out.

Cerridwen gives you special instruction, showing you many things within the reflection of the cauldron. Gaze deeply into the cauldron. Ask your questions.

She instructs you in the proper way of stirring the Brew of Awen. She explains the cauldron and the fire to you. The two ends of the handles represent the two horns of the God, the two sides of the God. The three legs represent the Triple Goddess of the Heavens, Earth and Underworld. The fire is the inner fire of creation. The metal is forged from the blood and bones of the earth, metals of copper, tin, and iron. The rim is outlined in pearls, the drops of wisdom. The waters are the waters of life. They are cooled by the breath of the nine maidens, the nine witches, the sisters of Avalon.

Cerridwen, Tegid, and their children leave you in the hut upon the island, in the lake, with the old man Morda. There you are to stir the cauldron. Stir the cauldron as the fire of Morda burns and brews. Gaze into the spinning waters.

Three drops rush out to you burning your thumb. You instinctively bring your thumb to your mouth, drinking the drops of wisdom and the rest of the brew turns to deadliest poison, cracks the cauldron, and poisons the land. Instantly you know that Cerridwen will know, return, and wear your guts as her garters. You leave Morda and flee the wrath of Cerridwen.

You move widdershins across the sacred circle, undoing yourself. To the North you go and move swiftly across the land as the hare, but she follows you as the Greyhound.

You move to the West and jump into the waters, becoming a salmon. She follows you as the Otter.

You move to the South to the open sky and become a Wren. She becomes a Hawk and follows you.

Clever with the new wisdom you have, and the new power, you see the threshing floor of a grainery in the East and dive down to it, becoming a single grain among thousands, safely hiding.

But Cerridwen becomes the Black Hen, and devours up the grain, including you.

Floating in the womb of Cerridwen, in the oven of the grain, you lay. In nine months time, you are reborn as the Child of Light, as the Taleisin, the Bright and Shining Brow, open and seeing the world through new eyes. Come into the world now with new light, with new life, and look through these new eyes.

Cone of Power

Any majick for the community or individuals.

Priest/ess brings the group to attention, and together we raise the cone of power. With that, all raise their hands upward to the sky, release the energy, and kneel to the ground to touch the sacred Earth, grounding and blessing the land.

Circle of Healing

Name the people you wish to send healing light to in the community, and as a group, do so together.

Release the Gods and Spirits

Thank and release the Goddess and God.

Devocation of the Gods Danu, Dagda, Cerridwen, Crearwy, Morvran, Morda, and Taliesin

Release the Quarters

Take the peyton in your left hand, face North, and hold up the peyton. Say,

To the powers of the North, we thank and release the element of Earth and the Hare and Greyhound. So Mote it Be!

Face West and hold up the peyton in your left hand. Say,

To the powers of the West, we thank and release the element of Water and the Salmon and Otter. So Mote it Be!

Face South and hold up the peyton in your left hand. Say,

To the powers of the South, we thank and release the element of Air and the Wren and Hawk. So Mote it Be!

Face East and hold up the peyton in your left hand. Say,

To the powers of the East, we thank and release the element of Fire and the Grain and Black Red-Crested Hen. So Mote it Be!

Complete the circle, returning to the North. Circle back to the front of the altar widdershins, acknowledge Spirit by saying,

And we thank Spirit, always with us, So Mote it Be!

Release the Circle in the traditional way.

Work:
- Write your own Yule Ritual.
- Read *Pywll, Prince of Dyfed,* from *The Mabinogion.*
- Learn about and possibly seek out with your meditations and majick the deities Rhiannon, Pryderi, Pywll, King Arthur, and the Avalonian Sister Tyronoe.
- Work with the animal spirits of Stag and Horse in majick and meditation.

Imbolc

Mythic City: Gorias
Wizard: Esras
Hallow Tool: Spear of Lugh/Dividing Sword
"Celtic" Element: Wind
"Celtic" Direction: East
Cabot Element: Fire
Cabot Direction: East

Irish Kingdom: Leinster
"Irish" Direction: East
"Irish" Element: Earth
Flag: Harp
Qualities: Abundance, Prosperity, Beauty
People: Land Owners and Farmers
Irish Goddess: Brigit
Sacred Site: Kildare
Irish Myth Cycle: Fenian Cycle

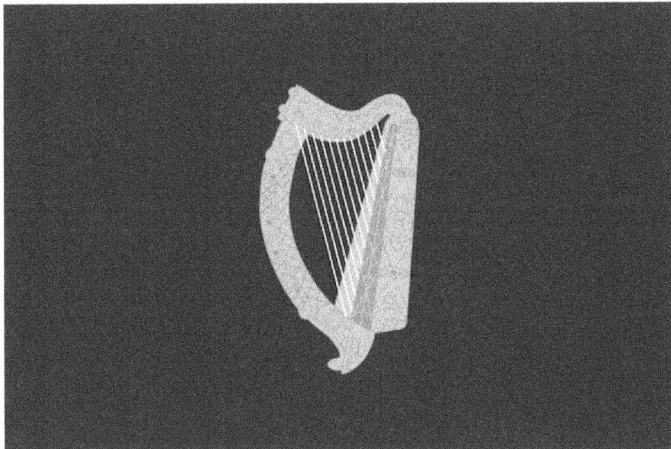

Flag of Leinster

Morgans of Avalon: Thitis
Arthurian Guides: Perceval, Galahad, and Bors
Areas of England: Yorkshire and the Humbler

Rites of Passage: Child Blessing
Totems: Greyhound
Primary Goddesses: Brigit
Primary Gods: Angus

Imbolc is the celebration of Bridget, later St. Bridget in the Irish Catholic traditions. We know her to be the goddess of poetry, healing and smithcraft, said to be the daughter of the great god, the Dagda. She was so beloved by the Irish people they couldn't give her up, so the church somehow managed to incorporate her into their own pantheon of saints rather than demonize her. There are many churches still dedicated to her, and her healing wells and sacred places have been adopted by the Christians. Still, we know her in her oldest forms.

Her sabbat, Imbolc, is the celebration of the spring. It doesn't feel like spring here in Massachusetts, yet in the traditional British calendar, Imbolc meant the spring was coming. We would light candles as an act of majick to embrace the growing light and help it grow. Our candlelight would also help warm and awaken the Earth Mother.

Imbolc: Festival of Awakening

Items Needed:
Imbolc Incense
Protection Potion
Altar
3 Imbolc Candles
3 Chalices
Milk
Wine/Juice
Blackberry Leaf Tea
Cauldron

People Needed:
Celebrant
White Priestess
Red Priestess
Black Priestess
Four Quarter Callers

The theme of this ritual is the triple power of the Goddess as manifest through the goddess Bridget. Looking at her three aspects as healer, poet, and smith, we will do community drinking and healing, using milk, wine (or juice), and herbal tea. Those who take the milk do so for healing. Those who take the wine (or juice) are seeking inspiration. Those who take the tea, related to the majick and craft of the blacksmith, are receiving energy to get something done.

Cleansing and Purification of the Space and People

Smudged with Imbolc Incense as they come in.

Anointed with protection potion.

Place potion and incense back on altar.

Imbolc Incense

2 Tablespoons of Benzoin
1 Tablespoon of Frankincense
1 Tablespoon of Blackberry Leaves
1 Teaspoon of All Heal
Pinch of Wheat
3 Drops of Camphor Oil

Casting of the Circle

Thrice with a wand or sword starting in the North

First Circle: *I cast this circle to protect us from any and all positive and negative energies that may come to do us harm.*

Second Circle: Silent.

Third Circle: *This circle is cast, So Mote it Be!*

Bow to the North.

Return to the altar and tap the wand three times on the altar.

Calling the Quarters

Take the peyton in your left hand, face North, and hold up the peyton. Say,

To the powers of the North, we call upon the element of Earth and the Bear. We welcome you to this circle. So Mote it Be!

Face East and hold up the peyton in your left hand. Say,

To the powers of the East, we call upon the element of Fire and the Fox. We welcome you to this circle. So Mote it Be!

Face South and hold up the peyton in your left hand. Say,

To the powers of the South, we call upon the element of Air and the Starling. We welcome you to this circle. So Mote it Be!

Face West and hold up the peyton in your left hand. Say,

To the powers of the West, we call upon the element of Water and the Salmon. We welcome you to this circle. So Mote it Be!

Complete the circle, returning to the North. Circle back to the front of the altar, and acknowledge Spirit by saying,

And Spirit, always with us, So Mote it Be!

Evocation of the Gods and Spirits

Anoint your Goddess and God candle with protection potion three times, from top to bottom, saying,

I anoint this candle with the energies of the Goddess/God.

Light the candle saying,

I strike this candle with the light of the Goddess/God. So Mote it Be!

I call upon the Great Mother Danu, Mother of All and Flowing Source of Life.
I call upon the Great Father, Dagda, Master of Seasons and Keeper of Life and Death.
The Dagda, Father of the Triple Bridget, Known as Brid in Days of Old
I call upon Bridget, Goddess of Healing.
I call upon Bridget, Goddess of Poetry and Inspiration.
I call upon Bridget, Goddess of Smithcraft and Majick
I call upon the Light and Fire of the God, burning bright and waxing as the year grows.
So Mote it Be!

Anoint and charge your Imbolc candles — Three Candles:

We charge these candles for the Triple Bridget, the Goddess of Three Lights, three ways. We light these candles by her power, and for the light of the Waxing God who shines and guides us in all things. May we receive the triple blessings as we turn the Wheel of the Year.

We call upon those who have come before us, ancestors of blood and ancestors of spirit.

Sacrament of Tara and Avalon
Chalice filled with milk. Two other chalices are present, one of red wine (or fruit juice) and one of a general herbal healing elixir, such as blackberry tea.

Place the peyton in the center of the altar. Place the chalice upon the peyton. While facing North, place your arms out in a receptive position, palms up. Say,

This is Tara (lift left hand), this is Avalon (lift right hand). I am Sovereign in this space. We are Sovereign in this space.

Take your wand or athame, and hold it with a triangular grasp. Raise it up and say,

I draw into this circle and water all of the most correct and harmonious energies of the universe.

Keeping the grasp as it is, stir the water in a clockwise direction three times. Say,

I bless these waters, the waters of life.

Touch thumb to water then to lips three times for the three drops of awen. Raise the cup and say,

By the Triple Blessings of Awen, the Three Rays of Inspiration
By the powers of Healing, Poetry, and Transformation
Brewed to Perfection in the Sacred Cauldron, the Sacred Grail
Warmed by the Breaths of Nine Witches
A libation to the Gods and the Ancient Ones. Iska Ba!

Invocation of the Bridget into the three Priestesses
Community chants the invocation:

Triple Goddess, Maiden, Mother, Crone
Bless Us Please, in our Hearth and Home.
Goddess Fire, Healer, Poet, Smith
Bless Us Please, with all your gifts.

Priest: Touch each priestess from the brow, heart and belly.

To the White Priestess. Priest: *To you I invoke Bridget as the Healer, Nourisher, and Counselor. May those who are touched by you find comfort and health. So Mote it Be!*

To the Red Priestess. Priest: *To you I invoke Bridget as the Poet, Sweet Inspiration of Awen. May those who are touched by you find words, music, and art within them, and share their inspiration with the world. So Mote it Be!*

To the Black Priestess. Priest: *To you I invoke Bridget as the Blacksmith, Mistress of Cunning Craft and Power. May those who are touched by you find the power to change the world, and change the world wisely. So Mote it Be!*

Community members choose one priestess to work with, choosing one aspect of Bridget. They approach the goddess, speak their intention, and drink from the cup. The priestess may offer oracular words of inspiration or remain silent, depending on the situation. The priestess may also lay hands upon the community member, offering a blessing or healing.

When done, the priestesses combine the remaining liquids of their chalices into the cauldron and pour it out to the Earth if outside.

Cone of Power

Any majick for the community or individuals.

Priest/ess brings the group to attention, and together we raise the cone of power. With that, all raise their hands upward to the sky, release the energy, and kneel to the ground to touch the sacred Earth, grounding and blessing the land.

Circle of Healing Light

Name the people you wish to send healing light to in the community, and as a group, do so together.

Devocation of Gods and Spirits

Thank and release the Ancestors and Spirits.

Thank and release the Goddess and God as Danu, Dagda, Bridget and the Young God of Light.

Release the Quarters

Take the peyton in your left hand, face North, and hold up the peyton. Say,

To the powers of the North, we thank and release the element of Earth and the Bear. So Mote it Be!

Face West and hold up the peyton in your left hand. Say,

To the powers of the West, we thank and release the element of Water and the Salmon. So Mote it Be!

Face South and hold up the peyton in your left hand. Say,

To the powers of the South, we thank and release the element of Air and the Starling. So Mote it Be!

Face East and hold up the peyton in your left hand. Say,

To the powers of the East, we thank and release the element of Fire and the Fox. So Mote it Be!

Complete the circle, returning to the North. Circle back to the front of the altar widdershins, and acknowledge Spirit by saying,

And we thank Spirit, always with us, So Mote it Be!

Release the circle.

Work:
- Write your own Imbolc Ritual.
- Read from the Fenian Myth Cycle and the Creation Myth Cycle.
- Work more closely with the element of Fire and the Spear/Wand. Call upon Esras the Teacher of Gorias to help you in gaining greater mastery of elemental Fire.
- Learn about and possibly seek out with your meditations and majick the Goddess Bridget, and the God Angus, as well as the Arthurian Grail knights Perceval, Galahad and Bors, and the Avalonian Sister Thitis.
- Work with the animal spirit of the Greyhound in majick and meditation.

OSTARA

Mabinogion Branch: Branwen, daughter of Llŷr
Welsh Gods and Goddesses: Bran, Branwen
Mystery of the Branch: Resurrection — Life from Death

Culhwch and Olwen Totem: Eagle
Morgans of Avalon: Cliton
Arthurian Guides: Guinevere
Areas of England: East Midlands

Rites of Passage: Coming of Age
Totems: Red Fox
Primary Goddess: Branwen
Primary God: Bran

Ostara is a borrowed name for this holiday, becoming popular in modern Witchcraft. The word Ostara comes from the Teutonic goddess Eostre, to celebrate the coming of the spring. Today we associate Ostara with the rising of the flowers from the underworld, a source of color, light, and life from what once appeared so barren in the winter.

Astrologically, the Sun has moved into the sign of Aries, which is the first sign of the zodiac. While our Witch's new year is on Samhain, we can think of this as an astrological new year, or the start of a new astrological cycle. Aries is the sign that starts things, initiating change and movement. So when the Sun enters Aries, spring is truly initiated.

Ostara: Resurrection of the Land

Items Needed:
Traditional Altar
Ostara Incense
Protection Potion
Ostara Candle
Flowers or Floral Water for the Altar
Water or Apple Juice

People Needed:

Celebrant

Four Quarter Callers

Spirit Caller

The theme of this ritual is a Celtic version of the tale of Persephone. Instead of the goddess Persephone, the harbinger of spring is the eternal boy-god Mabon, the Son, returning to the land with Modron, the Mother. They return through the seven caers and bring the light and life force from the dark into the light.

Cleansing and Purification of the Space and People

Smudged with Ostara Incense as they come in.

Anointed with protection potion or floral waters such as rose or lavender.

Place potion and incense back on altar.

Ostara Incense

2 Tablespoons of Dragon's Blood

1 Tablespoon of Amber Resin

1 Tablespoon of Orange Peel

1 Tablespoon of Lavender Flowers

1 Teaspoon of Jasmine Flowers

1 Teaspoon of Pink Rose Flowers

5 Drops of Orange Essential Oil

2 Drops of Jasmine Essential Oil

Casting of the Circle

Thrice with a wand or sword starting in the North:

First Circle: *I cast this circle to protect us from any and all positive and negative energies that may come to do us harm.*

Second Circle: Silent.

Third Circle: *This circle is cast, So Mote it Be!*

Bow to the North.

Return to the altar and tap the wand three times on the altar.

Calling of the Quarters

Take the peyton in your left hand, face North, and hold up the peyton. Say,

To the powers of the North, we call upon the element of Earth and the Stag. We welcome you to this circle. So Mote it Be!

Face East and hold up the peyton in your left hand. Say,

To the powers of the East, we call upon the element of Fire and the Owl. We welcome you to this circle. So Mote it Be!

Face South and hold up the peyton in your left hand. Say,

To the powers of the South, we call upon the element of Air and the Eagle. We welcome you to this circle. So Mote it Be!

Face West and hold up the peyton in your left hand. Say,

To the powers of the West, we call upon the element of Water and the Salmon. We welcome you to this circle. So Mote it Be!

Complete the circle, returning to the North. Circle back to the front of the altar, and acknowledge Spirit by saying,

And Spirit, with the Blackbird, always with us, So Mote it Be!

Evocation of the Gods and Spirits

Anoint your Goddess and God candle with protection potion three times, from top to bottom, saying,

I anoint this candle with the energies of the Goddess/God.

Light the candle saying,

I strike this candle with the light of the Goddess/God. So Mote it Be!

I call upon the Great Mother Danu, Mother of All and Flowing Source of Life.
I call upon the Great Father, Dagda, Master of Seasons and Keeper of Life and Death.
I call upon the Great Mother as Modron and her Son, Mabon, Child of Promise.
I call upon the Gods of the Witches, Cerridwen, Mistress of the Cauldron of Regeneration and Gwydion, Master of Light and Majick. We call upon Arianrhod of the Silver Wheel and Starry Castle, Heart of the Otherworld. So Mote it Be!

Anoint and charge your Ostara candle:

We charge this candle for the Child of Light, the Child of Hope and Promise who is reborn from the Depths of the Mother. We light this candle by the power of the Goddess, withdrawing her life from the world around us to dwell in the depths of the world below and bring new life. May we all safely travel through the seven castles, to be reborn as the God is reborn, renewing the land of Abred as we turn the Wheel of the Year.

We call upon those who have come before us, ancestors of blood and ancestors of spirit.

Sacrament of Tara and Avalon
Chalice Filled with Water or Apple Juice.

Place the peyton in the center of the altar. Place the chalice upon the peyton. While facing North, place your arms out in a receptive position, palms up. Say,

This is Tara (lift left hand), this is Avalon (lift right hand). I am Sovereign in this space. We are Sovereign in this space.

Take your wand or athame, and hold it with a triangular grasp. Raise it up and say,

I draw into this circle and water all of the most correct and harmonious energies of the universe.

Keeping the grasp as it is, stir the water in a clockwise direction three times. Say,

I bless these waters, the waters of life.

Touch thumb to water then to lips three times for the three drops of awen. Raise the cup and say,

By the growing green of the Earth
We call forth the blessings of Ostara
Brewed to Perfection in the Sacred Cauldron, the Sacred Grail
Warmed by the Breaths of Nine Witches
A libation to the Gods and the Ancient Ones. Iska Ba!

Returning the Child of Light to the Land: Guided Journey to the Otherworld

The Lord of Light has been reborn at Yule. He has nursed at Imbolc. Now we prepare his return as Mabon, Son of the Mother. We are all Children of the Mother, waiting to be reborn, to return to the land, to return to flesh, blood, breath and bone. We have guided him downward like the psychopomp, and now we guide him back to the world of Abred. We bring with him the blessings of the Oldest of Creatures.

We guide the Son of the Mother, within and without.
We bring the Light from the Heart of Darkness.
We lead the Child of Light stolen from his Mother, returned now.
We lead all Children of Light, Mabon Ap Modron, Pryderi, and Lleu.
We bring with him the Blessings of the Oldest of Creatures and the Ancient Ones.

We start in the Center and invite Blackbird, Creature of the Fifth Age, to come with us. Blackbird, guide us on the path to bring Mabon back.

We move to the North and invite Stag, Creature of the Fourth Age, to come with us. Stag, guide us on the path to bring Mabon back.

We move to the East and invite Owl, Creature of the Third Age, to come with us. Owl, guide us on the path to bring Mabon back.

We move to the South and invite Eagle, Creature of the Second Age, to come with us. Eagle, guide us on the path to bring Mabon back.

We move to the West and invite Salmon, Creature of the First Age, to come with us. Salmon, guide us on the path to bring Mabon back.

Together, with the Creatures of the Great Ages, we descend to Find Mabon. Come through the seven gates you know well, you have passed through them before. We have all passed through them.

We descend together, spiraling downward, spiraling downward, spiraling downward.

We enter a dark descending tunnel, with only the light of our spirits to guide us.

By our sides are the blackbird, the stag, the owl, the eagle, and the salmon, guiding us through the gates of the Underworld, of Annwn.

*We approach the gate of the first castle, Caer Orchen,
the Castle of Dread, the Castle of Shelving Tide, Castle of the Sloping Sides.
This Castle is our Root to all things Material, Sensual, and Physical.
The Guardian gives you safe passage.*

*We approach the gate of the second castle, Caer Fandy-Manddwy,
The Castle on High, the Sea Castle, the Castle of Starry Prisons.
This Castle of the Sea is where we pass through the astral oceans.
This Castle is our Intimacy where we make connections to all life.
The Guardian gives you safe passage.*

*We approach the gate of the third castle, Caer Goludd,
The Castle of Gloom, the Castle of Trials, the Castle of Death.
This Castle of Trials is where we learn the axis of Power and Fear.
The Guardian gives you safe passage.*

*We approach the gate of the fourth castle, Caer Rigor,
The Castle of the Royal Horn, the Royal Castle.
This Castle of Royals is where we learn to love perfectly.
This Castle is where we find the Royal Heart loving all.
The Guardian gives you safe passage.*

*We approach the gate of the fifth castle, Caer Fredwyd,
Castle of the Perfected Ones, Castle of Carousal, Castle of Revelry.
This Castle of Carousal is where we celebrate with the Mighty Dead who have gone before.*

This Castle is where we open to the Voice of Wisdom from within and from the past.
The Guardian gives you safe passage.

We approach the gate of the sixth castle, Caer Pedryfan,
The Revolving Castle, Four-Cornered and Revolving Sky Castle,
The Four-Squared Burial Castle.
This Castle of Revolving is where we see with True Sight.
The Guardian gives you safe passage.

We approach the gate of the seventh castle, Caer Sidi,
Castle of the Sidhe, Castle of the Zodiacal Wheel, Castle of the Inner Stars.
This Castle of Stars is where we began and where we shall end.
This Castle is where the Queen of the Starry Heavens resides.
This Castle is the Starry Kingdom in the Heart of the Underworld,
Where the Divine Fire resides.
The Guardian gives you safe passage.

Come in to the Starry Castle.
You are greeted by She who is of the Silver Wheel.
She who Shapes Form from the Mist.
She who is Arianrhod, Starry Weaver.
Take this time to commune with the Silver Goddess

She reveals to you Mabon, Son of Modron, both within the Caer and within yourself.
See Mabon within and without.
Feel Mabon within and without.
Know Mabon within and without.
Commune with the Child of Light, Hope, and Promise.
Take the child by the hand and guide him up with you. Come up and out of the seven gates, the
seven castles.

Pass freely through the gate of seventh castle, Caer Sidi,
This Castle of Stars.

Pass freely through the gate of sixth castle, Caer Pedryfan,
This Revolving Castle of True Sight.

Pass freely through the gate of the fifth castle, Caer Fredwyd,
This Castle of Carousal with the Wise and Mighty Dead.

Pass freely through the gate of the fourth castle, Caer Rigor,
This Castle of the Royal Heart.

Pass freely through the gate of the third castle, Caer Goludd,
This Gloomy Castle of Power and Fear.

Pass freely through the gate of the second castle, Caer Fandy-Manddwy,
This Sea Castle of Intimacy.

Pass freely through the gate of the first castle, Caer Orchen,
This Dread Castle of all things Material.

Only Seven Returned from Caer Sidi.
No more. No less.
Only Seven Returned from Caer Sidi.
Seven within. Seven without.
Seven holy powers challenged and blessed, suffered and kissed.
Only Seven Returned from Caer Sidi.

With Mabon and the Salmon of the West, of the First Age, we bring True Wisdom,
The Wisdom of the Hazel,
The Wisdom of True Knowing.

With Mabon and the Eagle of the South, of the Second Age, we bring True Sight,
The Sight of the Heavens,
The Sight of the Swift and Keen Eye.

With Mabon and the Owl of the East, of the Third Age, we bring the Inner Light,
The Light of Fire,
The Light of the Secret Flame.

With Mabon and the Stag of the North, of the Fourth Age, we bring Inner Strength,
The Strength of the Body,
The Strength of the Soul.

With Mabon and the Blackbird of the Center, of the Fifth Age, we bring Spirit,
Spirit of the Mother,
Spirit of the Son.

Return and open your eyes.

Cone of Power
Any majick for the community or individuals.

Priest/ess brings the group to attention and together we raise the cone of power. With that, all raise their hands upward to the sky, release the energy, and kneel to the ground to touch the sacred Earth, grounding and blessing the land.

Circle of Healing Light
Name the people you wish to send healing light to in the community and as a group, do so together.

Devocation of Gods and Spirits
Thank and release the Ancestors and Spirits

Thank and release the Goddess and God as Modron and Mabon

Devocation of the Gods Danu, Dagda, Cerridwen, Gwydion and Arianrhod

Release the Quarters
Take the peyton in your left hand, face North, and hold up the peyton. Say,

To the powers of the North, we thank and release the element of Earth and the Stag. So Mote it Be!

Face West and hold up the peyton in your left hand. Say,

To the powers of the West, we thank and release the element of Water and the Salmon. So Mote it Be!

Face South and hold up the peyton in your left hand. Say,

To the powers of the South, we thank and release the element of Air and the Eagle. So Mote it Be!

Face East and hold up the peyton in your left hand. Say,

To the powers of the East, we thank and release the element of Fire and the Owl. So Mote it Be!

Complete the circle, returning to the North. Circle back to the front of the altar widdershins, and acknowledge Spirit by saying,

And we thank Spirit, always with us, and the Blackbird, So Mote it Be!

Release the Circle.

Work:
- Write your own Ostara Ritual.
- Read *Branwen, daughter of Llŷr* from *The Mabinogion*.
- Learn about and possibly seek out with your meditations and majick the goddess Branwen and the god Bran, along with Guinevere and the Avalonian Sister Cliton.
- Work with the animal spirits of the Red Fox and Eagle in majick and meditation.

BELTANE

Mythic City: Finias
Wizard: Uiscias
Hallow Tool: Sword of Nuada/Spear
"Celtic" Element: Fire
"Celtic" Direction: South
Cabot Element: Air
Cabot Direction: South

Irish Kingdom: Munster
"Irish" Direction: South
"Irish" Element: Water
Flag: Three Crowns
Qualities: Creativity, Music, Art, Horsemanship
People: Artisans, Craftspeople and Laborers
Irish Goddess: Cailleach
Sacred Site: Cliffs of Moher
Irish Myth Cycle: Fenian Cycle

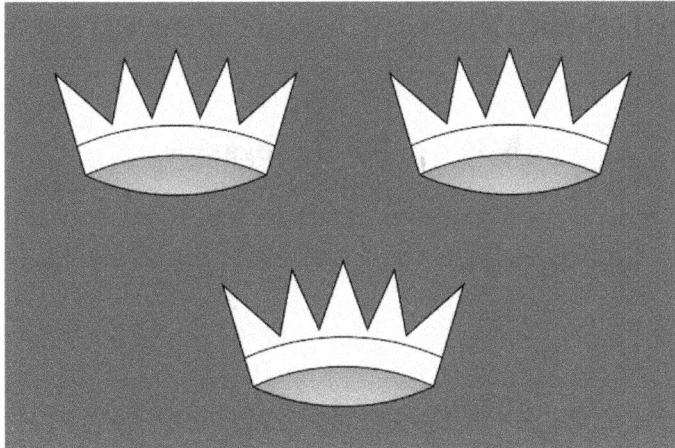

Flag of Munster

Morgans of Avalon: Thetis
Arthurian Guides: Lancelot
Areas of England: East of England

Rites of Passage: Hand Fasting
Totems: Hawk
Primary Goddesses: Cailleach
Primary Gods: Belenos

Beltane is one of our most beloved holidays, along with Samhain. As Samhain marked the start of the New Year and the beginning of winter for the Celts, Beltane is the halfway point in the year, but marks the true start to the warm growing season, the summer, in the simple winter/summer worldview of the early Celts. It survived into our May Day celebrations, and today we still use things like the May Pole dance to celebrate Beltane. Beltane is a time of joy and celebration, to come together with community. Our ancestors used to pass themselves and all their animals upon the farm between two sacred fires, purifying them from any lingering effects of winter illness. So some Witches do a lot of purification work at Beltane, with incense and fire. Others feast, dance, party, and come together with loved ones. The deeper teachings tell us this is the sacred union of the Goddess and God, what the ancients sometimes called the hierogamos, to renew the land and kingdom. While hierogamos is not a word from the Celts, you find the same mysteries in the Arthurian lore of our ancestors, between the sacred Priest-King and Priestess-Queen.

Beltane: The Hierogamos

Items Needed:
Standard Altar
Beltane Incense
Protection Potion
Beltane Candle
2 Sets of Cakes, for men and women, with a lot baked into one in each batch.
Milk, honey, oil, wine and yeast
Sod/Turf from the Land

People Needed:
Celebrant
Four Quarter Callers
May King
May Queen
Dancers

The theme of this ritual is the hierogamos, the sacred union of the Goddess and God, performed by the community through the Maypole Dance.

Cleansing and Purification of the Space and People

Smudged with Beltaine Incense as they come in.

Anointed with protection potion.

Place potion and incense back on altar.

Beltane Incense

2 Tablespoons of Amber Resin
2 Tablespoons of Red Sandalwood
1 Tablespoon of Orris Root
1 Tablespoon of Yarrow Flowers
1 Tablespoon of Rose Petals
5 Drops of Amber Oil
3 Drops of Rose Essential Oil

Casting of the Circle

Thrice with a wand or sword starting in the North

First Circle: *I cast this circle to protect us from any and all positive and negative energies that may come to do us harm.*

Second Circle: Silent.

Third Circle: *This circle is cast, So Mote it Be!*

Bow to the North.

Return to the altar and tap the wand three times on the altar.

Calling of the Quarters

Take the peyton in your left hand, face North, and hold up the peyton. Say,

To the powers of the North, we call upon the element of Earth and the Stag. We welcome you to this circle. So Mote it Be!

Face East and hold up the peyton in your left hand. Say,

To the powers of the East, we call upon the element of Fire and the Fox. We welcome you to this circle. So Mote it Be!

Face South and hold up the peyton in your left hand. Say,

To the powers of the South, we call upon the element of Air and the Crow. We welcome you to this circle. So Mote it Be!

Face West and hold up the peyton in your left hand. Say,

To the powers of the West, we call upon the element of Water and the Snake. We welcome you to this circle. So Mote it Be!

Complete the circle, returning to the North. Circle back to the front of the altar, and acknowledge Spirit by saying,

And Spirit, always with us, So Mote it Be!

Evocation of the Gods and Spirits

Anoint your Goddess and God candle with protection potion three times, from top to bottom, saying,

I anoint this candle with the energies of the Goddess/God.

Light the candle saying,

I strike this candle with the light of the Goddess/God. So Mote it Be!

I call upon the Great Mother Danu, Mother of All and Flowing Source of Life.
I call upon the Great Father, Dagda, Master of Seasons and Keeper of Life and Death.
I call upon the Goddess as the May Queen, the Maiden of the White and Green.
I call upon the God as the May King, the Man of Oak Leaves, Crowned in Light.
So Mote it Be!

Anoint and charge your Beltane candle:

We charge this candle for the Union of the Young Lovers, the Union of God and Goddess, May King and May Queen, Life and Light in the land of Abred. May we too find union with light and life in the realm of Mother Earth, as we turn the Wheel of the Year.

We call upon those who have come before us, ancestors of blood and ancestors of spirit.

Sacrament of Tara and Avalon

Place the peyton in the center of the altar. Place the chalice upon the peyton. While facing North, place your arms out in a receptive position, palms up. Say,

This is Tara (lift left hand), this is Avalon (lift right hand). I am Sovereign in this space. We are Sovereign in this space.

Take your wand or athame, and hold it with a triangular grasp. Raise it up and say,

I draw into this circle and water all of the most correct and harmonious energies of the universe.

Keeping the grasp as it is, stir the water in a clockwise direction three times. Say,

I bless these waters, the waters of life.

Touch thumb to water then to lips three times for the three drops of awen. Raise the cup and say,

By the Fire of the Head, Heart, and Hands,
We bring the blessings of Beltane,
Brewed to Perfection in the Sacred Cauldron, the Sacred Grail,

Warmed by the Breaths of Nine Witches,
A libation to the Gods and the Ancient Ones. Iska Ba!

Blessing of the Cakes

Pass the wand over the cakes, drawing a pentacle.

I bless these cakes in honor of the God and Goddess. May the flesh of the God found in this grain guide us to the new King of the May and Queen of the May.

Pass the first plate of cakes to the men. Find the May King by lot.

Pass the second plate to the women. Find the May Queen by lot.

Invocation of the May King and Queen

Touch the King-Priest with the wand at the brow, left foot, right shoulder, left shoulder, right foot and brown again.

Into this man chosen by the Gods, I invoke the King of the Green, the Lord of Oak, the Crowned Prince of Light. May he bless these proceedings and renew the land with the Queen, in the Dance that never ends.

Touch the Queen-Priestess with the wand at the belly, heart and brow.

Into this woman chosen by the Gods, I invoke the Queen of the Land, the Lady of Flowers, the Crowned Lady of Green. May she bless these proceedings and renew the land with the King, in the Dance that never ends.

Together, the King and Queen pour out onto the sod/turf of the land the milk, honey, oil, wine, and yeast, to be blessed for the fields.

Turning the Wheel of the Year with the Beltaine May Pole Dance

Cone of Power

Any majick for the community or individuals.

Priest/ess brings the group to attention, and together we raise the cone of power. With that, all raise their hands upward to the sky, release the energy, and kneel to the ground to touch the sacred Earth, grounding and blessing the land.

Circle of Healing Light

Name the people you wish to send healing light to in the community, and as a group, do so together.

Devocation of Gods and Spirits

Release the May King and May Queen by reversing the ritual wand movements.

I thank and release the May King/Queen from this man/woman, may there always be peace between us. So Mote it Be!

Thank and release the Ancestors and Spirits of the Land.

Thank and release the Goddess and God as the May King and Queen.

Devocation of the Gods Danu, Dagda, Cerridwen, Gwydion, and Arianrhod.

Release the Quarters

Take the peyton in your left hand, face North, and hold up the peyton. Say,

To the powers of the North, we thank and release the element of Earth and the Stag. So Mote it Be!

Face West and hold up the peyton in your left hand. Say,

To the powers of the West, we thank and release the element of Water and the Snake. So Mote it Be!

Face South and hold up the peyton in your left hand. Say,

To the powers of the South, we thank and release the element of Air and the Crow. So Mote it Be!

Face East and hold up the peyton in your left hand. Say,

To the powers of the East, we thank and release the element of Fire and the Fox. So Mote it Be!

Complete the circle, returning to the North. Circle back to the front of the altar widdershins, and acknowledge Spirit by saying,

And we thank Spirit, always with us, So Mote it Be!

Release the Circle.

Work:

- Write your own Beltane Ritual.
- Read from the Fenian Myth Cycle and the Creation Myth Cycle.
- Work more closely with the element of Air and the Sword/Athame. Call upon Uiscias the Teacher of Finias to help you in gaining greater mastery of elemental Air.
- Learn about and possibly seek out with your meditations and majick the Goddess Cailleach, and the Gods Belenos and Nuada. Also work with the Arthurian knight Lancelot and the Avalonian Sister Thetis.
- Work with the animal spirit of the Hawk in majick and meditation.

LITHA

Mabinogion Branch: Manawydan, son of Llŷr
Welsh Gods and Goddesses: Manawydan, Pryderi, Rhiannon
Mystery of the Branch: Cause and Effect

Culhwch and Olwen Totem: Owl
Morgans of Avalon: Gliten
Arthurian Guides: Modred
Areas of England: South East

Rites of Passage: Home Blessings
Totems: Hound/Dog
Primary Goddesses: Medb
Primary Gods: Cúchulainn

Litha is a modern name for the Summer Solstice. It is the peak of the Sun's power during the course of the year, and the time when the setting Sun, twilight, seems to last the longest. Twilight is the time of the faeries, a wonderful time when, like other key moments in the year, the veil appears to be thin between the worlds. At this time, we feel more connected to the dimensions of the Faery realm. Just like in Shakespeare's *A Midsummer's Night Dream,* we are visited by the Faery Queen and Faery King, and their court. We must be respectful of this elder race. Midsummer is also the time when the Oak King and Holly King must battle, and the Oak King gives up his throne to the dark Holly King, who will initiate the waning year.

Litha: Battle of Light and Darkness

Items Needed:
Standard Altar
Litha Incense
Litha Candle
Protection Potion

People Needed:
Celebrant
Four Quarter Callers

The theme of this ritual is the transition of the light symbolized by the God of Light and Life waning, giving sway to the dark god aspect, also known as the Battle between the Oak King and Holly King. Through this transition, this liminal balance point, we find the mysteries of the Fey, and have an opportunity to commune with the elder race.

Cleansing and Purification of the Space and People

Smudged with Litha Incense as they come in.

Anointed with protection potion.

Place potion and incense back on altar.

Litha Incense

2 Tablespoons of Benzoin

1 Tablespoon of Tragacanth Powder

1 Tablespoon of Apple Wood and Leaves

1 Tablespoon of Elecampagne

1 Tablespoon of Yarrow

1 Tablespoon of Lavender

1 Tablespoon of Rose Petals

4 Drops of Lavender Essential Oil

1 Drop of Rose Essential Oil

Casting of the Circle Thrice

With a wand or sword starting in the North.

First Circle: *I cast this circle to protect us from any and all positive and negative energies that may come to do us harm.*

Second Circle: Silent.

Third Circle: *This circle is cast, So Mote it Be!*

Bow to the North.

Return to the altar and tap the wand three times on the altar.

Calling of the Quarters

Take the peyton in your left hand, face North, and hold up the peyton. Say,

To the powers of the North, we call upon the element of Earth and the Green Dragon. We welcome you to this circle. So Mote it Be!

Face East and hold up the peyton in your left hand. Say,

To the powers of the East, we call upon the element of Fire and the Red Dragon. We welcome you to this circle. So Mote it Be!

Face South and hold up the peyton in your left hand. Say,

To the powers of the South, we call upon the element of Air and the Yellow Dragon. We welcome you to this circle. So Mote it Be!

Face West and hold up the peyton in your left hand. Say,

To the powers of the West, we call upon the element of Water and the Blue Dragon. We welcome you to this circle. So Mote it Be!

Complete the circle, returning to the North. Circle back to the front of the altar, and acknowledge Spirit by saying,

And Spirit, with the Silver Dragon, always with us, So Mote it Be!

Evocation of the Gods and Spirits

Anoint your Goddess and God candle with protection potion three times, from top to bottom, saying,

I anoint this candle with the energies of the Goddess/God.

Light the candle saying,

I strike this candle with the light of the Goddess/God. So Mote it Be!

I call upon the Great Mother Danu, Mother of All and Flowing Source of Life.
I call upon the Great Father, Dagda, Master of Seasons and Keeper of Life and Death.
I call upon the Goddess through the Queen of Elphame, of Faery, Lady of Elder.
I call upon the God through the King of Light and King of Darkness, of Oak and Holly, of Sap and Blood. So Mote it Be!

Anoint and charge your Litha candle:

We charge this candle for the Queen of the deep Earth and the flux and flow of Light and Dark. May we too grow and change with the light and with the dark and find the mystery of the deep Earth and the elder race as we turn the Wheel of the Year.

We call upon those who have come before us, ancestors of blood and ancestors of spirit.

Sacrament of Tara and Avalon

Place the peyton in the center of the altar. Place the chalice upon the peyton. While facing North, place your arms out in a receptive position, palms up. Say,

This is Tara (lift left hand), this is Avalon (lift right hand). I am Sovereign in this space. We are Sovereign in this space.

Take your wand or athame, and hold it with a triangular grasp. Raise it up and say,

I draw into this circle and water all of the most correct and harmonious energies of the universe.

Keeping the grasp as it is, stir the water in a clockwise direction three times. Say,

I bless these waters, the waters of life.

Touch thumb to water then to lips three times for the three drops of awen. Raise the cup and say,

By the stars of the meadows,
We call forth the solstice blessings,
Brewed to Perfection in the Sacred Cauldron, the Sacred Grail,
Warmed by the Breaths of Nine Witches,
A libation to the Gods and the Ancient Ones. Iska Ba!

Journey to the Realm of Elphame

Use the Crystal Countdown to enter into alpha. Use this meditation to commune with the Faery beings.

Envision the God standing, facing the Sun. He is strong. He is a powerful King. He is in harmony with the Goddess of the Land, but as he stands, his shadow is cast. The shadow is longer, and darker, than any shadow you have seen before. He turns his back to the Sun and faces his shadow, which seems to grow horns, like the Hunter, and rises up. His shadow rises up and becomes a god as well. As the shadow rises, the God of Light seems more translucent, less solid and real.

The Dark God strikes the first blow and a battle begins. Witness the battle between the two sides of the God of Life and the God of Death. The Witnesses are as important as the battle itself as the balance of light shifts on this day.

The Dark God vanquishes the Light God, and in that final blow, a light erupts from the ground, enveloping them both. This is not the light of the Sun and stars, but the inner Earth light that dwells within all matter, sacred and holy. In the light opens a gateway, and you are invited into the gateway.

The path of light spirals in and down, in and down, in and down....

You are led to the Realm of Fey, above the deepest dwelling of the Underworld where Mabon resided, but below the realm of mortals, the realm of cycles and seasons, untouched by Time and glowing with an otherworldly inner light.

The path leads deeper into the realm of Fey; take notice of who and what you see, and don't stray off the path or take any food or drink.

You are brought to the Court of the Queen of Elphame, the Queen of Fay, more beautiful than any woman you have seen, yet mercurial in her shape and form. Perhaps beside her is the God, light and dark balanced in harmony, within the form of the King of Elphame, both horned and filled with light.

Commune with the leaders of the Elder Race of Fey. Be polite as you would to king and queen. Do everything with respect. If your intuition bids you to do so, receive any gifts or prophecy offered, or politely decline if your intuition objects.

Thank the King and Queen of Fey. Do you have an offering or blessing for them before you go? Offer this now and say your farewells.

Follow the path of light back, winding through the realm of Fey.

Follow the path spiraling up and out, up and out, up and out.

Come back to the well of light within the Earth.

Come back to the circle.

Cone of Power

Any majick for the community or individuals.

Priest/ess brings the group to attention, and together we raise the cone of power. With that, all raise their hands upward to the sky, release the energy, and kneel to the ground to touch the sacred Earth, grounding and blessing the land.

Circle of Healing Light

Name the people you wish to send healing light to in the community, and as a group, do so together.

Devocation of Gods and Spirits

Thank and release the Ancestors and Spirits of the Land.

Thank and release the Goddess and God.

Devocation of the Gods Danu, Dagda, Queen of Elphame, Oak King and Holly King.

Release the Quarters

Take the peyton in your left hand, face North, and hold up the peyton. Say,

To the powers of the North, we thank and release the element of Earth and the Green Dragon. So Mote it Be!

Face West and hold up the peyton in your left hand. Say,

To the powers of the West, we thank and release the element of Water and the Blue Dragon. So Mote it Be!

Face South and hold up the peyton in your left hand. Say,

To the powers of the South, we thank and release the element of Air and the Yellow Dragon. So Mote it Be!

Face East and hold up the peyton in your left hand. Say,

To the powers of the East, we thank and release the element of Fire and the Red Dragon. So Mote it Be!

Complete the circle, returning to the North. Circle back to the front of the altar widdershins, and acknowledge Spirit by saying,

And we thank Spirit, always with us, and the Silver Dragon, So Mote it Be!

Release the Circle.

Work:
- Write your own Litha Ritual.
- Read *Manawydan, son of Llŷr* from *The Mabinogion*.
- Learn about and possibly seek out with your meditations and majick the goddesses Rhiannon and Medb and the gods Manawydan, Llyr, Pryderi and Cúchulainn as well as with Modred and the Avalonian Sister Gliten.
- Work with the animal spirits of the Owl and Hound/Dog in majick and meditation.

LUGHNASSADH

Mythic City: Murias
Wizard: Semias
Hallow Tool: Dagda's Cauldron/Hollow
"Celtic" Element: Water
"Celtic" Direction: West
Cabot Element: Water
Cabot Direction: West

Irish Kingdom: Connacht
"Irish" Direction: West
"Irish" Element: Air
Flag: Griffon, Hand, Dagger
Qualities: Learning, Magic, Eloquence
People: Wise Ones
Irish Goddess: Medb
Sacred Site: Knocknarea
Irish Myth Cycle: Ulster Cycle

Flag of Connacht

Morgans of Avalon: Glitonea
Arthurian Guides: Gawain
Areas of England: South West

Rites of Passage: Croning/Wizarding
Totems: Otter
Primary Goddesses: Arianrhod, Blodeuwedd
Primary Gods: Lleu

Lughnassadh is named after the funeral feast, not of Lugh, but his foster mother, Tailitu, who used her vast powers to clear the land of Ireland of stones, so the fields could be planted and food grown to survive the winter. She was so exhausted from the feat that she expired, but we honor and celebrate her gift to us through the harvest feast. Traditionally the holiday is celebrated by a much longer festival filled with games of skill and mastery—storytelling, athletic championships, races, and crafts. After all, a funeral, like in good Irish tradition, is a party celebrating life as well.

Lughnassadh: Sacrifice of the Grain

Items Needed:
Standard Altar
Broom
Lughnassadh Incense
Lughnassadh Candle
Protection Potion
Stones
Basket of Grains, Fruit, and Herbs
Platter with Cakes
Spear (Optional)

People Needed:
Celebrant
Circle Sweeper
Four Quarter Callers

The ritual theme of Lughnassadh is the harvest, the sacrifice of the first grains being cut and the diminishing light, forcing us to be skillful in our preparation for the coming darkness. Lugh is the god of great skill, and he will help us in our preparations.

Cleansing and Purification of the Space and People

Smudged with Lughnassadh Incense as they come in.

Anointed with protection potion.

Place potion and incense back on altar.

Circle Sweeping

Priestess or priest sweeps the circle by taking the broom at the front of the altar and moving in a clockwise direction says:

I sweep away any and all unwanted or harmful energies from this space.

The broom is then returned to the front of the altar.

Lughnassadh Incense

2 Tablespoons of Frankincense

1 Tablespoon of Gold Copal

1 Tablespoon of Marigold Flowers

1 Pinch of Wheat Flour

6 Drops of Frankincense Essential Oil

Casting of the Circle

Thrice with a wand or sword starting in the North. You could also use a ritual spear to cast and release the circle.

First Circle: *I cast this circle to protect us from any and all positive and negative energies that may come to do us harm.*

Second Circle: Silent.

Third Circle: *This circle is cast, So Mote it Be!*

Bow to the North.

Return to the altar and tap the wand three times on the altar.

Calling of the Quarters

Take the peyton in your left hand, face North, and hold up the peyton. Say,

To the powers of the North, we call upon the element of Earth and the Stag. We welcome you to this circle. So Mote it Be!

Face East and hold up the peyton in your left hand. Say,

To the powers of the East, we call upon the element of Fire and the Hound. We welcome you to this circle. So Mote it Be!

Face South and hold up the peyton in your left hand. Say,

To the powers of the South, we call upon the element of Air and the Eagle. We welcome you to this circle. So Mote it Be!

Face West and hold up the peyton in your left hand. Say,

To the powers of the West, we call upon the element of Water and the Salmon. We welcome you to this circle. So Mote it Be!

Complete the circle, returning to the North. Circle back to the front of the altar, and acknowledge Spirit by saying,

And Spirit, with the Crow, always with us. So Mote it Be!

Evocation of the Gods and Spirits

Anoint your Goddess and God candle with protection potion three times, from top to bottom, saying,

I anoint this candle with the energies of the Goddess/God.

Light the candle saying, I strike this candle with the light of the Goddess/God. So Mote it Be!

I call upon the Great Mother Danu, Mother of All and Flowing Source of Life.
I call upon the Great Father Dagda, Master of Seasons and Keeper of Life and Death.
I call upon the Goddess Tailitu, Clearer of the Fields, Giver of Blessings and Food.
I call upon the God Lugh, Master of the Many Talents, Bearer of the Spear.
So Mote it Be!

We call upon those who have come before us, ancestors of blood and ancestors of spirit.

Anoint and charge your Lughnassadh candle:

As the days grow darker and soon the nights will become cold, we charge this candle in celebration of all that we have here and now, and for the promise of our continued health, wealth, and happiness in the dark season.

Sacrament of Tara and Avalon

Place the peyton in the center of the altar. Place the chalice upon the peyton. While facing North, place your arms out in a receptive position, palms up. Say,

This is Tara (lift left hand), this is Avalon (lift right hand). I am Sovereign in this space. We are Sovereign in this space.

Take your wand or athame, and hold it with a triangular grasp. Raise it up and say,

I draw into this circle and water all of the most correct and harmonious energies of the universe.

Keeping the grasp as it is, stir the water in a clockwise direction three times. Say,

I bless these waters, the waters of life.

Touch thumb to water then to lips three times for the three drops of awen. Raise the cup and say,

Lammas,
By the golden grain,
We honor all the blessings before us.
Brewed to Perfection in the Sacred Cauldron, the Sacred Grail,

Warmed by the Breaths of Nine Witches,
A libation to the Gods and the Ancient Ones. Iska Ba!

The Blessings of the Grains

Priest/ess holds up stones in hands, saying,

Blessed be these stones. They have been obstacles on our path, rocks within our field. Blessed be Tailitu for removing these stones from our field. These stones become our ovens, our hearth, our foundation. Blessed be Tailitu for transforming our challenges into our boons! Blessed be Tailitu!

Priest/ess holds up the basket of grains, fruit, and herbs, saying,

Blessed be the harvest. I charge these grains, these fruits, these herbs with majick! Blessed be the ground from which they grow. May all partake in the blessings of the harvest. May all learn to plant seeds, grow, and harvest what they need. Blessed be Lugh. Blessed be the many skilled one! Blessed be Lugh!

Priest/ess holds up the platter of cakes, saying,

Blessed be the cakes that have been baked upon the stones. Blessed be the light that has been released from the seed. Blessed be the child of light. Blessed be Taliesin! Blessed be Mabon! Blessed be Pryderi! Blessed be Angus! Blessed be all the children of light. Blessed be the Ancient Ones.

Pass the cakes around the circle clockwise with the words:

Blessed is Tailitu. Blessed is Lugh. Blessed is the Child of Light!

Cone of Power

Any majick for the community or individuals.

Priest/ess brings the group to attention, and together we raise the cone of power. With that, all raise their hands upward to the sky, release the energy, and kneel to the ground to touch the sacred Earth, grounding and blessing the land.

Circle of Healing Light

Name the people you wish to send healing light to in the community, and as a group, do so together.

Devocation of Gods and Spirits

Thank and release the Ancestors and Spirits of the Land.

Thank and release the Goddess and God.

Devocation of the Gods Danu, Dagda, Queen of Elphame, Oak King, and Holly King.

Release the Quarters

Take the peyton in your left hand, face North and hold up the peyton. Say,

To the powers of the North, we thank and release the element of Earth and the Stag. So Mote it Be!

Face West and hold up the peyton in your left hand. Say,

To the powers of the West, we thank and release the element of Water and the Salmon. So Mote it Be!

Face South and hold up the peyton in your left hand. Say,

To the powers of the South, we thank and release the element of Air and the Eagle. So Mote it Be!

Face East and hold up the peyton in your left hand. Say,

To the powers of the East, we thank and release the element of Fire and the Hound. So Mote it Be!

Complete the circle, returning to the North. Circle back to the front of the altar widdershins, and acknowledge Spirit by saying,

And we thank Spirit, always with us, and the crow, So Mote it Be!

Release the Circle.

Work:

- Write your own Lughnassadh Ritual.

- Read from the Ulster Myth Cycle and the Creation Myth Cycle.
- Work more closely with the element of Water and the Cup/Cauldron. Call upon Murias the Teacher of Semias to help you in gaining greater mastery of elemental Water.
- Learn about and possibly seek out with your meditations and majick the Goddesses Medb, Ariahnrhod, Blodeuwdd, and the Gods Lugh and Lleu. Also work with the Arthurian knight Gawain and the Avalonian Sister Gawain.
- Work with the animal spirit of the Otter in majick and meditation.

MABON

Mabinogion Branch: Math, Son of Mathonwy
Welsh Gods and Goddesses: Math, Gwydion, Lleu, Arianhrhod, Blodeuwedd, Gronw
Mystery of the Branch: Creation — Something from Nothing

Culhwch and Olwen Totem: Salmon
Morgans of Avalon: Monroe
Arthurian Guides: Nimue
Areas of England: West Midlands

Rites of Passage: Crossing Over
Totems: Black Hen
Primary Goddesses: Cerridwen
Primary Gods: Taliesin

Mabon is arguably the star of the myth cycle known as *The Mabonogion,* which bears his name, though he barely appears in it. Mabon is considered the child of light, the child of promise from the great mother Modron. He's stolen away into darkness and must find release through those seeking him in the underworld. Traditionally he is found by King Arthur. Mabon's story echoes in the kidnapping of Pryderi, son of Rhiannon, and the darkness of Taliesin faces in the hut, womb, and leather bag. Mabon is the great theme of the lost child in the darkness, and the autumn equinox celebrates his theme as the light returns to the depths of the Earth for another cycle to be renewed.

Mabon: Journey to Annwn, The Seven Caers of the Underworld

Items Needed:
Traditional Altar
Mabon Incense
Mabon Candle
Protection Potion

People Needed:
Celebrant
Four Quarters

Spirit Caller

The theme of this ritual is the journey to the underworld of Annwn, following the footsteps of King Arthur and his band to find the child god Mabon. It combines imagery from Arthur's journey to the underworld in the Spoils of Annwn, as well as the totemic imagery in the Arthurian quest for Mabon. It is reminiscent of the seven-gated underworld journeys of the Sumerian goddess Inanna and parallels the Ostara Sabbat ritual of return for the Child of Light.

Cleansing and Purification of the Space and People

Smudged with Mabon Incense as they come in.

Anointed with protection potion.

Place potion and incense back on altar.

Mabon Incense
2 Tablespoons of Black Copal
1 Tablespoon of Pine Resin
1 Teaspoon of Dragon's Blood
1 Tablespoon of Oak Bark
1 Teaspoon of Apple Wood
1 Tablespoon of Vetiver
1 Tablespoon of Pine Needles
10 Drops of Pine Oil
5 Drops of Vetiver Oil

Casting of the Circle

Thrice with a wand or sword starting in the North.

First Circle: *I cast this circle to protect us from any and all positive and negative energies that may come to do us harm.*

Second Circle: Silent.

Third Circle: *This circle is cast, So Mote it Be!*

Bow to the North.

Return to the altar and tap the wand three times on the altar.

Calling of the Quarters

Take the peyton in your left hand, face North, and hold up the peyton. Say,

To the powers of the North, we call upon the element of Earth and the Stag. We welcome you to this circle. So Mote it Be!

Face East and hold up the peyton in your left hand. Say,

To the powers of the East, we call upon the element of Fire and the Owl. We welcome you to this circle. So Mote it Be!

Face South and hold up the peyton in your left hand. Say,

To the powers of the South, we call upon the element of Air and the Eagle. We welcome you to this circle. So Mote it Be!

Face West and hold up the peyton in your left hand. Say,

To the powers of the West, we call upon the element of Water and the Salmon. We welcome you to this circle. So Mote it Be!

Complete the circle, returning to the North. Circle back to the front of the altar, and acknowledge Spirit by saying,

And Spirit, with the Blackbird, always with us, So Mote it Be!

Evocation of the Gods and Spirits

Anoint your Goddess and God candle with protection potion three times, from top to bottom, saying,

I anoint this candle with the energies of the Goddess/God.

Light the candle saying,

I strike this candle with the light of the Goddess/God. So Mote it Be!

I call upon the Great Mother Danu, Mother of All and Flowing Source of Life.
I call upon the Great Father Dagda, Master of Seasons and Keeper of Life and Death.
I call upon the Great Mother as Modron and her Son, Mabon, Child of Promise.
I call upon the Gods of the Witches, Cerridwen, Mistress of the Cauldron of Regeneration and Gwydion, Master of Light and Majick. We call upon Arianrhod of the Silver Wheel and Starry Castle, Heart of the Otherworld. So Mote it Be!

Anoint and charge your Mabon candle:

We charge this candle for the Child of Light, the Child of Hope and Promise to be reborn from the Depths of the Mother. We light this candle by the power of the Goddess, withdrawing her life from the world around us to dwell in the depths of the world below and bring new life. May we all safely travel through the seven castles, to be reborn as the God is reborn, a child anew through the womb of the Great Mother as we turn the Wheel of the Year.

We call upon those who have come before us, ancestors of blood and ancestors of spirit.

Sacrament of Tara and Avalon
Place the peyton in the center of the altar. Place the chalice upon the peyton. While facing North, place your arms out in a receptive position, palms up. Say,

This is Tara (lift left hand), this is Avalon (lift right hand). I am Sovereign in this space. We are Sovereign in this space.

Take your wand or athame, and hold it with a triangular grasp. Raise it up and say,

I draw into this circle and water all of the most correct and harmonious energies of the universe.

Keeping the grasp as it is, stir the water in a clockwise direction three times. Say,

I bless these waters, the waters of life.

Touch thumb to water then to lips three times for the three drops of awen. Raise the cup and say,

By the shadows beyond the veil,
We seek the wisdom of the darkness,
Brewed to Perfection in the Sacred Cauldron, the Sacred Grail,
Warmed by the Breaths of Nine Witches,
A libation to the Gods and the Ancient Ones. Iska Ba!

The Quest for the Lost Child

Guided Journey to the Otherworld. The celebrant leads the guided meditation, with each of the four quarters speaking the part of their corresponding animal guide in the vision, creating a combination of a mystery passion play and guided journey with multiple voices and participants. Start by guiding everyone down into alpha with the Crystal Countdown.

The Lord of Light has been slain. Cut down with the first grain upon the threshing floor. His golden spirit is returned to the underworld like a newborn child, awaiting return. We must usher the spirit of our Lord to the Womb of the Mother. We must guide him, psychopomps, through the siege perilous, through the seven gates, until he is returned to the waiting arms of the Mother. He is lost in the Underworld, as often we are lost in the Underworld. We must seek the wisdom of the oldest creatures. We must open the gates and provide safe passage for his rebirth.

We seek the Son of the Mother, within and without.
We seek the Light in the Heart of Darkness.
We seek the Child stolen from the Mother and imprisoned in the Cold

We seek him as Mabon Ap Modron, as Pryderi, as Lleu.
We seek him through the Ages of the World by the Wisdom of the Animal Teachers.

We start in the Center, with the Blackbird, Creature of the Fifth Age. Blackbird, tell us if you know of Mabon, the son of Modron, who was taken when three nights old from between his Mother and the wall?

Blackbird: *When first I came to this place, there was a blacksmith's anvil here. No work has been done on that anvil save by me sharpening my beak on it every night. There is not even a bit of that anvil left, and in all that time, I have never heard of Mabon, son of Modron. But I do know of one older than I and I will take you to him.*

To the North we travel, seeking out the Stag, Creature of the Fourth Age. Stag, tell us if you know of Mabon, the son of Modron, who was taken when three nights old from between his Mother and the wall?

Stag: *When I first came to this place, there was only a single antler on each side of my head, and no tree grew here save a single oak. That oak tree grew large and strong, with hundreds of branches. Long ago it fell, and nothing is left but that stump, and in all that time, I have never heard of Mabon, son of Modron. But I do know of one older than I, and I will take you to him.*

To the East we travel, seeking out the Owl, Creature of the Third Age. Owl, tell us if you know of Mabon, the son of Modron, who was taken when three nights old from between his Mother and the wall?

Owl: *When I first came to this place, this great valley before us was a wooded glen. The race of man came and destroyed it. Then a second forest grew up. The forest here today is the third forest that has grown here. As for me, my wings have worn down to nothing but stump, and in all that time, I have never heard of Mabon, son of Modron. But I do know of one older than I, and I will take you to him.*

To the South we travel, seeking out the Eagle, Creature of the Second Age. Eagle, tell us if you know of Mabon, son of Modron, who was taken when three nights old from between his Mother and the wall?

Eagle: *When I first came to this place long ago, I had a stone that I would stand on and peck at. Today, there is nothing left of the stone. In all that time, I haven't heard of Mabon, son of Modron, except when I went hunting for food in the lake. I sank my talons into large salmon, expecting to carry it off. Instead it dragged me down into the water and almost destroyed me. I went back with my relatives to destroy it, but it asked for peace and came to have tridents pulled out of its pack. Unless the salmon knows something of Mabon, son of Modron, I know none that can help you.*

To the West we traveled, seeking out the Salmon, Creature of the First Age, Oldest of All Living Creatures. Salmon, tell us if you know of Mabon, son of Modron, who was taken when three nights old from between his Mother and the wall?

Salmon: *I swim the streams between this world and that, to feed on the Hazelnuts of Wisdom. I have found the place where the Son of the Mother is hidden. The way is dangerous, through seven gates, through seven castles, amid many dangers and many treasures. If you would not believe me, ride with me there.*

Together, with the Creatures of the Great Ages, we descended to find Mabon.

We descend together, spiraling downward, spiraling downward, spiraling downward.

We enter a dark descending tunnel, with only the light of our spirits to guide us.

By our sides are the blackbird, the stag, the owl, the eagle, and the salmon, guiding us through the gates of the Underworld, of Annwn.

We approach the gate of the first castle, Caer Orchen,
the Castle of Dread, the Castle of Shelving Tide, Castle of the Sloping Sides.
This Castle of Dread is where we must divest ourselves of the body, of earthly concerns.
This Castle is our Root to all things Material, Sensual, and Physical.
This Castle is where we open the gate to the Spirit World.

This Castle is where we release our attachments to the physical world to truly enjoy.
A guardian stops you at the gate, preventing you from passing.
How does the guardian appear? Is the guardian familiar, frightening, or otherwise something you recognize as a key to help you master this gate?
You must make an offering to the guardian before you can pass.
What do you want to hold onto most from this life? Offer it to the guardian.

We approach the gate of the second castle, Caer Fandy-Manddwy
The Castle on High, the Sea Castle, the Castle of Starry Prisons.
This Castle of the Sea is where we pass through the astral oceans.
This Castle is our Intimacy where we make connections to all life.
This Castle is where we learn to trust and immerse ourselves in the coming mystery
A guardian stops you at the gate, preventing you from passing.
How does the guardian appear? Is the guardian familiar, frightening, or otherwise something you recognize as a key to help you master this gate?

You must make an offering to the guardian before you can pass.

What prevents you from trusting yourself and trusting others? Offer it to the guardian.

We approach the gate of the third castle, Caer Goludd

The Castle of Gloom, the Castle of Trials, the Castle of Death.

This Castle of Trials is where we learn the axis of Power and Fear.

This Castle is where we face our darkness.

This Castle is where we embrace our power and overcome the death of the self.

A guardian stops you at the gate, preventing you from passing.

How does the guardian appear? Is the guardian familiar, frightening, or otherwise something you recognize as a key to help you master this gate?

You must make an offering to the guardian before you can pass.

What do you fear the most? Offer it to the guardian.

We approach the gate of the fourth castle, Caer Rigor

The Castle of the Royal Horn, the Royal Castle.

This Castle of Royals is where we learn to love perfectly.

This Castle is where we find the Royal Heart, loving all.

This Castle is where we seek harmony and balance.

A guardian stops you at the gate, preventing you from passing.

How does the guardian appear? Is the guardian familiar, frightening, or otherwise something you recognize as a key to help you master this gate?

You must make an offering to the guardian before you can pass.

What stops you from loving all? Offer it to the guardian.

We approach the gate of the fifth castle, Caer Fredwyd

Castle of the Perfected Ones, Castle of Carousal, Castle of Revelry.

This Castle of Carousal is where we celebrate with the Mighty Dead who have gone before.

This Castle is where we open to the Voice of Wisdom from within and from the past.

This Castle is where we express that wisdom to all holy races of flesh and spirit.

A guardian stops you at the gate, preventing you from passing.

How does the guardian appear? Is the guardian familiar, frightening, or otherwise something you recognize as a key to help you master this gate?

You must make an offering to the guardian before you can pass.
What stops you from hearing and speaking the wisdom of your ancestors?
Offer it to the guardian.

We approach the gate of the sixth castle, Caer Pedryfan
The Revolving Castle, Four-Cornered and Revolving Sky Castle,
The Four-Squared Burial Castle.
This Castle of Revolving is where we see with True Sight.
This Castle is where we see all times, all places, all things.
This Castle is where we die and are reborn through our vision.
A guardian stops you at the gate, preventing you from passing.
How does the guardian appear? Is the guardian familiar, frightening, or otherwise something you
recognize as a key to help you master this gate?
You must make an offering to the guardian before you can pass.
What stops you from truly seeing all worlds as they are? Offer it to the guardian.

We approach the gate of the seventh castle, Caer Sidi
Castle of the Sidhe, Castle of the Zodiacal Wheel, Castle of the Inner Stars.
This Castle of Stars is where we began and where we shall end.
This Castle is where the Queen of the Starry Heavens resides.
This Castle is the Starry Kingdom in the Heart of the Underworld
Where the Divine Fire resides.
A guardian stops you at the gate, preventing you from passing.
How does the guardian appear? Is the guardian familiar, frightening, or otherwise something you
recognize as a key to help you master this gate?
You must make an offering to the guardian before you can pass.
What stops you from finding the starry divinity within you? Offer it to the guardian.

Come in to the Starry Castle.
You are greeted by She who is of the Silver Wheel.
She who Shapes Form from the Mist.
She who is Arianrhod, Starry Weaver.
Take this time to commune with the Silver Goddess

She reveals to you Mabon, Son of Modron, both within the Caer and within yourself.

See Mabon within and without

Feel Mabon within and without.

Know Mabon within and without.

Commune with the Child of Light, Hope, and Promise.

Do whatever he asks to prepare his way and coming Rebirth at Yule

And return at Ostara.

When done, his light guides the way out of the seven gates, the seven castles.

Pass freely through the gate of the seventh castle, Caer Sidi,

This Castle of Stars.

You are crowned by the Guardian who acknowledges your Sovereignty

Pass freely through the gate of the sixth castle, Caer Pedryfan,

This Revolving Castle of True Sight.

You are anointed with salve on your eyes and brow to see truly always.

Pass freely through the gate of the fifth castle, Caer Fredwyd,

This Castle of Carousal with the Wise and Mighty Dead.

You are given a torc or choker necklace to remember to always speak with wisdom.

Pass freely through the gate of the fourth castle, Caer Rigor,

This Castle of the Royal Heart.

You are given a medallion that hangs at your heart of Perfect Love.

Pass freely through the gate of the third castle, Caer Goludd,

This Gloomy Castle of Power and Fear.

You are given a golden bracelet, to shine and light your way.

Pass freely through the gate of the second castle, Caer Fandy-Manddwy,

This Sea Castle of Intimacy.

You are given a cord, your link to the first womb.

Pass freely through the gate of the first castle, Caer Orchen,
This Dread Castle of all things Material.
You are given a royal robe, concealing all these things yet granting power in the world.

Only Seven Returned from Caer Sidi.
No more. No less.
Only Seven Returned from Caer Sidi.
Seven within. Seven without.
Seven holy powers challenged and blessed, suffered and kissed.
Only Seven Returned from Caer Sidi.

Cone of Power

Any majick for the community or individuals.

Priest/ess brings the group to attention, and together we raise the cone of power. With that, all raise their hands upward to the sky, release the energy, and kneel to the ground to touch the sacred Earth, grounding and blessing the land.

Circle of Healing Light

Name the people you wish to send healing light to in the community, and as a group, do so together.

Devocation of Gods and Spirits

Thank and release the Ancestors and Spirits of the Land.

Thank and release the Goddess and God as Modron and Mabon.

Devocation of the Gods Danu, Dagda, Cerridwen, Gwydion and Arianrhod.

Release the Quarters

Take the peyton in your left hand, face North, and hold up the peyton. Say,

To the powers of the North, we thank and release the element of Earth and the Stag. So Mote it Be!

Face West and hold up the peyton in your left hand. Say,

To the powers of the West, we thank and release the element of Water and the Salmon. So Mote it Be!

Face South and hold up the peyton in your left hand. Say,

To the powers of the South, we thank and release the element of Air and the Eagle. So Mote it Be!

Face East and hold up the peyton in your left hand. Say,

To the powers of the East, we thank and release the element of Fire and the Owl. So Mote it Be!

Complete the circle, returning to the North. Circle back to the front of the altar widdershins, and acknowledge Spirit by saying,

And we thank Spirit, always with us, and the Blackbird, So Mote it Be!

Release the Circle.

Work:
- Write your own Mabon Ritual.
- Read *Math, Son of Mathonwy* from *The Mabinogion.*
- Learn about and possibly seek out with your meditations and majick the goddesses Arianhrhod, Blodeuwedd, and Cerridwen, and the gods Math, Gwydion, Lleu, Gronw, and Taliesin as well as Nimue and the Avalonian Sister Monroe.
- Work with the animal spirits of the Black Hen and Salmon in majick and meditation.

THE SACRED CENTER

Mythic City: Tara
Wizard: None
Hallow Tool: Crown
"Celtic" Element: Spirit
"Celtic" Direction: Center
Cabot Element: Spirit
Cabot Direction: Center

Irish Kingdom: Meath
"Irish" Direction: Center
"Irish" Element: Spirit
Flag: King on Throne
Qualities: Kingship, Stewardship, Sacredness
People: Chieftans
Irish Goddess: Eiru
Sacred Site: Uisneach Hill
Irish Myth Cycle: Mythological Cycle

Flag of Meath

Mabinogion Branch: Hanes Taliesin
Welsh Gods and Goddesses: Cerridwen, Taliesin
Mystery of the Branch: Initiation and Inspiration

Culhwch and Olwen Totem: Blackbird
Morgans of Avalon: Morgan
Arthurian Guides: Fisher King
Areas of England: London

Rites of Passage: Initiation
Totems: Your Totem
Primary Goddesses: Your Matron
Primary Gods: Your Patron

The Ritual of the Sacred Center is the Ritual of Initiation.

Work:

- If you are petitioning for initiation in the Cabot Tradition, prepare by making sure all your necessary work is done before applying. Spiritually prepare for initiation by reflecting upon the meaning of spiritual initiation and what your motivations are for seeking this out.
- Reread the *Hanes Taliesin* and reflect upon the story as a tale of initiation.
- Reread tales from the Irish Mythological Cycle and reflect upon its stories.
- Learn about and possibly seek out with your meditations and majick the goddesses and gods you feel closest to in your own spiritual work. Also look to the Fisher King of Arthurian lore and the chief sister of Avalon, Morgan, as teachers and initiators.
- Work with the animal spirits you feel are your strongest teachers and healers in majick and meditation. Also seek out the Blackbird as an animal of initiation.

RECOMMENDED READING LIST FOR THE MYSTERIES AND MYTHS OF THE WHEEL OF THE YEAR

Books marked with * are required reading. Out-of-print books can be found through keyword searches at Bibliofind.com. Many public domain translations of mythological texts can be found free at *http://www.sacred-texts.com*

Primary Source Texts

Irish/Scottish

Early Irish Myths and Sagas by Jeffrey Gantz

The Tain: Translated from the Irish Epic Tain Bo Cuailnge by Thomas Kinsella

Gods and Fighting Men by Isabella Gregory

A Treasury of Irish Myth, Legend and Folklore by W.B. Yeats

Myles Dillon, The Cycles of the Kings by Dillon Myles

Welsh

The Mabinogi and Other Medieval Welsh Tales by Patrick K. Ford*

The Black Book of Carmarthen by John Evans

Arthurian

The History of the Kings of Britain by Geoffrey of Monmouth with Lewis Thorpe (Translator)

Chrétien de Troyes: Arthurian Romances translated by William W. Kibler and Carleton W. Carroll

Sir Gawain and the Green Knight by Marie Borroff (Translator)

Lancelot-Grail: The Old French Arthurian Vulgate and Post-Vulgate in Translation

Le Morte D'arthur by Sir Thomas Malory

Secondary Source Texts

Celebrate the Earth by Laurie Cabot*

Wheel of the Year by Pauline and Dan Campanelli*

The Complete Idiot's Guide to Celtic Wisdom by Carl McColman*

Women in Celtic Myth by Mora Caldecott*

Celtic Myth and Magick by Edain McCoy*

Red Haired Girl from the Bog by Patricia Monaghan*

Celtic Myth and Religion by Sharon Paice Macleod*

A Dictionary of Irish Mythology by Peter Ellis

Dictionary of Celtic Mythology by James MacKillop

The Aquarian Guide to the British and Irish Mythology by John and Caitlin Matthews

Mabon and the Mysteries of Britain by John and Caitlin Matthews*

Taliesin by John and Caitlin Matthews*

Celtic Gods, Celtic Goddesses by R.J. Stewart

Ladies of the Lake by Caitlin Matthews*

Arthur and the Sovereignty of Britain by Caitlin Matthews*

The Celtic Lunar Zodiac: How to Interpret Your Moon Sign by Helena Paterson*

The Handbook of Celtic Astrology by Helena Paterson

The Celts by Jean Markale*

The Celts by T.G.E. Powell*

III.
Clergy Training

The training of clergy is done best in person, from minister to future minister. The material within this Book of Shadows is simply a guideline, emphasizing points to keep in mind when training to be clergy. It is drawn from the Cabot Clergy training course by Memie Cabot Watson, lectures from Laurie Cabot, and additional information from Penny Cabot and Christopher Penczak.

HOW TO MAKE A DIFFERENCE

Institutions and government are failing us. So how do we progress? How do we change the world? It takes an individual. It takes someone who won't take no for an answer who has something to offer the world, someone who stands up for it. It takes someone who continues to practice it, to share it, to show it to everyone. And you are out there; every one of you has something to offer to the world. Don't wait for someone to tell you, "Yes, ok, you can do that." They may not even know your talent. They may not even know the concepts that you have. You need to teach them. They can't say no if they don't understand it. But they will say no to you.

When I started to step out and I wanted to open a Witch shop, one of my family lawyers said I couldn't open a Witch shop. He told me someone would come in there and kill me. I said, "I don't think so." Of course he didn't know anything about majick or protection shields or what our life is about at all. He simply knew that the propaganda and the misinformation were so thorough that the general public knew nothing at all about Witchcraft. And that would put me in harm's way. What kept me from harm's way was the majick, and the need for majick in everyone's life. You know, when you first saw a Walt Disney movie and they waved wands and all the magic happened, something in you as a child said, "It's real." You know it's real, and that's innate knowledge. It is real. It can happen. And then you were told, "No, that's just a movie. Majick wands don't work." Yes, they do. Maybe not the way Walt Disney saw it, but they do work. What works is your own majick. That means it doesn't have to be about Witchcraft, it has to be about what you have to offer the world. What is it that you can create that goes beyond what anyone else has done? It may be in your creative self. You must stand up for it. You cannot take no for an answer.

WHAT IT MEANS TO BE A HIGH PRIESTESS/HIGH PRIEST IN THE CABOT KENT HERMETIC TEMPLE

Responsibility: This means to do everything you can do to achieve your goals and not let your ego get in the way. Always keep in mind that it be done for the good of all, harming none. It is taking responsibility for your thoughts, words, and actions as you are the creator of your destiny. You want to make sure you are a reliable individual and are trustworthy to yourself and your peers. Remember the three-fold law.

Respect: You must have respect for yourself and for others at all times. Remember, respect is earned and not taken for granted or demanded.

Leadership: Set an example as a leader, being able and capable to lead individuals in rituals and matters at hand. We teach our wisdom and knowledge to those that seek; we do not hide our knowledge. It is not about being on a power trip. Leadership is also having organizational skills by integrating and being able to put things into perspective.

Community Service: It is a very important part about being a High Priestess or High Priest. We set ourselves into the eye of the community and lead by example. We help others in need through our Temple and community, and we guide individuals to learn and grow.

Controversy and Gossip: This is disrespectful and can be hurtful not only to yourself, but also to others, and it ultimately reflects on the Temple. Avoid conflicts at all costs. If you get yourself into a conflict, you need to resolve the matter with clear thinking, a calm manner, and conflict resolutions. If the issue is with a fellow Cabot Witch and cannot be resolved in a peaceful manner, then the persons involved must speak to a certified Cabot counselor. Further counseling might be needed. The final decision will be made by the elder and must be followed. You are not a counselor on Temple politics until you are certified as one.

Mentoring: A mentor is a trusted friend, a counselor, or teacher. You become a person who can guide others with inspiration and motivation. A mentor is there for the person when truly needed, so it is important not to pass judgment, to have a compassionate ear, to remain patient, and to listen. Apply ethics and proper morals when giving advice. Be honest and discreet while mentoring. You may seek advice on mentoring from Elders of the Temple. You must be certified to counsel or teach in the Temple.

Ethics: Understand and apply the Cabot Code of Ethics at all times.

Trusting: Trust your intuition and being sovereign over yourself and your sacred space. Always do things with ethics in mind, and always remember the cause and effects of what you do. Aim to be a trustworthy person by your words and actions.

Laws: We follow, respect, and abide by the ethical laws of The Cabot Kent Hermetic Temple and the local, state, and federal laws.

— Reprinted with permission from Memie Cabot Watson, H.Ps.

What does it mean to be clergy? What does it mean, this day and age, when Witches reclaim their rightful role as clergy to their community? We were the priestesses and priests of the ancient temples, the Druids and the seers of the ancient tribes. Yet we are still learning how to be clergy in our reclaimed traditions in a mostly secular world, alongside other, more recognized religions.

The word "clergy" comes from the French, who allowed those who were recognized as clergy freedom from paying taxes due to their common role in promoting the good in society by worshipping God and caring for others. Today, churches and religious organizations are granted tax exempt status with the same fundamental understanding. Such groups provide support to the poor, the sick, the destitute, and those in prisons while simultaneously growing their own organization and promoting their own beliefs, philosophies, and rituals.

Clergy are asked usually to preside over rituals when called upon and teach religious doctrine and traditions within their community. The terms for the person filling this societal role have changed and been added to over time, and include clergy, cleric, reverend, or High Priestess and High Priest. Christianity has specific names for specific roles of the clergy, including deacon, priest, preachers, ministers, and pastors. In the Jewish traditions, religious leaders are known as

Rabbi. Both Judaism and Christianity have ministers of music, known as cantors, or in Judaism, also called a hazzan.

Members of the Clergy have three main functions:

1. Introducing others to the Temple
2. Conducting rites of passage
3. Providing guidance and mentorship

Beyond these three primary roles, clergy are called upon to visit the sick and dying, minister to prisoners in correctional institutions, give interviews to the media, organize and conduct community service, offer emotional support, and provide a model for their religion in the public sphere.

In Witchcraft, when our societal role was diminished with the growth of Christianity, we took the role of the village wise woman or wise man, dispensing aid informally at the edge of the village. Much of our ministry today tends to reflect that, combining roles of the cunning woman or cunning man with more traditional clergy. Many ordained Witchcraft High Priestesses and High Priests take the honorific of Reverend, and place H.Ps. or H.P. after their name.

We can look at our role as clergy divided in the following areas of service:

Divination Readings

Spiritual Counsel and Pastoral Care

Guidance and Mentorship

Rites of Passage Rituals

Public Ritual of Sabbats and Esbats

Home Rituals (Home Cleansings, Animal Blessings)

Teaching

Public Relations and Media

Social Justice Activism

Environmentalism

Social Service Support (Hospital, Military, and Prison Ministry)

Interfaith Service

Community Service

Clergy and Community

Beyond the technical meaning and role of clergy, we must look at the deeper spiritual calling of clergy. It's not for everyone. When we follow the old ways of clergy, meaning the Druids of ancient Celtic Societies, we are called to serve community. What we think of as the Celtic community was actually many different tribes and groups sharing similar culture, story, art, and religion; it was most likely the Druidic tradition that kept an underlying connection and unity among them. That is why the Romans targeted the Druids as the key to conquering the disparate Celtic groups.

The spirit of clergy is the spirit to form and serve community. I've found three keys to helping serve the community from this spiritual perspective:

1. Selflessness
2. The Art of Compromise
3. Compassion

To a certain extant, one must be selfless to serve the community. Things can get toxic when we make our service all about serving our own ego. When we take the position of High Priestesses or High Priests, it is no longer about us personally, but how we facilitate community and the good of all. Your actions, including your majick, should be done for the sake of community, for the greater good. You often have to put your own desires aside and create situations where others can grow, develop, and shine, while you are often in the background in a supportive role. You have to use your intuition to bring together compatible people for projects, to succeed in mutually agreed upon community goals. It is the goal of clergy to help the development of projects and to give others the tools needed to create circumstances where the work flows and is successful for all.

The art of compromise is a very difficult art to learn. Witches are often strong-willed individuals, used to marching to our own beat and usually dismissing any effort to control us. It helps to understand that compromise is not about control, but mutual agreement. Yes, it sometimes requires concessions from both sides, but it is truly about balance and understanding. As ministers, we usually have to be the one negotiating compromise between two community members. We have to understand that each person involved has their own personality, perception, and needs in the situation. Compromise takes all those factors into consideration to create a situation that works for all when conflict and misunderstanding arise.

Compassion is the final key, and in fact, a key to the mysteries of the Witch. Compassion fills the cup of the Holy Grail which we seek. Compassion is the balm that heals us and helps us facilitate true healing in others. Compassion is genuine sympathy for the suffering of others, a kindness and empathy that stems from unconditional love. Compassion doesn't mean a lack of boundaries or pity. Sometimes the most compassionate thing one can do is to hold someone accountable for their actions, including ourselves. But we must also be willing to forgive and welcome again. Selflessness and compromise help us embody compassion, and truly embodying compassion make us more selfless, and more likely to compromise. These three principles are like the three legs the cauldron of community stands upon, the three poles of the tripod from which it hangs. I think of the triple stone monument of Kent, Kit's Coty House, which consists of three standing stones with a fourth across the top of the lower three, giving it support. We need a minimum of three points to build a structure.

THE PERSONAL, INTERPERSONAL, AND TRANSPERSONAL

When working as clergy, we should keep in mind the three levels described in modern psychology as the personal, interpersonal, and transpersonal. The personal level is just that, dealing with the individual and their own experiences. Personal realm issues deal with the individual needs, desires, hopes, dreams, failings, and satisfaction. The interpersonal deals with our relationships with other people, how we communicate, how we empathize and deal with expectations and experiences with others, and how they deal with us. The transpersonal realm deals with the larger dimensions of life, beyond our relationship with just ourselves or others. Transpersonal issues deal with the greater community, the world, our larger spirituality, and our role and place in the scheme of things.

One thing that often happens in majickal training is the need for personal healing. We focus so much on personal, individual sovereignty and self-esteem, as we come from a society that doesn't teach this to us, that we sometimes suffer as our practice grows. Many times we have a profound spiritual experience that pushes us to do the work of a High Priestess or High Priest. The profound peak is very transpersonal. The problem we then encounter is that we've skipped the natural progression of working on our interpersonal communication and empathy skills. We lack social awareness with other individuals and small groups. We feel we are beyond it because we had such a profound experience, but when we have to work in cooperation with people, we can lack the skills to do so.

Good ministers learn these skills and can recognize when this is the issue in others. Selflessness, compromise, and compassion become the keystones in this work with others. We need to learn how to model those qualities to others, and work from a clear understanding of them for ourselves. Only then can we effectively operate personally, interpersonally, and transpersonally. We've been operating in all three realms all the time, but we have to become conscious of the fact, and operate effectively.

WORKING WITH CLIENTS: GUIDANCE, MENTORSHIP, AND APPROPRIATE RELATIONSHIPS

When we are working with others in the role of a minister with a client, we must be clear in what services we are offering, what is expected from both parties, and what is outside of the bounds of the relationship. This is particularly true when we are offering guidance in the form of readings and majickal consultations, becoming mentors and teachers, and performing rituals.

Communication — Develop communication skills. Be able to engage in truly meaningful and effective communication. Be able to listen and offer appropriate responses. Use critical thinking and avoid the trap of filling the session only with your own talking. Many come to clergy because they need to be heard. Use supportive language, although you can be direct. Do not judge or impose your own thoughts upon a client. Help people move through their own process.

Clear Roles — Understand your role in any given situation before you. What are you offering? What is being asked of you? Do they match? If not, be clear with your client about everyone's roles and responsibilities. Make sure this is communicated at the start of any relationship.

Contact — If a client is not comfortable in your presence, seek out the assistance of other clergy members whom they might be able to share their thoughts and feelings. Don't let your ego get in the way of helping someone. There are times when you will need to have two clergy members in the room pending the meeting.

Schedule — Make an appropriate schedule to work with longer-term clients. Book visits as necessary. Make yourself appropriately available, but do not allow your own boundaries to be crossed.

Ethics — Obviously refrain from exploiting and manipulating clients for your benefit consciously or unconsciously. Always keep client information private. Follow the established ethical codes.

Payment and Fees — Usually there is a fee when performing services such as guided meditation, teaching, readings, rituals, and rites of passage. Make sure your fee is appropriate and reasonable for the services you are providing. If the client is not able to pay, try to work out a sliding scale price based upon what is reasonable for them. Depending on the service, you might need to travel, such as the travel for rites of passage, and can ask to be compensated for your time and travel expenses.

Touch — Avoid physical touch with clients unless the form of service you are providing is a hands-on healing or a rite of passage where touch is necessary. You must always get permission from a client before touching them.

Minors — If ministering to minors, please make sure you always have the parent or legal guardian present for you and have the parent/guardian sign a release form for the services you are providing.

Records — Keep records of your work, including your rites of passage and pastoral care. Records should be kept in a safe place in case access to them is needed once again.

TEACHING WITCHCRAFT AND MAJICK

When I came to Salem, Massachusetts, one of the first rituals I did was a majick circle to project for my life's goals, to envision the end result of my life's work. I did a spell to teach Witchcraft as a science to the world. I didn't focus on how, when, or where. I had not developed a curriculum for teaching. But that was my goal.

With those forces set in motion, two weeks later I was invited out to see a friend of mine perform. She was a singer in a band performing in a little honky-tonk bar in Rhode Island. I went out to see her perform, and the whole time, I was wondering "Why am I here?" I didn't particularly want to be there. The guy at the next table was drunk, and I was trying to avoid eye contact with him.

Eventually he walked over to the table while my friend was still singing on stage. He looked at me and said, "You're a Witch, aren't you?" At that time I didn't wear as much make-up as I do now. I looked a little less public, but I was still a public Witch in my black. He instinctually knew. At first I wanted to tell him to go away, but something made me not say that. Something made me talk with him. He was making sense and he was a nice guy.

My girlfriend came down off the stage with her band and she was about ready to say, "Excuse me, sir," when I stopped her. We started talking about Witchcraft. He then announced that he was the head of continuing education at Wellesley High School and wanted to give me a six-week course on Witchcraft. I was stunned. I had just done this projection, but had no idea it would manifest so quickly. I didn't know anything about creating the curriculum he had asked for. He explained to me in detail what a curriculum was, and gave me his name, address, and phone number so that I could send it to him. I went home, wrote up a six-week course, and sent it to him. Soon enough, I was hired by the prestigious Wellesley High School to teach in their continuing education department.

Soon after the course was done, I met a woman named Alice Keegan, whose father, unknown to me, was the president of Salem State College. The Wellesley experience gave me confidence to teach little classes in my first shop in Salem, and that material would eventually become my Witchcraft I course. Alice attended a lot of my shop classes. Alice came to me one day and said that her father would like to speak to me. She was going to Catholic school at the time, and I thought there was a problem. I agreed, and soon I was meeting her mother and father. Her father asked me what I was teaching and soon offered me a spot for a ten-week course on Witchcraft at Salem State College, with the stipulation that the second year I teach it, it would be an accredited course. While I got my library card for Salem State that said "faculty" on it—a card I still have—sadly the media attention got to be too much for the college administration, and I was not asked to teach it the following year. The media did create a frenzied circus around the idea of a Witch teaching in a state college. Though I was teaching the science of the Craft, not the religion, I can still understand why people were concerned about the mixture of church and state in a college. But it was a huge start. It got me on my life's path as a teacher, and I haven't looked back since.

Teaching is a special vocation. It's a calling, and not all Witches are called to it. Yes, we are called to educate the public, but if you find that teaching is a part of your life's work, stick with it and project for your life's goal as a teacher. The doors will open for you.

For those teaching the Cabot Tradition as Certified Teachers, here are some things to keep in mind:

- It is preferred that your classes contain a minimum of six students, and no more than twelve per class. It makes it easier to share and to create a group experience, without getting overwhelming for the students or the teacher.

- As your students come into class, welcome them and encourage them to get to know those around them.

- If you have stragglers, please let them know that tardiness is not accepted, and that latecomers to ritual are not allowed in circle once the ritual has begun. It is for this reason that we are so strict on timeliness.

- As the students are signing in and getting settled, do a visual around the room. Make certain you can see each student to the point of where you can make eye contact with all of them. Whenever possible, have student chairs arranged in a manner where you as the instructor can see everyone. A semi-circle is an ideal seating plan.

- Encourage students to take notes, especially on things they may observe throughout the room during the course of the classes, as well as anything they may feel at any given time. These things can later be entered into their journal or Book of Shadows as a reference for them in future majickal workings/classes.

- Go around the room and assess how each student did. Be positive in your critique. Suggest they note all the results of each meditation in this class for their Book of Shadows.

- Remember, be very descriptive when guiding meditations. What should they be seeing, hearing, smelling, and feeling? Paint a picture on all levels.

- Talk about working health cases. Put them at ease.

- Share your own stories and experiences in working majick and psychic development.

TRANSFORMING IGNORANCE AND PREJUDICE

If the path of the Witchcraft minister is yours as it is mine, you must understand that we are not yet in a political place where we have power or where we are totally safe from prejudice, avarice, and greed. All the things that have been set upon us since our ancestors are still present to a certain extent. We work our Craft in a constant state of explaining our beliefs and customs. Witchcraft is a nature-based religion, and today we practice for the good of all. We do not have a devil or any absolute evil deity in our belief structure at all. We have to educate people that the devil figures are really Christian deities, not ours.

Here in America where all religions are supposedly safe, we are recognized by the Federal government as a religion. However, the lack of information and knowledge is still prevalent and creates a problem. People hang onto these old stereotypes of the Witch, sometimes out of ignorance and sometimes out of prejudice. They do not want to see us in any other light. Even here in Salem, Massachusetts, where you think the education and awareness would be the highest, we have had newscasters report when someone had performed graffiti with a pentacle that the criminals used "the mark of the devil." I beg to differ. That's not the mark of the devil; it is the symbol of Witchcraft. Some of the armed forces of the United States carry that same exact symbol, and it has be recognized as a religious symbol. There are many Witches and Pagans in the military and police.

As priestesses and priests of the Craft, we must know our facts and truths, and work to inform others in the media when there are misconceptions about who we are and what we do. We must approach things from a calm and rational manner, even when others do not. We need to transform ignorance and prejudice with education, with modeling what Witchcraft is, and by sharing how we are contributing members of our overall communities. Remember, you are the public face of Witchcraft and must act accordingly to bring our work forward to the next generation.

INTERFAITH WORK

Interfaith work, as a minister, is working with the ministers and community members of other religions to build understanding, tolerance, and work on mutual community goals. High Priestesses and High Priests should take their place among the world religions and get involved in interfaith work for the betterment of all.

Intrafaith work is making alliances and doing mutual work with other denominations within our own larger religious groups, including other traditions of Witchcraft and Paganism.

COMMUNITY SERVICE

You must do a Community Service Project, approved by the Cabot Council or your instructor, to be considered for initiation. Community service should be a regular part of the work of a minister or aspiring minister. We start with aiding others in their projects, ranging for helping set up for sabbats and other events, to later taking charge of committees and leading new projects.

HOSPITAL VISITS

Witchcraft clergy making hospital visits is not a typical experience for most hospital staff, but thankfully it's a growing phenomenon as patients are becoming more comfortable requesting clergy from their own traditions.

We can classify hospital (and home wellness) visits into the following four categories:

Crucial Visits: These visits include giving comfort and guidance to those who are dying, or those traumatized by violence. These clients are those who need immediate support and comfort. Generally crucial visits are not long unless death is at hand, and you are asked to help cross them over.

Needed Visits: These visits are not as sensitive or immediate. They can include visits prior to surgery, or the day after.

Optional Visits: These visits are for those who are not in the hospital long or are under no immediate danger or crisis. These visits provide support and comfort.

Token Visit: Token visits invoke making visits for no practical reason other than to please people, keeping the peace, or satisfy tradition. You are not necessarily ministering to another's need, but donating your time as a friend or colleague.

It can also be helpful to keep the following in mind when performing a hospital visit as clergy:

- Contact the hospital staff or administration when formally requested to visit as clergy.

- Carry your ministerial credentials with you.

- While the wearing of robes is appropriate, often the length of ritual robes makes it unfeasible. Wear black and your Cabot sash. Convey an air of professionalism and respect with your choice of clothes.

- If the door is closed or privacy curtain is drawn, knock and announce yourself, asking permission to enter.

- Offer encouragement and comfort to the patient. Provide support in the form of sympathy, empathy, and solidarity. Realize many will be afraid, discouraged, lonely, or in pain.

- Realize you are ministering to not only the patient in the hospital, but also to the members of the family. Be aware that not all families are accepting of their loved one's religious choices, so keep those boundaries in mind.

- Pay attention to cues to understand when the patient is tired and wants you to go. Look for yawning, heavy eyelids, and verbal cues. Do not overstay your welcome.

- Keep up your own majickal shields; hospitals can be very energetically chaotic places. Use your own talismans, stones, and charms to keep yourself centered and clear in difficult times and places.

CRITICAL THINKING

Critical or analytical thinking is the ability to see and analyze a situation to quickly and effectively solve problems and adapt to new information. Through the use of critical thinking, you apply reason and logic to new or unfamiliar ideas, opinions, and situations. Critical thinking includes:

Attitude — The attitude you need to consider others and their problems in a thoughtful way. You need to be able to keep an open mind. You must acknowledge your own personal goals, motives, biases, and emotions that might sway your opinions and thought processes.

Examination — Examination of any beliefs in light of the evidence before you. It generally requires that you recognize problems and meet those problems directly.

Reason — Knowledge in using logic and reasoning skills and how to apply those methods. You must approach things rationally and analyze the information before you.

With critical thinking in a ministerial capacity, you are identifying the root issues from the information given to you by a client, looking at the patterns from the Principle of Cause and Effect, and drawing conclusions to offer potential solutions to the issue at hand. Gather all the information needed from the client that is required for helping you work with their problems. Obtain more information by asking appropriate questions to help you arrive at an appropriate solution. Make sure your suggestions and advice address the issues on hand.

MAJICKAL THINKING

"Magical Thinking" is a term in the psychological world for when someone is disassociating from logic and reason. Basically in many ways it's considered irrational. the opposite of critical thinking. Many see it as indicative of other disorders. Yet Witches have a definition of Majickal Thinking that is very helpful, and it's good to be aware of when such irrational creative thinking is indicating a disassociation from the facts of someone's current reality, and what is truly majick. Witches understand where they are as they project intentions for where they want to be and what they want to manifest.

True, healthy majickal thinking helps us also approach our ministry, and life, through the eyes of the Witch, learning to use our intuition and majick to create effective changes and effective attitudes. Majick does start with self-love and self-esteem, so that is the foundation for a Cabot's majickal thinking, and is not disassociated with reality. When working with others, learn to craft rituals and ceremonies, meditations and spells to help empower a client. Approach situations from a spiritual and majickal lens, as well as a logical and rational one. Use all the tools at your disposal.

CONFLICT RESOLUTION

Ministers must work together to resolve any conflicts between themselves, or when acting as a mediator in the conflicts of others in the community. The goal of successful conflict resolution is neutralizing the conflict and potentially creating mutually beneficial relationships for all involved. Keep the following in mind when doing any conflict resolution:

- Ask questions.
- Clarify the nature of the problem.
- Build trust.
- Do not jump to conclusions.
- Do not stereotype those involved.
- Do not pressure anyone or feel pressured to do anything without agreement.
- Be flexible.
- Listen to the ideas from others.
- Be able to witness other people's emotions without feeling attacked.
- Be able to express your emotions without attacking.
- Understand the history of the situation and how it influences the present.
- Find points where all can agree.
- Offer reasonable solutions for moving forward in both the short-term and long-term.

Listening and Boundaries as a Minister

Listening skills are an important part of being a clergy member and offering support. Learn active listening skills and be able to hold space and witness when another is engaging in their own process, directing them to outside facilitation and support as needed. Keep in mind that any session is not about you or your own issues, however much you might empathize with the person before you. This time is about your client and how best to aid them spiritually.

While mentorship includes teaching ethics and offering support, it's important to realize you are a spiritual counselor offering pastoral care as a minister, not a psychological counselor. Direct people to the appropriate medical and psychological support when necessary. You are not a psychologist, so do not pretend or assume to be one. People seek you out because of your knowledge, but present your credentials accurately. Majickal knowledge is helpful under certain circumstances, but other forms of knowledge and expertise are needed in other situations.

Be clear in what services you can offer and what services are not comfortable or qualified to offer. It is easy to become overwhelmed by not understanding your own role and responsibilities in the situation. You cannot take responsibility for anyone else, but simply offer support, guidance, and access to other resources.

RITES OF PASSAGE RITUALS

The following are the foundation stones of specific rites of passage as done in the Cabot Tradition of Witchcraft. Of course ministers are going to vary them to suit the people using them, to make sure they are appropriate, but these rituals show the most important elements of each rite of passage.

Each one's life passage can be associated with one of the sabbats in the Wheel of the Year. It can be helpful as ministers to be contemplating the cycle of our life along with the cycle of the year as we celebrate the eight sabbats.

Passage	Ritual	Corresponding Sabbat
Funeral	Passing on into Avalon-Summerland	Samhain
Birth Ritual	Belly Blessing	Yule
Child Blessing	Wiccaning	Imbolc
Coming of Age	Princess/Prince Rite	Ostara
Marriage	Handfasting	Beltane
Home	House Blessings, Animal Blessing	Litha
Elderhood	Croning, Wizarding	Lughnassadh
Last Rites	Crossing Over	Mabon
Clergy	Initiation	Center

The rituals are written simply, as ministers should have the basics of the liturgy already known. They can be performed by a single officiant, though having a pairing of a High Priestess and High Priest alternating the roles is ideal. While these are the official rites in the Cabot Tradition, they must be adapted to suit the needs of the people present whenever necessary.

FUNERAL: PASSING ON INTO AVALON-SUMMERLAND

Funeral ceremonies are both for the deceased, to raise the energy and open the way to ease the transition and give clarity of choice to what is next in the process of crossing, and for the loved ones who are mourning and need a sacred space to process their grief and share in family and community. This ritual is a celebration of a life that has now begun a new journey and, until we are once again together, we send out their sprit back to Avalon.

We see Avalon as the sacred Otherworld of the gods, ancestors, and faeries. It is connected deeply to the concept of Summerland, where one may return upon death, rest, and possibly return for a new life.

The preparation for the funerary rites will depend on what the funeral home will allow for incenses, oils, and other rituals tools. Many funeral homes understand religious requirements, but are also sensitive to the needs of others who will also be using the space.

Items Needed:
White Robes for Officiants
Altar with Flowers and White Candles
Photo of the Deceased
Apple Wands for the Officiants
Speak to the Dead Potion

• Cast the traditional full majick circle with the four quarters.

• Light the Goddess and God candles. Call upon the God to open the way to Avalon and call upon the Sisters of Avalon.

We call upon the Goddess, the Lady Morgaine, chief of the Nine Sisters, to aid us in this rite.
We call upon the God, Cernnunos, to open the gate and lead the way.
So Mote it Be!

• Light all other candles. Have one candle next to, or before, the photo of the deceased.

• Perform the Sacrament of Tara and Avalon and a libation to the Ancient Ones.

Avalon is his/her new home, where all is of peace and harmony with the universe. We ask you to go with your guides to the Otherworld, but let us always hear your voice and feel your presence when you decide to visit or stay among us.

• Vision Working for the Deceased.

Officiant to call upon the Goddess for the journey:

We call upon the Goddess Morgaine, come to this majick space. Bring the boat to the shores of Tara.

Officiants ask those present to close their eyes and envision in the mind's eye the mists rising... and the deceased also descending...

We watch the spirit of (name deceased) as he/she steps into the boat and drifts into the mist. Morgaine guard and keep this Witch (name deceased), she/he who is a Priest/tess of Avalon, and guide them on their journey back to rest and peace.

May she lead you to the Great Castle of Avalon. There within you shall be led to the Great Hall. There you will be greeted by loved ones, by the ancestors rejoicing and feasting for your arrival, as the Otherworld is safe and filled with wisdom.

We call you to the veil, and we cherish your life beyond and value your wisdom ad guidance.

Blessed be.

• Western Gate

The officiants petition Morgaine (ideally the High Priestesses) and Cernnunos (ideally the High Priest) as they lift their apple wands together and turn to face the western quarter. They open the gate to the ancestors with their majick.

All present in the circle raise their hands and turn to the western quarter as well.

May we call upon your wisdom and power to help the living?
Know that you shall be loved and forever remembered.

All say together the final salutation:

Merry Meet, Merry Part and Merry Meet Again.

Wands are lowered, and the western gate is closed.

If casket is in the circle, an officiant anoints it with Speaking to the Dead potion. Then each person attending passes the casket and places an offering on or around it (usually flowers or specifically roses of the Goddess).

All of the candles are extinguished except for the Goddess and God candles, and the one before the photo.

The deceased's remains are blessed and any tools or artifacts are either placed in the coffin or given to the family.

• The Goddess and God are thanked and released.

• The quarters are released, but this time, start in the West and end in the North.

• The circle is released.

Blessings to the family for the gift of the spirit that they loved so and have now sent back home to the Goddess and God, back to Avalon... And so it is...and so it shall be!

Let the candles burn out, if possible. If not, extinguish and move them to a home altar. Relight them and let them burn down entirely.

BIRTH RITUAL, OR BELLY BLESSINGS RITUAL

There is not a specific Cabot tradition for Blessing the Belly of the pregnant mother as such circumstances and needs are so specific and unique. As clergy, work with the mother-to-be to create a unique ritual for her own spiritual path and journey on the road to motherhood. Often such rituals include anointing the belly, or using non-toxic pigment to mark the belly with symbols and sigils of blessing.

Be extremely careful with any herbal substances, including oils, as many medicinal oils and herbs of majick are considered abortifacient, and can harm the pregnant mother and child. Be sure everything is completely safe and non-toxic.

Ideally call upon the great Mother Goddesses—Danu and Modron can be a part of the ritual, as well as the goddess Brid, who is the goddess of midwives and childbirth. Rhiannon is particularly protective of children due to what happened with her and Pryderi. Any of the gods of medicine would also be appropriate, such as Dian Cetch, Miach, and Airmid. Mothers that are beloved goddesses to Witches but who have difficult stories with their children are usually not called upon in such rituals, such as Arianrhod or Cerridwen.

Many modern Witches and Pagans also seek to ritualize the birth itself, with the aid of open medical staff, midwives, and doulas. Likewise, such ritual support is unique as each birth is unique, and can be adapted to suit the situation and care of the mother, child, and family.

You can use this ritual for inspiration and guidance:

Items Needed:
Safe, Non-toxic Anointing Oil (Olive Oil will suffice)
Altar with Flowers and Red Candles for the Mother

• Cast the traditional full majick circle with the four quarters.

• Light the Goddess and God candles. Call upon the Goddess to bless the Mother and Child and the God to protect.

We call upon the Goddess, the Danu, the Great Mother, to bless this Mother-to-be, to bless this Child!
We call upon the God, the Dagda, to protect and provide.
So Mote it Be!

• Perform the Sacrament of Tara and Avalon and a libation to the Ancient Ones.

• Blessing of the Belly:

Officiant to call upon the Goddess by lighting all the red candles for the mother:

We call upon the Red Queen, the Sovereign Mother, to bring the blessings and protection of Motherhood upon this woman. Blessed be her womb. Blessed be her child. Blessed be the birth.

Anoint the mother with the oil, providing additional blessings. If working in a group of women, all the women may take a turn to bless the mother-to-be and her unborn child. Traditional images would be waxing Moon crescents, full Moon circles, spirals, and stars.

Blessings can end with the Mother giving a blessing to her own unborn child, spending time in alpha welcoming the child, and sharing the love of the circle with the child, so the child knows s/he is welcome in the world and will be cherished.

Allow the candles to continue to burn. If they are not burned away by the end of the celebration, the mother-to-be should take them home and continue to burn them to release their blessings.

- The Goddess and God are thanked and released.

- The quarters are released.

- The circle is released.

- Celebrate with the group.

CHILD BLESSING: WICCANING

A child blessing is the act of welcoming a child into the community and offering the blessings and protections of the community upon the child. The child is also blessed with the potential of spiritual foster "parents" or those charged to aid the child in their spiritual journey, whatever that may be.

In preparation for the welcoming and blessing of a child, the parents must first have an astrological natal chart of the child completed. The child's astrological sign will determine the composition of the unique anointing oil crafted for the rite. Also from the chart we will see what elements the child may lack in, so that we can add our blessings to them by incorporating them into spiritual gifts of the ritual. We see the Child Blessing ritual akin to the myth of Sleeping Beauty. If the gathered Witches left out a particular area to bless the child, it was often what the child turned out to not be good at doing.

In preparation, the child should be bathed and dressed only in a diaper, swaddled in a black wrap, so that he/she may be able to be anointed. The parents may choose God/dess parents who will guide the child through the spiritual journey, just as they do in many other traditions.

Items Needed:
Child's Unique Anointing Oil
Gifts and Tools for the Child

• Circle is ritually cleansed, possibly with a broom.

• Cast the traditional full majick circle with the four quarters.

• Light the Goddess and God candles. Call upon the Goddess and God as the Divine Parents.

We call upon the Goddess, the Great Mother, the First Mother, to bring her blessings to this rite.
We call upon the God, the Great Father, the First Father, to bring his blessings to this rite.
So Mote it Be!

• Perform the Sacrament of Tara and Avalon and a libation to the Ancient Ones.

• The child is welcomed and acknowledged by all present.

• Spiritual Gift Giving:

The parents pass the child to each person in the circle. As the child is passed, each person places a hand on the child's forehead and the bottom of his/her feet, and bestows the child a spiritual gift. This gift is something that the persons themselves have, such as a beautiful voice, sense of humor, love of animals, or other less tangible blessings.

• Chakra Blessing:

After the gifts of spirit have been presented, the child is taken back to the officiants where he or she is anointed with their astrological oil on the seven chakras.

I anoint and bless your root chakra.
Blessed be your feet as you are your own person.

I anoint and bless your spleen chakra.
Blessed be where you feel your creative forces in all aspects of your being.

I anoint and bless your solar plexus chakra.
Blessed be where you hold your personal power and manifest your goals.

I anoint and bless your heart chakra.
Blessed be where you express love.

I anoint and bless your throat chakra.
Blessed be where you speak and listen.

I anoint and bless your third eye chakra.
Blessed be where you channel your intuition and see.

I anoint and bless your crown chakra.
Blessed be where you understand and create wisdom.

• The tools and gifts that were placed on the altar are blessed and presented to the child.

• All of the candles are extinguished.

• The Goddess and God are thanked for their blessing and guidance, and then released.

• The quarters are released.

• The circle is released.

• The circle is open and the celebration and opening of other gifts commences.

COMING OF AGE: PRINCESS/PRINCE RITE

The Coming of Age ritual recognizes young men and women coming into their sovereignty as their own princesses and princes. The astrological chart should have been done at the Child Blessing, but if not, make sure you have the chart done and with you for the ritual.

This ritual is usually done at age thirteen. Thirteen is a power number for a Witch, and represents an age of transition. Biologically, for girls, the coming of age is usually near their first menstrual period, which can be from the ages of 12-15. It marks a time of coming into womanhood. For boys, the transition is more subtle, and can be done anywhere from age 13-21.

At this time, the first set of full majickal tools is given to the newly crowned Princess or Prince. Family and friends will save and pass on their own tools, make new ones, or buy new ones for the celebration. These will be passed on in the ritual.

Place any other gifts for the child under the altar, so they will be charged by the circle's majick.

Items Needed:
Drum
Bell
Chalice
Wand
Athame
Sword
Scissors
Red Ribbon
Prince/Princess' Silver Crown
Pre-Written Scroll tied with Black Cord
Rose Quartz and Amethyst for Prince/Princess' Hands
Blue Feather
Majick Bag
Astrological Oil from Child Blessing unique to the Prince/Princess
Astrological Blend of Herbs for the Prince/Princess
New Pentacle for the Prince/Princess
First Set of Majick Tools for the Prince/Princess — Cup, Wand, Stones, Peyton, Athame (Not Sharp)
Candles in the Colors Red, Black, White, Pink, Purple
Altar with Flowers, Clear Quartz, Wand, Chalice, Athame, Incense Thurible, Protection Potion

The officiant should write a blessing for the Prince/Princess upon parchment.

• Use the drum and bell to call forth the Witches to circle.

• Cast the circle with an Excalibur sword, with the Prince/Princess standing inside the circle in front of the altar with parents.

• Quarters are called with flowers in the hands of the four Witches calling the quarters who then turn and place the flowers on the altar.

• All participants are anointed with protection potion.

• Officiant anoints the Prince/Princess with protection potion and says:

I anoint your head to bring knowledge and wisdom.
I anoint your neck to hold you upright with courage.
I anoint your right wrist to give you power of majick.
I anoint your left wrist to give you insight and psychic power.

• The officiant performs the sacrament of Tara and Avalon and libation to the Ancient Ones.

• The officiant lights all the candles upon the altar and says:

I place this crown upon your head to show you your own sovereignty.

• The coefficient places stones, rose quartz and amethyst, in the hands of Prince/Princess.

• Red ribbon is tied around mother and child. The officiant then cuts the ribbon saying,

You are now on your journey to adulthood. You are sovereign and shall make your own majick.
You shall call to the Ancient Ones for guidance.

The newly crowned Prince/Princess steps towards the altar while the parents step backwards.

• The scroll blessing is read by the officiant or another community member. Then the parchment is rolled back up and tied with a black cord. The scroll with black cord is placed upon the altar. Officiant says:

Blessings to your maidenhood/manhood.

• A blue feather is placed on the altar. Officiant says:

The bluebirds of Rhiannon shall bring you happiness.

• The two stones are taken from the Prince/Princess and placed in a majick bag. The herbal blend is placed into the majick bag. The scroll is placed into the majick bag.

The officiant touches the Prince/Princess with a special oil crafted for their own particular astrological chart and claims:

You are now a Prince/Princess of the Cabot Clan.

A few drops of oil are placed within the majick bag, and the bag is given as a talisman to the Prince/Princess. The first pentacle is placed around the neck of the Prince/Princess. Any majickal tools are gifted to the Prince/Princess.

• All of the candles are extinguished.

• The Goddess and God are thanked for their blessing and guidance, and released.

• The quarters are released.

• The circle is released.

• The circle is open and the celebration and opening of any other gifts commences.

MARRIAGE: HANDFASTING

In preparation for handfasting, the couple must first consult in advance with their High Priest and High Priestess. Handfasting is a very serious rite of passage and must be entered into according to the free will of each individual. The state laws governing marriage licenses must be completed, and the paperwork must be given to the officiant to fill out and send to the local city hall after the ceremony is performed. Be sure to have two witnesses on hand to sign the appropriate paperwork.

The couple will need a cord for each of them in their astrological colors. The cords should be nine feet each, and they should be braided by the couple before their ceremony and be ready to place on the altar the day of the handfasting. A broom for the couple should be made, to bring blessing to their home after the handfasting. Most other tools should be from the couple as well, starting with the wedding rings and personally crafted vows, decorative pillows for kneeling, and a handfasting chalice.

Items Needed:
Two 9 Foot Cords, one for each in their appropriate astrological colors
Prepared Personal Vows (On Parchment if Necessary)
Wedding Rings

Chalice
Two Pillows for Kneeling
Broom for the Couple to Keep in the Home
Flowers for Altar and Circle Space

The bride and her attendant wait outside the circle in the east. The groom stands in the inner circle at the altar.

• Cast the traditional full majick circle with the four quarters.

• Light the Goddess and God candles. Call upon the Goddess and God as the Divine Parents.

We call upon the Goddess, the Great Mother Danu, to bring her blessings to this rite..
We call upon the God, the Great Father, the Dagda, to bring his blessings to this rite.
So Mote it Be!

• Perform the Sacrament of Tara and Avalon and a libation to the Ancient Ones.

• Opening the Portal:

The Officiant goes to the eastern quarter and open a portal in the circle for the bride to enter asking,

Do you come according to your own free will?

If yes, she enters and follows the officiant back to the central altar to be with the groom. Her attendant follows her.

• Cleansing of the Circle:

The bride's attendant takes the broom and ritually sweeps the circle, symbolizing a new beginning.

• Vows:

The officiant anoints the couple and then asks them each to kneel upon the pillow. The couple exchanges their vows to each other.

• Handfasting:

The braided cords are taken by the officiant from the altar and wrapped loosely around the wrists of the couple with a blessing. The rings are placed in the chalice of spring water, and the chalice is placed gently between their hands. Each takes a sip of water. The officiant takes the chalice back and places it upon the altar, and then gently unwinds the cords around their hands, keeping a loose knot, like an infinity loop, in place. Officiant places the cord over the couple's heads with the loose knot and says:

You are now bound in infinity, So Mote it Be!

Officiant then ties the knot in the cord over their heads and places the entire cord back upon the altar.

• Ring Exchange:

The couple is then handed the chalice once again. They each remove their spouse's ring from the chalice and place the ring on each other's finger. They are then acknowledged as handfasted. They rise and kiss. Each guest in the circle may wish a blessing upon them.

• The Goddess and God are thanked for their blessing and guidance, and released.

• The quarters are released.

• The couple jumps over the broom to symbolize jumping into their new life together.

• The circle is then opened.

• Time to celebrate!

HOME CLEARING: CABOT HOUSE BLESSING

by Memie Cabot Watson, Rev. H.P.S

A house blessing is an ancient tradition that is practiced by most if not all religions. Each religion has their method of blessing a home. At times you will also hear it called a house cleansing or house clearing. Blessing the home is usually done inside the house by using the elements of earth, air, fire, water, and spirit, and then calling upon the Ancient Ones for their guidance.

A house blessing is done to create sacred space in new home or to rid your current home of incorrect energies that were left behind by other occupants who inhabited the house prior to your moving in, such as angry tenants, a death in the home, divorce, or domestic violence.

Some Witches, prior to moving, start preparing their sacred space by grounding themselves, meditating, and asking guidance from the Ancient Ones.

Prior to moving in, we would use a besom to cleanse the space, sweeping out the old of unwanted and incorrect energies and in with the new, protection, love, happiness, and peace. With each passing of the besom/witches broom, we not only visualize our space being cleansed, we also state the words:

I sweep any and all unwanted harmful and incorrect energies from this space, and as I sweep, let no harm enter to do us any harm. So Be It!

And this is done in every room of the house. Once this is done, you can cast a majick circle. For the blessings I would cast a majick circle around the house visualizing the white light of protection around each room, the whole house, and the property, creating a protective shield.

Next we would anoint ourselves with protection potion, and smudge with frankincense and myrrh. Frankincense and myrrh is one of the strongest incense combinations that helps cleanse, clear, heal, purify, and protect you and your sacred space. You can also use a lavender spritz if desired, made with essential oils and distilled water in a spray bottle. It creates peace and calmness in the household and helps those sensitive to smoke.

Do this with each element of the quarters (earth, air, fire, water and spirit), going from room to room, and corner to corner, as energies tend to collect in the corners.

When calling upon the earth element, we use a peyton and visualize the pentacle as an extension being drawn on each wall of the home. The peyton is usually made from clay, wood or metal, so it is the ideal tool of earth and protection. It represents all the elements and is used for protection.

For fire, take a candle or a small bowl of lit twigs, and likewise move from room to room and corner to corner, blessing and protecting the home. It will bring energy and power.

For air, take incense for new beginnings, communication, inspiration, and creativity. We use a special house blessing incense blend.

House Blessing Incense

1 Tablespoon of Pink Rose Petals
1 Tablespoon of Frankincense
1 Tablespoon of Myrrh
1 Teaspoon of Sunflower Petals
3 Drops of Money Oil
3 Drops of Protection Oil
3 Drops of Love Oil

For water, use a bowl of water or salt water for understanding, transformation, and healing.

You could also place quartz crystals in each corner of every room prior to starting or during the cleansing. I leave the crystals in the room for seven days. Seven is a number that helps you confront obstacles with strength and transformation, while the quartz serves as a powerful healing, energizer, and amplifier.

You could, if you wanted to, make a whole ritual out of the house blessing and even have the family members help you with the cleansing of their house, particularly if you were doing the blessing/cleansing for someone else. We do this while using the qualities of the elements; in doing so you could state your intentions from room to room with words as simple as:

From the North, South, East, and West. This sacred space is now consecrated and blessed.

After the cleansing is done, we release the circle and thank the Ancient Ones for their guidance. Pour the water back to the Earth as an offering to the Goddess.

You can also do any of the following if you desire as a part of your house blessings:

Hang Herbs of Protection — Rosemary, Thyme, Lavender

Hang Horseshoe Amulet — Upward pointing creates protection and brings luck

Witch's Bottle — Charms for Protection in front and back doors, buried in dirt.

Give any remaining incense to the occupants of the home after you leave, so they can continue the majick.

ANIMAL BLESSING

by Memie Cabot Watson Rev. H.P.S

Pet blessings are celebrations of our furry friends who are our companions on the planet physically and spiritually. As our companions in life, we bless them with our majick to make sure they have a good home, food, water, and toys, as well as health and well-being. Blessing work can be simply to ensure blessings of our beloved friends, or to bring greater healing in times of need.

Animal blessings are usually done near Ostara and Mabon. Bridget is called upon as the Goddess of spring and new beginnings, but you can also call upon the little known Celtic goddess Flidais, as she is the goddess of wildlife and nature. Other deities might have specific totemic associations. Bridget has been associated with lambs and foxes. Epona and Macha are linked with horses, and Rhiannon with birds. Call upon whatever deities seem appropriate to you.

The ritual can be done inside or outside, depending on the animals being blessed. Logistically they should be on a leash, or in a carrier or birdcage if gathered together in a group, to prevent fighting and injury. They can be done inside of a majick circle when feasible, but it's not required.

Items Needed:
Candle
Matches

Light a candle in the pet's name with the words:

May you bring compassion, peace, and love to your home.
May you bring strength to your family in times of need.

Say to the owner:

May (name animal) brighten your day when you are feeling down.
May (name animal) bring you joy, happiness, and warmth.

Say to the animal:

May you have peace, love, and healing wherever you may roam.
You are now blessed and blessed be.

Depending on the amount of animals attending, you can adapt this to a larger group of animals except for the names of family members.

ELDERHOOD

Elderhood is the rite to recognize a level of wisdom and experience in life. Elderhood can mean two very different things. One means the chronological age a person has reached, in terms of a rite of passage ritual. We honor those who have reached a level of experience by the virtue of being alive. Their number of years in the Craft, as a practicing Witch, does not matter.

The second type of elderhood recognizes the wisdom and maturity of someone in majick and Witchcraft, being an elder of a specific tradition. Different traditions have different time periods used to mark traditional elderhood, and some base it upon merit. A dedicated practitioner of ten years taking leadership roles and responsibilities in the community is more of an elder than a lazy practitioner of twenty years.

The following rites are more in alignment with chronological elderhood, recognizing the rite of passage of entering into our elder years.

CRONING

The croning ritual is best done on the new Moon. Some will perform croning rites only with other women in attendance, while others do it with mixed genders, depending on the request of the one undergoing the croning.

Items Needed:
Full Altar
Athame
Bell
Besom
Peyton
Chalice
Cauldron

Protection Potion

Wisdom Oil

Candle in the colors white, red, silver, purple and two black

Sea Salt in Bowl

Four Stones

Three Black Feathers

Black Cord for Measure

• Circle is ritually cleansed, possibly with a broom counterclockwise, to remove past obstacles and clear the space.

• Anoint everyone present with protection potion.

• Drum and ring the bell to call forth the crone to enter the circle space. The crone must enter the ritual space full prepared for this rite.

• Cast the traditional full majick circle with a wand or sword.

• Quarter Calling and Blessings:

Four Witches call to the four quarters in a traditional way, but each one holds one of the four stones while doing so.

The crone in the center of the circle takes all three black feathers from the altar, to present them to each of the four quarters, moving clockwise and starting in the north, asking for guidance, knowledge, and strength to carry onward. Each of the four blesses her in turn.

• Call to the Gods:

Officiant lights the Triple Goddess candles of white for the maiden, red for the mother, and black for the crone.

Officiant or another member of the ritual reads the *Cabot Call of the Goddess* and then the *Cabot Call of the God.*

Crone anoints the candles of purple, silver, and black with the Wisdom Oil and says:

Dark Goddess the black swan,
Bright Goddess of light
Singing Goddess of power
These candles call your spirit to this sacred space and honor you.

Wisdom Oil

2 Drams of Hazel Nut Oil
7 Drops of Myrrh Essential Oil
4 Drops of Lavender Essential Oil
1 Drop of Sage Essential Oil
Pinch of Blessed Thistle
Pinch of Solomon's Seal
Pinch of Comfrey Root
Chip of Raw Emerald or Quartz

• Perform the Sacrament of Tara and Avalon and a libation to the Ancient Ones. The crone receives the three drops.

• Cast the Spell of the Crone:

Call forth the crone with drums and bells and the crone says:

Crone, I call upon the ancient and old, my ancestors, I draw you near to share the twilight of life...

Sea Salt is sprinkled into the cauldron like the sands of life.

Then the new crone must recite the Spell of the Crone:

Spell of the Crone
by Rev. Mimi Millet, HPs

The circle was cast with the wisdom of three,
The maiden, the mother, the crone live in me.
By the fire I sit with the crone all alone,

Reflecting my past, and my future unknown.
A circle of stones has been gathered with love,
I dance in your powers so below and above.
The Sun has been shining upon me all morn'
My measure has increased, my wisdom reborn.
My arms are wide open — my teacher, my friend,
Come share in my dreams and hopes till the end.
Three feathers I've gathered to offer to you,
Three sips of devotion, compassion be true.
Although we just met, I know in my heart,
We're always together and never apart.
So Mote it Be!

The officiants take the measure of the crone and say,

Your measure has been taken. Measure and your life shall be measured by your deed. Your measure is a gift to the Cabot Tradition; we are honored; we shall place your measure with the Cabot Archives so it shall ever be.

• All of the candles are extinguished.

• The Goddess and God are thanked for their blessing and guidance, and released.

• The quarters are released.

• The circle is released.

• The circle is open and the celebration and opening of gifts commences.

• Celebrate. Feast. Give any gifts you have to celebrate the new crone!

WIZARDING

Unlike the Croning Ritual, the Wizarding Ritual does not have a specific time it should be done. Often it is done at public sabbat ceremonies, except Beltane and Samahain, or it can be done at any other time and location, as desired by the new wizard. While traditionally croning occurs at the end of menstruation, for the wizard, a minimum of fifty years is required.

Traditionally this ritual is performed by a group of six to thirteen men from the community, including Witches and non-Witches, with one of these men being the personal choice from the man receiving the wizarding of the ceremony. The ritual only has one woman in the circle, so if there is a High Priestess conducting the ritual, she is the one woman for the ceremony. The rest must be men for the men's mysteries.

Items Needed:
Crown — Purchased or Hand-Made
Blindfold
Stone for the Stone of Destiny
Gold Candle
Standard Altar

• Officiant calls all to gather to the circle, while the future wizard is blindfolded and brought to the north in silence by his specially chosen attendant.

• Officiant speaks about the role of the wizard in the community and the tradition of crowning an elder.

• Cast the traditional full majick circle with the sword. Future wizard is led by his attendant to the front (north) of the altar, next to the Stone of Destiny and across from the officiant. The blindfold is removed.

• The four quarters are called, with animal totems or elemental dragons.

• Call to the Goddess and God:

Light the Goddess and God candles. Call upon the Goddess and God.

I charge this candle with the light of Danu. I strike this candle with the gift of flame and continued life.

I charge this candle with the light of the Dagda. I strike this candle with the recognition of (name)'s wisdom and years as a witch.

• Light and Inspiration of the Wizard:

Gold Candle is anointed and lit by the officiant

This candle represents the crowning of the wizard, the wise one.

• Perform the Sacrament of Tara and Avalon and a libation to the Ancient Ones.

Officiant draws down the athame into the chalice. After taking of the chalice water, the officiant passes it to the wise one in front of the altar. He takes of the water, and the chalice is passed back to the officiant to be placed back upon the altar.

• Recite the Cabot Call of the God.

• Crowning of the Wizard:

Officiant asks the wise one to kneel upon the Stone of Destiny. The officiant takes the crown from the altar and holds it over the wise one's head and says:

I now crown you for your 50 years of wisdom (and dedication to the Cabot Tradition, if applicable).

As a Wise One, I place this crown upon your head.

Places crown on his head.

We ignite you mind, body, and spirit with the power of the Ancient Ones, our ancestors to continue your life as a Wise One!

You may rise.

All clap.

• Wisdom Offering:

Officiant asks all the participants, starting in the north and moving clockwise, to share their wisdom and guidance for the newly crowned wizard to aid him on his inner journey into elderhood. Gifts for the wizard can also be presented at this time.

• All of the candles are extinguished.

• The Goddess and God are thanked for their blessing and guidance, and released.

• The quarters are released.

• The circle is released.

• Celebrate with the new wizard.

LAST RITES: CROSSING OVER

Giving last rites, which differ from a funeral ritual, is the act of helping one cross over when their time is near. It focuses upon the one who is actively dying more so than the family, friends, and community. Usually the ritual involves a consecration, easing the transition, and is often performed these days in hospital or hospice.

Unlike a formal ritual, it happens mostly in vision, while in an alpha state. It is a call to the spirits and gods and an opening of the way. This is usually done for those who are Witches or Pagan, and not for those of different faith traditions who have their own rites and rituals, with imagery more appropriate to those beliefs.

If possible, hold the hand of the person who is preparing to pass. Speak quietly but reassuringly, even if they are unable to respond. If possible, you can anoint them with a simple consecration oil. A blend of frankincense and myrrh is excellent, though do not use a protection potion with iron in it, as iron helps ground people back into their body. Though complex, this is an excellent formula for aiding transition:

Last Rites Oil

1 Dram of Base Oil

7 Drops of Frankincense Essential Oil

5 Drops of Myrrh Essential Oil

3 Drops of Benzoin Essential Oil

2 Drops of Vetiver Essential Oil

1 Drop of Rose Oil

1 Pinch of Marshmallow Root

1 Pinch of Solomon Seal

3 Apple Seeds

Quartz or Rose Quartz Crystal Chip

When consecrating the body, start at the feet and move upward, working through the energies of the seven chakras, encouraging a clear passage for the awareness to leave via the brow or ideally the crown, rather than the lower chakras. The oil helps open the way and provide a sense of spiritual support and comfort.

Get into an alpha state, and bring your awareness to the west. Imagine a gate opening, if not already open, and the loving presence of the spirits and beloved dead coming to attend the one who is crossing. Usually you don't even have to do this, as it's already occurring naturally. Telepathically speak to the one who is crossing, acknowledging that if they are ready, they are free to go. Many simply need permission to go, as they are holding on unconsciously for the sake of their loved ones. Ask the spirits who have gathered if there is anything further you could or should be doing to aid the process for the highest good, harming none, and follow their guidance and advice.

Stay as long as you feel necessary. Some need another person there to pass in peace. Others need to be alone to finally pass. Do as your guidance and intuition lead you.

CABOT KENT HERMETIC TEMPLE LAW MEMORANDUM: WITCHCRAFT AS A RELIGION IN THE UNITED STATES

Statement of Facts

Witchcraft in the United States is a living, growing religion. As a religion, Witchcraft is protected by the Constitution. The Law has the obligation to serve and protect Witches in their religious endeavors, equally as much as it protects the rights and freedoms of other groups.

In the United States today, Witches are entitled to the same rights and protections as other groups under the First and Fourteenth Amendment.

Issue I: Is Witchcraft recognized as a legitimate religion in the United States?

Issue II: Does the practice of Witchcraft fall within the parameters of the First Amendment's protection clause?

Issue III: Are Witches entitled to rights under the equal protection clause of the Fourteenth Amendment?

Issues IV: Are Witches entitled to the same rights and protection under State Laws, applicable to where they live, as they are under Federal Law?

Issue I:

Witchcraft is recognized in the United States as a legitimate religion. In 1985, Dettmer v. Landon (617 F. Supp. 529) the District Court of Virginia pursuant to rule 52 (a) of the Federal Rules of Civil Procedure, ruled that Witchcraft is a legitimate religion and falls within a recognizable religious category. In 1986, in the Federal Appeals court, fourth circuit, Butzner, J. affirmed the decision (592 F. 2d 934). Since in most cases Federal Law, even case law, supersedes state law in this type of matter, the affirmation by Judge Butzner clearly sets Witchcraft as a religion under the protection of constitutional rights: "The Church of Wicca (or Witchcraft) is clearly a religion for First Amendment purposes. Members of the Church sincerely adhere to a fairly complex set of doctrines relating to the spiritual aspect of their lives, and in doing so they have 'ultimate concerns' in much the same way as followers of more accepted religions. Their ceremonies and leadership structure, their rather elaborate set of articulated doctrine, their belief in the concept of another world, and their broad concern for improving the quality of life for others gives them at least some facial similarity to other more widely recognized religions.

"While there are certainly aspects of Wiccan philosophy that may strike most people as strange or incomprehensible, the mere fact that a belief may be unusual does not strip it of Constitutional protection. Accordingly the Court concludes that the Church of Wicca, of which the plaintiff is a sincere follower, is a religion for the purpose of the free exercise clause." Williams, J 1985 Dettmer v Landon Supra: "We agree with the district court that the doctrine taught by the Church of Wicca is a religion." Butzner, J. 1986 4th Curcuit. Dettmer v Landon Supra.

Issue II:

The first amendment of the United States Constitution guarantees the right to freedom of religious belief. The USCA states that a practice is a religion if it is for an individual a belief system for their whole life. The Constitution does not wish to dictate what an individual should hold as a belief system or how it is practiced and will not enter into a ruling on that. "Courts may not inquire into worthiness of parties' religious belief to ascertain whether they merit First Amendment protection, but need only consider whether beliefs are 'religious' in parties' own scheme of things and whether their beliefs are sincere. USCA Const. Amend. (Kaplan v Hess 694 F. 2d. 842/224 U.S. app. D.C 281)" "To be a bona fide religious belief entitled to protection under either the First Amendment or Title VII, a belief must be sincerely held" and within the believers own scheme of things religious. USCA Const. Amend. 1: Civil Rights Act 1964 §§ 701 et seq., 717 as amended 42 USCA § 2000e-16"

Issue III:

The equal protection clause is guaranteed to all people and groups. If one group of people is entitled to equal protection, then all groups are. Witchcraft is accepted as a religion; therefore, Witches are entitled to the same protections as all other religious groups under the equal protection clause of the Fourteenth Amendment. "First and Fourteenth Amendments insure without qualifications that a state may not forbid the holding of any religious belief or opinion, nor may it force anyone to embrace any religious belief or to say or believe anything in conflict with its religious tenets. USCA Const. Amend. 1, 14, Africa v. Anderson 542 F. Suppl 224." (16 FPD 12-16)

Issue IV:

USCA ARTICLE VII § 2 states:

"This Constitution, and the Laws of the United States which shall be made in pursuance thereof; and all treaties made or which shall be made, under the authority of the United States, shall be The Supreme Law of the Land; and the judges in every state shall be bound thereby, anything in the Constitution or laws of any state to the contrary notwithstanding."

In light of the fact that Dettmer v. Landon supra, being a Federal l Adjudicated case, it is thereby protected by the Constitution. No state can override this Federal adjudication. No Witch can be denied his/her civil liberty and right to be a Witch, open and free, in any state in the land, within the parameters of the Law.

COMMONWEALTH OF MASSACHUSETTS LAW

This is an example of how state law supports and protects the rights guaranteed to individuals by the United States Constitution and Federal Law. **

Ch. 265 §37. Interfering with Any Right or Privilege Secured by Constitution or Laws of the Commonwealth.

No person, whether or not acting under color of law, shall by force or threat of force, willfully injure, intimidate or interfere with, or attempt to injure, intimidate or interfere with, or oppress or threaten any other person in the free exercise or enjoyment of any right or privilege secured to him by the constitution or laws of the commonwealth or by the constitution or laws of the United States. Any person convicted or violating this provision shall be fine not more than one thousand dollars or imprisoned not more than one year or both; and if bodily injury results, shall be punished by a fine of not more than ten thousand dollars or by imprisonment for not more than ten years, or both. (Added by L. 1979, chap. 801 (2), eff. 2/14/80.)

CH. 265 §39. Intimidation

Whoever commits an assault or a battery upon a person or damages the real or personal property of another for the purpose of intimidation because of said person's race, color, religion, or national origin, shall be punished by a fine of not more than five thousand dollars or not more than three times the value of the property destroyed or damaged, whichever is greater, or by imprisonment in a house of correction for not more than two and one-half years, or both. (Added by L. 1983, chap. 165 (I), eff. 9/8/83.)

Ch 266 *§127A. Injury to Religious, Educational, etc., Institutions

Any person who willfully, intentionally and without right, or wantonly and without cause, destroys, defaces, mars, or injures a church, synagogue or other building, structure or place used for the purpose of burial or memorializing the dead, or a school, educational facility or community center or the groups of adjacent to and owned or leased by any of the foregoing or any personal property contained in any of the foregoing shall be punished by a fine of not more than two thousand dollars or not more than three times the value of the property so destroyed, defaced, marred or injured, whichever is great or by imprisonment in a house of correction for not more than two and one-half years, or both; provided, however, that if the damage or loss of such property exceeds five thousand dollars, such person shall be punished by a fine of not more than three times the value of the property so destroyed, defaced, marred or injured or by imprisonment in a state prison for not more than five years, or both.

*(added by L. 1983, chap. 165 (2), eff. 9/8/83)

** Information provided for the CKHT by Captain Paul Murphy, Salem Police Department, Salem Massachusetts.

Conclusion:

Witchcraft is a legally recognized religion in the United States and Witches are entitled to every right and protection for freedom of religion, including freedom from harassment and prejudice as every other recognized religion in the United States.

The United States Constitution, under the First and Fourteenth Amendments, supports the right of all people in the United States to practice their own belief system and to enjoy this in each their own manner.

Lawyers and Law Enforcement Agencies have the obligation to protection the right of all people in their religious endeavors, no matter what they may be, without bias or prejudice. Witches desire only to retain their right of religious privacy and to practice their Craft as they see fit within the parameters of the law.

The Cabot Kent Hermetic Temple would like to thank Patricia A Barki, Legal Intern, Legal Department of the Cabot Kent Hermetic Temple for her research and authorship of this Law Memorandum. Text © 2007 by CKHT All Rights Reserved. This law memorandum or part thereof may not be reproduced in any form whatsoever without permission in writing from the publisher. Reprinted here with permission from the Cabot-Kent Hermetic Temple.

RECOMMENDED READING LIST FOR CLERGY

Teaching
Spiritual Mentoring by Judy Harrow

A Teaching Handbook for Wiccans and Pagans by Thea Sabin

Groups
Coven Craft by Amber K

Truth or Dare: Encounters with Power, Authority, and Mystery by Starhawk

The Empowerment Manual: A Guide for Collaborative Groups by Starhawk

Extreme Facilitation: Guiding Groups Through Controversy and Complexity by Suzanne Ghais

Wicca Covens: How to Start and Organize Your Own by Judy Harrow

Ritual
Creating Circles and Ceremonies by Oberon Zell-Ravenheart and Morning Glory Zell-Ravenheart

Neopagan Rites: A Guide to Creating Public Rituals that Work by Isaac Bonewits

Women's Rites, Women's Mysteries: Intuitive Ritual Creation by Ruth Barrett

Handfasting and Wedding Rituals by Raven Kaldera and Tannin Schwartzstein

Ministering
The Living Temple of Witchcraft: Vol. I and Vol. II by Christopher Penczak

The Priesthood: Parameters and Responsibilities by Nema

A Handbook for Wiccan Clergy by Kevin Gardner

The Wiccan Minister's Manual, A Guide for Priests and Priestesses by Kevin Gardner

The Pagan Clergy's Guide for Counseling, Crisis Intervention and Otherworld Transitions by Kevin Gardner

Circle Round: Raising Children in Goddess Traditions by Starhawk

The Pagan Book of Living and Dying by Starhawk

Legal
Pagans and the Law by Dana D. Ellers

Pagan Religions: A Handbook for Diversity Training by Kerr Cuhulain

Spiritual, Biographical, and Inspirational

Crones Don't Whine: Concentrated Wisdom for Juicy Women by Jean Shinoda Bolen

Devoted To You: Honoring Deity in Wiccan Practice by Judy Harrow

How To Be Glorious: Day By Day Empowerment by Kerr Cuhulain

Modern Knighthood by Kerr Cuhulain

Diary of a Witch by Sybil Leek

Witchfather: Vols. I and II by Philip Heselton

Fire Child: The Life and Magic of Maxine Sanders 'Witch Queen' by Maxine Sanders

King of the Witches: The World of Alex Sanders by June Johns

High Priestess: The Life and Times of Patricia Crowther by Patricia Crowther

Ameth: The Life and Times of Doreen Valiente by Jonathan Tapsell

The Wizard and the Witch by John C. Sulak

Bull of Heaven by Michael Lloyd

INITIATION

As they rode together Arthur said, 'I have no sword,' but Merlin bade him be patient and he would soon give him one. In a little while they came to a large lake, and in the midst of the lake Arthur beheld an arm rising out of the water, holding up a sword. 'Look!' said Merlin, 'that is the sword I spoke of.' And the King looked again, and a maiden stood upon the water. 'That is the Lady of the Lake,' said Merlin, 'and she is coming to you, and if you ask her courteously she will give you the sword.' So when the maiden drew near, Arthur saluted her and said, 'Maiden, I pray you tell me whose sword is that which an arm is holding out of the water? I wish it were mine, for I have lost my sword.'

'That sword is mine, King Arthur,' answered she, 'and I will give it to you, if you in return will give me a gift when I ask you.'

'By my faith,' said the King, 'I will give you whatever gift you ask.' 'Well,' said the maiden, 'get into the barge yonder, and row yourself to the sword, and take it and the scabbard with you.' For this was the sword Excalibur. 'As for my gift, I will ask it in my own time.' Then King Arthur and Merlin dismounted from their horses and tied them up safely and went into the barge, and when they came to the place where the arm was holding the sword Arthur took it by the handle, and the arm disappeared. And they brought the sword back to land. As they rode the King looked lovingly on his sword, which Merlin saw, and smiling, said, 'Which do you like best, the sword or the scabbard'? 'I like the sword,' answered Arthur. 'You are not wise to say that,' replied Merlin, 'for the scabbard is worth ten of the sword, and as long as it is buckled on you you will lose no blood, however sorely you may be wounded.' So they rode into the town of Carlion, and Arthur's Knights gave them a glad welcome, and said it was a joy to serve under a King who risked his life as much as any common man.

— The Sword Excalibur from *King Arthur: Tales of the Round Table*

Requirements for Witchcraft III Initiation:

• Must complete Witchcraft III As a Religion Class, including passing in and have all homework graded acceptable
• Must complete the additional Ministerial Course on the Role and Responsibility of Clergy
• Must complete Wheel of the Year work within the Temple

- Have a letter of recommendation by an Initiate in the Tradition
- Pass Initiation Interview with Elder
- Must Petition for Initiation and be accepted

Reflect upon the power and meaning of initiation. Look at the paths that have brought you to this place. Reflect up on the self-healing of Witchcraft I. It required self-healing and the development of psychic and meditative abilities in alpha. What did you learn? How did you change?

Reflect upon your majickal experiences in Witchcraft II. It required taking responsibilities for your needs and manifesting what you desire to care for yourself and satisfying your wants. You learned to perform ceremony and become your own priestess or priest. What did you learn? How did you change?

Reflect upon the long journey of the Third Degree, and the call to ministry as a High Priestess or High Priest. Think about the healing that occurs with the deep mysteries. Look to our myths of Taliesin, the tales of the lost child like Mabon, and the quest for the Holy Grail. Reflect upon the cycle of the Wheel of the Year. Reflect upon your training to better minister to others. What did you learn? How did you change?

Are you ready?

THIRD DEGREE RITUAL TOOLS

The following tools are used in Third Degree initiation ritual:

Excalibur Sword

All initiates must have an Excalibur sword for their initiation. The sword is the crucial symbol of the initiated priest and tool of a sovereign leader in the Cabot Tradition. Excalibur was a gift from the Lady of the Lake to King Arthur, as a token of the union of the human and Otherworld's partnership. It is the sword of light and truth. The Witches of Kent have kept the Light of Excalibur in our blades, and now the Cabot Witches bring that light out into the open, into the public, with full traditional Excalibur swords. During the ritual of initiation, the light of your initiator's Excalibur is passed to your own sword, and you use the sword to dedicate your power to the work of the Earth and the Goddess.

Traditionally one keeps a little thyme in the sword case for additional blessings.

Witch's Cord

A sign of the Third Degree Witch in the Cabot tradition is the Witch's Cord. Unlike other traditions where it is used as a belt, we place the cord around our neck. The cord is between four and a half and nine feet, and a triple braid of white, red, and black, which many Witches individually decorate by hanging small items from it, while others keep it plain. The three colors are for the Triple Goddess as the white maiden, the red queen mother, and the black crone. It is placed around our neck in ritual reminding us about the sacred space we are all in, and functionally can be used to mark out the space of a sacred circle.

High Priest/ess Robe

While the robe for the second degree is all black, with a sash and possibly a Cabot Kent Hermetic Temple patch on the left side, the Third Degree robe will have red lining in the sleeve and Royal Stewart piping. Upon graduation you receive your Third Degree patch, signifying completion of the Third Degree, and later an initiation patch, to signify successful petition for initiation.

Cabot Kent Hermetic Temple Patch

The triangle of wisdom is colored yellow for wisdom and communication, green for nature and the faerie realm, and blue for peace and prosperity, with the red triquetra in the center, a symbol of clergy (see below) for us. The triangle is adorned with a yellow ankh, a symbol of everlasting life and the Egyptian mysteries, linking our work with those of ancient Egypt. One who takes initiation in the Third Degree is to be active in the Cabot Kent Hermetic Temple, and if a person does not already have the patch, they should obtain it through their support of the Temple and place it upon the left shoulder/arm of the robe.

Third Degree Patch

The patch for the completion of the Third Degree is a four-fold Celtic Knot with a red pentagram entwined within it. It represents a greater mastery with the four elements through the powers of the Witch and the intelligence of the Divine Mind. It is placed on the lower right sleeve.

Initiation Patch

The initiation patch for those who successfully undergo initiation in the Cabot Tradition is the triple knot entwined with a circle, also known as the triquetra. The patch is a red symbol upon black and placed near the right shoulder. The triple knot forms three vesica pisces, the sacred geometry shape that is a seed for creation and representative of the great Goddess. The three points represent the maiden, mother and crone, as well as the three points necessary for initiation—the mysteries of Witchcraft III, the Wheel of the Year, and the clergy training. The circle is the power of the Divine Mind linking all and the circle of community an initiate vows to serve.

The Measure

The measure is one of the few things we have integrated from Gardnerian Wicca specifically, though we don't use it quite the same way. While a measured line with knots is made during initiation to safeguard vows of secrecy, so the measure can be a majickal devices used against an oath breaker, we use it as a sign of measuring the loyalty, integrity, and intention on a spiritual level, at the same time the physical measure it taken. It is to always remind the initiate they have put themselves before the gods and must not be found wanting. They must fulfill what they have set before them to do as High Priestesses and High Priests.

The Oath

The oath, or Cabot Tradition Initiation Vow, is not only recited in the ritual, but is a signed and dated vow with your initiator and sponsor-witness, saved with your measure in the Cabot-Kent Hermetic Temple archives.

I do vow before my Elders and the Lord and the Lady
that I shall Honor the Cabot Tradition of Religion
and take this for my Only Religion.
To dedicate my life to the majick and teachings
Of my Elder, Rev. Laurie Cabot
And our Ancestors, The Witches of Kent, England.
I am mindful that my measure has been taken.

Other symbols that have been used in the past with the Cabot Tradition include a majick ring of initiation, either a crown ring to embody sovereignty or a star ring symbolic of Arianrhod, as a Goddess of Initiation. Any Cabot who desires either of these rings is welcome to obtain them and use them ritually.

The Mark of Avalon Ritual Tattoos

It is traditional that many Cabot Witches choose to mark their initiation with ritual tattooing. We have created two marks for initiated High Priestesses and High Priests. Some choose to mark their face, while others tattoo other areas of their body. When someone tattoos their face, it is a complete dedication to their path of life. A tattoo is permanent. Although many priests and priestesses take it upon themselves to have the mark, it is not required in the Cabot Tradition; it is, however, highly respected. These marks are only for the Third Degree and should not be done by those who have not completed their initiation.

For the High Priestesses, we have the Mark of Avalon. The Mark of Avalon is to keep and honor our sacred ways. Upon the forehead of many Cabot priestesses is the symbol of the two moons with the three drops, a symbol of our Goddess.

High Priestess Mark of Avalon

The High Priests of the Cabot Tradition have a mark of the God and Goddess on their arm. It is the symbol of Taurus, with a pentagram within the circle, making a pentacle together. Above the horns are the three drops of Awen.

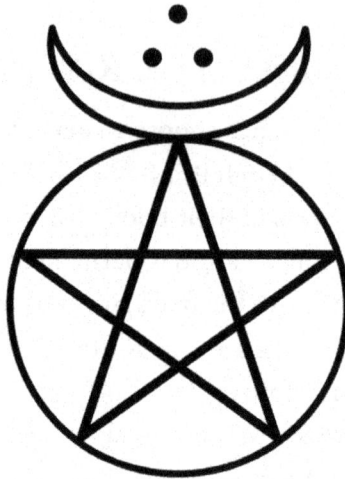

High Priest Mark of the God and Goddess

THIRD DEGREE INITIATION RITUAL

The potential initiate must have completed all work and be accepted for initiation, and have all materials necessary, including Excalibur sword, braided Witch's Cord, and soil from home or a sacred and special place.

Usually the ritual takes place with a full complement of Third Degree initiates to guard, guide, and witness the initiation rite. The initiation ritual is unique and inspired by the moment, the initiator and the initiates present. This is a simple guide for the necessary elements, but over the years, I've varied the words and actions through the inspiration of awen, to suit the majick of those who are present and what they need to be truly initiated Witches.

Items Needed:
Excalibur Sword
Soil from your Home or Sacred Place
Large Cauldron

Stone as the Stone of Destiny
Anointing Oil
Braided Cord
Measuring Cords and Scissors
Full Altar

• Preparation:

Space is prepared and the altar is set. Space is cleansed and cleared. Gifts for the initiate are placed under the altar to be charged, and gifts from the initiate to the initiator can also be set under the altar. Soul brought from the home or sacred place of all initiates is placed into the large cauldron.

Initiate is prepared, fully robed and corded and standing in the center before the altar with the initiator.

• Initiation Circle Casting — Circle of Swords or Kent Casting Method:

When done in a group setting, the circle is cast by the Light of Excalibur by a group of initiates. When in a smaller group where a circle of swords if not possible, if four initiates are available the Kent Casting Method can be used, or a traditional circle can be cast.

A variation of the Circle of Swords is to have all Third Degree initiates in a circle with their swords, facing outward. Swords are raised and initiates face outward from the circle. Circle is cast with the raising of the sword, with the hilt in the left hand and the point of the sword to the hilt of the Witch to their right side. The High Priest/ess says:

The circle is cast in the Light of Excalibur.

All swords are placed upon the ground, point to hilt, create a circle of swords, and the Witches turn spin clockwise to face the inside of the circle again.

The initiate places Excalibur in front, with the hilt to the left and the point to the right.

• The four quarters are called, with animal totems.

• Calling upon the Goddess and God. Light the black and white candles.

• Perform the Sacrament of Tara and Avalon and a libation to the Ancient Ones.

• Declaration of Initiation:

Initiator says:

You are here in this sacred space to title your journey in the Cabot Tradition of Witchcraft.
This initiation gives you the responsibility to carry on the Cabot Tradition.
From this day forward, you will be a leader of selflessness, of spirit, of compromise, and of
compassion.

• Anointing:

Initiator anoints the initiate with sacred oil, a mixture of frankincense and myrrh, upon the wrists, brow, and the back of the head.

• Passing the Light of Excalibur:

Initiator bids the initiate to kneel and be prepared.

Stand before me
Kneel on the Stone of Destiny
And raise your sword.

The initiator strikes the initiate's Excalibur sword on both sides with their own Excalibur sword. With the clanging of metal and the flashing of light upon the reflections of the sword, the blessed Light of Excalibur, guarded by the Witches of Kent, is passed from sword to sword.

• Initiation as a High Priest/ess:

The initiate lowers the sword and bows the head to the initiator, still kneeling upon the Stone of Destiny. The initiator performs the accolade, or dubbing, ceremony to confer "knighthood" as a keeper of the Light of Excalibur and a true High Priestess or High Priest. Initiator takes their own

Excalibur and touches the flat of the blade to the right shoulder, then slowly raises it up and over the head to the left shoulder, and then to the forehead of the initiate. The initiator says:

I now name you Witch!

• Returning your Power to the Earth:

The initiator says:

As many who have walked the path have done before you, place your sword into the cauldron of sacred earth and what say you?

The initiate plunges the sword into the cauldron of the earth and says:

I declare myself Witch.
I return my wisdom, power, and majick to the Earth,
To nurture,
To heal,
To bring the Goddess to the living Earth
And all upon it.

The initiator says:

You may rise.

And the initiate rises up again.

• Vow

Initiator recites the Cabot Tradition Initiation Vow, which is repeated line by line by the new initiate.

I do vow before my Elders and the Lord and the Lady
that I shall Honor the Cabot Tradition of Religion
and take this for my Only Religion.
To dedicate my life to the majick and teachings

Of my Elder, Rev. Laurie Cabot
And our Ancestors, The Witches of Kent, England.
I am mindful that my measure has been taken.
I am mindful that my measure shall be taken.

• Measure:

Priest/esses aiding the initiate stretch a length of cord from the crown to the bottom of the heel, cutting and knotting it, and then another from outstretched finger tip to outstretched finger tips, taking the measure and gathering the two threads up. The initiator says:

Remember your measure has been taken before and before the gods!

Initiate steps back into the circle of initiates, joining the ranks of the High Priestesses and High Priests of the Cabot Tradition

• All of the candles are extinguished.

• The Goddess and God are thanked for their presence and blessing.

• The quarters are released.

• The circle is undone.

*Every ending is the beginning
And for Witches this is law.
Where they enter in,
from there they must withdraw.*

About the Author

Laurie Cabot is a pioneer in the modern Witchcraft movement. As a teacher, author, and activist, she was one of the first to inform the public on who and what Witches are, and what they believe and practice, through many appearances on radio and television, including the *Oprah Winfrey Show*. She has championed the rights of Witches and Pagans through establishing the Witch's League for Public Awareness, and later Project Witches Protection, educating the media on inaccurate and demeaning portrayals of Witches and educating government representatives on the religious rights of Witches.

Residing in Salem, Massachusetts, Laurie has been a publicly active Witch, running several Witchcraft shops where she offered psychic readings, as well as hosting numerous classes and public rituals, including the first ever Salem Witch's Ball. She teaches "Witchcraft As A Science" to all, emphasizing meditation and psychic development, and established her own Cabot Tradition of Witchcraft. Former Governor of Massachusetts, Michael S. Dukakis, awarded her the Patriot Award for public service and declared her the "official Witch of Salem, Massachusetts." She later established the Cabot-Kent Hermetic Temple as a federally recognized religious organization for furthering the Witchcraft community and culture. She is the author of four other books, including the classic *Power of the Witch*. For more information, visit *www.lauriecabot.com.*

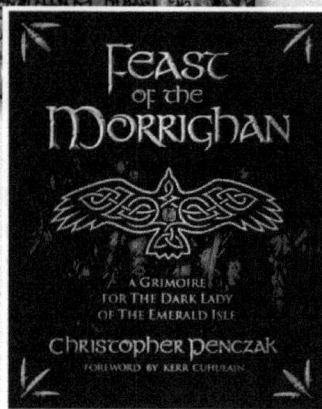

www.ingramcontent.com/pod-product-compliance
Lightning Source LLC
Chambersburg PA
CBHW081107240326
41723CB00007B/399

9781940755052